Lecture Notes in Artificial Intelligence     5919

Edited by R. Goebel, J. Siekmann, and W. Wahlster

Subseries of Lecture Notes in Computer Science

Lars Braubach   Jean-Pierre Briot
John Thangarajah (Eds.)

# Programming Multi-Agent Systems

7th International Workshop, ProMAS 2009
Budapest, Hungary, May 10-15, 2009
Revised Selected Papers

 Springer

Series Editors

Randy Goebel, University of Alberta, Edmonton, Canada
Jörg Siekmann, University of Saarland, Saarbrücken, Germany
Wolfgang Wahlster, DFKI and University of Saarland, Saarbrücken, Germany

Volume Editors

Lars Braubach
University of Hamburg
Hamburg, Germany
E-mail: braubach@informatik.uni-hamburg.de

Jean-Pierre Briot
LIP6, Paris 6 - CNRS
Paris, France
E-mail: jean-pierre.briot@lip6.fr

John Thangarajah
RMIT University
Melbourne, Australia
E-mail: johthan@cs.rmit.edu.au

Library of Congress Control Number: 2010932226

CR Subject Classification (1998): I.2, D.2, C.2.4, I.2.11, I.6, D.1

LNCS Sublibrary: SL 7 – Artificial Intelligence

ISSN       0302-9743
ISBN-10    3-642-14842-5 Springer Berlin Heidelberg New York
ISBN-13    978-3-642-14842-2 Springer Berlin Heidelberg New York

springer.com

© Springer-Verlag Berlin Heidelberg 2010
Printed in Germany

Typesetting: Camera-ready by author, data conversion by Scientific Publishing Services, Chennai, India
Printed on acid-free paper       06/3180

# Foreword

The earliest work on agents may be traced at least to the first conceptualization of the actor model by Carl Hewitt. In a paper in an AI conference in the early 1970s, Hewitt described actors as entities with knowledge and goals. Research on actors continued to focus on AI with the development of the Sprites model in which a monotonically growing knowledge base could be accessed by actors (inspired by what Hewitt called "the Scientific Computing Metaphor"). In the late 1970s and well into 1980s, controversy raged in AI between those arguing for declarative languages and those arguing for procedural ones. Actor researchers stood on the side of a procedural view of knowledge, arguing for an open systems perspective rather than the closed world hypothesis necessary for a logical, declarative view. In the open systems view, agents had arms length relationships and could not be expected to store consistent facts, nor could the information in a system be considered complete (the "negation as failure" model).

Subsequent work on actors, including my own, focused on using actors for general purpose concurrent and distributed programming. In the late 1980s, a number of actor languages and frameworks were built. These included Act++ (in C++) by Dennis Kafura and Actalk (in Smalltalk) by Jean-Pierre Briot. In recent times, the use of the Actor model, in various guises, has proliferated as new parallel and distributed computing platforms and applications have become common: clusters, Web services, P2P networks, client programming on multicore processors, and cloud computing. These applications have motivated the use of actors as it is proving to be more natural to program large-scale actor systems than write programs with large numbers of threads, locks, and shared variables. Among the many actor languages and frameworks now being used or developed are Erlang, E, Scala, Salsa, Kilim, ActorFoundry, and Axum, besides many other frameworks in Python, Java, and Ruby.

Work on agents from its earliest stages has concentrated on distributed problem solving. Unlike the turn actor research had taken by focusing on the development of actors as a programming model, the agents research community worked on ways in which agents could be used to solve problems more abstractly. By embedding more abstract declarative notions of knowledge within agents, it can be said that while at their core agents remain procedural, agents are also overcoming the schism between the declarative and the procedural camps.

It can be safely asserted that research in agents as "intelligent" actors gathered momentum in the 1990s. However, the bulk of this research focused on building models and algorithms. The community relied on theoretical analyses and simulations as their primary tools. The need for building intelligent agent languages and development tools continued to grow. It is true that the formal programming model for agents is actors, in that agents are autonomous, operate asynchronously, are distributed, may create new agents and acquire knowledge about other agents, all properties of the actor programming model. However, supporting multi-agent programming requires more than this: agents have a complex semantics which needs to be supported by providing ways of easily specifying concepts such as mental models, beliefs, goals, intentions, and plans. Although certain frameworks for agents, such as BDI, have also become popular, programming support for these frameworks remains a work in progress. Part of the reason for this is the need for research which will enable us to understand how to build debugging, profiling, and monitoring tools for agents.

The ProMAS community is addressing this critical need. The current volume is a good representative of the state of the art; it documents both the progress that has been made and the challenges that lie ahead. For example, research on the notion of commitments shows how a more semantic model of communication can be interpreted to specify behaviors of agents instead of the traditional rigid method of specifying interactions by building specific protocols. Research in reasoning and verification of agents has also focused on the semantic content of agent behavior, applying techniques such as constraint solving, hybrid automata, situation calculus, and other formal methods.

In the final analysis, research on multi-agent systems should not be viewed as research in a specialized area; rather it as an ambitious enterprise whose goal is to change the future of computing. Multi-agent programming is a way of more abstractly expressing general purpose real-world programs which are concurrent and distributed, open to interaction, and extensible. By enabling more declarative specifications in the small and resilience through cooperation in the large, agent programming provides the robustness currently missing from software. To reach that vision, multi-agent research must focus not only on making actors more intelligent, it must focus on providing models and tools which enable large organizations or ensembles of agents to be programmed effectively.

November 2009                                                        Gul Agha
                          University of Illinois at Urbana-Champaign

# Preface

These are the proceedings of the International Workshop on Programming Multi-Agent Systems (ProMAS 2009), the seventh of a series of workshops that has the main objective of giving an overview of current research for programming multi-agent systems and providing an interactive discussion forum for agent researchers.

The ProMAS workshop series aims at promoting and contributing to the establishment of multi-agent systems as a mainstream approach to the development of industrial-strength software. More specifically, the workshop facilitates the discussion and exchange of ideas concerning the concepts, techniques, and tools that are important for establishing multi-agent programming platforms that are useful in practice and have a theoretically sound basis.

In its previous editions, ProMAS constituted an invaluable occasion bringing together leading researchers from both academia and industry to discuss issues on the design of programming languages and tools for multi-agent systems. We were very pleased to be able to again present a range of high-quality papers at ProMAS 2009. After six successful editions of the ProMAS workshop series, which took place at AAMAS 2003 (Melbourne, Australia), AAMAS 2004 (New York, USA), AAMAS 2005 (Utrecht, The Netherlands), AAMAS 2006 (Hakodate, Japan), AAMAS 2007 (Honolulu, Hawai'i), and AAMAS 2008 (Estoril, Portugal), the seventh edition took place during May 11–12 in Budapest, Hungary, in conjunction with AAMAS 2009, the main international conference on autonomous agents and multi-agent systems. ProMAS 2009 received 34 submissions. Each of these papers was carefully reviewed by three members of the Program Committee. As a result, nine contributions were accepted as full presentations and seven as short ones. Due to the high number of quality contributions received this year, it was decided to extend ProMAS 2009 to a two-day workshop.

At the workshop, in addition to the presentation of regular papers, Munindar Singh (North Carolina State University) gave an invited talk about *commitment communication*. The main idea is that communication relations are often specified in a too constrained way when traditional description techniques like AUML sequence diagrams are used. In this case, too much attention is paid to the exact definition of how an interaction takes place, i.e., what the possible message sequences are. In contrast to this rigid way, a commitment-based specification is proposed. Commitments are a mechanism for specifying the different responsibilities of the participating communication parties. The communication then follows the commitments made by these parties, which means the focus of the interaction shifts from flow orientation to reason orientation. In this way, the concrete message ordering loses importance and alternatives may be exploited. We are also happy that Munindar Singh accepted the invitation for an invited paper on this topic and provided it for this ProMAS proceedings volume.

Following the workshop, we set up a new submission, evaluation, and revision process for publishing these proceedings. The authors of the papers accepted at the workshop were invited to submit revised papers. Each paper was reviewed by a member of the Program Committee and by the editors. Authors were then requested to further revise their submissions and the resulting papers are what forms this volume.

This volume also includes a foreword by Gul Agha (University of Illinois at Urbana-Champaign). In his foreword, Gul Agha traces back work on multi-agent programming to the early proposal about actors by Carl Hewitt in the early 1970s and discusses the relations between multi-agent programming and actor programming, pointed out as a possible programming model foundation. He also discusses the needs for better understanding and for building debugging, profiling and monitoring tools for large-scale multi-agent programs.

The workshop addressed a broad range of mostly practical topics. This year the topics included practical examples of applying agent technology in interesting application domains such as computer games and boat monitoring. Another focus was on typical programming aspects such as debugging and profiling, which are common in standard programming languages but very new to agent languages. Finally, more formal aspects were also covered e.g., those that address artifact environments and verification with hybrid automata.

We thank the authors whose contributions made this book possible. Also, we thank the members of the Program Committee for their dedication on successive rounds of reviewing papers.

As for previous editions, we hope that the work described in these proceedings will contribute to the overall goal of stimulating the uptake of agent programming languages and the adoption of agent-based tools for real-world applications.

January 2010                                                      Lars Braubach
                                                              Jean-Pierre Briot
                                                             John Thangarajah

# Organization

The ProMAS 2009 workshop was held May 11–12, 2009, in Budapest, Hungary. The workshop was part of the AAMAS 2009 Workshop Program.

## Program Chairs

Lars Braubach                   University of Hamburg, Germany
Jean-Pierre Briot               LIP6, University Paris 6 - CNRS, France
John Thangarajah                RMIT University, Australia

## Steering Committee

Rafael Heitor Bordini           Federal University of Rio Grande do Sul, Brazil
Mehdi Dastani                   Utrecht University, The Netherlands
Jürgen Dix                      Clausthal University of Technology, Germany
Amal El Fallah Seghrouchni      LIP6, University Paris 6 - CNRS, France

## Program Committee

Matteo Baldoni                  University of Turin, Italy
Guido Boella                    University of Turin, Italy
Juan Botía Blaya                Universidad de Murcia, Spain
Keith Clark                     Imperial College, UK
Rem Collier                     University College Dublin, Ireland
Louise Dennis                   University of Liverpool, UK
Ian Dickinson                   HP Labs, Bristol, UK
Berndt Farwer                   Durham University, UK
Michael Fisher                  University of Liverpool, UK
Jorge Gómez-Sanz                Universidad Complutense de Madrid, Spain
Vladimir Gorodetsky             Russian Academy of Sciences, Russian Federation
Dominic Greenwood               Whitestein Technologies, Switzerland
James Harland                   RMIT University, Australia
Koen Hindriks                   Delft University of Technology, The Netherlands
Benjamin Hirsch                 TU-Berlin, Germany
Jomi Fred Hübner                ENS Mines Saint-Etienne, France
João Leite                      Universidade Nova de Lisboa, Portugal
Viviana Mascardi                University of Genova, Italy
John-Jules Meyer                Utrecht University, The Netherlands
David Morley                    SRI International, USA
Jörg Müller                     Clausthal University of Technology, Germany
Peter Novák                     Clausthal University of Technology, Germany

| Andrea Omicini | University of Bologna, Italy |
| Frédéric Peschanski | LIP6, University Paris 6 - CNRS, France |
| Michele Piunti | ISTC - CNR and DEIS Università di Bologna, Italy |
| Agostino Poggi | University of Parma, Italy |
| Alexander Pokahr | University of Hamburg, Germany |
| Alessandro Ricci | DEIS, Università di Bologna, Italy |
| Ralph Rönnquist | Intendico Pty Ltd, Australia |
| Sebastian Sardina | RMIT University, Australia |
| Ichiro Satoh | National Institute of Informatics, Japan |
| Munindar P. Singh | NCSU, USA |
| Tran Cao Son | New Mexico State University, USA |
| Kostas Stathis | Royal Holloway, UK |
| Paolo Torroni | University of Bologna, Italy |
| Gerhard Weiß | SCCH GmbH, Austria |
| Wayne Wobcke | University of New South Wales, Australia |
| Neil Yorke-Smith | SRI International, USA |
| Yingqian Zhang | Delft University of Technology, The Netherlands |
| Olivier Boissier | ENS Mines Saint-Etienne, France |
| Birna van Riemsdijk | Delft University of Technology, The Netherlands |
| Leon van der Torre | University of Luxembourg, ILIAS, Luxembourg |

## Auxiliary Reviewers

| | |
| --- | --- |
| Alferes, José | Hepple, Anthony |
| Bromuri, Stefano | Kaiser, Silvan |
| Chopra, Amit | Remondino, Marco |
| Gabaldon, Alfredo | Torres, Viviane |
| Ghizzioli, Roberto | |

# Table of Contents

# Programming Multiagent Systems without Programming Agents

Munindar P. Singh[1] and Amit K. Chopra[2]

[1] North Carolina State University
singh@ncsu.edu
[2] Università degli Studi di Trento
akchopra.mail@gmail.com

**Abstract.** We consider the programming of multiagent systems from an architectural perspective. Our perspective emphasizes the autonomy and heterogeneity of agents, the components of multiagent systems, and focuses on how to specify their interconnections in terms of high-level protocols. In this manner, we show how to treat the programming of a multiagent system as an architectural endeavor, leaving aside the programming of individual agents who might feature in a multiagent system as a secondary concern.

## 1 Introduction

This paper presents a new way of thinking about the programming of multiagent systems. Most existing approaches either seek to apply traditional software engineering or to apply traditional artificial intelligence metaphors and abstractions. In contrast, this paper takes a uniquely multiagent systems perspective. It focuses on how to describe the interactions among agents in a manner that facilitates their loose coupling, and thus naturally respects their autonomy and heterogeneity.

Like traditional software engineering approaches, this paper gives primacy to interfaces and contracts. But unlike traditional approaches, it formulates these at a high level. Like traditional artificial intelligence approaches, it considers high-level abstractions that need not make sense in all applications and specifically are not pursued in traditional software engineering. Unlike traditional artificial intelligence, it gives prominence to social and organizational abstractions as opposed to cognitive ones, and offers a way to judge the compliance of agents.

Before we talk about what constitutes a multiagent architecture, it is helpful to consider how architecture fits into software engineering and how we understand it here. An *architecture* is motivated by requirements of the stakeholders of the systems that instantiate it as well as by the environment in which it is instantiated [1]. Traditional engineering draws an important distinction between functional and nonfunctional requirements. The former deal with functionality that is somehow relevant to the problem domain—for example, a sorting service would differ from a matrix inversion service on functional grounds. The latter deal with aspects of how that functionality is delivered—for example, with what latency, throughput, and availability. The associated idea in traditional engineering is that all approaches would meet the functional requirements but architectures would largely vary based on the nonfunctional requirements that they support [2].

L. Braubach, J.-P. Briot, and J. Thangarajah (Eds.): ProMAS 2009, LNAI 5919, pp. 1–14, 2010.

However, the above distinction—although a useful one—is far from perfect. It is not always clear, as is well known, how to distinguish functional from nonfunctional requirements. For example, if we are relying upon a numerical computation service to determine how much to decelerate an automobile so it avoids a collision, the apparently nonfunctional requirement of latency is very much functionally critical.

More importantly, when we think of a multiagent system in the broad sense, it is not at all clear whose requirements we are dealing with. A traditional software system would usually have multiple stakeholders: some users, some user advocates, some administrators, some developers (including, for us, designers, implementers, and maintainers). The developers are a bit of an outlier in this list in that they are not users of the system but they do impose requirements such as the maintainability of a system, which arguably an end user has no direct interest in—at least within a usage episode. However, when end users have an interest in having a system keep up with evolving requirements, maintainability becomes key to them as well. Regardless, the various stakeholders negotiate (perhaps in absentia via the developers) to determine and prioritize system requirements. The ultimate product—the system—is a tightly integrated whole that ought to meet its (suitably negotiated) requirements.

In sharp contrast with a traditional software system, it is generally not appropriate to think of a multiagent system as being designed in its totality to serve one integrated set of requirements. This is because in a typical multiagent system, the stakeholders are autonomous entities and do not necessarily serve the interests of a common enterprise. Many of the stakeholders are projected into the designed system as autonomous entities, that is, as agents. These agents are generally heterogeneous, meaning that they not only exhibit diverse designs and implementations but also instantiate apparently idiosyncratic decision policies.

It is worth emphasizing this point further. We are concerned with the programming of multiagent systems that not only involve multiple autonomous stakeholders, but also keep those stakeholders isolated from one another in the sense that the stakeholders may potentially hold divergent stakes in the different components. Service-oriented applications—banking, auctions, flight reservation, e-business in general, e-health, foreign exchange transactions, and so on—are prime examples of such systems; so are normative systems and virtual organizations. There are indeed multiagent systems, especially in cooperative applications involving distributed sensing, teamwork, and so on, that resemble a tightly integrated whole in the sense described above. For such applications, the system is decomposed into multiple agents because of some feature of the environment, such as the distributed nature of the information to be obtained or actions to be performed [3], or simply to facilitate a separation of concerns among different active modules [4]. Such applications do not emphasize the autonomous nature of agents and thus are not of primary concern here. In the following, the term *multiagent systems* refers exclusively to systems with multiple stakeholders, at least some of whom are isolated.

For the above reasons, traditional software architectures and their concomitant design methodologies are not readily applicable to the design and implementation of multiagent systems. Our present interest is to consider the aspects of multiagent systems that are *unique* to multiagent systems in the realm of software engineering [5]. For this reason, we claim that any approach that focuses on traditional programming artifacts works at too low a level to be of great value. In the same vein, any approach that focuses on building an integrated solution is generally inapplicable for multiagent systems. In contrast to integration, we seek approaches that emphasize the interoperation of autonomous and heterogeneous components.

Consequently, we advocate an approach for programming multiagent systems that does not look within individual agents at all. Instead, this approach talks about the interactions among agents. The interactions could themselves be captured through fiat in the worst case, through design-time negotiation among some of the stakeholders, or through runtime negotiation among the participating agents (based ultimately on some design-time negotiation at least to nail down the language employed within the negotiation). Our primary focus here is on the middle category above although the concepts we promote can work in the other categories as well.

## 2    Architecture in General

Let us begin with a brief study of an *architecture* in conceptual terms. Understood abstractly, an architecture is a description of how a system is organized. This consists primarily of the ingredients of the system, that is, its *components* and the *interconnections* it supports among the components. An *architectural style* is an abstraction over an architecture. A style identifies the following:

- *(Architectural) Constraints* on components and interconnections.
- *Patterns* on components and interconnections.

An architectural style yields a description language (possibly, also a graphical notation) in which we can present the architectures of a family of related systems and also the architecture of a particular system.

An *open architecture* is one whose components can change dynamically. Therefore, the openness of an architecture arises from its specifying the interconnections cleanly. In other words, the *physical* components of the architecture all but *disappear*; in their stead, the *logical* traces of the components remain. We define *protocols* as the kinds of interconnections that arise in open information environments.

### 2.1   Criteria for Judging Interconnections

The purpose of the interconnections is to support the interoperation of the components that they connect. How may we judge different kinds of interconnections? Our assessment should depend upon the level of interoperation that the interconnections support.

In particular, given our motivation for multiagent systems in Section 1, we identify the following criteria.

- *Loose coupling:* support heterogeneity and enables independent updates to the components.
- *Flexibility:* support autonomy, enabling participants to extract all the value they can extract by exploiting opportunities and handling exceptions.

- *Encapsulation:* promote modularity, thereby enabling independent concerns to be modeled independently, thus facilitating requirements tracing, verification, and maintainability.
- *Compositionality:* promote reuse of components across different environments and contexts of usage, thereby improving developer productivity.

We take the view that two or more components *interoperate* when each meets the expectations that each of the others places on it. An important idea—due to David Parnas from the early days of software architecture—is that interoperation is about each component satisfying the assumptions of the others [6]. Parnas specifically points out that interoperation is neither about control flow nor about data flow.

Unfortunately—and oddly enough—most if not all, subsequent software engineering research considers *only* control or data flow. As we explained in the foregoing, such approaches emphasize low-level abstractions that are ill-suited for multiagent systems. However, considering expectations abstractly and properly opens up additional challenges. Specifically,

- How may we characterize the expectations of components regarding each other except via data and control flow?
- How may we verify or ensure that the expectations of a component are being met by the others?

### 2.2   Protocols, Generally

The main idea is that a protocol encapsulates the interactions allowed among the components. In this sense, a protocol serves two purposes. On the one hand, a protocol *connects* components via a conceptual interface. On the other hand, a protocol *separates* components by providing clean partitions among the components viewed as logical entities. As a result, wherever we can identify protocols, we can (1) make interactions explicit and (2) identify markets for components. That is, protocols yield standards and their implementations yield products.

Let us consider protocols in the most general sense, including domains other than software, such as computer networking or even power systems. In networking, conventional protocols such as IEEE 802.11g and the Internet Protocol meet the above criteria. They determine what each component may expect of the others. They help identify markets such as of wireless access points and routers. In power systems, example protocols specify the voltage and frequency an electrical component can expect from a power source and the ranges of acceptable impedances it must operate within.

## 3   Proposed Approach

What are some key requirements for an architecture geared toward multiagent systems? Clearly, the components are *agents*, modeled to be *autonomous* (independent in their decision making) and *heterogeneous* (independently designed and constructed). Further, the environment of a multiagent system provides support for

- Communication: inherently *asynchronous*.
- Perceptions.
- Actions.

For Information Technology environments, we can treat all of the above as communications. The key general requirement for a multiagent system is that its stakeholders require the agents to *interoperate*. The specifics of interoperation would vary with the domain. In our approach, these would be captured via the messages and their meanings that characterize the interactions among the members of the desired multiagent system.

### 3.1 Specifying Multiagent System Protocols

In light of the above criteria, we can approach the problem of specifying multiagent system protocols in the following main ways. Following traditional methodologies, we can take a *procedural* stance, which would specify the *how* of the desired interaction. Examples of these approaches that are well-known even in current practice include finite state machines and Petri nets. In general, the procedural approaches over-specify the desired interactions, thus limiting flexibility and coupling the components more tightly than is necessary.

Alternatively, we can take a *declarative* stance, which would specify the *what* of the desired interaction, meaning what it seeks to accomplish. Examples of declarative approaches are those based on the various forms of logic: predicate, modal, temporal, and such. A logic-based approach is not necessarily higher level than the procedural approaches. What matters primarily or even solely is what the conceptual model is that the formalization seeks to capture. We advocate declarative approaches based on high-level conceptual abstractions that promote loose coupling and flexibility.

Our proposed approach can be summarized as *agent communication done right*. Communication in general and agent communication in particular can be understood as involving at least the following main aspects of language.

- *Syntax:* documents to be exchanged as messages. We can imagine these documents as being rendered in a standardized notation such as a vocabulary based on XML.
- *Semantics:* formal meaning of each message. We propose that at least for business applications, this desired meaning may be best expressed using abstractions based on the notion of *commitments* [7]. For other situations involving multiagent systems, the meaning could potentially be expressed via other suitable constructs in a like manner. However, even in nonbusiness settings, the commitments among agents can be valuable. In particular, the type of commitment known as dialectical may be suitable for applications involving the exchange of information or arguments, such as negotiation [8].

Our approach places considerable weight on the idea of minimizing operational constraints. Our motivation for this is to enhance the features listed in Section 2.1, specifically loose coupling, which promotes autonomy and heterogeneity. From our experience in formalizing various domains, it is worth remarking—and it would prove surprising to many—that few operational constraints are truly needed to capture the essential requirements of an application.

## 3.2  Ensuring Interoperation via Traditional Representations

Traditional software engineering approaches apply only at the level of control and data flow among the components. Usually the concomitant flows are specified procedurally, although they can be captured declaratively. Regardless, as we argued in Section 2.1, control and data flows prove to be a poor notion of interoperation for multiagent systems. However, it is important to recognize that traditional approaches *can support* interoperation, albeit at a low level. Further, they carry a concomitant notion of compliance as well.

In contrast, the traditional agent-oriented approaches—based as they are on traditional artificial intelligence concepts—place onerous demands on the agents. Because these approaches emphasize the cognitive concepts such as beliefs, goals, desires, or intentions, they presuppose that the agents be able to interoperate at the cognitive level. In other words, the traditional agent-oriented approaches require that the cognitive state of an agent be

- Externally *determinable*, which is impossible without violating the heterogeneity of the agents.
- In constant *mutual agreement*, which is impossible without violating autonomy and asynchrony.

Consequently, we claim that these approaches offer no viable notion of interoperation (or of compliance [9]). In this manner, they reflect a step backwards from the traditional software engineering approaches.

For the above reasons, the BDI approaches are *not* suitable for architecture. They (1) violate heterogeneity by presuming knowledge of agent internals; (2) prevent alignment in settings involving asynchrony; (3) tightly couple the agents with each other; and (4) lead to strong assumptions such as sincerity in communication that prove invalid in open settings.

## 3.3  Interoperation via Commitments

Commitments yield a notion of compliance expressly suited for multiagent systems. Agent compliance amounts to the agent not violating any of its commitments towards others. A protocol specified in terms of commitments does not dictate specific operationalizations in terms of when an agent should send or expect to receive particular messages; as long as the agent discharges its commitments, it can act as it pleases [10].

We introduce some notation and elementary reasoning rules for commitments.

- The expression C(debtor, creditor, antecedent, consequent) represents a commitment; it means that debtor is committed to the creditor for the consequent if the antecedent is brought about. For example, C(EBook, Alice, $12, BNW) means that EBook is committed to Alice for the book *BNW* (for *Brave New World*) in return for a payment of $12.
- C(debtor, creditor, $\top$, consequent) represent an unconditional commitment. For example, C(EBook, Alice, $\top$, BNW) means that EBook is committed to Alice for the book *BNW*.

- DETACH: $C(x, y, r, u) \wedge r \rightarrow C(x, y, \top, u)$: if the antecedent holds, then the debtor become unconditionally committed to the consequent. For example (reading $\Rightarrow$ as logical consequence), $C(\text{EBook}, \text{Alice}, \$12, \text{BNW}) \wedge \$12 \Rightarrow C(\text{EBook}, \text{Alice}, \top, \text{BNW})$.
- DISCHARGE: $u \rightarrow \neg C(x, y, r, u)$: if the consequent holds, the commitment is *discharged*—it does not hold any longer—no matter if it is conditional or not. For example, both of the following hold. $\text{BNW} \Rightarrow \neg C(\text{EBook}, \text{Alice}, \$12, \text{BNW})$. And, $\text{BNW} \Rightarrow \neg C(\text{EBook}, \text{Alice}, \top, \text{BNW})$

The flexibility of a (complying) agent is limited by the need to interoperate with others. To fully exploit the flexibility afforded by commitments, we must necessarily formalize interoperability in terms of commitments. For if we continued to rely upon the notions of interoperability as formalized for components—in terms of a component being able to simply send and receive messages as assumed by others—we would be introducing operational constraints on the communication among agents, thus limiting their flexibility.

To motivate our definition of interoperation in terms of commitments, we observe that there are two primary sources of asymmetry in a multiagent system. On the one hand, communications are inherently directed with the direction of causality usually being treated as flowing from the sender to a receiver (but see Baldoni et al. [11] for a more general, alternative view). On the other hand, commitments are directed with the direction of expectation being from the creditor of a commitment to its debtor.

Accordingly, we propose a notion of interoperation that we term *(commitment) alignment* [12]. Alignment, as we define it, is fundamentally asymmetric. The intuition it expresses is that whenever a creditor computes (that is, infers) a commitment, the presumed debtor also computes the same commitment. The formalization of this definition involves some subtlety, especially on the notion of what we mean by *whenever*. Specifically, we capture the intuition that at the moments or system snapshots at which we judge the alignment or otherwise of any two agents, we make sure that the agents have received the same relevant information. Thus all messages sent must have been received, and each agent ought to have shared any information it has received that is materially relevant to the commitments in which it participates. In particular, a creditor should propagate information about partial or total detachments, which strengthen a commitment. And, a debtor should propagate information about partial or total discharges, which weaken or dissolve a commitment.

In this manner, our approach can achieve alignment even in the face of asynchrony—meaning unbounded message delays but messaging that is order-preserving for each pair of sender and receiver. The approach works as follows. When a debtor autonomously creates a commitment, it sends a corresponding message, which eventually lands at the creditor. Here the debtor is committed before the creditor learns of the debtor being committed, so alignment is preserved. When a creditor detaches a commitment, thereby strengthening it, a message corresponding to the detach eventually arrives at the debtor. Here the debtor is committed when it receives the detach message.

The foregoing motivates a treatment of *quiescence* wherein we only consider well-formed points in executions where each message has landed. When a debtor or creditor learns that a commitment is discharged or detached, respectively, it must immediately notify the other (*integrity*, which ensures no quiescence until the information has propagated).

In broad terms, our ongoing research program calls for the development of what we term *CSOA*, a commitment-based service-oriented architecture [13]. CSOA is focused on the notion of a *service engagement*. When thought of in business terms, a service engagement involves multiple business partners carrying out extensive, subtle interactions in order to deliver value to each other. Business services are to be contrasted with technical services such as on Web or the Grid, which emphasize lower level questions of connectivity and messaging without regard to the business content of the interactions.

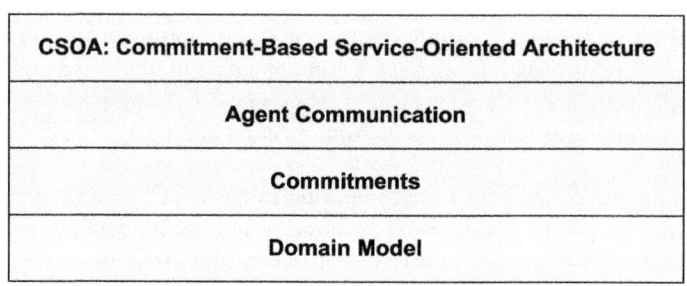

**Fig. 1.** Proposed architecture schematic, conceptually

Figure 1 shows how we imagine the layers of our architecture in conceptual terms. For a given application, the *domain model* describes the roles involved and the vocabulary, including the business documents that agents adopting the role would exchange. The *commitments* layer understands the documents in terms of their business contents. The *agent communication* layer deals with the primitive commitment operations such as Create, Delegate, and so on, and other communication primitives such as Request, Declare, and so on; the primitives in this layer would be more or less standard. Finally, the *CSOA* layer deals with composite service engagement patterns built from the primitive commitment operations. For example, a book-selling application would involve at least the roles *Buyer* and *Seller*. An *Offer* for some book from the *Seller* could be mapped to a commitment from the *Seller* to the *Buyer*, similar to the one above from EBook to Alice. A CSOA pattern for the book-selling application could encode refunds from the *Seller*.

## 4   Programming Multiagent Systems

Based on the foregoing, we can now introduce a conceptually straightforward way in which to program a multiagent system.

### 4.1   Step 1: Specify the Communications

We define a protocol and specify it as follows.

- Specify roles to describe abstracted versions of the agents who will participate in the multiagent system at runtime.
- Specify messages as the surface communications among various pairs of roles.
- Specify the meanings of each message declaratively in terms of commitments and other relevant propositions.
- Specify any additional constraints on the messages such as the conventions of the relative orders among the messages, and how information carried in one message flows to another message in the protocol.

The above commitment-based specification approach is reasonable for the following reasons. Based on the notion of commitments, we can unambiguously determine if a particular enactment satisfies the specified protocol or not. We can also determine if any of the agents is noncompliant. Further, if needed, we can refine and compose protocols to produce protocols that better address our stakeholder requirements.

## 4.2  Step 2: Instantiate the System

The next step in this methodology is to instantiate and configure a multiagent system so as to be able to enact its computations. To instantiate and enact a multiagent system, identify agents to play roles in the protocol that characterizes the multiagent system. We refer to a unique protocol because when there are multiple protocols, they can be considered for this discussion as having been composed into a single definitive protocol. In practice, we do not require the creation of a monolithic composed protocol. The instantiation of a multiagent system could proceed one of three ways in terms of the agents who are involved. These agents could be any combination of (1) preexisting agents proceeding on their own initiative; (2) newly instantiated agents based on preexisting code-bases; and (3) custom-designed agents to suit the needs of the stakeholders who contribute them to the multiagent system. Different stakeholders could follow any of the above approaches in constructing the agents they field in the given system. In any case, each agent would apply the decision-making policies of the stakeholder whom it represents computationally within the multiagent system.

## 4.3  Enactment and Enforcement

The agents collectively enact this programming model by individually applying their policies to determine what messages to send each other. As explained above, the meaning of each message specifies how it corresponds to operations on commitments.

The above approach can be readily realized in runtime tools, which can be thought of as commitment middleware [14]. The middleware we envisage would offer primitives encapsulated as programming abstractions by which each agent can

- Communicate with other agents.
- Maintain the commitments in which it features as debtor or creditor.
- Propagate the information necessary to maintain alignment among the agents.
- Verify the compliance of debtors with commitments where it is the creditor.

Such a middleware would enable writing programs directly in terms of commitments. Instead of an agent effecting communication with others through such low-level primitives as *send* and *receive*, the agent would perform commitment operations.

Our commitment-based architecture does not require that there be a central authority to enforce commitments. In general, in settings with autonomous agents, no agent can be sufficiently powerful to force another agent to act in a certain manner. Enforcement in such settings realistically amounts to arbitration and applying penalties where appropriate.

A commitment is made in a certain *context*, which defines the rules of encounter for the agents who feature in it [13]. We model the context as an agent in its own right. Viewed in this light, the context can perform several important functions, not necessarily all of them in the same setting. The context can be a monitor for tracking commitments, which assumes it observes all communications. Alternatively, the context may serve as arbiter for any disputes between the contracted parties.

In some settings, the context may also act as a sanctioner who penalizes agents who violate their commitments. The context may cause a new *penalty* commitment (with the same debtor as the violated commitment) to come into force. Ultimately, there is little the context can do, except possibly to eject a malfeasant agent from the interaction. The context may observe the violation itself or may learn of it from the creditor, who would have escalated the commitment to the context. For example, a buyer on eBay (the marketplace) may escalate a dispute with a seller to eBay (the corporate entity, serving as the context). The protocol for escalating and dispute resolutions may be considered as part of a larger Sphere of Commitment [15]. However, often, penalties are left unspecified. For example, a buyer's agent may simply notify the buyer that the seller has violated some commitment, at which point the buyer may take up the matter with eBay. A more common approach is to use reputation as a form of social censure for malfeasant agents. In well-structured settings such as eBay, which might support a notion of reputation, there is also the option of ejecting a malfeasant agent.

Figure 2 illustrates a way to operationalize our architecture in schematic terms. A commitment middleware resides above messaging and makes sure that agents maintain their alignment by exchanging relevant information. The agents function within a suitably powerful sphere of commitment which, as explained above, potentially ensures they comply with their commitments.

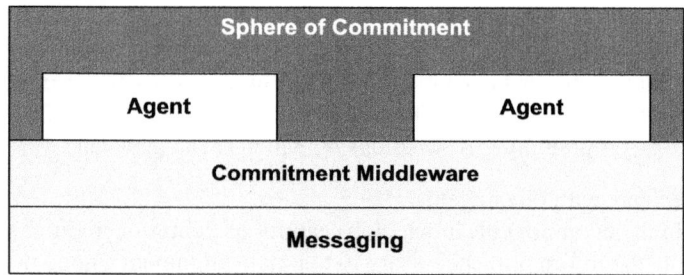

**Fig. 2.** Proposed architecture schematic, operationally

## 4.4   Summary of Benefits

We highlight the benefits of our approach according to the criteria presented in Section 2.1. Formalizing interoperability in terms of commitment alignment promotes a *looser* coupling among agents than is possible with traditional approaches. In particular, many of the message ordering constraints that are typically taken for granted in real-life applications, for example, that the *accept* or the *reject* of an *offer* must follow the *offer*, are no longer necessary. In effect, when we loosely couple agents, they can update their commitments independently of each other.

Commitments support a high-level notion of compliance, and thus support flexible enactment. In earlier work on commitments, the flexibility afforded by commitments could not be fully exploited as concerns of concurrency obscured the picture somewhat. With interoperation formalized in terms of commitments, agents can fully exploit this flexibility.

Encapsulation and compositionality have to do with the efficient software engineering of protocols [16]. In essence, each protocol is a discrete artifact, independent from requirements and from other protocols. A protocol may thus be made available in a repository, and depending on a particular application's requirements, composed with other protocols and instantiated.

## 5   Discussion: Conclusions and Future Work

First, we observe that existing multiagent systems engineering approaches, in attempting to develop practical systems, adopt traditional software engineering ideas wholesale. In this manner, they tend to neglect the key features that characterize multiagent systems, specifically, the autonomy and the heterogeneity of their participants.

Second, when existing approaches recognize the high-level nature of the descriptions of agents and their interactions, they seek to differentiate themselves from traditional software engineering by introducing concepts from traditional artificial intelligence, specifically, concepts such as beliefs, goals (or desires), and intentions. In this manner, they continue to poorly accommodate the asynchrony, autonomy, and heterogeneity that characterize real-life multiagent systems.

We advocate an approach in which high-level concepts yield interconnections that support multiagent system applications. These concepts are centered on commitments and help model the interactive nature of multiagent systems directly. A key challenge is that we realize such concepts correctly in order to achieve interoperation.

The key to building large-scale multiagent systems lies in adequately formalizing agent communication, not the internal decision making of agents. Whether an agent is capable of reasoning about beliefs or whether the agent is specified as an automaton is neither relevant nor discernible to another agent. A desirable development would be if both agent communication and reasoning could be specified in terms of high-level abstractions, and the runtime infrastructure would directly support the abstractions. This would obviate the need to translate between different levels of abstraction, as advocated in model-driven approaches, and would truly usher in the age of agent-oriented software engineering. For this, we would have to formally relate agent reasoning with agent communications. This challenge is beginning to be addressed in the recent literature [17,18].

Considerations of multiagent systems require fresh approaches in requirements modeling. Instead of classifying requirements simply as functional or nonfunctional, one also needs to consider whether the requirement is *contractual*—implying a commitment between two of the stakeholders—or noncontractual. A requirement could be functional and contractual (for example, EBook's offer entails such a commitment), or nonfunctional and contractual (for example, the requirement that the book be delivered using priority service), and so on. Indeed, as pertains to multiagent systems, the contractual dimension seems to be more significant than the functional one.

In business engagements, the context plays an important role—it instills some measure of confidence in compliance by the interacting parties. In commitments of a personal nature, the context may be implicit. Further, there may not be any explicitly specified penalty commitments. For example, if Rob commits to picking up Alice from the airport, but does not show up on time, Alice may cancel her dinner engagement with him or she may simply note Rob to be unreliable. The point to be taken here is that commitments are valuable because they enable reasoning about compliance; their value does not derive from their being enforced or not. Neither penalty nor arbitration are semantically integral to commitments.

## 5.1  A Remark on Notation

Architectural approaches inherently lead to ways to describe systems. Thus they naturally lead and should lead to notations. Notation, although important, remains secondary to the concepts. When we describe an architecture, what matter most are the concepts using which we do so. It is more important to develop a suitable metamodel than to specify a detailed notation that lacks an appropriate metamodel.

We notice a tendency in agent-oriented software engineering where, in attempting to develop practical systems, researchers adopt traditional notations wholesale as well. There is indeed value in adopting traditional notations, but *only* where such notations apply. The field of multiagent systems exists—and research into the subfield of programming multiagent systems is a worthwhile endeavor—only because traditional approaches are known to be inadequate for a variety of practical information systems, especially large-scale open, distributed systems. In other words, existing notations are not complete for these purposes. Therefore, a worthwhile contribution of multiagent system research is to invent suitable notations backed up by expressive metamodels.

## 5.2  Directions

CSOA is an architecture style that treats business (not technical) services as agents, and includes patterns for service engagements. Along the lines of CSOA, we have recently begun to develop a business modeling language [17]. This language is based on a metamodel that provides first-class status to business partners and their respective commitments, expressing their contracts. It also includes support for some CSOA patterns such as for delegating commitments that are core to the precise, yet high-level specification of a service engagement.

Upcoming research includes a study of ways in which to express a multiagent system in terms of the business relationships among agents as conglomerates of commitments, and formal methods to verify the computations realized with respect to business models.

## Acknowledgments

Munindar Singh's research was partially supported by a gift from the Intel Research Council. Amit Chopra's research was partially supported by the Integrated FP6-EU project SERENITY contract 27587.

## References

1. Zachman, J.A.: A framework for information systems architecture. IBM Systems Journal 26(3), 276–292 (1987)
2. Filman, R.E., Barrett, S., Lee, D.D., Linden, T.: Inserting ilities by controlling communications. Communications of the ACM 45(1), 116–122 (2002)
3. Durfee, E.H.: Practically coordinating. AI Magazine 20(1), 99–116 (Spring 1999)
4. Singh, M.P., Huhns, M.N.: Automating workflows for service provisioning: integrating AI and database technologies. IEEE Expert 9(5), 19–23 (October 1994)
5. Huhns, M.N., Singh, M.P., Burstein, M.H., Decker, K.S., Durfee, E.H., Finin, T.W., Gasser, L., Goradia, H.J., Jennings, N.R., Lakkaraju, K., Nakashima, H., Parunak, H.V.D., Rosenschein, J.S., Ruvinsky, A., Sukthankar, G., Swarup, S., Sycara, K.P., Tambe, M., Wagner, T., Gutierrez, R.L.Z.: Research directions for service-oriented multiagent systems. IEEE Internet Computing 9(6), 65–70 (2005)
6. Parnas, D.L.: Information distribution aspects of design methodology. In: Proceedings of the International Federation for Information Processing Congress, Amsterdam, North Holland, vol. TA-3, pp. 26–30 (1971)
7. Singh, M.P.: An ontology for commitments in multiagent systems: Toward a unification of normative concepts. Artificial Intelligence and Law 7(1), 97–113 (1999)
8. Singh, M.P.: Semantical considerations on dialectical and practical commitments. In: Proceedings of the 23rd Conference on Artificial Intelligence (AAAI), Chicago, pp. 176–181. AAAI Press, Menlo Park (July 2008)
9. Singh, M.P.: Agent communication languages: Rethinking the principles. IEEE Computer 31(12), 40–47 (1998)
10. Yolum, P., Singh, M.P.: Flexible protocol specification and execution: Applying event calculus planning using commitments. In: Proceedings of the 1st International Joint Conference on Autonomous Agents and MultiAgent Systems, Bologna, pp. 527–534. ACM Press, New York (July 2002)
11. Baldoni, M., Baroglio, C., Chopra, A.K., Desai, N., Patti, V., Singh, M.P.: Choice, interoperability, and conformance in interaction protocols and service choreographies. In: Proceedings of the 8th International Joint Conference on Autonomous Agents and MultiAgent Systems (AAMAS), Budapest, pp. 843–850, IFAAMAS (May 2009)
12. Chopra, A.K., Singh, M.P.: Multiagent commitment alignment. In: Proceedings of the 8th International Joint Conference on Autonomous Agents and MultiAgent Systems (AAMAS), Budapest, pp. 937–944, IFAAMAS (May 2009)

13. Singh, M.P., Chopra, A.K., Desai, N.: Commitment-based service-oriented architecture. IEEE Computer 42(11), 72–79 (2009)
14. Chopra, A.K., Singh, M.P.: An architecture for multiagent systems: An approach based on commitments. In: Braubach, L., Briot, J.-P., Thangarajah, J. (eds.) ProMAS 2009. LNCS (LNAI), vol. 5919, pp. 15–30. Springer, Heidelberg (2009)
15. Singh, M.P.: Multiagent systems as spheres of commitment. In: Proceedings of the International Conference on Multiagent Systems (ICMAS) Workshop on Norms, Obligations, and Conventions (December 1996)
16. Desai, N., Chopra, A.K., Singh, M.P.: Amoeba: A methodology for modeling and evolution of cross-organizational business processes. ACM Transactions on Software Engineering and Methodology (TOSEM) 19(2), 6:1–6:45 (2009)
17. Telang, P.R., Singh, M.P.: Business modeling via commitments. In: Vo, Q.B. (ed.) SOCASE 2009. LNCS, vol. 5907, pp. 111–125. Springer, Heidelberg (2009)
18. Robinson, W.N., Purao, S.: Specifying and monitoring interactions and commitments in open business processes. IEEE Software 26(2), 72–79 (2009)

# Elements of a Business-Level Architecture for Multiagent Systems

Amit K. Chopra[1] and Munindar P. Singh[2]

[1] Università degli Studi di Trento
akchopra.mail@gmail.com
[2] North Carolina State University
singh@ncsu.edu

**Abstract.** Existing architectures for multiagent systems emphasize low-level messaging-related considerations. As a result, the programming abstractions they provide are also low level. In recent years, commitments have been applied to support flexible interactions among autonomous agents. We present a layered multiagent system architecture based on commitments. In this architecture, agents are the components, and the interconnections between the agents are specified in terms of commitments, thus abstracting away from low level details. A crucial layer in this architecture is a commitment-based middleware that plays a vital role in ensuring interoperation and provides commitment-related abstractions to the application programmer. Interoperation itself is defined in terms of commitment alignment. This paper details various aspects of this architecture, and shows how a programmer would write applications to such an architecture.

## 1 Introduction

An *architecture* is an abstract description of a system. The fundamental idea of an architecture is that it identifies *components* and their *interconnections* [1]. An *open* architecture is one that emphasizes the interconnections, leaving the components unspecified except to the extent of their interconnections. In this manner, an open architecture yields systems whose components can be readily substituted by other components.

When we understand multiagent systems from the standpoint of architecture, it is clear that the components are *agents* (or, rather, abstractly *roles*). Traditionally, the interconnections have been modeled in operational terms derived from an understanding of distributed systems. Consequently, the multiagent systems that result are over-specified and behave in an inflexible manner. With such systems, it is difficult to accommodate a richer variety of situations. What is required is the specification of interconnection in terms of higher-level abstractions.

For concreteness, we consider cross-organizational business processes as an application of multiagent systems that provide the happy mix of significance and complexity to demonstrate the payoff of using the proposed approach. The last few years have developed compelling accounts of the fundamental autonomy and heterogeneity of business partners, and the concomitant need to model these partners' interest. The related studies of interaction protocols hint at how we might engineer multiagent systems in such settings [2,3,4]. A feature of these approaches is their basis in commitments. Commitments

L. Braubach, J.-P. Briot, and J. Thangarajah (Eds.): ProMAS 2009, LNAI 5919, pp. 15–30, 2010.
© Springer-Verlag Berlin Heidelberg 2010

yield a business-level notion of compliance: as long as agents discharge their commitments, they are free to interact as they please. However, the relationship of protocols with architectures has not yet been adequately worked out. This requires an understanding of interoperability in terms of commitments.

We make a fresh start on multiagent systems via an architecture. Once we realize that we would only consider the components as agents understood flexibly, the associated interconnections must inevitably be the business relationships between the agents. One can imagine that some notional business value flows across such relationships, just as data flows over the traditional connectors of distributed computing. Thinking of the business relationships as interconnections yields an architecture for what we term *service engagements* [5].

The above architecture is conceptual in nature. Two natural questions arise: what programming abstractions does the architecture support, and how may we operationalize it over existing infrastructure that is no different from that underlying traditional approaches. Answering the above questions is the main contribution of this paper.

## 1.1  Middleware: Programming Abstractions

From a top-down perspective, an important layer of any architecture is middleware. Middleware supports programming abstractions for the architecture in a way that ensures interoperability between components in the architecture. A relatively simple middleware is one that provides reliable message queuing services, freeing the programmer from the burden of, for example, implementing persistent storage and checking for acknowledgments. These days, reliable message queuing is just one of many abstractions supported in enterprise middleware. In cross-organizational business processes, the common middleware is centered on the abstractions of messaging. The resulting architectural style is termed the *Enterprise Service Bus (ESB)*. ESBs emphasize messaging abstractions and patterns—for example, Apache Camel supports the enterprise integration patterns in [6]. Further, ESBs support an event-driven architecture so as to promote loose coupling between business applications. ESBs provide various kinds of translation services, routing, and security, among other things, thus saving the application programmer a good deal of repetitive effort. Some ESB implementations, such as provided by Oracle, also support business protocols such as RosettaNet [7].

Ideally, middleware should offer abstractions that follow closely the vocabulary of the domain. ESBs purport to support business applications; however, they lack business-level abstractions. The abstractions they support, e.g., for RosettaNet, involve message occurrence and ordering but without regard to the meanings of the messages. Thus RosettaNet can be thought of as a protocol grammar. Other protocols, e.g., Global Data Synchronization Network (GDSN) [8], would correspond to alternative grammars. Each grammar is arbitrary and its correctness or otherwise is not up for consideration.

Figure 1 shows the conceptual arrangement of a service-oriented architecture based on such ESBs. Programmers design business *processes* (for example, in BPEL) based on a public interface specification (for example, in WS-CDL or based on a protocol such as RosettaNet). Messaging-based middleware, such as described above, hides the details of the infrastructure from process programmers.

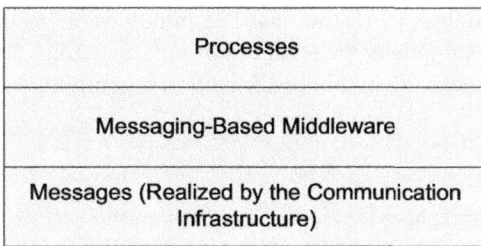

**Fig. 1.** Current enterprise middleware, conceptually

## 1.2   Overview of Approach

We assume a conventional infrastructure based on messaging, such as is already made available by middleware such as the Java Messaging Service and specified in the emerging standard known as the Advanced Message Queuing Protocol (AMQP) [9]. This infrastructure supports point-to-point messaging over channels that preserve pairwise message order and guarantee eventual delivery. It is important to emphasize that such infrastructure is commonly available in existing implementations.

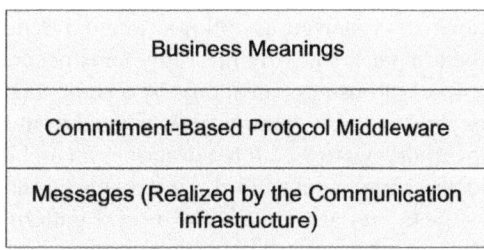

**Fig. 2.** Commitment middleware, conceptually

The essential idea underlying our approach is that we can thus view system architecture at two levels of abstraction: business and infrastructure. The business level deals with meaning whereas the infrastructure provides the operationalization. Accordingly, we view the function of middleware as bridging this conceptual gap. Figure 2 shows that our middleware lies in the middle between meaning and messaging. In our approach, business meaning is expressed in terms of commitments. Commitments arise in virtually all cross-organizational business applications. Thus, reasoning about commitments would be applicable to all of them. Commitments underlie two correctness criteria: *compliance* and *alignment*. Agents are compliant as long as they discharge their commitments; such a notion of compliance naturally takes into account agents' autonomy. Agents are aligned as long they agree on whatever commitments as may result from their communications. Alignment is, in fact, a key form of business interoperability [10,11].

The proposed middleware provides commitment-based abstractions. The middleware supports not only the basic commitment operations [12], but also high-level patterns that build on the commitment operations. The middleware ensures that if applications are determined interoperable at the level of business meaning, then infrastructure-level concerns such as asynchrony do not break the interoperability.

### 1.3   Contributions

The contribution of this paper lies in making explicit the architecture that commitment alignment, as a notion of business-level interoperability, supports. This includes the specification of agent interfaces and the question of their compatibility, the design of the middleware that bridges between the business level and the infrastructural level, and the programming abstractions that are made available to application programmers. In all of these elements, the architecture presented is significantly different from current multiagent architectures. We also outline how the middleware may be extended with common business patterns and additional kinds of alignment. To illustrate how the architecture supports a new way of programming, consider that traditional agent communication is treated simply in terms of sending and receiving messages. However, with our proposed architecture, it would be possible to encode communication in terms of commitment operations and patterns. The benefit accrued is of a nature similar to that accrued by being able to write agents (their internal reasoning, in particular) in terms of BDI abstractions rather than low-level procedural abstractions.

The rest of this paper is organized as follows. Section 2 describes commitments formally, what alignment means, and why misalignments occur. Some misalignments can be detected at the level of business meanings by a static analysis of the interfaces, whereas others that occur due to the nature of distributed systems must be prevented by careful design of the middleware. Section 3 describes an architecture based on commitments. It describes the components and the interconnections and the layers in the architecture. Section 4 describes a sample set of useful patterns that the middleware supports. Section 5 discusses the relevant literature.

## 2   Commitment Alignment

Interoperability among participants means that each participant fulfills the expectations made by the others. To understand an architecture, it is important to understand what interoperability in the architecture means. In our approach, an agent represents each participant, and the expectations of an agent take the form of commitments. Existing work on service interoperability treats expectations solely at the level of messages [13,14,15].

Let us explain how commitments yield expectations. A commitment is of the form $C(debtor, creditor, antecedent, consequent)$, where $debtor$ and $creditor$ are agents, and $antecedent$ and $consequent$ are propositions. This means that the debtor commits (to the creditor) to bringing about the consequent if the antecedent holds. For example, $C(EBook, Alice, \$12, BNW)$ means that EBook commits to Alice that if she pays $12, then EBook will send her the book *Brave New World*. Agents interact by sending each other messages. The messages have meanings in terms of how they affect the agents' commitments toward each other. For example, an offer message from EBook to Alice may bring about the aforementioned commitment.

Now imagine that at some point in their interaction, Alice infers that EBook is committed to sending her the book she paid for, but EBook infers no such commitment. Their interaction would break down at the level of business meaning. In other words, Alice and EBook would not be interoperable. In general, a key requirement for interoperability is that the interacting agents remain aligned with respect to their commitments. Commitment alignment is a key form of business-level interoperability. Agents are aligned if whenever one agent (as creditor) infers a commitment from a second agent, the second agent (as debtor) also infers that commitment. If we can guarantee *a priori* that agents never—at no point during any possible interaction—get misaligned, only then the agents are interoperable.

In general, agents may get misaligned because of their *heterogeneity*, *autonomy*, and *distribution*.

**Heterogeneity.** Agents may assign incompatible meanings to the messages they are exchanging. To be able to successfully interact, the agents must agree on what their communications count as. Heterogeneity is the cause of misalignment in Example 1.

*Example 1.* For Alice, an *Offer* message from EBook counts as a commitment from EBook to ship a book in return for payment. Whereas for EBook, *Offer* does not count as any such commitment; but an explicit *Accept* from Alice does. Thus, when EBook sends Alice an *Offer* message, Alice infers the commitment, but EBook does not—a misalignment.                                    ∎

Heterogeneity is addressed by statically analyzing if the interfaces of agents are compatible [10].

**Autonomy.** Agent autonomy must be accommodated; however, accommodating autonomy is nontrivial. The reason is that autonomy operationally means that they are free to send messages. In turn, this means that communication between agents is asynchronous. Thus, in general, agents may observe messages in different orders. Since messages are understood in terms of their effects on commitments, the agents involved may become misaligned. This is the cause of misalignment in Example 2.

*Example 2.* EBook sends an *Offer* to Alice, where the offer means a commitment that if Alice pays, then EBook will send the book. Alice sends the payment (message) for the book. Concurrently, EBook cancels the offer by sending *CancelOffer*. Alice observes EBook's cancellation after sending the payment; so she regards it as spurious. EBook observes Alice's payment after sending its cancellation, so EBook considers the payment late. As a result, Alice infers that EBook is committed to sending her the book, but EBook does not infer that commitment. Thus, EBook and Alice are misaligned.                                    ∎

An ideal approach to addressing the challenge of autonomy should work without curbing autonomy. In contrast, existing approaches to reasoning about commitments in distributed systems typically rely on some kind of synchronization protocol; synchronization, however, inhibits autonomy. Chopra and Singh [11] formalize the inferences made upon observing commitment-related messages in such a way that, in spite of autonomy, agents remain aligned.

**Distribution.** In a distributed system, some agents may have more information about relevant events than others. This is the cause of misalignment in Example 3.

*Example 3.* Alice commits to Bob that if the sky is clear at 5PM, then she will meet him at the lake. At 5PM, Bob observes (a message from the environment) that the sky is clear, and therefore infers that Alice is unconditionally committed to meeting him at the lake. However, Alice does not know that the sky is clear, and therefore does not infer the unconditional commitment. Bob and Alice are thus misaligned. ∎

Chopra and Singh [11] state *integrity constraints*, which are constraints upon agent behavior necessary to handle distribution. The constraints are of two kinds: (1) a debtor must inform the creditor about the discharge of a commitment, and (2) a creditor must inform the debtor about the detach of a commitment. One should not consider alignment until such information has been propagated.

## 2.1   Characterizing Alignment

A set of agents is aligned if in all executions, at *appropriate* points during their execution, if a creditor infers a commitment from its observations, the debtor also infers the commitment from its own observations [11]. An "appropriate" point in the execution of a multiagent system is given by consistent observations of the various agents where two additional properties hold. One, alignment may only be considered at those points where no message is in transit. Such points are termed *quiescent*. Two, alignment may only be considered at those points that are *integral* with respect to the stated information propagation constraints. The motivation behind the above properties is simply that it would surprise no one if two agents failed to infer matching commitments when they had made differing observations: either because some message was in transit that only its sender knew about or because some message was not sent, and some agent had withheld material facts from another.

## 2.2   Background on Commitments

A commitment is of the form $C(x, y, r, u)$ where $x$ and $y$ are agents, and $r$ and $u$ are propositions. If $r$ holds, then $C(x, y, r, u)$ is *detached*, and the commitment $C(x, y, \top, u)$ holds. If $u$ holds, then the commitment is *discharged* and doesn't hold any longer. All commitments are *conditional*; an unconditional commitment is merely a special case where the antecedent equals $\top$. Singh [16] presents key reasoning postulates for commitments.

The commitment operations are reproduced below (from [12]). CREATE, CANCEL, and RELEASE are two-party operations, whereas DELEGATE and ASSIGN are three-party operations.

- CREATE$(x, y, r, u)$ is performed by $x$, and it causes $C(x, y, r, u)$ to hold.
- CANCEL$(x, y, r, u)$ is performed by $x$, and it causes $C(x, y, r, u)$ to not hold.

- RELEASE$(x, y, r, u)$ is performed by $y$, and it causes $C(x, y, r, u)$ to not hold.
- DELEGATE$(x, y, z, r, u)$ is performed by $x$, and it causes $C(z, y, r, u)$ to hold.
- ASSIGN$(x, y, z, r, u)$ is performed by $y$, and it causes $C(x, z, r, u)$ to hold.

Let us define the set of messages that correspond to the basic commitment operations. Let $\Phi$ be a set of atomic propositions. In the commitment operations, $r$ and $u$ are formulas over $\Phi$ using $\wedge$ and $\vee$. $Create(x, y, r, u)$ and $Cancel(x, y, r, u)$ are messages from $x$ to $y$; $Release(x, y, r, u)$ from $y$ to $x$; $Delegate(x, y, z, r, u)$ from $x$ to $z$; and $Assign(x, y, z, r, u)$ from $y$ to $x$. Suppose $c = C(x, y, r, u)$. Then $Create(c)$ stands for $Create(x, y, r, u)$. We similarly define $Delegate(c, z)$, $Assign(c, z)$, $Release(c)$, and $Cancel(c)$. $Inform(x, y, p)$ is a message from $x$ to $y$, where $p$ is conjunction over $\Phi$. Observing an $Inform(p)$ causes $p$ to hold, which may lead to the discharge or detach of a commitment.

Below, let $c_B = C(EBook, Alice, \$12, BNW)$; $c_G = C(EBook, Alice, \$12, GoW)$; $c_0 = C(EBook, Alice, \$12, BNW \wedge GoW)$. (*BNW* stands for the book *Brave New World*; *GoW* stands for the book *Grapes of Wrath*).

## 3   Multiagent System Architecture

Figure 3 shows our proposal for a multiagent system architecture. At the level of business meaning, the components are the agents in the system representing the interacting business partners. As pertains to programming using our architecture, at the top, we have agents and at the bottom the communication layer; the middleware sits in between. This layered architecture is characterized by three kinds of interfaces.

- At the business level, the interface is between agents and is expressed via meanings. The business analyst and the software developer who programs using commitments

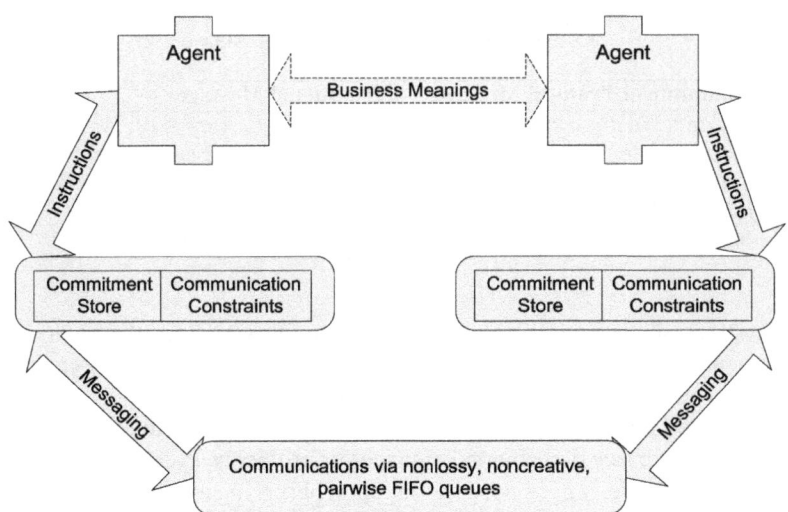

**Fig. 3.** Understanding Commitment-Based Architecture

would think at this level (of business relationships), and would be unaware of any lower layer.

- At the implementation level, the interface is between our middleware and the communication infrastructure and is based on traditional messaging services. In a traditional distributed system, a software developer would need to think at this level. In our approach, only the implementor of our middleware thinks at this level.
- Between the agent and the middleware, the interface is largely in terms of instructions from the agent to the middleware: when an agent tells the middleware to apply a commitment operation or one of the additional patterns based on commitments such as *Escalate* (patterns described later).

Two nice features of our approach are that (1) the instructions use the same vocabulary as the business meanings and (2) we specify middleware that guarantees alignment as long as the instructions are limited to the commitment operations or patterns. Below, we describe each components (agents), interconnections (interfaces), and layers in detail.

### 3.1   Agents

Agents represent business partners. They provide and consume real-world services by participating in service engagements. The principal elements of interest in an agent are its interface and its reasoning engine.

**Interface.**   An agent's interface describes the messages it expects to exchange with other agents, along with the business meanings of such messages. Table 1 shows Alice's interface specification. The left column is the actual protocol whereas the right column shows a traditional understanding of those messages. For example, $Create(EBook, Alice, \$12, BNW)$ message from EBook to Alice corresponds to an offer from EBook.

**Table 1.** An example interface for Alice

| Commitment Protocol Message | Traditional Message |
|---|---|
| $Create(EBook, Alice, \$12, BNW)$ | $Offer(EBook, Alice, \$12, BNW)$ |
| $Create(Alice, EBook, BNW, \$12)$ | $Accept(Alice, EBook, BNW, \$12)$ |
| $Release(EBook, Alice, \$12, BNW)$ | $Reject(Alice, EBook, \$12, BNW)$ |
| $Inform(EBook, Alice, BNW)$ | $Deliver(EBook, Alice, BNW)$ |
| $Inform(Alice, EBook, \$12)$ | $Pay(Alice, EBook, \$12)$ |

The interface shown in Table 1 is admittedly quite simple in that it does not talk about the penalties for the violation or cancellation of a commitment. Penalties would be encoded as additional commitments in the interface.

Notice that the interface does not contain some of the procedural constructs commonly found in interface description languages or protocols, such as sequence, choice, and so on. For example, it does not say, that upon observing an offer Alice has a *choice* between accepting or rejecting the offer—there is simply no need to say so. A rejection sent after Alice accepts the offer and EBook sends the book should have no effect—Alice should remain committed to pay. The formalization of commitments in [11] captures such intuitions, and makes the statement of procedural constructs in interfaces largely unnecessary. A second reason such constructs are introduced is to simply make the interaction synchronous. However, such constructs are rendered superfluous by the approach for reasoning about commitments in asynchronous settings [11]. Finally, threading constructions such as fork and join are clearly implementation details, and have no place in an interface. Of course, if an application demands a procedural construct, it could be introduced. For example, Alice may not trust booksellers and her interface might constrain delivery of books before payment. Alice will then be noninteroperable at the messaging-level with booksellers who require payment first; however, it would not affect alignment, that is, commitment-level interoperability [17].

As described earlier, misalignments arise when agents ascribe incompatible meanings to messages. An application programmer would specify an interface and publish it. Before interacting with other agents, the agent would presumably check for compatibility with the other agents.

**Engine.** The engine drives the agent. It represents the private policies of the agent; these govern when an agent should pass an instruction to the middleware, how instruction parameters should be bound, how an agent should handle returned callbacks (described below) and so on. In fact, the engine is the place for all the procedural details. For example, Alice's policy may enforce a choice between accept and reject upon receiving an offer, or dictate that payment be sent only after receiving books.

Writing the engine is where the principal efforts of a programmer are spent. The implementation of the engine could take many forms. It could be a BPEL, Jess, JADE, or a BDI implementation such as Jason, for example. The details are irrelevant as long as it is consistent with reasoning about commitments.

From the programming perspective, the engine is coded in terms of the *meaning* of a message, not the message itself. In other words, the API that the programmer uses to interface with the middleware is in terms of commitment operations and other patterns built on top of the commitment operations. When the meaning concerns the sending of the message, the meaning may be thought of as an instruction (API) from the agent's engine to the middleware. The middleware then sends the appropriate messages. Analogously, for an incoming message, the engine registers a callback with the middleware that returns when the commitment operation corresponding to the message has been executed. Thus, the programmer's API is a business-level one, one of the goals we set out to achieve.

### 3.2 Middleware

To relate meanings to messages, the middleware takes on the responsibility for representing and reasoning about commitments. The middleware consists of a commitment reasoner, maintains a commitment store, and is configured with communication constraints needed for the commitment operations and the further patterns (described later). The middleware computes commitments as prescribed in [11], and thus ensures that no misalignments arise because of autonomy and distribution. Further, as described above, the middleware's interface with the agent is instruction and callback-based.

The commitment reasoner presents a query interface to the agent (specifically the agent's engine), which can be used to inquire about commitments in the store. The engine can use such a information to decide on a course of action. For example, Alice's policy might be such that she sends payment only if $C(EBook, Alice, \$12, BNW)$ holds.

The middleware maintains a *serial*, point-to-point communication interface with each other agent in the system through the communication layer. This means that an agent's middleware processes messages involving another particular agent—sent or received—one at a time. This is necessary to ensure consistency of the commitment store.

## 3.3 Communication Layer

The role of the communication layer is to provide reliable, ordered, and noncreative delivery of messages. Reliability implies that each sent message is eventually delivered; ordered implies that any two messages sent by an agent to another will arrive in the order in which they were sent, and noncreative means messages are not created by the infrastructure. Such a communication layer can be readily implemented by available reliable message queuing solutions.

## 3.4 Programming the Middleware: Example Scenario

Going back to our purchase example, suppose EBook wishes to sell BNW to Alice. The scenario may be enacted as follows.

1. EBook computes that it wants to make Alice an offer for BNW on internal grounds, such as excess inventory or the goal of making a profit.
2. At the level of business meaning, EBook sends an offer to Alice. At the computational level, this is effected by EBook instructing its middleware to create the corresponding commitment $C(EBook, Alice, \$12, BNW)$.
3. The middleware then sends Alice corresponding message $Create(EBook, Alice, \$12, BNW)$.
4. The message travels along the communication infrastructure and arrives at Alice's endpoint of the message queue.
5. At the computational level, Alice's middleware receives the message from the communication layer, computes the corresponding commitment, and triggers Alice's callback on the creation of that commitment to return, in effect returning to the business level.
6. Alice may reason on the commitment and may decide to accept the offer, based on her private considerations such as goals.
7. Alice responds by accepting—by instructing her middleware to create $C(Alice, EBook, BNW, \$12)$; and so on.

Table 2 shows sample code for EBook. Although it is not possible to write such code yet (as the middleware hasn't been implemented yet), it captures the spirit of programming with a business-level API. In other examples, the more complex communication constraints would also apply.

**Table 2.** A snippet of EBook's code

```
if (preferredShopper(shopper) and inStock(book)) {

    Proposition price = lookupPrice(book);

    //register handler with middleware for accept from the shopper
    register(created(shopper, EBook, book, price), handler1);

    //Send an offer to the shopper
    Create(EBook,shopper,price,book);

    }
...


//Handler for accept
handler1(Debtor shopper, Proposition book, Proposition price) {

    //shopper accepted, so send the book
    Inform(EBook, shopper, book);
}
```

## 4  Abstractions Supported by the Middleware

As mentioned before, the middleware supports sending notifications to debtors and
creditors about detaches and discharges, respectively. The middleware also supports
other integrity constraints critical to alignment. The middleware supports all commitment operations, including delegation and assignment, which are three-party operations,
and guarantees that even in asynchronous settings, the operations occur without giving
causing misalignments. Alignment is guaranteed because the middleware embodies the
techniques for alignment developed in [11]. Here, we discuss even high-level abstractions in the form of commitment patterns and additional forms of alignment that the
middleware could practically support.

### 4.1  Patterns

We sketch some of the patterns here; these derive from those presented by Singh *et al.*
[5]. Below, we describe a sample set of patterns that can readily be supported by the
middleware.

Figure 4 shows the pattern for updating a commitment. At the programming level,
this corresponds to the debtor sending an *Update* instruction to the middleware. At the
computational level, the debtor's middleware sends two messages: one to cancel the
existing commitment, and another to create a new commitment in its place.

Figure 5 shows the pattern for escalating a delegated commitment. Consider that
Alice has delegated $c_B$ to Charlie. (In the figures, a commitment with the name prefix $d\_$
is the delegated version of a commitment. Since $c_B = C(EBook, Alice, \$12, BNW)$,
in Figure 5, $d\_c_B = C(Charlie, Alice, \$12, BNW)$.) The delegatee (Charlie) may find

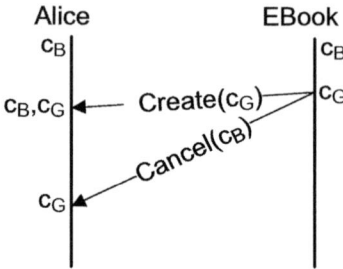

**Fig. 4.** Update pattern

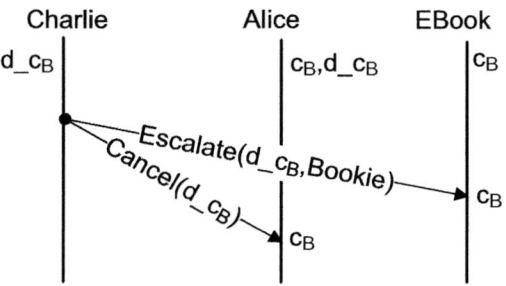

**Fig. 5.** Escalate pattern

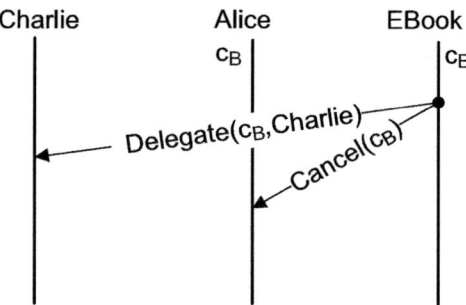

**Fig. 6.** Delegating without responsibility pattern

itself unable to fulfill the commitment. Here, the delegatee sends an *Escalate* instruction to the middleware. The middleware then sends a message notifying the delegator of the escalation of the commitment, and a *Cancel* message to the creditor.

Figure 6 shows the pattern for delegating a commitment without retaining responsibility. Here, the debtor instructs the middleware to accomplish *DelegationWithoutResponsibility*. Along with the *Delegate* instruction to the delegatee, the middleware sends a *Cancel* message to the creditor thus absolving the debtor of any further responsibility. (Presumably, upon receiving the *Delegate*, Charlie will send $Create(d\_c_B)$ to Alice.)

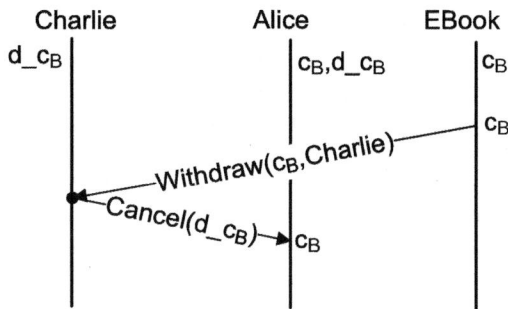

**Fig. 7.** Withdraw pattern

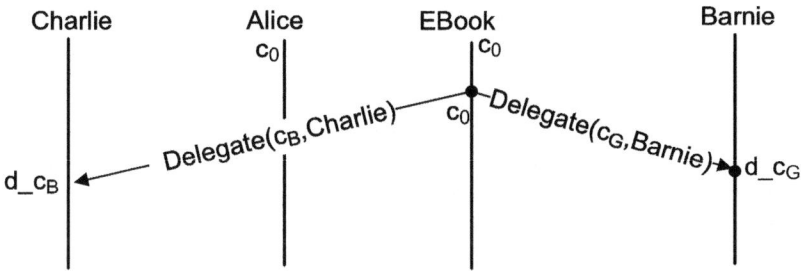

**Fig. 8.** Division of labor pattern

Figure 7 shows the pattern for withdrawing a delegated commitment. The delegator sends a *Withdraw* instruction to the middleware. The middleware then sends a *Withdraw* message to the delegatee. The delegatee's middleware, upon receiving this message, sends a *Cancel* to the creditor. The callback for *Withdraw* would return in the delegatee.

Figure 8 shows the pattern for division of labor: different parts of the commitment are delegated to different parties. Here, the delivery of $BNW$ is delegated to Charlie and that of $GoW$ is delegated to Barnie.

### 4.2   Other Forms of Alignment

Alignment as described in the previous sections and in [11] is essentially a creditor-debtor relation. When a creditor-debtor misalignment arises, there is the possibility of a violation of a commitment, and therefore, noncompliance. The following additional forms of alignment may be supported as additional patterns in the middleware. These forms of alignment may not necessarily result in noncompliance as it relates to commitment violation; nonetheless, these forms are useful for maintaining coherence in virtual organization settings, and are commonly effected in practice.

**Debtor-debtor Alignment.**  For example, suppose EBook delegates the commitment to send Alice a book to another bookseller Charlie. Then, EBook might want to be notified when Charlie discharges the commitment by sending the book, and vice versa.

Such alignment may be formalized in terms of debtor-debtor alignment: two agents who are related by a delegation relation remain aligned with respect to the discharge of the commitment. To effect such alignment would mean that the middleware would have to be configured with the additional constraint that if a debtor delegates a commitment to another agent, then whenever one of them discharges the commitment, it notifies the other.

Considering alignment in a *debtor group* could also be a useful notion. When two or more agents are committed for the same thing (thus the group), then whenever one discharges the commitment, it notifies the entire group.

**Creditor-creditor Alignment.**  In a similar vein, suppose Alice assigns the commitment made to her by EBook to Bob. Alice may want to be notified when Bob sends the payment, and vice versa.

This alignment is between creditors, and it is formalized and effected analogously to debtor-debtor alignment.

**Contextual Alignment.**  Each commitment has a social or legal context. Although we have omitted the context from the commitment so far, each commitment is in general a relation between three agents, the debtor, the creditor, and the context, and is expressed as $C(debtor, creditor, context, antecedent, consequent)$. The context's role is the enforcement of the commitment. If EBook and Alice are operating on eBay, then eBay is the context of their interaction. Applications such as eBay, in which the context itself plays an active role, typically have the requirement that the context should also be aligned with respect to the commitment.

Contextual alignment involves three parties; stronger guarantees, such as causal delivery [18] may be required from the communication layer.

## 5   Discussion: Conclusions and Future Work

In this paper, we have presented a multiagent system architecture based on interaction and commitments. CSOA as an architectural style was first proposed in [5]; the current paper elaborates on that theme by taking into account the results on commitment alignment [11]. In particular, we have discussed a middleware that can compute commitments and guarantee alignment between agents even in completely asynchronous settings. Notably, the middleware provides high-level programming abstractions that build on commitment operations. We have also sketched alternative kinds of alignments that the middleware could practically support, thus further alleviating the programmer's burden.

Our architecture is unique in that commitments form the principal interconnections between agents. We deemphasize the implementation of the agent's engine. Agent programming languages, for example 2APL [19], remain largely based on BDI and do not support commitments. As mentioned before, such languages can be used to create an agent's engine. Enhancing agent programming frameworks such as JADE with high-level abstractions, for example, as illustrated in [20], is no doubt useful. However, when one talks of multiagent systems, that invariably involves interaction and commitments. Therefore, a programming language or a framework for multiagent systems should ideally support reasoning about commitments, and have commitment-related abstractions.

Even when interactions protocols are supported in agent-oriented methodologies and platforms, it is at the level of specific choreographies, and not of meaning (for example, [21,22,23,24]). Tropos [25] uses the notion of goals to abstract away from agent reasoning and specific plans; however, when it comes to architectural specifications, Tropos resorts to data and control dependencies. Dastani *et al.* [26] show how to model a rich family of coordination connectors for multiagent systems, formalized as data and control flow abstractions. They do not consider the meaning of messages and thus lack the business-level semantics that distinguishes our work. Winikoff supports commitments in SAAPL by providing mappings from commitments to BDI-style plans, but the commitment reasoning supported is fairly limited [4]. Fornara *et al.* [27] base the semantics of communicative acts in terms of commitments. However, the operational semantics of commitments themselves do not consider asynchronous settings. As a consequence, an architecture based on the communicative acts would require strong assumptions such as synchrony.

In general, the treatment of communication at a low level in terms of data and control flow is complementary to our work. We can explain this in terms of correctness properties [17]. At a business level, commitment alignment is the correctness property as pertains to interoperability; at the level of data and control, interoperability is often characterized in terms of liveness and safety. On the one hand, agents may be aligned (with respect to their commitments) but deadlocked, each waiting for the other to take the next step. On the other hand, agents may be deadlock-free but misaligned.

The main priority for our research is the implementation of the proposed architecture. The language used here to give meanings to communications is sufficiently expressive for our purposes. We are investigating more powerful languages, however, for more subtle situations.

**Acknowledgments.** This research was partially supported by the Integrated FP6-EU project SERENITY contract 27587.

# References

1. Shaw, M., Garlan, D.: Software Architecture: Perspectives on an Emerging Discipline. Prentice-Hall, Upper Saddle River (1996)
2. Yolum, P., Singh, M.P.: Flexible protocol specification and execution: Applying event calculus planning using commitments. In: Proceedings of the 1st International Joint Conference on Autonomous Agents and MultiAgent Systems, pp. 527–534. ACM Press, New York (July 2002)
3. Desai, N., Mallya, A.U., Chopra, A.K., Singh, M.P.: Interaction protocols as design abstractions for business processes. IEEE Transactions on Software Engineering 31(12), 1015–1027 (2005)
4. Winikoff, M.: Implementing commitment-based interactions. In: Proceedings of the 6th International Joint Conference on Autonomous Agents and Multiagent Systems, pp. 1–8 (2007)
5. Singh, M.P., Chopra, A.K., Desai, N.: Commitment-based SOA. IEEE Computer 42 (2009), http://www.csc.ncsu.edu/faculty/mpsingh/papers/
6. Hohpe, G., Woolf, B.: Enterprise Integration Patterns: Designing, Building, and Deploying Messaging Solutions. Addison-Wesley Longman Publishing Co., Inc., Amsterdam (2003)
7. RosettaNet: Home page (1998), www.rosettanet.org

8. GDSN, http://www.gs1.org/productssolutions/gdsn/
9. AMQP: Advanced message queuing protocol (2007), http://www.amqp.org
10. Chopra, A.K., Singh, M.P.: Constitutive interoperability. In: Proceedings of the 7th International Conference on Autonomous Agents and Multiagent Systems, pp. 797–804 (2008)
11. Chopra, A.K., Singh, M.P.: Multiagent commitment alignment. In: Proceedings of the 8th International Joint Conference on Autonomous Agents and MultiAgent Systems (AAMAS), Columbia, SC, pp. 937–944, IFAAMAS (May 2009)
12. Singh, M.P.: An ontology for commitments in multiagent systems: Toward a unification of normative concepts. Artificial Intelligence and Law 7, 97–113 (1999)
13. Fournet, C., Hoare, C.A.R., Rajamani, S.K., Rehof, J.: Stuck-free conformance. In: Alur, R., Peled, D.A. (eds.) CAV 2004. LNCS, vol. 3114, pp. 242–254. Springer, Heidelberg (2004)
14. Bravetti, M., Zavattaro, G.: A theory for strong service compliance. In: Murphy, A.L., Vitek, J. (eds.) COORDINATION 2007. LNCS, vol. 4467, pp. 96–112. Springer, Heidelberg (2007)
15. Baldoni, M., Baroglio, C., Chopra, A.K., Desai, N., Patti, V., Singh, M.P.: Choice, interoperability, and conformance in interaction protocols and service choreographies. In: Proceedings of the 9th International Conference on Autonomous Agents and Multiagent Systems (2009)
16. Singh, M.P.: Semantic considerations on dialectical and practical commitments. In: Proceedings of the 23rd Conference on Artificial Intelligence, pp. 176–181 (2008)
17. Singh, M.P., Chopra, A.K.: Correctness properties for multiagent systems. In: Baldoni, M., Son, T.C., van Riemsdijk, M.B., Winikoff, M. (eds.) DALT 2008. LNCS (LNAI), vol. 5397. Springer, Heidelberg (2009)
18. Schiper, A., Birman, K., Stephenson, P.: Lightweight causal and atomic group multicast. ACM Transactions on Computer Systems 9(3), 272–314 (1991)
19. Dastani, M.: 2APL: A practical agent programming language. Autonomous Agents and Multi-Agent Systems 16(3), 214–248 (2008)
20. Baldoni, M., Boella, G., Genovese, V., Grenna, R., van der Torre, L.: How to program organizations and roles in the jade framework. In: Bergmann, R., Lindemann, G., Kirn, S., Pĕchouček, M. (eds.) MATES 2008. LNCS (LNAI), vol. 5244, pp. 25–36. Springer, Heidelberg (2008)
21. Zambonelli, F., Jennings, N.R., Wooldridge, M.: Developing multiagent systems: The Gaia methodology. ACM Transactions on Software Engineering Methodology 12(3), 317–370 (2003)
22. Padgham, L., Winikoff, M.: Prometheus: A practical agent-oriented methodology. In: Henderson-Sellers, B., Giorgini, P. (eds.) Agent-Oriented Methodologies, pp. 107–135. Idea Group, Hershey (2005)
23. Garcia-Ojeda, J.C., DeLoach, S.A., Robby, Oyenan, W.H., Valenzuela, J.L.: O-maSE: A customizable approach to developing multiagent development processes. In: Luck, M., Padgham, L. (eds.) Agent-Oriented Software Engineering VIII. LNCS, vol. 4951, pp. 1–15. Springer, Heidelberg (2008)
24. Alberti, M., Chesani, F., Gavanelli, M., Lamma, E., Mello, P., Torroni, P.: Verifiable agent interaction in abductive logic programming: the SCIFF framework. ACM Transactions on Computational Logic 9(4) (2008)
25. Bresciani, P., Perini, A., Giorgini, P., Giunchiglia, F., Mylopoulos, J.: Tropos: An agent-oriented software development methodology. Autonomous Agents and Multi-Agent Systems 8(3), 203–236 (2004)
26. Dastani, M., Arbab, F., de Boer, F.S.: Coordination and composition in multi-agent systems. In: Proceedings of the 4rd International Joint Conference on Autonomous Agents and Multiagent Systems (AAMAS), pp. 439–446. ACM, New York (2005)
27. Fornara, N., Viganò, F., Colombetti, M.: Agent communication and artificial institutions. Autonomous Agents and Multi-Agent Systems 14(2), 121–142 (2007)

# A Computational Semantics for Communicating Rational Agents Based on Mental Models

Koen V. Hindriks and M. Birna van Riemsdijk

EEMCS, Delft University of Technology, Delft, The Netherlands
{k.v.hindriks,m.b.vanriemsdijk}@tudelft.nl

**Abstract.** Communication is key in a multi-agent system for agents to exchange information and coordinate their activities. In the area of agent programming, the challenge is to introduce communication primitives that are useful to a programmer of agent programs as well as semantically well-defined. Moreover, for agents that derive their choice of action from their beliefs and goals it is natural to introduce primitives that support communication related to both of these attitudes. We introduce a communication approach for multi-agent systems based on *mood operators* instead of the usual speech act labels and a semantics based on the idea that a message can be used to *(re)construct a mental model* of the sender. An operational semantics is provided that specifies the precise meaning of the primitives. Finally, to facilitate *coordination* in multi-agent systems, we introduce the concept of a *conversation* to synchronize actions and communication among agents. Conversations provide a limited resource at the multi-agent level, and provide a natural approach for multi-agent systems to coordinate agent activities.

## 1 Introduction

Communication is key in a multi-agent system for agents to exchange information and coordinate their activities. For this reason, the design of constructs that facilitate communication in agent programming languages also is an important aspect that must be addressed in these programming languages. In particular, for agents that derive their choice of action from their beliefs and goals it is natural to introduce communication primitives that support communication related to both of these attitudes.

We argue that it is not sufficient to provide only communication primitives that facilitate the *exchange of messages*, but it is also necessary to provide explicit support for the *coordination* of agent communication and activities. It often occurs that agents need to decide on which agent will perform a particular task, whether it is the turn of an agent to make a move, or synchronize their activities for other reasons. It is useful to provide programming constructs that facilitate such coordination.

In this paper we address both aspects discussed above, and propose a communication language that facilitates both information exchange as well as the coordination of agent activities. We take a definite *engineering stance* here. Although we think it is very important to introduce communication primitives

L. Braubach, J.-P. Briot, and J. Thangarajah (Eds.): ProMAS 2009, LNAI 5919, pp. 31–48, 2010.

that are semantically well-defined and motivated adequately from a theoretical point of view, our main concern is to provide *useful* communication facilities to a programmer of rational agents. An approach is presented that addresses each of these issues: the meaning of the communication constructs are defined using a formal semantics, are theoretically motivated, and - so we believe - address the pragmatic component as the primitives introduced are relatively easy to grasp, which will facilitate programmers that will need to make good use of these constructs.

The paper is organized as follows. In section 2 we briefly discuss related work in agent programming languages with respect to communication. Then in section 3 we present our approach for integrating agent communication into an agent programming language informally first and motivate some of our choices. Section 4 introduces the formal semantics for the various communication facilities. Section 5 illustrates all communication constructs, using the dining philosophers as an example. Finally, section 6 concludes the paper.

## 2    Communication in Agent Programming Languages

It has been common in agent programming to integrate communication constructs into the programming language using constructs that are based on *speech act theory* [1,2]. This theory has underpinned much work on agent communication languages such as KQML [3] and FIPA [4], two of the most well-known agent communication languages available. The JADE implementation [5] that is said to be compliant with the FIPA specifications is one of the most used platforms for implementing agents, as it not only facilitates the FIPA list of speech acts but also provides a middleware infrastructure that facilitates message exchange. One of the distinguishes features of any approach based on speech acts is the list of *performative labels* that may be used to label possible speech acts that an agent can perform, such as *inform*ing, *ask*ing, and *request*ing to name but a few of the more well-known speech acts.

One of the approaches to integrating communication into an agent programming language is to explicitly integrate the communication primitives that a platform such as JADE provides. The interpreters of quite a few agent programming languages are built on top of JADE in order to have a middleware layer that facilitates message exchange. It is then relatively easy to provide the communication primitives of JADE as constructs that can be used in an agent program. This is more or less the approach taken in the programming language Jadex [6]. Communication in JACK [7] also seems to be based on a similar approach, but the implementation has not been based on JADE but on a specific implementation for JACK itself.

The integration of communication has been necessarily somewhat pragmatic in order to be able to deal with the specifics of each programming language. In particular, the means to handle received messages and the effects of messages vary across languages. In 2APL, a successor of 3APL [8], the format of messages as specified in FIPA is basically preserved [9], and the same performative labels available in FIPA may be used as 2APL is built on top of JADE. Messages that are received are stored in a message base and so-called procedure call rules are used to allow an agent to react or respond to messages received. Different from the languages discussed above, the semantics of communication in 2APL is formally specified. The meaning of communication primitives and messages is defined by as a simple "mailbox" semantics: communicating a message means that the message is added to a mailbox and the programmer then needs to write rules to handle these messages.

Interestingly, a somewhat different approach is used for providing communication in the agent language Jason[10]. Although the approach is based on speech acts as well, instead of providing a long list of performative labels the programmer of a Jason agent can choose from a relatively small number of available labels, derived from KQML. We think restricting the set of labels to a limited set in the context of agent programming is a sensible thing to do for two reasons: (i) Offering a broad range of performative labels may confuse a programmer and complicate the design of agents, and (ii) it is difficult to avoid subtle differences in the semantics for two or more labels that are hard to distinguish by programmers.[1] For the set of labels available in Jason a formal semantics is defined that in some respects is similar to that specified in FIPA as far as the effects of communication are concerned. However, Jason does not require any specific preconditions to be true before an agent may send a message. A Jason-specific feature is the use of so-called "annotations" to label a message with the identity of the source of this information. These annotations were motivated specifically by the design of the communication semantics [10]. For example, the *tell* message inserts the content $c$ of the message into the receiver's belief base, labeled with an annotation $s$ to identify the source of this information; that is, $c[s]$ is inserted into the belief base. As another example, the *achieve* message inserts the content of the corresponding message in the event base. Moreover, the *ask* primitive provides a limited means to synchronize agents as the asking agent may wait for an answer from the agent that is being asked to address the message. Finally, abstract functions are introduced to determine whether a message is "socially acceptable", and only socially acceptable messages are processed.

Summarizing, all approaches in agent programming are based on the speech act paradigm, and more or less are based on KQML/FIPA. Some agent programming languages, such as 2APL and Jason, also provide a formal semantics that specifies precisely what happens when a message is sent. Although FIPA also specifies the preconditions and rational effects of the performance of specific speech acts, in practice there is no programming language that actually implements these specifications. This is in part due to the fact that certain features required by FIPA are not supported by agent programming languages, and in part due to more fundamental issues that gave rise to a shift from the sender to that of the receiver.

---

[1] An example to illustrate this issue is the subtle difference in meaning of the `confirm` and `inform` speech acts in FIPA [4].

The agent programming language that we take as our starting point in the remainder of this paper is the GOAL language [11]. This language has in common with 2APL and Jadex that agents have mental states that consist of *declarative beliefs and goals*. The presence of declarative beliefs and goals naturally induces the question how a rational agent can be provided with primitives that support communicating information related to both these mental attitudes, an issue that has not been explicitly addressed in the context of agent programming. Mental states also provide the means to define a semantics of communication that makes explicit the idea that a receiver reconstructs a mental model of the sender, in line with the noted shift from sender to receiver. The semantics that we will introduce here explicitly uses messages received to *model the sender*. Another contribution of this paper is the introduction of an explicit mechanism for synchronizing and coordinating agent activities based on the concept of a *conversation*. This concept seems related to that of an artefact or possibly workspace in the simpA language [12], and may be effectively implemented using constructs provided in this language.

## 3   Design of Communication Approach

As discussed, in agent programming a shift from the sender to the receiver has made. The reason for this shift may be explained by some of the criticisms that have been leveled against the use of speech act semantics for implementing agent communication, see e.g. [13,14].

The key idea of speech act theory that message exchanges are acts is implemented in most approaches to communication in agent programming by using *speech act labels* to tag messages. We believe that a second shift is needed and the use of speech act labels is better replaced by a different labelling. Note that we do not argue against differentiating message types by means of labelling messages per se. One of our main reasons for replacing speech act labels by a different labelling is that the interpretation typically associated with speech act labels as a specification of pre- and postconditions of actions does not provide a proper basis for implementing communication between agents. Speech act theory may be adequate as a *descriptive* theory that specifies the conditions that identify the particular type of communicative act that has been performed when a sentence is uttered (or message exchanged). We believe, however, that it is less useful to take the theory to provide a *recipe* for executing actions specified by means of pre- and postconditions as is traditional in computing science.[2] Attempts to do so run into some by now well-known problems. For example, the so-called *sincerity conditions* that should hold with respect to the sender usually are dropped in order to be able to make practical use of the labels that are used to classify various acts. Conditions like this have not been incorporated

---

[2] To highlight the difference we intend to convey here, an example may be useful: A label such as *misinform* or *lie* makes perfect sense in a *descriptive* theory but not so much as part of a message that is being transmitted, as usually one attempts to hide that one is deceiving.

into an operatorional semantics for communication for two reasons. First, it is impossible for a receiving agent to *verify* whether an agent speaks truthfully upon receiving a message of the form $inform(..)$, making the variety of labels not very useful for the purpose of identifying the act that has been performed (the reason for naming these labels as they have been) [13,14]. Second, a sender would be unnecessarily constrained by imposing such conditions and would no longer be able to "inform" an agent of a statement it believes to be false, i.e. lie.

There is a second, more pragmatic reason to deviate from the speech act paradigm in the context of agent programming, namely the fact that introducing a relatively high number of performative labels with possibly subtle semantical differences complicates agent design. The choice of labels, moreover, is different from theory to theory and it is not clear which set is to be preferred (compare e.g. KQML and FIPA). We argue below that these issues can be resolved by using *mood operators* instead of speech act labels, a choice that also has a strong basis in linguistic theory.

We briefly discuss an alternative approach to the FIPA-style semantics based on so-called *social commitments*, see e.g. [15,16,17]. There is a huge literature on the topic of *social semantics* which is impossible to survey here. A social semantics for speech acts may be contrasted with a semantics based on mental states. Whereas social commitments, the main entities in a social semantics, are supposed to be *public*, mental states are supposed to be *private*. An advantage of social commitments therefore is that there is no need to reconstruct and attribute them to other agents [15]. The basic idea of social commitments is that speech acts do have public and objective effects with which both sender and receiver can always be confronted again; a receiver may always say, for example, something like: "You told/asked/requested me so". Although the processing of the message by the receiver has moved to the background here, from the perspective of agent programming this is not necessarily an advantage. As agent-oriented programming may also be paraphrased as "programming with mental states", it is important to clarify how social commitments relate to the mental attitudes of agents. We recognize that a social semantics may be complementary to a semantics based on mental attitudes and some work to revolve this issue has been reported in, for example, [18]. The main issue seems to be how to relate commitments which are supposed to be *publicly available* to mental states which are supposed to be *private*. This issue, we believe, is not easily resolved, and in this paper, we focus on a semantics that is based on mental models as they represent the entities that an agent computes with in agent programming.

### 3.1   Communication Semantics

We take an *engineering stance* towards the design of a communication semantics that fits well with the agent-oriented programming paradigm. Related to this, issues such as how useful communication primitives are to a programmer, whether such primitives facilitate communication about the beliefs and goals of rational agents, and the range of applications that these primitives have need to be considered. This means that communication primitives should support, e.g., the exchange of reasons for acting based on beliefs and goals, and should be provided with a relatively easy to grasp semantics that fits basic intuitions.

The starting point for the semantics introduced here is the idea that a message can be used to *(re)construct a mental model* of the sender. The content of a message is not a speech act per se but a speech act is inferred from a message. This idea is somewhat related to the *inferential* approach to speech act theory advocated in [19]. In particular, some of our ideas are inspired by the work in theoretical linguistics of Harnish [20] and we aim to provide a framework for agent communication based on some of these ideas. It should however also be noted that we have simplified this work in line with some of the pragmatic issues discussed above. A second idea is to use *mood operators* instead of speech act labels. Here, we take inspiration from natural language to differentiate between various communication modes. Mood, in the sense that we use it here in line with linguistic theory, refers to "sentential form with a function". We follow [20] and limit the discussion to the three *major moods* in natural language:

- *declarative* mood, e.g. "Snow is white." Typically, the literal and direct use of a declarative sentence is to make statements (about the environment).
- *interrogative* mood, e.g. "Is it snowing?". One of the typical literal and direct uses of an interrogative is, for example, to inquire about a state of affairs.
- *imperative* mood, e.g. "Leave the room!". Typically, the literal and direct use of an imperative is to direct someone to establish a state of affairs.

These moods are recognized as central in their communicative importance and occur most frequently [20], and for this reason we include these moods in a language for agent communication. Corresponding to each of these moods, mood operators are introduced. We use $:\phi$ to indicate declarative mood, $?\phi$ to indicate declarative mood, and $!\phi$ to indicate imperative mood.[3]

Returning to one of our main goals, that of defining a semantics for agent communication, we start by discussing some of the ideas presented in [20]. Harnish presents a set of strategies accounting for the *literal and direct* use of declaratives, imperative and interrogative sentences. As a first approximation, Harnish suggests that a hearer upon perceiving that $S$ utters "Leave the room!" is allowed to infer that $S$ is *directing* that someone to leave the room, and the request (etc) is *complied with* just in case someone leaves the room. These strategies thus allow to infer the *force* and the *condition of satisfaction* related to the uterrance. Harnish suggests that this process proceeds in two stages: "first, there is an inference from form to expressed attitude; then there is an inference from expressed attitude to force". The expressed attitude of a declarative $:\phi$ is a belief that $\phi$, of an interrogative $?\phi$ it is a desire that hearer tells whether that $\phi$, and of an imperative $!\phi$ it is a desire that hearer makes it the case that $\phi$. Inferences to (illocutionary) force in stage two then are restricted and only support inferences to those speech acts whose conditions require the expressed attitude [20].

We adapt the proposal of Harnish here in two ways, which better meets our pragmatic concerns to provide a relatively easy to understand semantics. First,

---

[3] This notation has also been used by Pendlebury [21].

we do not want to complicate the representational means needed to express these conditions, i.e. at this stage we do not want to complicate things by introducing modal operators in the databases that agents maintain but leave this for future work. Of course, the meaning should still be intuitive and match common sense; we propose the following: upon receiving a message $:\phi$ $r$ concludes that sender $s$ believes $\phi$; from $?\phi$ $r$ concludes that $s$ does not know whether $\phi$; and, from $!\phi$ $r$ concludes that $s$ has $\phi$ as a goal, and does not believe $\phi$ to be the case. Second, we do not incorporate stage two into our semantics. The actual conclusion as to which speech act has been performed is left to the agent; that is, the programmer needs to either supply the agent with explicit inference rules to derive speech act types, or leave these implicit in the design of the agent (which we expect will be easier in practice). A message thus possibly allows for multiple interpretations as to which speech act is performed [20].

We further motivate and illustrate the proposed semantics briefly using an example (see also [22]). Consider the utterance "The house is white" and let $p$ denote the proposition that is expressed. In line with the discussion above about the literal and direct use of an utterance such as "The house is white", the effect of this utterance in our proposed semantics is that the receiver updates his model of the sender in such a way that it models the sender as believing $p$. Obviously, this is not always a safe assumption to make, as the sender may be lying, but it is also not overly presumptuous. Other "effects" such an utterance might have on the mental state of a receiver could be: (i) The receiver comes to believe that the house is white, (ii) The receiver comes to believe that the sender had the intention to make the receiver believe that the house is white,and (iii) The utterance has no effect on the receiver, i.e. its mental state is not changed as a result of the utterance. Even though each of these other interpretations may be waranted given specific circumstances of the speaker and the hearer and the knowledge they have about each other, these interpretations do not correspond with the literal and direct use of an utterance [20]. In general, we consider effect (i) too strong, as it implicitly assumes that the sender always convinces the receiver; effect (ii) too indirect, and not very useful from a programmer's point of view either as rather involved reasoning on the part of the agent seems to be required to make good use of such indirect conclusions about the sender's state of mind; and, finally, effect (iii) too weak, as it is not very useful for programming communication among agents since no effect would occur.

Summarizing, the communication semantics that we propose records the *expressed attitude* of the sender in a *mental model* of that sender maintained by the receiving agent. Declaratives express a belief of the sender, interrogatives a lack of belief, and imperatives desires or goals. Messages thus never directly impact the beliefs or goals of a receiving agent. We do allow, of course, that an agent updates his own beliefs and goals using his model of that of other agents. An agent also may use the mental models of other agents it maintains to decide which action to perform next, which is illustrated in the program of section 5).

## 3.2 Conversations

A second contribution of this paper is the concept of a *conversation* to facilitate the synchronization of actions and communication in a multi-agent system, which is particularly important to coordinate agent activities.

As is well-known, in concurrent systems one needs mechanisms to ensure that processes cannot access a particular resource simultaneously. A similar need arises in multi-agent systems, but this has received little attention in the agent programming community so far. Emphasis has been put on the fact that agent communication is *asynchronous*. However, in order to ensure that only one agent has access to a particular resource at any time, agents need to be able to coordinate their activities and *synchronize* their actions.[4] Of course, asynchronous communication allows to implement synchronization between agents. We argue, however, that it is useful to have predefined primitives available in an agent programming language that facilitate coordination and synchronization, as is usual in concurrent programming [23]. We introduce a mechanism that fits elegantly into the overall setup of communication primitives introduced above, using the notion of a *conversation*.

# 4    A Communication Semantics Based on Mental Models

In this section, we make the informal semantics discussed above precise in the context of GOAL.

## 4.1 Mental Models and Mental States

Mental models play a key role in this semantics and are introduced first. GOAL agents maintain mental models that consists of *declarative* beliefs and goals. An agent's beliefs represent its environment whereas the goals represent a state of the environment the agent wants. Beliefs and goals are specified using some knowledge representation technology. In the specification of the operational semantics we use a propositional logic $\mathcal{L}_0$ built from a set of propositional atoms *Atom* and the usual boolean connectives. We use $\models$ to denote the usual consequence relation associated with $\mathcal{L}_0$, and assume a special symbol $\bot \in \mathcal{L}_0$ which denotes the false proposition. In addition, the presence of an operator $\oplus$ for adding $\phi$ to a belief base and an operator $\ominus$ for removing $\phi$ from a belief base are assumed to be available.[5] A mental model associated with a GOAL agent needs to satisfy a number of *rationality constraints*.

---

[4] Note that *perfectly symmetrical solutions to problems in concurrent programming are impossible because if every process executes exactly the same program, they can never 'break ties'* [23]. To resolve this, solutions in concurrency theory contain asymmetries in the form of process identifiers or a kernel maintaining a queue.

[5] We assume that $\Sigma \oplus \phi \models \phi$ whenever $\phi$ is consistent, and that otherwise nothing changes, and that $\Sigma \ominus \phi \not\models \phi$ whenever $\phi$ is not a tautology, and that otherwise nothing changes. Additional properties such as minimal change, etc. are usually associated with these operators (see e.g. [24]) but not considered here.

**Definition 1.** *(Mental Model)*
*A mental model is a pair $\langle \Sigma, \Gamma \rangle$ with $\Sigma, \Gamma \subseteq \mathcal{L}_0$ such that:*

- *The beliefs are consistent:* $\qquad\qquad\qquad \Sigma \not\models \bot$
- *Individual goals are consistent:* $\qquad\qquad \forall \gamma \in \Gamma : \gamma \not\models \bot$
- *Goals are not yet (believed to be) achieved:* $\forall \gamma \in \Gamma : \Sigma \not\models \gamma$

In a multi-agent system it is useful for an agent to maintain mental models of other agents. This allows an agent to keep track of the perspectives of other agents on the environment and the goals they have adopted to change it. A mental model maintained by an agent $i$ about another agent $j$ represents what $i$ thinks that $j$ believes and which goals it has. Mental models of other agents can also be used to take the beliefs and goals of these agents into account in its own decision-making. An agent may construct a mental model of another agent from the messages it receives from that agent or from observations of the actions that that agent performs (e.g., using intention recognition techniques). Here we focus on the former option.

We assume a multi-agent system that consists of a fixed number of agents. To simplify the presentation further, we use $\{1, \ldots, n\}$ as names for these agents. A *mental state* of an agent is then defined as a mapping from all agent names to mental models.

**Definition 2.** *(Mental State)*
*A mental state $m$ is a total mapping from agent names to mental models, i.e.*
$m(i) = \langle \Sigma_i, \Gamma_i \rangle$ *for $i \in \{1, \ldots, n\}$.*

For an agent $i$, $m(i)$ are its own beliefs and goals, which was called the agent's mental state in [25].

A GOAL agent is able to inspect its mental state by means of *mental state conditions*. The mental state conditions of GOAL consist of atoms of the form $\mathbf{bel}(i, \phi)$ and $\mathbf{goal}(i, \phi)$ and Boolean combinations of such atoms. $\mathbf{bel}(i, \phi)$ where $i$ refers to the agent itself means that the agent itself believes $\phi$, whereas $\mathbf{bel}(i, \phi)$ where $i$ refers to another agent means that the agent believes that agent $i$ believes $\phi$. Similarly, $\mathbf{goal}(i, \phi)$ is used to check whether agent $i$ has a goal $\phi$.[6]

**Definition 3.** *(Syntax of Mental State Conditions)*
*A mental state condition, denoted by $\psi$, is defined by the following rules:*

$$i ::= \textit{any element from } \{1, \ldots, n\} \mid \boldsymbol{me} \mid \boldsymbol{allother}$$
$$\phi ::= \textit{any element from } \mathcal{L}_0$$
$$\psi ::= \mathbf{bel}(i, \phi) \mid \mathbf{goal}(i, \phi) \mid \psi \wedge \psi \mid \neg \psi$$

The meaning of a mental state condition is defined by means of the mental state of an agent. An atom $\mathbf{bel}(i, \phi)$ is true whenever $\phi$ follows from the belief base of the mental model for agent $i$. An atom $\mathbf{goal}(i, \phi)$ is true whenever $\phi$ follows

---

[6] In a multi-agent setting it is useful to introduce additional labels instead of agent names $i$, e.g. $\mathbf{me}$ to refer to the agent itself and $\mathbf{allother}$ to refer to all other agents, but we will not discuss these here in any detail.

from *one* of the goals of the mental model for agent $i$. This is in line with the usual semantics for goals in GOAL, which allows the goal base to be inconsistent (see [25] for details). Note that we overload $\models$.

**Definition 4.** *(Semantics of Mental State Conditions)*
*Let $m$ be a mental state and $m(i) = \langle \Sigma_i, \Gamma_i \rangle$. Then the semantics of mental state conditions is defined by:*

$$
\begin{aligned}
m &\models \mathbf{bel}(i, \phi) & &\text{iff } \Sigma_i \models \phi \\
m &\models \mathbf{goal}(i, \phi) & &\text{iff } \exists \gamma \in \Gamma_i \text{ such that } \gamma \models \phi \\
m &\models \neg \psi & &\text{iff } m \not\models \psi \\
m &\models \psi \wedge \psi' & &\text{iff } m \models \psi \text{ and } m \models \psi'
\end{aligned}
$$

## 4.2 Actions

GOAL has a number of built-in actions and also allows programmers to introduce user-specified actions by means of STRIPS-style action specifications. The program discussed in Section 5 provides examples of various user-specified actions. In the definition of the semantics we will abstract from action specifications specified by programmers and assume that a fixed set of actions $Act$ and a (partial) transition function $T$ is given. $T$ specifies how actions from $Act$, performed by agent $i$, update $i$'s mental state, i.e., $T(i, a, m) = m'$ for $i$ an agent name, $a \in Act$ and $m, m'$ mental states. All actions except for communicative actions are assumed to only affect the mental state of the agent performing the action.

The built-in actions available in GOAL (adapted to distinguish between mental models) that we need here include $\mathbf{ins}(i, \phi)$, $\mathbf{del}(i, \phi)$, $\mathbf{adopt}(i, \phi)$, $\mathbf{drop}(i, \phi)$ and communicative actions of the form $\mathbf{send}(i, msg)$ where $i$ is an agent name and $msg$ is a message of the form $:\phi$, $?\phi$ or $!\phi$. The semantics of actions from $Act$ and built-in actions performed by agent $i$ is formally captured by a mental state transformer function $M$ defined as follows:

$$
\begin{aligned}
M(i, a, m) &= \begin{cases} T(i, a, m) & \text{if } a \in Act \text{ and } T(i, a, m) \text{ is defined} \\ \text{undefined} & \text{otherwise} \end{cases} \\
M(i, \mathbf{ins}(j, \phi), m) &= m \oplus_j \phi \\
M(i, \mathbf{del}(j, \phi), m) &= m \ominus_j \phi \\
M(i, \mathbf{adopt}(j, \phi), m) &= \begin{cases} m \cup_j \phi & \text{if } \phi \text{ is consistent and } m \not\models \mathbf{bel}(i, \phi) \\ \text{undefined} & \text{otherwise} \end{cases} \\
M(i, \mathbf{drop}(j, \phi), m) &= m -_j \phi \\
M(i, \mathbf{send}(j, msg), m) &= m
\end{aligned}
$$

where $m \times_j \phi$ means that operator $\times \in \{\oplus, \ominus, \cup, -\}$ is applied to mental model $m(j)$, i.e. $m \times_j \phi(i) = m(j) \times \phi$ and $m \times_j \phi(k) = m(k)$ for $k \neq j$. To define the application of operators to mental models, we use $Th(T)$ to denote the logical theory induced by $T$, i.e. the set of all logical consequences that can be derived from $T$. Assuming that $m(i) = \langle \Sigma, \Gamma \rangle$, we then define: $m(i) \oplus \phi = \langle \Sigma \oplus \phi, \Gamma \setminus (Th(\Sigma \oplus \phi)) \rangle$, $m(i) \ominus \phi = \langle \Sigma \ominus \phi, \Gamma \rangle$, $m(i) \cup \phi = \langle \Sigma, \Gamma \cup \{\phi\} \rangle$, and $m(i) - \phi = \langle \Sigma, \Gamma \setminus \{\gamma \in \Gamma \mid \gamma \models \phi\} \rangle$. Note that sending a message does not have any effect on the sender. There is no need to incorporate any such effects in the semantics of **send** since such effects may be *programmed* by using the other built-in operators.

It is useful to be able to perform multiple actions simultaneously and we introduce the $+$ operator to do so. The idea here is that multiple mental actions may be performed simultaneously, possibly in combination with the execution of a *single* user-specified action (as such actions may have effects on the external environment it is not allowed to combine multiple user-specified actions by the $+$ operator). The meaning of $a + a'$ where $a, a'$ are actions, is defined as follows: if $M(i, a, m)$ and $M(i, a', m)$ are defined and $M(i, a', M(i, a, m)) = M(i, a, M(i, a', m))$ is a mental state, then $M(i, a+a', m) = M(i, a', M(i, a, m))$; otherwise, $a + a'$ is undefined.

In order to select actions for execution, an agent uses action rules of the form **if** $\psi$ **then** a, where a is a user-specified action, a built-in action, or a combination using the $+$-operator. An agent $\mathcal{A}$ is then a triple $\langle i, m, \Pi \rangle$ where $i$ is the agent's name, $m$ is the agent's mental state, and $\Pi$ is the agent's program (a set of action rules).

### 4.3   Operational Semantics: Basic Communication

We first introduce a single transition rule for an agent performing an action. Transitions "at the agent level" are labelled with the performed action, since this information is required "at the multi-agent level" in the case of communication.

**Definition 5.** (Actions)
*Let $\mathcal{A} = \langle i, m, \Pi \rangle$ be an agent, and **if** $\psi$ **then** $a \in \Pi$ be an action rule.*

$$\frac{m \models \psi \quad M(i, a, m) \text{ is defined}}{m \xrightarrow{a} M(i, a, m)}$$

Using Plotkin-style operational semantics, the semantics at the multi-agent level is provided by the rules below. A configuration of a multi-agent system consists of the agents of the multi-agent system $\{\mathcal{A}_1, \ldots, \mathcal{A}_n\}$ and the environment $E$, which is used to store messages that have been sent and are waiting for delivery.[7] The environment is used to model *asynchronous* communication, i.e., no handshake is required between sender and receiver of a message. Transitions at the multi-agent level are not labelled. Actions other than the **send** action only change the agent that executes them, as specified below.

**Definition 6.** (Action Execution)
*Let "a" be an action other than send(j, msg).*

$$\frac{\mathcal{A}_i \xrightarrow{a} \mathcal{A}'_i}{\mathcal{A}_1, \ldots, \mathcal{A}_i, \ldots, \mathcal{A}_n, E \longrightarrow \mathcal{A}_1, \ldots, \mathcal{A}'_i, \ldots, \mathcal{A}_n, E}$$

The following transition rule specifies the semantics of sending messages.

---

[7] Other aspects of the environment might also be modeled, but that is beyond the scope of this paper.

**Definition 7.** (Send)

$$\frac{\mathcal{A}_i \overset{send(j,msg)}{\longrightarrow} \mathcal{A}_i}{\mathcal{A}_1, \ldots, \mathcal{A}_i, \ldots, \mathcal{A}_n, E \longrightarrow \mathcal{A}_1, \ldots, \mathcal{A}_i, \ldots, \mathcal{A}_n, E \cup \{send(i, j, msg)\}}$$

The premise of the rule indicates that agent $\mathcal{A}_i$ sends a message to agent $\mathcal{A}_j$. To record this, $send(i, j, msg)$ is added to the environment, including both the sender $i$ and the intended receiver $j$. Also note that a message that is sent more than once has no effect as the environment is modeled as a set here (this is the case until the message is received).[8]

Three rules for receiving a message are introduced below, corresponding to each of the three message types. In each of these rules, the conclusion of the rule indicates that the mental state of the receiving agent is changed. If agent $j$ receives a message from agent $i$ that consists of a declarative sentence, it has the effect that the mental model $m(i)$ of the mental state of the receiver $j$ is modified by updating the belief base of $m(i)$ with $\phi$. In addition, any goals in the goal base of $m(i)$ that are implied by the updated belief base are removed from the goal base to ensure that the rationality constraints associated with mental models are satisfied.

**Definition 8.** (Receive: Declaratives)

$$\frac{send(i, j, {:}\phi) \in E}{\mathcal{A}_1, \ldots, \langle j, m, \Pi \rangle, \ldots, \mathcal{A}_n, E \longrightarrow \mathcal{A}_1, \ldots, \langle j, m', \Pi \rangle, \ldots, \mathcal{A}_n, E \setminus \{send(i, j, {:}\phi)\}}$$

*where:*

- $m'(i) = \langle \Sigma \oplus \phi, \Gamma \setminus Th(\Sigma \oplus \phi) \rangle$ *if* $m(i) = \langle \Sigma, \Gamma \rangle$, *and*
- $m'(k) = m(k)$ *for* $k \neq i$.

The condition $m'(k) = m(k)$ for $k \neq i$ ensures that only the mental model associated with the sender $i$ is changed.

The rule below for interrogatives formalizes that if agent $i$ communicates a message $?\varphi$ of the interrogative type, then the receiver $j$ will assume that $i$ does not know the truth value of $\phi$. Accordingly, it removes $\phi$ using the $\ominus$ operator from the belief base in its mental model of agent $i$ to reflect this.

**Definition 9.** (Receive: Interrogatives)

$$\frac{send(i, j, ?\phi) \in E}{\mathcal{A}_1, \ldots, \langle j, m, \Pi \rangle, \ldots, \mathcal{A}_n, E \longrightarrow \mathcal{A}_1, \ldots, \langle j, m', \Pi \rangle, \ldots, \mathcal{A}_n, E \setminus \{send(i, j, ?\phi)\}}$$

*where:*

- $m'(i) = \langle ((\Sigma \ominus \phi)) \ominus \neg\phi, \Gamma \rangle$ *if* $m(i) = \langle \Sigma, \Gamma \rangle$, *and*
- $m'(k) = m(k)$ *for* $k \neq i$.

---

[8] The implicit quantifier **allother** may be used to define a broadcasting primitive: **broadcast**$(msg) \overset{df}{=}$ **send**$(\textbf{allother}, msg)$. In the rule above, in that case, for all $i \neq j$ $send(i, j, msg)$ should be added to $E$, but we do not provide the details here.

*Remark.* An alternative, more complex semantics would not just conclude that agent $i$ does not know $\phi$ but also that $i$ wants to know the truth value of $\phi$, introducing a complex proposition $K_i\phi$ into the model of the goal base of that agent. As explained above, this would require including modal operators $K_i\phi$ in the goal base, and we leave such complications for future work.

The rule below for imperatives formalizes that if agent $i$ communicates a message $!\phi$ with imperative mood operator, then the receiver $j$ will conclude that $i$ does not believe $\phi$, and also that $\phi$ is a goal of $i$. Accordingly, it removes $\phi$ using the $\ominus$ operator and adds $\phi$ to its model of the goal base of agent $i$.

**Definition 10.** (Receive: Imperatives)

$$send(i, j, !\phi) \in E$$
$$\overline{\mathcal{A}_1, \ldots, \langle j, m, \Pi \rangle, \ldots, \mathcal{A}_n, E \longrightarrow \mathcal{A}_1, \ldots, \langle j, m', \Pi \rangle, \ldots, \mathcal{A}_n, E \backslash \{ send(i,j,!\phi) \}}$$

*where:*
- $m'(i) = \langle \Sigma \ominus \phi, \Gamma \cup \{\phi\} \rangle$ *if* $\phi \not\models \bot$ *and* $m(i) = \langle \Sigma, \Gamma \rangle$;
  *otherwise,* $m'(i) = m(i)$.
- $m'(k) = m(k)$ *for* $k \neq i$.

Note that this semantics does not refer to the *actual* mental state of the sender, nor does it define when a sender should send a message or what a receiver should do with the contents of a received message (other than simply record it in its mental model of the sending agent).

## 4.4    Operational Semantics: Conversations

As explained, the idea of a conversation is that an agent can engage only in a limited number of conversations at the same time. By viewing a conversation as a resource, the number of conversations that an agent can participate in simultaneously thus introduces a limit on access to that resource. For our purposes, it suffices to restrict participation to at most one conversation at any time.

More specifically, a parameter representing a unique conversation identifier can be added when sending a message, i.e., **send**$(c : j, msg)$ specifies that the message $msg$ should be sent to agent $j$ as part of the ongoing conversation $c$. We also allow conversations with groups of more than two agents which is facilitated by allowing groups of agent names $\{\ldots\}$ to be inserted into **send**$(c : \{\ldots\}, msg)$. A message that is sent as part of an ongoing conversation $c$ is handled similarly to a message that is not part of a specific conversation. Whenever a conversation $c$ has been closed (see below), sent messages that are intended to be part of that conversation are "lost", i.e. nothing happens. To initiate a conversation, the term **new** can be used instead of the conversation identifier. That is, whenever an agent $i$ performs a **send**(**new** : $g, msg$) action where $g$ is an agent or a group of agents, agent $i$ initiates a new conversation. Because agents can only engage in a limited number of conversations at the time, it may be that an initiated conversation is *put on hold initially* because one of the agents that should participate already participates in another conversation.

Semantically, to be able to model that a conversation is ongoing, we split the environment into a set $A$ of *active conversations*, a queue $Q$ of *pending conversations*, and a set $M$ of other pending messages. A message to initiate a new conversation is added to the queue *if* at least one agent that should participate is already present in the set $A$ or the queue $Q$. The check on $Q$ guarantees that a conversation is not started when another conversation requiring the participation of one of the same agents is still on hold in the queue ("no overtaking takes place"). Otherwise, the message is directly added to the set of active conversations.

Whenever a message $send(c : i, g, msg)$ that initiated a conversation is part of the set $A$, written $c \in A$, we will say that *conversation c is ongoing*, and when such a message is part of the queue $Q$, written $c \in Q$, we will say that *conversation c is put on hold*. Since the rules for receiving messages remain essentially the same, we only provide the rules for sending a message at the multi-agent level. The following rule specifies the semantics of sending a message that is part of an ongoing conversation.

**Definition 11.** (Send: Ongoing Conversation)

$$\frac{\mathcal{A}_i \xrightarrow{send(c:j,msg)} \mathcal{A}_i' \quad c \in A}{\mathcal{A}_1, \ldots, \mathcal{A}_i, \ldots, \mathcal{A}_n, \langle A, Q, M \rangle \longrightarrow \mathcal{A}_1, \ldots, \mathcal{A}_i', \ldots, \mathcal{A}_n, \langle A, Q, M' \rangle}$$

*where* $M' = M \cup \{send(c : i, j, msg)\}$.

The following transition rule specifies the semantics of messages that are used to initiate conversations. We use $+$ (e.g., $Q+send(c : i, g, msg)$) to add a message to the tail of a queue. The set of active conversations $A$ and the queue $Q$ store information about participants in conversations, as this may be derived from $send(c : i, g, msg)$, where agents $i$ and $g$ are participants. We write $agent(A, Q)$ to denote the set of agents in $A$ and $Q$. The reserved **new** label is used to have the system automatically generate a new conversation identifier.

**Definition 12.** (Send: Initiating a Conversation)
*Let $g$ be a set of agent names, and $c$ a new conversation identifier not yet present in $A$ or $Q$.*

$$\frac{\mathcal{A}_i \xrightarrow{send(\mathbf{new}:g,msg)} \mathcal{A}_i'}{\mathcal{A}_1, \ldots, \mathcal{A}_i, \ldots, \mathcal{A}_n, \langle A, Q, M \rangle \longrightarrow \mathcal{A}_1, \ldots, \mathcal{A}_i', \ldots, \mathcal{A}_n, \langle A', Q', M' \rangle}$$

*where if* $(\{i\} \cup g) \cap agents(A, Q) = \emptyset$ *then* $A' = A \cup \{send(c : i, g, msg)\}$, $Q' = Q$ *and* $M' = \bigcup_{k \in g} send(c : i, k, msg)$, *and otherwise* $A' = A$, $Q' = Q + send(c : i, g, msg)$, *and* $M' = M$.

This semantics specifies that we cannot simply allow a conversation between two agents to start when these agents are not part of an ongoing conversation, as this may prevent a conversation between another group of agents involving the same agents from ever taking place. The point is that it should be prevented that "smaller" conversations always "overtake" a conversation between a larger group of agents that is waiting in the queue.

As conversations are a resource shared at the multi-agent level, it must be possible to free this resource again. To this end, we introduce a special action

**close**$(c)$ which has the effect of removing an ongoing conversation from the set $A$ and potentially adding conversations on hold from the queue $Q$ to $A$. This is the only essentially new primitive needed to implement the conversation synchronization mechanism.

We need an additional definition: we say that $F$ is a *maximal fifo-set of messages* derived from a queue $Q$ relative to a set of agent names $Agt$ if $F$ consists of *all* messages $send(c : i, g, msg)$ from $Q$ that satisfy the following constraints: (i) $(\{i\} \cup g) \cap Agt = \emptyset$, and (ii) there is no earlier message $send(c' : i', g', msg')$ in the queue $Q$ such that $(\{i\} \cup g) \cap g' \neq \emptyset$.

**Definition 13.** (Send: Closing a Conversation)

$$\frac{\mathcal{A}_i \xrightarrow{close(c)} \mathcal{A}_i'}{\mathcal{A}_1, \ldots, \mathcal{A}_i, \ldots, \mathcal{A}_n, \langle A, Q, M \rangle \longrightarrow \mathcal{A}_1, \ldots, \mathcal{A}_i', \ldots, \mathcal{A}_n, \langle A', Q', M \rangle}$$

*where, assuming that $F$ is the maximal fifo-set derived from $Q$ relative to agents$(A)$, if $send(c : i, g, msg) \in A$ then $A' = (A \setminus \{send(c : i, g, msg)\}) \cup F$ and $Q' = Q \setminus F$, and otherwise $A' = A$ and $Q' = Q$.*

Note that the transition rule for closing a conversation only allows the initiator of a conversation, i.e. agent $\mathcal{A}_i$, to close the conversation again. (Otherwise agents that want to start their own conversation immediately might try to get it going by closing other conversations.) Finally, as it is important that the initiating agent as well as other participating agents are aware that a conversation has started or is ongoing, we assume a special predicate $conversation(c, i)$ is available, where $c$ denotes a unique conversation identifier and $i$ the initiating agent, which can be used in the belief base of an agent to verify whether a conversation is ongoing or not. We do not provide the formal details here due to space restrictions (see the next section for an example).

## 5   The Dining Philosophers

The dining philosophers is a classic problem in concurrency theory [23]. In the Table below, a complete GOAL program (for one of the philosopher agents) is listed that implements a solution. The currently implemented version of GOAL uses Prolog as a knowledge representation language, which we also use here. We use numbers to refer to the action rules of the GOAL program.

A number of philosophers are sitting at a round table where they each engage in two activities: thinking and eating (1,2). Our philosophers only think when they are not hungry and get hungry after thinking a while (see the action specifications). At the table an unlimited supply of spaghetti is available for eating. A philosopher needs two forks, however, to be able to eat (3). Forks are available as well, but the number of forks equals the number of philosophers sitting at the table (one fork is between each two philosophers). It is thus is never possible for all of the philosophers to eat at the same time and they have to coordinate. The problem is how to ensure that each philosopher will eventually be able to eat.

```
main i { % i, a number between 1 and N, is the name of the philosopher agent
  knowledge{
    neighbour(X,left) :- i>1, X is i-1.
    neighbour(X,left) :- i=1, X is N.        % N is the number of philosophers.
    neighbour(X,right) :- i<N, X is i+1.
    neighbour(X,right) :- i=N, X is 1.
    neighbours(X,Y) :- neighbour(X,left), neighbour(Y,right).
    forkAvailable(D) :- hold(fork,D) ; on(fork,table,D).
    forksAvailable :- forkAvailable(left), forkAvailable(right).
  beliefs{ hold(fork,left). }
  goals{ hold(fork,left), hold(fork,right). }

  program{
    1. if true then think.          % can only think when not hungry (see action spec)
    2. if true then eat.            % can only eat when hungry and holding forks

    3. if bel(hungry) then adopt(hold(fork,left), hold(fork,right)).

    % Initiate conversation with neighbors if you want to eat but forks are not
    % available by sending an imperative: See to it that I hold the fork.
    4. if goal(hold(fork,_)), bel(not(forksAvailable)), neighbours(X,Y))
          then send(new:{X,Y},!hold(fork)).

    % Ongoing conversation initiated by philosopher itself.
    % Only in this case the philosopher will pick up forks.
    5. if bel(neighbour(X,D), not(hold(fork,D))), bel(X, on(fork,table))
          then ins(on(fork,table,D)).
    6. if bel(conversation(Id,i)) then pickUp(fork,D) + send(Id:X, .hold(fork)).
    % Close the conversation if I hold both forks and neighbours have noticed this.
    7. if bel(conversation(Id,i), hold(fork,left), hold(fork,right), neighbours(X,Y))
            bel(X,not(on(fork,table))), bel(Y,not(on(fork,table)))
          then close(Id).

    % Ongoing conversation initiated by a neighbouring philosopher
    % Only in this case a philosopher will put down a fork.
    8. if bel(conversation(Id,X)), goal(X, hold(fork))
          then putDown(fork,D) + send(Id:X, .on(fork,table), not(hold(fork))).
    9. if bel(conversation(Id,X), neighbour(X,D)), bel(X, hold(fork))
          then del(on(fork,table,D)) + send(Id:X, ?on(fork,table)).
  }
  action-spec{
    think{pre{not(hungry)}post{hungry}}
    pickUp(fork,D){pre{on(fork,table,D)}post{hold(fork,D),not(on(fork,table,D))}}
    eat{pre{hungry,hold(fork,left), hold(fork,right)}post{not(hungry)}}
    putDown(fork, D){pre{hold(fork,D)}post{on(fork,table,D),not(hold(fork,D))}}
  }
}
```

The solution uses the conversational metaphor for coordinating activities. In the solution we present, the dining philosophers are assumed to be decent agents that are always willing to listen to the needs of their fellow philosophers at the table, and provide them with the forks when they indicate they require the forks to eat. If a philosopher needs the forks to eat but they are not available, he will initiate a conversation with his neighbors and indicate that he needs the forks (4).[9] According to Definition 12, a conversation will be started if no conversation initiated by the agent is part of the queue or ongoing, thus preventing a philosopher from continuously asking for the forks. Each of the philosophers

---

[9] In the sent messages the direction of the forks (left, right) has been dropped as this is just a matter of perspective, useful for keeping track of which fork has been picked up or put down from a single philosopher's perspective. From the point of view of two philosophers, a fork is just "in between" them.

competing for the works will thus be able to initiate at most one conversation to aks for works, which are ordered automatically in the queue and the request to start a conversation thus will be eventually initiated. If a philosopher $i$ is eating and receives a request for forks from a fellow philosopher $X$ as part of a new conversation, $i$ will finish eating and put down the fork in between $X$ and himself and notify $X$ of this fact (8). A philosopher $i$ will put down a fork only upon being requested. As long as the conversation is ongoing, $i$ will not pick up the fork again. The philosopher that initiated the conversation will pick up the fork after being informed by his neighbor that the fork is on the table (6).[10] The initiator of the conversation informs his neighbors that he picked up the fork (6). Upon receiving a message from both neighbors that they do not know whether the fork is on the table or not (reflected in the mental models of the neighbors), the initiator closes the conversation (7), and another conversation involving one of the philosophers may be started. Rules 5 and 9 are used to update the philosopher's own beliefs on the basis of its mental models of other philosophers (which are changed due to the sending of messages).

# 6  Conclusion

In this paper, we have introduced an alternative semantics for communication in agent programming languages, based on the idea that a received message can be used to (re)construct a mental model of the sender. We have made this idea precise for the GOAL agent programming language. Also, we have introduced the concept of a conversation to synchronize actions and communication in a multi-agent system. We have shown how these new constructs can be used to program a solution for a classic problem in concurrency theory. We are currently implementing these ideas to allow further experimentation and testing.

# References

1. Austin, J.L.: How to Do Things with Words. Oxford University Press, Oxford (1962)
2. Searle, J.: Speech acts. Cambridge University Press, Cambridge (1969)
3. Labrou, Y., Finin, T.: A semantics approach for KQML - a general purpose communication language for software agents. In: Proceedings of the Third International Conference on Information and Knowledge Management (CIKM 1994). ACM, New York (1994)
4. FIPA: Fipa communicative act library specification. Technical Report SC00037J, Foundation for Intelligent Physical Agents, Geneva, Switzerland (2002)
5. Bellifemine, F.L., Caire, G., Greenwood, D.: Developing Multi-Agent Systems with JADE. Wiley, Chichester (2007)
6. Braubach, L., Pokahr, A., Lamersdorf, W.: Software Agent-Based Applications, Platforms and Development Kits

---

[10] In fact, only when having initiated a conversation to require the forks, will a philosopher pick up a fork in our solution.

7. Howden, N., Ronnquist, R., Hodgson, A., Lucas, A.: JACK intelligent agents - summary of an agent infrastructure. In: Wagner, T., Rana, O.F. (eds.) Proceedings of the 5th ACM International Conference on Autonomous Agents, Workshop on Infrastructure for Agents, MAS and Scalable MAS, pp. 251–257 (2001)
8. Hindriks, K.V., de Boer, F.S., van der Hoek, W., Meyer, J.J.C.: Agent Programming in 3APL. Autonomous Agents and Multi-Agent Systems 2(4), 357–401 (1999)
9. Dastani, M.: 2APL: a practical agent programming language . Journal Autonomous Agents and Multi-Agent Systems 16(3), 214–248 (2008)
10. Vieira, R., Moreira, A., Wooldridge, M., Bordini, R.H.: Formal Semantics of Speech-Act Based Communication in an Agent-Oriented Programming Language. Artificial Intelligence Research 29, 221–267 (2007)
11. Hindriks, K.V.: Programming Rational Agents in GOAL. In: Multi-Agent Programming: Languages, Tools and Applications, pp. 119–157. Springer, Heidelberg (2009)
12. Ricci, A., Viroli, M., Piancastelli, G.: simpa: A simple agent-oriented java extension for developing concurrent applications. In: Dastani, M.M., El Fallah Seghrouchni, A., Leite, J., Torroni, P. (eds.) LADS 2007. LNCS (LNAI), vol. 5118, pp. 176–191. Springer, Heidelberg (2008)
13. Singh, M.: Agent Communication Languages: Rethinking the Principles. IEEE Computer 31(12), 40–47 (1998)
14. Wooldridge, M.: Semantic Issues in the Verification of Agent Communication Languages. Autonomous Agents and Multi-Agent Systems 3(1), 9–31 (2000)
15. Colombetti, M.: A commitment–based approach to agent speech acts and conversations. In: Proc. Workshop on Agent Languages and Communication Policies, 4th International Conference on Autonomous Agents (Agents 2000), pp. 21–29 (2000)
16. Singh, M.P.: A social semantics for agent communication languages. In: Issues in Agent Communication, pp. 31–45. Springer, Heidelberg (2000)
17. Chopra, A., Singh, M.: Constitutive interoperability. In: Proceedings of the 7th International Joint Conference on Autonomous Agents and MultiAgent Systems (AAMAS 2008), pp. 797–804 (2008)
18. Boella, G., Damiano, R., Hulstijn, J., van der Torre, L.: Role-based semantics for agent communication: embedding of the 'mental attitudes' and 'social commitments' semantics. In: Proceedings of the fifth international joint conference on Autonomous agents and multiagent systems, pp. 688–690 (2006)
19. Bach, K., Harnish, R.M.: Linguistic Communication and Speech Acts. The MIT Press, Cambridge (1979)
20. Harnish, R.M.: Mood, Meaning and Speech Acts. In: Foundations of Speech Act Theory: Philosophical and Linguistic Perspectives, pp. 407–459. Routledge, New York (1994)
21. Pendlebury, M.: Against the power of force: reflections on the meaning of mood. Mind 95, 361–372 (1986)
22. Wooldridge, M.: An introduction to multiagent systems. John Wiley and Sons, LTD, West Sussex (2002)
23. Ben-Ari, M.: Principles of Concurrent and Distributed Programming. Prentice-Hall, Englewood Cliffs (1990)
24. Gärdenfors, P.: Knowledge in Flux: Modelling the Dynamics of Epistemic States. MIT Press, Cambridge (1988)
25. de Boer, F., Hindriks, K., van der Hoek, W., Meyer, J.J.: A Verification Framework for Agent Programming with Declarative Goals. Journal of Applied Logic 5(2), 277–302 (2007)

# Multi-Agent Systems: Modeling and Verification Using Hybrid Automata

Ammar Mohammed and Ulrich Furbach

Universität Koblenz-Landau, Artificial Intelligence Research Group, D-56070 Koblenz
{ammar,uli}@uni-koblenz.de

**Abstract.** Hybrid automata are used as standard means for the specification and analysis of dynamical systems. Many researches have approached them to formally specify reactive Multi-agent systems situated in a physical environment, where the agents react continuously to their environment. The specified systems, in turn, are formally checked with the help of existing hybrid automata verification tools. However, when dealing with multi-agent systems, two problems may be raised. The first problem is a state space problem raised due to the composition process, where the agents have to be parallel composed into an agent capturing all possible behaviors of the multi-agent system prior to the verification phase. The second problem concerns the expressiveness of verification tools when modeling and verifying certain behaviors. Therefore, this paper tackles these problems by showing how multi-agent systems, specified as hybrid automata, can be modeled and verified using constraint logic programming(CLP). In particular, a CLP framework is presented to show how the composition of multi-agent behaviors can be captured dynamically during the verification phase. This can relieve the state space complexity that may occur as a result of the composition process. Additionally, the expressiveness of the CLP model flexibly allows not only to model multi-agent systems, but also to check various properties by means of the reachability analysis. Experiments are promising to show the feasibility of our approach.

## 1 Motivation

Specifying behaviors of (physical) multi-agent systems is a sophisticated and demanding task, because of the high complexity of the interactions among agents and the dynamics of the environment. An important aspect of multi-agent systems is that the agents interact with a physical environment. Such interactions typically consist of continuous changes of behaviors of agents (e.g. a movement of a robot, or an agent is waiting for occurrence of an event), as well as discrete changes of behaviors. Those scenarios can be captured by means of hybrid automata [12]. Here the discrete changes are modeled using a form of transition diagrams dialect like statecharts [26], while the continuous changes are modeled using differential equations. Hybrid automata formal semantics make them accessible to formal validation of systems, especially for systems, which are situated in safety critical environments.Thus, it is possible to prove desirable features as well as the absence of unwanted properties for the modeled systems automatically with the help of hybrid automata verification tools [13,8,3].

L. Braubach, J.-P. Briot, and J. Thangarajah (Eds.): ProMAS 2009, LNAI 5919, pp. 49–66, 2010.
© Springer-Verlag Berlin Heidelberg 2010

Hybrid automata can be used to model and verify multi-agent plans (we call it modeling multi-agent systems), especially for those agents that are defined through their capability to continuously react to a physical environment, while respecting some time constraints. With the help of the verification's tools of hybrid automata, one can validate/verify and control multi-agent plans. For this reason, several researches, for example [6,7,9,22,23], have approached hybrid automata as a framework in order to model multi-agent systems in a dynamic environment, where the time is critical. There are authors, for example [18], who have modeled multi-agent systems with a simple form of hybrid automata that are called timed automata [2]. Nevertheless, two problems occur when applying hybrid automata to multi-agent systems. Firstly, multi-agent systems are specified as a network of synchronized hybrid automata that have to be parallel composed statically into an automaton (synonymy agent). By statically we mean that agents have to be parallel composed prior to the verification phase. Technically, the composition of hybrid automata is obtained from the cartesian product of the number of states of all concurrent automata, unless the automata have mutual synchronization messages. In this case, the states have to be considered simultaneously. As a result of the composition process, an agent captures all possible behaviors that may occur in the multi-agent systems. In turn, the resulting composed agent afterwards is checked by hybrid automata verification tools. Consequently, this composition process may lead to a state explosion problem.

The second problem concerns the expressiveness of the modeling tools. Standard hybrid automata tools are not flexible enough to model multi-agent systems. This is because they are special purpose tools, which model the agents' decision depending on the evaluation of the continuous dynamics. However, there are favorable situations of modeling multi-agent systems where the agents' decision steps do not depend on the evaluation of continuous dynamics, but on evaluation functions (e.g. shortest distance, max, or min) happening during the continuous dynamic. Imagine, for example, an agent who wants to cooperate with the nearest agent to conduct certain tasks in a rescue team of a multi-agent system. To our knowledge, this type of decision making is beyond the capabilities of the current hybrid automata verification tools. Therefore it is necessary to have expressive tools that can handle such situations. Ideally, modeling tools are favorable when they are flexibly able to verify the systems' requirements.

To this end, the purpose of this paper is to cope with the mentioned problems when approaching hybrid automata to model multi-agent systems. In particular, we present a novel approach which models hybrid automata based on constraint logic programming. This approach is appropriate to represent multi-agent systems specified as hybrid automata. The novelty of the presented approach is that the composition of hybrid automata is built dynamically on the fly, where only the reached behaviors are captured dynamically, rather than building all possible behaviors in advance. On the other hand, the expressiveness of CLP does not only allow us to model multi-agent systems, but also to check various properties by representing requirements with a suitable query. We show the feasibility of our approach with experimentation on standard benchmarks taken from the hybrid automata context.

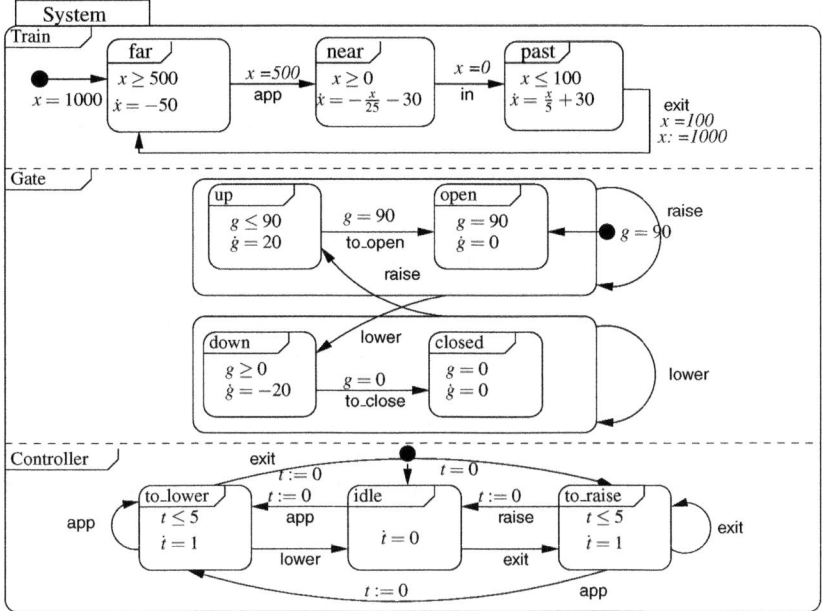

**Fig. 1.** Specification of the train gate controller as hybrid automata

### 1.1 Overview on the Rest of the Paper

In summary, the main contributions of this paper are as follows: First, an effective framework, implemented in CLP, is presented, which is suitable to model and verify multi-gent systems based on hybrid automata. Second, compositions of automata do not have to be computed explicitly prior to verifying multi-agent systems. Instead, the composition of automata is built dynamically during the verification phase, which can relieve the state explosion problem that may raise as the result of multi-agent systems. Last but not least, by employing CLP, constraints can be derived automatically, under which certain states of a system can be tested for reachability. This enhances standard model checking methodologies.

In the sequel, we first introduce a running example that will be used throughout the paper to illustrate our approach in Sec. 2. Then hybrid automata syntax and semantics are discussed in Sec. 3. In Sec. 4 a CLP implementation model is discussed, before showing how to specify and verify requirements in Sec. 5. The evaluation of our CLP implementation model is discussed in Sec. 6. Then Sec. 7 briefly reviews related works, before we end up with the conclusion Sec. 8.

## 2 Running Example

Before we present both syntax and semantic of hybrid automata, we first introduce an illustrating running example that we use throughout the paper, before we shows the basics formalism which we use to demonstrate the CLP implementation.

A train gate controller [14] is a reactive multi-agent system consisting of three agent components: the train, the gate, and the controller. In this system, a road is crossing a train track, which is guarded by a gate, which must be lowered to stop the traffic when the train approaches, and raised after a train passed the road. The gate is supervised by a controller that has the task to receive signals from the train and to issue lower or raise signals to the gate. Initially, a train is at a distance of 1000 meters away from the gate and moves at a speed 50 meter per second. At 500 meters, a sensor on the tracks detects the train, sending a signal *app* to the controller. The train slows down, obeying the differential equation $\dot{x} = -\frac{x}{25} - 30$. After a delay of five seconds, which is modeled by the variable $t$, the controller sends the signal *lower* to the gate, which begins to descend from 90 degrees to 0 degrees at a rate of -20 degrees per second. After crossing the gate, the train accelerates according to the differential equation $\dot{x} = \frac{x}{5} + 30$. A second sensor placed 100 meters past the crossing detects the leaving train, sending a signal *exit* to the controller. After five seconds, the controller raises the gate.

The specification of the previous multi-agent system is graphically illustrated as concurrent hybrid automata in Fig. 1. The variable $x$ represents the distance of the train from the gate. The variable $t$ represents the delay time of the controller, while the position of the gate in radius degrees is represented by the variable $g$.

# 3   Hybrid Automata Preliminaries

In this section, we show the basics syntax and the semantics of hybrid automata.

## 3.1   Hybrid Automaton: Syntax

A hybrid automaton is represented graphically as a state transition diagram dialect like statecharts, augmented with mathematical formalisms on both transitions and locations. Formally speaking, a hybrid automaton (agent in continuous domain) is defined as follows.

**Definition 1 (basic components).** *A hybrid automaton is a tuple $H = (X, Q, Inv, Flow, E, Jump, Reset, Event, Init)$ where:*

- *$X = \{x_1, x_2, ..., x_n\}$ is a finite set of n real-valued variables that model the continuous dynamics of the automaton wrt. time.*
- *$Q$ is a finite set of control locations. For example, the locations of the train automaton (Fig. 1) has the locations far, near, and past.*
- *Inv is a mapping which assigns an invariant condition to each location $q \in Q$. The invariant condition $Inv(q)$ is a predicate over the variables in $X$. The control of a hybrid automaton remains at a location $q \in Q$, as long as $Inv(q)$ holds. For instance, the location far in the train automaton has the invariant $x \geq 500$.*
- *Flow is a mapping, which assigns a flow condition to each control location $q \in Q$. The flow condition $Flow(q)$ is a predicate over $X$ that defines how the variables in $X$ evolve over the time t at location q.*

    *It constrains the time derivative of the continuous part of the variables at location q. Basically, we represent the flow as a constraint relation of the real variables* to the time. In the graphical representation, a flow of a variable $x$ is denoted as $\dot{x}$. For example, $\dot{x} = \frac{x}{5} + 30$ describes the speed of the train at the location past in the train automaton (Fig. 1).

- $E \subseteq Q \times Q$ is the discrete transition relation over the control locations.
- Jump is a mapping which assigns a jump condition (guard) to each transition $e \in E$. The jump condition $jump(e)$ is a predicate over $X$ that must hold to fire $e$. Omitting a jump condition on a transition means that the jump condition is always true and it can be taken at any point of time. Conventionally, writing $Jump(e)[v]$ means that the jump condition on a transition $e$ holds, if the valuations of variables on the transition are $v$.
- Reset is a mapping, which assigns values to variable to each transition $e \in E$. $Reset(e)$ is a predicate over $X$ that defines how the variables are reset. For example, the variable $X$ in the train automaton on the transition between locations past and far is reset to $X := 1000$. Resetting variables are omitted on transition, if the values of the variables do not change before the control goes from a location to another location.
- Event is a mapping which assigns an event to each tranisition $e \in E$ from a set of events $Event_H$.

  For instance, the train automaton contains the events app, in, and exist, on its transitions. These events define the composition of the automata.
- Init is the initial state of the automaton. It defines the initial location together with the initial values of the variables $X$. For example, the initial state of train is is the location far with initial value $x = 1000$.

Before describing the semantics of a hybrid automaton, it should be mentioned that the hybrid automata are classified according to the type of continuous flows such that;

- if $\dot{x} = c$ (constant), then the hybrid automaton is called linear hybrid automaton (a special case of linear hybrid automata are a timed automata [2], where $c = 1$).
- if $c_1 \leq \dot{x} \leq c_2$, then the hybrid automaton is called rectangular hybrid automaton.
- if $\dot{x} = c_1 x + c_2$, then the hybrid automaton is called non-linear hybrid automaton.

### 3.2 Hybrid Automaton: Semantics

Informally speaking, the semantics of a hybrid automaton is defined in terms of a labeled transition system between states, where a state consists of the current location of the automaton and the current valuation of the real variables. To formalize the semantics of the hybrid automaton, first we need to define the concept of a hybrid automaton's state.

**Definition 2 (State).** At any instant of time, a state of a hybrid automaton is given by $\sigma_i = \langle q_i, v_i, t \rangle$, where $q_i \in Q$ is a control location, $v_i$ is the valuation of its real variables, and $t$ is the current time. A state $\sigma_i = \langle q_i, v_i, t \rangle$ is admissible if $Inv(q_i)[v_i]$ holds.

A state transition system of a hybrid automaton $H$ starts with the initial state $\sigma_0 = \langle q_0, v_0, 0 \rangle$, where the $q_0$ and $v_0$ are the initial location and valuations of the variables respectively. For example, the initial state of the *train* (see Fig. 1 ) can be specified as $\langle far, 1000, 0\rangle$.

In fact, a hybrid automaton evolves depending on two kinds of transitions: continuous transitions, capturing the continuous evolution of states, and discrete transitions, capturing the changes of location. More formally, we can define hybrid automaton semantics as follows.

**Definition 3 (Operational Semantic).** *A transition rule between two admissible states* $\sigma_1 = \langle q_1, v_1, t_1 \rangle$ *and* $\sigma_2 = \langle q_2, v_2, t_2 \rangle$ *is defined as follows:*

**discretely:** *iff* $e = (q_1, q_2) \in E$, $t_1 = t_2$ *and* $Jump(e)[v_1]$ *holds, then variables are reset according to* $v_2$ *such that* $Inv(q_2)[v_2]$ *holds at location* $q_2$. *In this case an event* $a \in Event$ *occurs. Conventionally, it is written* $q_1 \xrightarrow{a} q_2$.

**continuously(time delay):** *iff* $q_1 = q_2$, *and* $t_2 > t_1$ *is the duration of time passed at location* $q_1$, *during which the invariant predicate* $Inv(q1)[v_1]$ *and* $Inv(q1)[v_2]$ *holds.*

Intuitively, an execution of a hybrid automaton corresponds to a sequence of transitions from a state to another. Therefore we define the valid run as follows.

**Definition 4 (Run:Micro level).** *A run of hybrid automaton* $\Sigma = \sigma_0\sigma_1\sigma_2,...$, *is a finite or infinite sequence of admissible states, where the transition from a state* $\sigma_i$ *to a state* $\sigma_{i+1}$ *is related by either a discrete or a continuous transition and* $\sigma_0$ *is the initial state.*

It should be noted that the continuous change in the run may generate an infinite number of reachable states. It follows that state-space exploration techniques require a symbolic representation way in order to represent the set of states in a appropriate way. In this paper, we use CLP to represent the infinite states symbolically as finite intervals. we call a symbolic interval as a region, which is defined as follows:

**Definition 5 (Region).** *Given a run* $\Sigma$, *a sub-sequence of states* $\Gamma = \sum_{j=1}^{m} \sigma_{i+j} \subseteq \Sigma$ *is called a region, if for all states* $\sigma_{i+j}$, $1 \leq j \leq m$, *it holds* $q_{i+j} = q$ *and if there exist a state* $\sigma_i$ *and a state* $\sigma_{i+m+1}$ *with respective locations* $q_1$ *and* $q_2$, *then it must hold* $q_1 \neq q$ *and* $q_2 \neq q$. *Conventionally, a region* $\Gamma$ *is written as* $\Gamma = \langle q, V, T\rangle$, *where* $t_{i+1} \leq T \leq t_{i+m}$ *is the interval of continuous time, and* $V$ *is the set of intervals* $V_k$ *of the interval defined by the values of* $x_k \in X$ *in the time interval* $T$. *A region* $\Gamma$ *is called admissible if each state* $\sigma \in \Gamma$ *is admissible.*

Now, the run of hybrid automata can be rephrased in terms of reached regions, where the change from one region to another is fired using a discrete step.

**Definition 6 (Run:Macro level).** *A run of hybrid automaton H is* $\Sigma_H = \Gamma_0\Gamma_1,...$ *a sequence of (possibly infinite ) admissible regions, where a transition from a region* $\Gamma_i$ *to a region* $\Gamma_{i+1}$ *is enabled (written as* $\Gamma_i \xrightarrow{a} \Gamma_{i+1}$), *if there is* $q_i \xrightarrow{a} q_{i+1}$, *where* $a \in Event$ *is the generated event before the control goes to the region* $\Gamma_{i+1}$. $\Gamma_0$ *is the initial region reached from a start state* $\sigma_0$ *by means of continuous transitions.*

The operational semantics is the basis for verification of a hybrid automaton. In particular, model checking of a hybrid automaton is defined in terms of the reachability analysis of its underlying transition system. The most useful question to ask about hybrid automata is the reachability of a given state. Thus, we define the reachability of states as follows.

**Definition 7 (Reachability).** *A region $\Gamma_i$ is called reachable in $\Sigma_H$, if $\Gamma_i \subseteq \Sigma_H$. Consequently, a state $\sigma_j$ is called reachable, if there is a reached region $\Gamma_i$ such that $\sigma_j \in \Gamma_i$.*

The classical method to compute the reachable states consists of performing a state space exploration of a system, starting from a set containing only the initial state and spreading the reachability information along control locations and transitions until fixed regions are obtained. Stabilization of a region is detected by testing if the current region is included in the union of the reached regions obtained in previous steps. It is worth mentioning that checking reachability for hybrid automata is generally undecidable. However, under various constraints, reachability is decidable for certain classes of hybrid automata including timed and initialized rectangular automata[15]. A rectangular automaton is initialized if each continuous variable is reset every time a discrete transition is taken.

### 3.3   Hybrid Automata: Composition

To specify complex systems, hybrid automata can be extended by parallel composition. Basically, the parallel composition of hybrid automata can be used for specifying larger systems (multi-agent systems), where a hybrid automaton is given for each part of the system, and communication between the different parts may occur via shared variables and synchronization labels. Technically, the parallel composition of hybrid automata is obtained from the different parts using a product construction of the participating automata. The transitions from the different automata are interleaved, unless they share the same synchronization label. In this case, they are synchronized during the execution. As a result of the parallel composition, a new automaton, called composed automaton, is created, which captures the behavior of the entire system. In turn, the composed automata are given to a model checker that checks the reachability of a certain state.

Intuitively, the composition of hybrid automata $H_1$ and $H_2$ can be defined in terms of synchronized or interleaved regions of the regions produced from run of both $H_1$ and $H_2$. As a result from the composition procedure, compound regions are constructed that consists of a conjunction of one region from $H_1$ and another from $H_2$. Therefore, each compound region takes the form $\Lambda = \langle(q_1, V_1), (q_2, V_2), T\rangle$ (shortly written as $\Lambda = \langle \Gamma_1, \Gamma_2, T\rangle$), which represents reached region at both control locations $q_1$ and $q_2$ the during a time interval T. Now the run of composed automata is the sequence $\Sigma_{H_1 \circ H_2} = \Lambda_0, \Lambda_1, ...$, where a transition between compound region $\Lambda_1 = \langle \Gamma_1, \gamma_1, T_1\rangle$ and $\Lambda_2 = \langle \Gamma_2, \gamma_2, T_2\rangle$ (written as $\Lambda_1 \xrightarrow{a} \Lambda_2$) is enabled, if one of the following holds:

- $a \in Event_{H_1} \cap Event_{H_2}$ is a joint event, $\Gamma_1 \xrightarrow{a} \Gamma_2$, and $\gamma_1 \xrightarrow{a} \gamma_2$. In this case , we say that the region $\Gamma_1$ is synchronized with the region $\gamma_1$.
- $a \in Event_{H_1} \setminus Event_{H_2}$ (respectively $a \in Event_{H_2} \setminus Event_{H_1}$ ), $\Gamma_1 \xrightarrow{a} \Gamma_2$ and $\gamma_1 \rightarrow \gamma_2$, such that both $\gamma_1$ and $\gamma_2$ have the same control location (i.e., they relate to each other using a continuous transition).

The previous procedures give the possibility to construct the composition dynamically during the run/verification phase. Obviously, computing the composition in such a way is advantageous. This is for the reason that only active parts of the state space will be taken into consideration during the run instead of producing the composition procedure prior to verification phase. This can relieve the state space problem raised from modeling multi-agent systems.The coming section shows how the previous procedure, with the help of constraint logic programming, can be performed.

## 4   CLP Model

In the following, we will show how to encode the syntax and semantics of hybrid automata, described in the previous section, as a Constraint Logic Program *CLP* [19].There are diverse motivations for choosing CLP. Firstly, hybrid automata can be described as a constraint system, where the constraints represent the possible flows, invariants, and transitions. Further, constraints can be used to characterize certain parts of the state space (e.g., the set of initial state or a set of unsafe state). Secondly, there are close similarities in operation semantics between CLP and hybrid automata. Ideally, state transition systems can be represented as a logic program, where the set of reachable states can be computed. Moreover, constraints enable us to represent infinite states symbolically as a finite interval. Hence, the constraint solver can be used to reason about the reachability of a particular state. In addition, CLP is enriched with many efficient constraint solvers for interval constraints and symbolic domains, where the interval constraints can used to represent the continuous evolution, whereas symbolic domains are appropriate to represent the synchronization events (communication messages). Last but not least, by employing CLP, the construction of the automata composition can be constructed on the fly (during checking models). In contrast to the standard hybrid automata composition technique that builds the composition prior to the verification phase, the technique used to construct the composition can relieve the state space problem raised from specifying and verifying MAS.

Our implementation prototype was built using ECLiPSe Prolog [21]. A preliminary implementation model was introduced in [25]. The prototype follows the definitions of both the formal syntax and semantics of hybrid automata, which are defined in the previous section. We start modeling each hybrid automaton individually. Therefore, we begin with modeling locations of automata that are implemented in the `automaton` predicate, ranging over the respective locations of the automaton, real-valued variables and the time:

```
%%% automaton(+Location,?Vars,+Vars0,+T0,?Time)
%%% models invariant and flow inside location
automaton(Location,Vars,Vars0,T0,Time):-
        Vars#c2(Vars0,(Time-T0)),
        c1(Inv),Time $>=T0.
```

Here, *automaton* is the name of automaton itself, and *Location* represents the ground name of the current locations of the automaton. *Vars* is a list of real variables participating in the automaton, whereas *Vars0* is a list of the correspondent initial values. $c1(Invs)$ is the invariant constraint on *Vars* inside the location. The constraint predicate $Vars\#c2(Vars0,(Time-T0))$, where $\# \in \{<,\leq,>,\geq,=\}$ are constraints, which represent the continuous flows of the variables in *Vars* wrt. time $T0$ and $Time$, given initial values *Vars0* of the variables *Vars* at the start of the flow. *T0* is the initial time at the start of the continuous flow, while $(Time - T0)$ represents the delay inside the location. It should be noted that after executing the predicate *automaton*, *Vars* and *Time* holds the reached valuations of the variables together with their the reached time respectively. The following is an example showing the concrete implementation of location *far* in the automaton *train* Fig. 1. The $ symbol in the front of (in)equalities is the constraint relation for interval arithmetic constraints (library *ic* in ECLiPSe Prolog).

```
train(far,[X],[X0],T0,Time):-
    X $= X0-50*(Time-T0),
    X $>=500, Time $>=T0.
```

According to operational semantics defined in Def. 3, a hybrid automaton has two kinds of transitions: *continuous* transitions, capturing the continuous evolution of variables, and *discrete* transitions, capturing the changes of location. For this purpose, we encode transition systems into the predicate *evolve*, which alternates the automaton between a discrete and a continuous transition. The automaton evolves with either discrete or continuous according to the constraints appeared during the run.

```
%%% evolve(+Automaton,+State,-Nextstate,+T0,-Time,?Event)
evolve(Automaton,(L1,Var1),(L2,Var2),T0,Time,Event) :-
    continuous(Automaton,(L1,Var1),(L1,Var2),T0,Time,Event);
    discrete(Automaton,(L1,Var1),(L2,Var2),T0,Time,Event).
```

When a *discrete* transition occurs, it gives rise to update the initial variables from *Var1* into *Var2*, where *Var1* and *Var2* are the initial variables of locations *L1* and *L2* respectively. Otherwise, a delay transition is taken using the predicate *continuous*. It is worth noting that there are infinite states due to the continuous progress. However, this can be handled efficiently as interval constraint that bounds the set of infinite reachable state as a finite interval (i.e., $0 \leq X \leq 250$).

In addition to the variables, each automaton is augmented with a set events called $Event_{Automaton}$. An example of this set of events of the automaton *train* is denoted as $Event_{train} = \{app, in, exit\}$. For this reason, each transition is augmented with the variable *Event*, which is used to define the parallel composition from the automata individuals sharing the same event. The variable *Event* ranges over symbolic domains. It guarantees that whenever an automaton generates an event, the corresponding synchronized automata have to be taken into consideration simultaneously. It should be mentioned that the declaration of automata events must be provided in the modeling example. For instance, the declaration of the possible events domains of Fig. 1. are coded as the following:

```
:- local domain(events(app,in,exit,raise,lower, to_open)).
```

The previous means that the domains of events are declared symbolically to capture the set of all possible applicable events to the underlying modeled system. The appropriate solver of symbolic domain deals with any defined constraints in terms of the declared domains. Now after defining the domains of events, a variable of type events can be declared as the following:

```
Event &::events,Event &=domain_value.
```

The previous means that a variable *Event* is declared with domain values defined by *events*, and is initialized with a specific value from its domain. The & symbol is a constraint relation for symbolic domains (library *sd* in ECLiPSe Prolog).

The following is the general implementation of the predicate *discrete*, which defines transitions between locations.

```
%%% discrete(+Automaton,+State1,-State2,+IntTime,-Time,-Event)
discrete(Automaton,(Loc1,Var1),(Loc2,Var2),T0,Time,Event):-
        automaton,(Loc1,Var1,Var,T0,Time),
        jump(Var), reset(Var2),
        Event &::events,Event &=domain_value.
```

In the previous predicate, *domain_value* must be a member in $Event_{Automaton}$.

The following is an instance showing the implementation of the *discrete* predicate between locations *far* and *near* in automaton *train*.

```
discrete(train,(far,[X0]),(near,[XX0]),T0,Time,Event):-
        train(far,[X0],[X],T0,Time),
        X $=500, XX0 $=X,
        Event &::events, Event &=app.
```

The description of the previous *discrete* predicate means that the transition between the locations *far* and *near* in the *train* automata takes place, if the continuous variable $X$, based on the initial value $X0$, satisfies the jump condition, which is given as $X = 500$. If such a case occurs, then the new variable, denoted as $XX0$, is updated and the event *app* is fired. The executed events afterwards synchronize the *train* automaton with the automata sharing the same event.

Once the locations and transition rules have been modeled, a state machine should be implemented, in order to execute the model. For this purpose, a driver program is implemented as shown in Fig. 2.

The *driver* is a state machine which is responsible for generating and controlling the behaviors of the concurrent hybrid automata, as well as to provide the reachable regions symbolically. The *driver* takes, as input argument, the starting state for each participating automaton (i.e. a control location as well as the list of initial valuations of the variables). In addition, it takes the starting time $T0$ to begin the execution, followed by the list of reached regions, which is needed for the purpose of the verification. It should be noted that during the course of driver's execution, there is a symbolic domain variable *Event* shared among automata, which is used by the appropriate solver to ensure that only one event is generated at a time. Precisely, when an automaton generates an event, thanks to a discrete transition of one of the predicates *evolve* of the concurrent automata, then the symbolic domain solver will exclude all the domain of values of the other automata that are not coincident with the generated event. This means that only one event is generated at a time. If more than one automaton generate different events at the same point of time, then the symbolic domain solver will handle only one of them at a time, but the other events will be handled using backtracking.

Since each automaton, at the end of its continuous evolution, generates an event by a discrete step, then the precedence of events that appear during the run are important to

```
%%% driver(+State1,+State2,...,+Staten,+T0,-Regions,+PastRegion).
%%% perform composition and reachability
driver((L1,Var01),(L2,Var02),...,(Ln,Var0n),T0,[Reg|NxtReg],PastReg) :-

    automaton1(L1,Var1,Var01,T0,Time),
    automaton2(L2,Var2,Var02,T0,Time),
    ... ,
    automatonn(Ln,Varn,Var0n,T0,Time),

    evolve(automaton1, (L1,Var01), (NxtL1,Nvar01),T0,T,Event),
    evolve(automaton2, (L2,Var02), (NxtL2,Nvar02),T0,T,Event),
    ... ,
    evolve(automatonn, (Ln,Var0n), (NxtLn,Nvar0n),T0,T,Event),

    +\ member((L1,L2,..,Ln,Var1,Var2,..,Varn,_,Event), PastReg),
    Reg = (L1,L2,..,Ln,Var1,Var2,..,Varn,Time,Event),
    NpastReg =[Reg|PastReg],

driver((NxtL1,Nvar01),(NxtL2,Nvar02),...,(NxtLn,Nvar0n),T,NxtReg,NpastReg).
```

**Fig. 2.** A state machine to driver the execution and reachability

both composition and the verification process. For this reason, an obvious way to deal with this precedence is to use constraints on the time of the generated events. To accomplish this, we constrain the execution of each automaton with a shared variable *Time*. The constraint solver, in turn, binds this variable with the minimum execution time among the automata. It follows that this variable *Time* eventually holds the minimum time needed to generated an event. The previous computation partitions the state space into regions, where the transition from one region to another depends on the minimum time needed to generate an event. Consequently, this shows how the automata composition can be implicitly constructed efficiently on the fly (i.e. during the computation).

It has been said that we are not only concerning with run and composition of the automata, but also with the their verification. For this purpose, the *driver* is augmented with the list of reached regions. At each step of the *driver*'s execution, a region, of the form ⟨*locations,Variables,Time,Event*⟩ is add to the list of reached regions. This region represents symbolically the set of reached states and times to each control location as mathematical constraints. Additionally, each region contains the generated event before the control goes to another region using a discrete step. Technically, the *driver* computes the set of reached regions until fixed regions are obtained. This is computed by checking, in each iteration of driver, if the reached region is not contained in the list of the previously reached regions. For this purpose, the last argument of the *driver* holds the list of past reached regions. Stemming from the decidability of hybrid automata [15], termination of the driver to reach to a fixed regions is not guaranteed generally. Fortunately, it does terminate for all the examples in the experimental result. However, to overcome the non termination problem generally, one can augment the predicate *driver* with some iteration depth in advance, where the driver is enforced to stop upon reaching this depth.

Reachable regions should contain only those variables, which are important for the verification of a given property. Therefore, the last argument list of the predicate *driver* can be expanded or shrunk as needed to contain the significant variables.

As soon as the *driver* has been built, the complete model should be invoked for the purpose of execution and hence verification. For this reason, the *driver* has to be invoked with a query starting from the initial states of the hybrid automata. An example showing how to query the driver on the running scenario (Fig. 1) takes the form:

```
?- driver((far,1000),(open,90),(idle,0),0,Reached,[]).
```

## 5   Verification as Reachability Analysis

Now we have an executable constraint based specification, which can be used to verify properties of a multi-agent system. Several properties can now be investigated. In particular, one can check properties on states using reachability analysis. Fundamentally, the reachability analysis consists of two basic steps. First, computing the state space of the automaton under consideration. In our case, this is done using the predicate *driver*. Second, searching for states that satisfy or contradict given properties. This is done using a standard prolog predicates like *member/2* and *append/3*. Therefore, we present CLP rules, which constitute our verification framework. The validation of these rules depends totally on the set of reached regions that we described them formally in Sec.3, and implemented in Sec.4.

In terms of *CLP*, a state is reached iff the constraint solver succeeds in finding a satisfiable solution for the constraints representing the intended state. In other words, assuming that *Reached* represents the set of all reachable states computed by the *CLP* model from an initial state, then the reachability analysis can be generally specified, using *CLP*, by checking whether *Reached* $\models \Psi$ holds, where $\Psi$ is the constraint predicate that describes a property of interest. In practice, many problems to be analyzed can be formulated as a reachability problem. For example, a safety requirement can be checked as a reachability problem, where $\Psi$ is the constraint predicate that describes forbidden states, and then the satisfiability of $\Psi$ wrt. *Reached* is checked. For instance, one can check that the state, where the train is near at distance $X = 0$ and the gate is open, is a disallowed state. Even a stronger condition can be investigated, namely that the state where the train is near at distance X=0 and the gate is down, is a forbidden state. The *CLP* computational model, with the help of the standard Prolog predicate *member/2*, gives us the answer *no* as expected, after executing the following query:

```
?- driver((far,1000),(open,0),(idle,0),0,Reached,[]),
   member((near,down,_,Time,_,X,),Reached), X $= 0.
```

Other properties concerning the reachability of certain states can be verified similarly.

Fundamentally, different properties can be checked in this framework As previously demonstrated, the set of reachable states *Reached* contains the set of finite, reachable regions. Within each region, the set of all states is represented symbolically as a mathematical constraint, together with the time delay. Therefore, constraint solvers ideally can be used to reason about the reachability of interesting properties within some region. For example, an interesting property is to find the shortest distance of the train to the gate before the gate is entirely closed. This can be checked by posing the following query:

```
?- driver((far,1000),(open,0),(idle,0),0,Reached,[]),
   member((near,_,_,Time,to_close,_),Reached), get_max(Time,Tm),
   member((near,_,_,Tm,_,X),Reached), get_min(X,Min).
```

The previous query returns $Min = 104.8$ meters, which is the minimum distance of the train that the model guarantees before the gate is completely closed.

Since the events and time are recorded particularly at reached regions, verifying timing properties or computing the delay between events are further tasks that can be done within the reachability framework too. For instance, we can find the maximal time delay between *in* and *exit* events, by stating the following query:

```
?- driver((far,1000),(open,0),(idle,0),Reached,[]),
   append(A,[(past,_,_,Time1,exit,_)|_],Reached),
   append(B,[(near,_,_,Time2,in,_)|_],A),
   get_max(Time1,Tmax1),get_max(Time2,Tmax2),
   Delay $= Tmax1-Tmax2.
```

The constraint solver answers *yes* and yields $Delay = 2.554$. This value means that the train needs at most 2.554 seconds to be in the critical crossing section before leaving it. Similarly, other timing properties can be verified.

## 6   Experimental Results

In the previous section, we have demonstrated how different properties can be verified within the *CLP* implementation framework.

We did several experiments comparing our approach with HyTech [16]. We chose HyTech as a reference tool, because it is one of the most well-known tools for the verification of hybrid automata, and it tackles verification based on reachability analysis similar to the approach in this paper. In HyTech however, the automata working in parallel are composed before they are involved in the verification phase. Obviously, this may lead to state explosion as stated earlier.

Now to use our approach to model and verify multi-agent systems, specified as hybrid automata, we have to demonstrate the feasibility of our proposed approach by experiments taken from the hybrid automata context. Therefore, we will refer to standard benchmarks of verification of real-time systems. Querying these benchmarks to check safety properties (cf. Fig. 3). First, in the *scheduler* example [11], it is checked whether a certain task (with number 2) never waits. Second, in the *temperature control* example [1], it has to be guaranteed, that the temperature always lies in a given range. Third, in the *train gate controller1* example [13], it has to be ensured that the gate is closed whenever the train is within a distance less than 10 meter toward the gate. In the *water level* example [1,11], the safety property is to ensure that the water level is always between given thresholds (1 and 12). A non-linear version of both train gate controller (described throughout this paper) and the thermostat are taken from [14]. The safety property of the former one is to prove the same property as in the linear version, whereas in the second one we need to prove that the temperature always lies between 0.28 and 3.76. The safety property of *Fisher's mutual exclusion protocol* [13] has to guarantee that never two processes are in the critical section at the same time. Last but not least, nuclear *Reactor* examples are taken from the verification examples of HyTech [16]. The safety property of both example is to ensure that only one of the rods of the reactor can be put in. For more details on the examples, the reader is referred to the cited literature.

| Example | HyTech | CLP |
|---|---|---|
| Scheduler | 0.12 | 0.07 |
| Temperature Controller | 0.04 | 0.02 |
| Train Gate Controller1 | 0.05 | 0.02 |
| Water Level | 0.03 | 0.01 |
| Train Gate Controller2 | - | 0.02 |
| Thermostat | - | 0.01 |
| Fisher protocol | 0.11 | 0.34 |
| Reactor1 | 0.01 | 0.01 |
| Reactor2 | - | 0.01 |

**Fig. 3.** Experimental results

The symbol − in Fig. 3 indicates that the example is inadequate to HyTech. This is because HyTech can not treat non-linear dynamics directly. Instead, It checks approximation versions of these examples.

When comparing HyTech to the approach depicted in this paper, several issues have to be taken into consideration. The first issue concerns the expressiveness of the dynamical model. HyTech restricts the dynamical model to linear hybrid automata in which the continuous dynamics is governed by differential equations. The nonlinear dynamics e.g. of the form $\dot{x} \bowtie c1 * x + c2$, where $c1, c2 \in \Re, c1 \neq 0, \bowtie \in \{<, \leq, >, \geq, =\}$ are first approximated either by a linear phase portrait or clock translation [17]. Then, the verification phase is done on the approximated model. On the other hand, *CLP* is more expressive, because it allows more general dynamics. In particular, *CLP* can directly handle dynamics expressible as a combination of polynomials, exponentials, and logarithmic functions explicitly without approximating the model. For instance the last equation can be represented in *CLP* form as $X \$\bowtie X0 - c2/c1 + c2/c1 * exp(c1 * (T - T0))$, where $(T - T0)$ is the computational delay. Although clearly completeness cannot be guaranteed, from a practical point of view, this procedure allows to express problems in a natural manner. The *CLP* technology can be fully exploited; it suspends such complex goals until they become solvable.

Another issue that should be taken into account is the type of verifiable properties. HyTech cannot verify simple properties that depend on the occurrence of events, despite of the fact that synchronization events are used in the model. On the other hand, simple real-time duration properties between events can be verified using HyTech. However, to do so, the model must be specified by introducing auxiliary variables to measure delays between events or the delay needed for a particular conditions to be hold. Bounded response time and minimal event separation are further properties that can be verified using HyTech. These properties, however, can only be checked after augmenting the model under consideration with what is called a *monitor* or *observer* automaton (cf. [13]), whose functionality is to observe the model without changing its behavior under consideration. It records the time as soon as some event occurs. Before the model is verified, the monitor automaton has to be composed with the original model, which in turns may add further complexity to the model. As demonstrated in this paper, however, there is no need to augment the model with an extra automaton for the reason that during the run, not only the states of variables are recorded, but also the events and the time, where the constraint solver can be used to reason about the respective property.

In addition to the benchmarks that demonstrate the feasibility of our approach, we have recently used our framework to model a case study that has been taken from a logistic domain [23]. In this case study, we have demonstrated how an agent, in a multi-agent scenario, selects the most appropriate plan, in case of occurring unexpected events during the plan's execution. The agent selects the plan that maximizes its utility function. The expressiveness of classical tools of hybrid automata lack to model such types of scenario. This is for the reason that these tools are special purpose tools that model continuous reactive systems. The Expressive of hybrid automata on multi-agent system, in terms of modeling and verification, are not the main concerns of these tools.

# 7  Related Works

Since we have presented and implemented an approach to model and verify multi-agent systems by means of hybrid automata, this section will relate our work to the other approaches of hybrid automata. The key relation to these approaches to multi-agent systems is that all of them can be used to model and validate multi-agent systems plans that are defined through their capability to continuously react in dynamic environments, while respecting some time constraints.

Several tools exist for formal verification of hybrid automata [13,8,3], where a multi-agent team can be verified. Differently to our approach, however, these tools compose the automata prior to the verification phase. Consequently, this gives rise to a state explosion problem, and hence limits to verify a group of agents.

We are not the first one who approached modeling and verifying hybrid automata using CLP. In contrast to our proposed approach, several authors propose the explicit composition of different concurrent automata by hand leading to one single automaton, before a CLP implementation is applied. This is a tedious work, especially in the case of multi-agent systems, where a group of agents exists. The latter case is exemplified in [27,20]. Other authors employ CLP for implementing hybrid automata [4,5,10], but restrict their attention to a simple class of hybrid systems (e.g. timed systems). They do not construct the overall behavior prior to modeling, but model each automaton separately. However, the run of the model takes all possible paths into consideration, resulting from the product of each component, which leads to unnecessary computation.

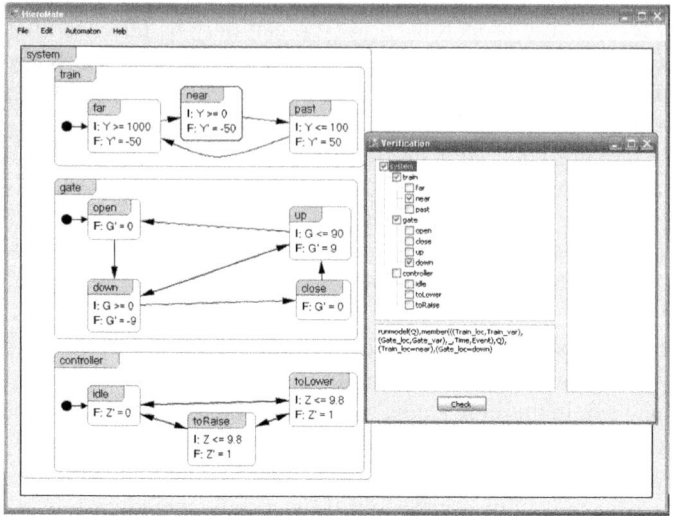

**Fig. 4.** A tool for modeling and Verification based on CLP

## 8   Conclusion

Multi-agent systems need to coordinate their plans especially in a safety critical environment, where unexpected events typically arise. Therefore, it is becoming increasingly important to react to those events in real time in order to avoid the risk that may occur during the planning. For this purpose, various researches have approached hybrid automata as a framework to model reactively multi-agent plans. In this paper, we have showed how multi-agent systems can be formally specified and verified as hybrid automata without explicitly composing the system prior to the verification phase. The previous helps to tackle the state space problem that may arise during the composition process. We have programmed our approach by means of constraint logic programming, where constraint solvers help us to build dynamically the entire behavior of a multi-agent system and to reason about its properties. Furthermore, we have showed how various properties can be verified using our CLP framework. In addition, we have conducted several experiments taken from the hybrid automata context to show the feasibility of our approach.

Currently we are developing and enhancing a tool environment that aims at simplifying both processes of modeling and verification. In this tool, a model together with its requirement are specified graphically, then the process of verification is achieved automatically. The graphical specifications are transformed into executable CLP codes, which follows the outline of this paper. This can avoid the tedious work, which results from specifying larger systems. Additionally, this can give the possibility to the non experts of CLP to model and verify multi-agent systems in terms of hybrid automata. A primary version of the tool (see Fig.4) appears in [24]. Moreover, we intend to model and verify some of case studies that model plans of group agents to reach a particular goal, for example the plan of agents in a rescue scenario [9]. As a further work, since

CLP is a suitable framework, where we can reason not only about the time behaviors of multi-agent systems, bout also about their knowledge, then the combination of both worlds is subjected to a future work.

# References

1. Alur, R., Courcoubetis, C., Henzinger, T.A., Ho, P.-H., Nicollin, X., Olivero, A., Sifakis, J., Yovine, S.: The algorithmic analysis of hybrid systems. In: ICAOS: International Conference on Analysis and Optimization of Systems – Discrete-Event Systems. LNCIS, pp. 331–351. Springer, Heidelberg (1994)
2. Alur, R., Dill, D.: A Theory of Timed Automata. Theoretical Computer Science 126(2), 183–235 (1994)
3. Behrmann, G., David, A., Larsen, K.G.: A tutorial on Uppaal. In: Bernardo, M., Corradini, F. (eds.) SFM-RT 2004. LNCS, vol. 3185, pp. 200–236. Springer, Heidelberg (2004)
4. Ciarlini, A., Frühwirth, T.: Automatic derivation of meaningful experiments for hybrid systems. In: Proceeding of ACM SIGSIM Conf. on Artificial Intelligence, Simulation, and Planning, AIS 2000 (2000)
5. Delzanno, G., Podelski, A.: Model checking in CLP. In: Cleaveland, W.R. (ed.) TACAS 1999. LNCS, vol. 1579, pp. 223–239. Springer, Heidelberg (1999)
6. Egerstedt, M.: Behavior Based Robotics Using Hybrid Automata. In: Lynch, N.A., Krogh, B.H. (eds.) HSCC 2000. LNCS, vol. 1790, pp. 103–116. Springer, Heidelberg (2000)
7. El Fallah-Seghrouchni, A., Degirmenciyan-Cartault, I., Marc, F.: Framework for Multi-agent Planning Based on Hybrid Automata. In: Mařík, V., Müller, J.P., Pěchouček, M. (eds.) CEEMAS 2003. LNCS (LNAI), vol. 2691, pp. 226–235. Springer, Heidelberg (2003)
8. Frehse, G.: PHAVer: Algorithmic verification of hybrid systems past HyTech. In: Morari, M., Thiele, L. (eds.) HSCC 2005. LNCS, vol. 3414, pp. 258–273. Springer, Heidelberg (2005)
9. Furbach, U., Murray, J., Schmidsberger, F., Stolzenburg, F.: Hybrid multiagent systems with timed synchronization – specification and model checking. In: Dastani, M.M., El Fallah Seghrouchni, A., Ricci, A., Winikoff, M. (eds.) ProMAS 2007. LNCS (LNAI), vol. 4908, pp. 205–220. Springer, Heidelberg (2008)
10. Gupta, G., Pontelli, E.: A constraint-based approach for specification and verification of real-time systems. In: Proceedings of IEEE Real-time Symposium, pp. 230–239 (1997)
11. Halbwachs, N., Proy, Y., Raymond, P.: Verification of linear hybrid systems by means of convex approximations. In: LeCharlier, B. (ed.) SAS 1994. LNCS, vol. 864, p. 223. Springer, Heidelberg (1994)
12. Henzinger, T.: The theory of hybrid automata. In: Proceedings of the 11th Annual Symposium on Logic in Computer Science, New Brunswick, NJ, pp. 278–292. IEEE Computer Society Press, Los Alamitos (1996)
13. Henzinger, T., Ho, P.-H., Wong-Toi, H.: A user guide to HyTech. In: Brinksma, E., Steffen, B., Cleaveland, W.R., Larsen, K.G., Margaria, T. (eds.) TACAS 1995. LNCS, vol. 1019, pp. 41–71. Springer, Heidelberg (1995)
14. Henzinger, T., Horowitz, B., Majumdar, R., Wong-Toi, H.: Beyond HYTECH: Hybrid Systems Analysis Using Interval Numerical Methods. In: Lynch, N.A., Krogh, B.H. (eds.) HSCC 2000. LNCS, vol. 1790, pp. 130–144. Springer, Heidelberg (2000)
15. Henzinger, T.A., Kopke, P.W., Puri, A., Varaiya, P.: What's Decidable about Hybrid Automata? Journal of Computer and System Sciences 57(1), 94–124 (1998)
16. Henzinger, T.A., Ho, P.-H., Wong-Toi, H.: HyTech: The Next Generation. In: IEEE Real-Time Systems Symposium, pp. 56–65 (1995)

17. Henzinger, T.A., Ho, P.-H., Wong-Toi, H.: Algorithmic analysis of nonlinear hybrid systems. IEEE Transactions on Automatic Control 43, 540–554 (1998)
18. Hutzler, G., Klaudel, H., Wang, D.Y.: Towards timed automata and multi-agent systems. In: Hinchey, M.G., Rash, J.L., Truszkowski, W.F., Rouff, C.A. (eds.) FAABS 2004. LNCS (LNAI), vol. 3228, pp. 161–172. Springer, Heidelberg (2004)
19. Jaffar, J., Lassez, J.: Constraint logic programming. In: Proceedings of the 14th ACM SIGACT-SIGPLAN symposium on Principles of programming languages, pp. 111–119. ACM, New York (1987)
20. Jaffar, J., Santosa, A., Voicu, R.: A clp proof method for timed automata. In: IEEE International on Real-Time Systems Symposium, vol. 0, pp. 175–186 (2004)
21. Krzysztof, M.W., Apt, R.: Constraint Logic Programming Using Eclipse. Cambridge University Press, Cambridge (2007)
22. Mohammed, A., Furbach, U.: Modeling multi-agent logistic process system using hybrid automata. In: Ultes-Nitsche, U., Moldt, D., Augusto, J.C. (eds.) MSVVEIS 2008: Proceedings of the 6th International Workshop on Modelling, Simulation, Verification and Validation of Enterprise Information Systems, MSVVEIS-2008, pp. 141–149. INSTICC Press (2008)
23. Mohammed, A., Furbach, U.: From reactive to deliberative multi-agent planning. In: Ultes-Nitsche, U., Moldt, D., Augusto, J.C. (eds.) Proceedings of the 7th International Workshop on Modelling, Simulation, Verification and Validation of Enterprise Information Systems, MSVVEIS 2009, pp. 67–75. INSTICC Press (2009)
24. Mohammed, A., Schwarz, C.: Hieromate: A graphical tool for specification and verification of hierarchical hybrid automata. In: Mertsching, B., Hund, M., Aziz, Z. (eds.) KI 2009. LNCS (LNAI), vol. 5803, pp. 695–702. Springer, Heidelberg (2009)
25. Mohammed, A., Stolzenburg, F.: Implementing hierarchical hybrid automata using constraint logic programming. In: Schwarz, S. (ed.) Proceedings of 22nd Workshop on (Constraint) Logic Programming, Dresden, pp. 60–71 (2008); University Halle Wittenberg, Institute of Computer Science. Technical Report 2008/08
26. Object Management Group, Inc.: UML Version 2.1.2 (Infrastructure and Superstructure) (November 2007)
27. Urbina, L.: Analysis of hybrid systems in CLP(R). In: Freuder, E.C. (ed.) CP 1996. LNCS (LNAI), vol. 1118, pp. 451–467. Springer, Heidelberg (1996)

# Probabilistic Behavioural State Machines

Peter Novák

Department of Informatics
Clausthal University of Technology
Julius-Albert-Str. 4, D-38678 Clausthal-Zellerfeld, Germany
peter.novak@tu-clausthal.de

**Abstract.** Development of embodied cognitive agents in agent oriented programming languages naturally leads to writing underspecified programs. The semantics of BDI inspired rule based agent programming languages leaves room for various alternatives as to how to implement the action selection mechanism of an agent (paraphrased from [5]).

To facilitate encoding of heuristics for the non-deterministic action selection mechanism, I introduce a probabilistic extension of the framework of *Behavioural State Machines* and its associated programming language interpreter *Jazzyk*. The language rules coupling a triggering condition and an applicable behaviour are extended with labels, thus allowing finer grained control of the behaviour selection mechanism of the underlying interpreter. In consequence, the agent program not only prescribes a set of mental state transitions enabled in a given context, but also specifies a probability distribution over them.

## 1 Introduction

Situated cognitive agents, such as mobile service robots, operate in rich, unstructured, dynamically changing and not completely observable environments. Since various phenomena of real world environments are not completely specifiable, as well as because of limited, noisy, or even malfunctioning sensors and actuators, such agents must operate with *incomplete information*.

On the other hand, similarly to mainstream software engineering, *robustness* and *elaboration tolerance* are some of the desired properties for cognitive agent programs. Embodied agent is supposed to operate reasonably well also in conditions previously unforeseen by the designer and it should degrade gracefully in the face of partial failures and unexpected circumstances (robustness). At the same time the program should be concise, easily maintainable and extensible (elaboration tolerance).

Agent programs in the reactive planning paradigm [15] are specifications of partial plans for the agent about how to deal with various situations and events occurring in the environment. The inherent incomplete information on one side, stemming from a level of knowledge representation granularity chosen at the agent's design phase, and striving for robust and easily maintainable programs on the other yield a trade-off of *intentional underspecification* of resulting agent programs.

L. Braubach, J.-P. Briot, and J. Thangarajah (Eds.): ProMAS 2009, LNAI 5919, pp. 67–81, 2010.

Most BDI inspired agent oriented programming languages on both sides of the spectrum between theoretically founded (such as *AgentSpeak(L)/Jason* [2], *3APL* [3] or *GOAL* [4]) to pragmatic ones (e.g., *JACK* [16] or *Jadex* [14]) facilitate encoding of underspecified, non-deterministic programs. Any given situation, or an event can at the same time trigger multiple behaviours, which themselves can be non-deterministic, i.e, can include alternative branches.

A precise and exclusive qualitative specification of behaviour triggering conditions is often impossible due to the, at the design time chosen and fixed, level of knowledge representation granularity. This renders the qualitative condition description a rather coarse grained means for steering agent's life-cycle. In such contexts, a quantitative heuristics steering the language interpreter's choices becomes a powerful tool for encoding developer's informal knowledge, or intuitions about agent's run-time evolutions. For example, it might be appropriate to execute some applicable behaviours more often than others, or some of them might intuitively perform better than other behaviours in the same context, and therefore should be preferably selected.

In this paper I propose a *probabilistic extension* of a rule-based agent programming language. The core idea is straightforward: language rules coupling a triggering condition with an applicable behaviour are extended with labels denoting a probability with which the interpreter's selection mechanism should choose the particular behaviour in a given context. The idea is directly applicable also to other agent programming languages, however here I focus on extension of the theoretical framework of *Behavioural State Machines* [10] and its associated programming language instance *Jazzyk*, which I use in my long-term research. One of elegant implications of the extension of the *BSM* framework is that subprograms with labelled rules can be seen as specifications of probability distributions over actions applicable in a given context. This allows steering agent's focus of deliberation on a certain sub-behaviour with only minor changes to the original agent program. I call this technique *adjustable deliberation*.

After a brief overview of the framework of *Behavioural State Machines* (*BSM*) with the associated programming language *Jazzyk* in Section 2, sections 3 and 4 introduce *P-BSM* and *Jazzyk(P)*, their respective probabilistic extensions. Section 5 discusses practical use of the *P-BSM* framework together with a brief overview of related work. Finally, a summary with final remarks concludes the paper in Section 6.

## 2   Behavioural State Machines

In [10] I introduced the framework of *Behavioural State Machines*. *BSM* framework draws a clear distinction between the *knowledge representation* and *behavioural* layers within an agent. It thus provides a programming framework that clearly separates the programming concerns of *how to represent an agent's knowledge* about, for example, its environment and *how to encode its behaviours* for acting in it. This section briefly introduces the *BSM* framework, for simplicity without treatment of variables. For the complete formal description of the *BSM* framework, see [10].

## 2.1 Syntax

*BSM* agents are collections of one or more so-called *knowledge representation modules* (KR modules), typically denoted by $\mathcal{M}$, each representing a part of the agent's knowledge base. KR modules may be used to represent and maintain various mental attitudes of an agent, such as knowledge about its environment, or its goals, intentions, obligations, etc. Transitions between states of a *BSM* result from applying so-called *mental state transformers (mst)*, typically denoted by $\tau$. Various types of mst's determine the behaviour that an agent can generate. A *BSM agent* consists of a set of KR modules $\mathcal{M}_1, \ldots, \mathcal{M}_n$ and a mental state transformer $\mathcal{P}$, i.e. $\mathcal{A} = (\mathcal{M}_1, \ldots, \mathcal{M}_n, \mathcal{P})$; the mst $\mathcal{P}$ is also called an *agent program*.

The notion of a KR module is an abstraction of a partial knowledge base of an agent. In turn, its states are to be treated as theories (i.e., sets of sentences) expressed in the KR language of the module. Formally, a KR module $\mathcal{M}_i = (\mathcal{S}_i, \mathcal{L}_i, \mathcal{Q}_i, \mathcal{U}_i)$ is characterised by a knowledge representation language $\mathcal{L}_i$, a set of states $\mathcal{S}_i \subseteq 2^{\mathcal{L}_i}$, a set of query operators $\mathcal{Q}_i$ and a set of update operators $\mathcal{U}_i$. A query operator $\models \in \mathcal{Q}_i$ is a mapping $\models : \mathcal{S}_i \times \mathcal{L}_i \to \{\top, \bot\}$. Similarly an update operator $\oplus \in \mathcal{U}_i$ is a mapping $\oplus : \mathcal{S}_i \times \mathcal{L}_i \to \mathcal{S}_i$.

Queries, typically denoted by $\varphi$, can be seen as operators of type $\models : \mathcal{S}_i \to \{\top, \bot\}$. A primitive query $\varphi = (\models \phi)$ consists of a query operator $\models \in \mathcal{Q}_i$ and a formula $\phi \in \mathcal{L}_i$ of the same KR module $\mathcal{M}_i$. Complex queries can be composed by means of conjunction $\wedge$, disjunction $\vee$ and negation $\neg$.

Mental state transformers enable transitions from one state to another. A primitive mst $\oslash \psi$, typically denoted by $\rho$ and constructed from an update operator $\oslash \in \mathcal{U}_i$ and a formula $\psi \in \mathcal{L}_i$, refers to an update on the state of the corresponding KR module. Conditional mst's are of the form $\varphi \longrightarrow \tau$, where $\varphi$ is a query and $\tau$ is a mst. Such a conditional mst makes the application of $\tau$ depend on the evaluation of $\varphi$. Syntactic constructs for combining mst's are: non-deterministic choice $|$ and sequence $\circ$.

**Definition 1 (mental state transformer).** *Let $\mathcal{M}_1, \ldots, \mathcal{M}_n$ be KR modules of the form $\mathcal{M}_i = (\mathcal{S}_i, \mathcal{L}_i, \mathcal{Q}_i, \mathcal{U}_i)$. The set of* mental state transformers *is defined as below:*

- **skip** *is a primitive mst,*
- *if $\oslash \in \mathcal{U}_i$ and $\psi \in \mathcal{L}_i$, then $\oslash \psi$ is a primitive mst,*
- *if $\varphi$ is a query, and $\tau$ is a mst, then $\varphi \longrightarrow \tau$ is a conditional mst,*
- *if $\tau$ and $\tau'$ are mst's, then $\tau | \tau'$ and $\tau \circ \tau'$ are mst's (choice, and sequence respectively).*

## 2.2 Semantics

The *yields* calculus, summarised below after [10], specifies an update associated with executing a mental state transformer in a single step of the language interpreter. It formally defines the meaning of the state transformation induced by executing an mst in a state, i.e., a mental state transition.

Formally, a *mental state* $\sigma$ of a *BSM* $\mathcal{A} = (\mathcal{M}_1, \ldots, \mathcal{M}_n, \tau)$ is a tuple $\sigma = \langle \sigma_1, \ldots, \sigma_n \rangle$ of KR module states $\sigma_1 \in \mathcal{S}_1, \ldots, \sigma_n \in \mathcal{S}_n$, corresponding to $\mathcal{M}_1, \ldots, \mathcal{M}_n$ respectively. $\mathcal{S} = \mathcal{S}_1 \times \cdots \times \mathcal{S}_n$ denotes the space of all mental states over $\mathcal{A}$. A mental state can be modified by applying primitive mst's on it and query formulae can be evaluated against it. The semantic notion of truth of a query is defined through the satisfaction relation $\models$. A primitive query $\models\phi$ holds in a mental state $\sigma = \langle \sigma_1, \ldots, \sigma_n \rangle$ (written $\sigma \models (\models\phi)$) iff $\models(\phi, \sigma_i)$, otherwise we have $\sigma \not\models (\models\phi)$. Given the usual meaning of Boolean operators, it is straightforward to extend the query evaluation to compound query formulae. Note that evaluation of a query does not change the mental state $\sigma$.

For an mst $\oslash\psi$, we use $(\oslash, \psi)$ to denote its semantic counterpart, i.e., the corresponding *update* (state transformation). Sequential application of updates is denoted by $\bullet$, i.e. $\rho_1 \bullet \rho_2$ is an update resulting from applying $\rho_1$ first and then applying $\rho_2$. The application of an update to a mental state is defined formally below.

**Definition 2 (applying an update).** *The result of applying an update* $\rho = (\oslash, \psi)$ *to a state* $\sigma = \langle \sigma_1, \ldots, \sigma_n \rangle$ *of a BSM* $\mathcal{A} = (\mathcal{M}_1, \ldots, \mathcal{M}_n, \mathcal{P})$, *denoted by* $s \bigoplus \rho$, *is a new state* $\sigma' = \langle \sigma_1, \ldots, \sigma_i', \ldots, \sigma_n \rangle$, *where* $\sigma_i' = \sigma_i \oslash \psi$ *and* $\sigma_i$, $\oslash$, *and* $\psi$ *correspond to one and the same* $\mathcal{M}_i$ *of* $\mathcal{A}$. *Applying the empty update* **skip** *on the state* $\sigma$ *does not change the state, i.e.* $\sigma \bigoplus \textbf{skip} = \sigma$.

*Inductively, the result of applying a sequence of updates* $\rho_1 \bullet \rho_2$ *is a new state* $\sigma'' = \sigma' \bigoplus \rho_2$, *where* $\sigma' = \sigma \bigoplus \rho_1$. $\sigma \overset{\rho_1 \bullet \rho_2}{\longrightarrow} \sigma'' = \sigma \overset{\rho_1}{\longrightarrow} \sigma' \overset{\rho_2}{\longrightarrow} \sigma''$ *denotes the corresponding compound transition.*

The meaning of a mental state transformer in state $\sigma$, formally defined by the *yields* predicate below, is the update set it yields in that mental state.

**Definition 3 (yields calculus).** *A mental state transformer* $\tau$ *yields an update* $\rho$ *in a state* $\sigma$, *iff* $yields(\tau, \sigma, \rho)$ *is derivable in the following calculus:*

$$\frac{\top}{yields(\textbf{skip}, \sigma, \textbf{skip})} \quad \frac{\top}{yields(\oslash\psi, \sigma, (\oslash, \psi))} \quad (primitive)$$

$$\frac{yields(\tau, \sigma, \rho),\ \sigma \models \phi}{yields(\phi \longrightarrow \tau, \sigma, \rho)} \quad \frac{yields(\tau, \sigma, \rho),\ \sigma \not\models \phi}{yields(\phi \longrightarrow \tau, \sigma, \textbf{skip})} \quad (conditional)$$

$$\frac{yields(\tau_1, \sigma, \rho_1),\ yields(\tau_2, \sigma, \rho_2)}{yields(\tau_1 | \tau_2, \sigma, \rho_1),\ yields(\tau_1 | \tau_2, \sigma, \rho_2)} \quad (choice)$$

$$\frac{yields(\tau_1, \sigma, \rho_1),\ yields(\tau_2, \sigma \bigoplus \rho_1, \rho_2)}{yields(\tau_1 \circ \tau_2, \sigma, \rho_1 \bullet \rho_2)} \quad (sequence)$$

*We say that* $\tau$ *yields an* update set $\nu$ *in a state* $\sigma$ *iff* $\nu = \{\rho | yields(\tau, \sigma, \rho)\}$.

The mst **skip** yields the update **skip**. Similarly, a primitive update mst $\oslash\psi$ yields the corresponding update $(\oslash, \psi)$. In the case the condition of a conditional mst $\phi \longrightarrow \tau$ is satisfied in the current mental state, the calculus yields one of the updates corresponding to the right hand side mst $\tau$, otherwise the no-operation **skip** update is yielded. A non-deterministic choice mst yields an update corresponding to either of its members and finally a sequential mst yields a sequence of updates corresponding to the first mst of the sequence and an update yielded by the second member of the sequence in a state resulting from application of the first update to the current mental state.

Notice, that the provided semantics of choice and sequence operators implies associativity of both. Hence, from this point on, instead of the strictly pairwise notation $\tau_1|(\tau_2|(\tau_3|(\cdots|\tau_k)))$, we simply write $\tau_1|\tau_2|\tau_2|\cdots|\tau_k$. Similarly for the sequence operation $\circ$.

The following definition articulates the denotational semantics of the notion of mental state transformer as an encoding of a function mapping mental states of a *BSM* to updates, i.e., transitions between them.

**Definition 4 (mst functional semantics).** *Let $\mathcal{M}_1,\ldots,\mathcal{M}_n$ be KR modules. A mental state transformer $\tau$ encodes a function $\mathfrak{f}_\tau : \sigma \mapsto \{\rho|yields(\tau,\sigma,\rho)\}$ over the space of mental states $\sigma = \langle\sigma_1,\ldots,\sigma_n\rangle \in S_1 \times \cdots \times S_n$.*

Subsequently, the semantics of a *BSM* agent is defined as a set of traces in the induced transition system enabled by the *BSM* agent program.

**Definition 5 (BSM semantics).** *A BSM $\mathcal{A} = (\mathcal{M}_1,\ldots,\mathcal{M}_n,\mathcal{P})$ can make a step from state $\sigma$ to a state $\sigma'$, iff $\sigma' = \sigma \bigoplus \rho$, s.t. $\rho \in \mathfrak{f}_\mathcal{P}(\sigma)$. We also say, that $\mathcal{A}$ induces a (possibly compound) transition $\sigma \xrightarrow{\rho} \sigma'$.*

*A possibly infinite sequence of states $\sigma_1,\ldots,\sigma_i,\ldots$ is a* run *of BSM $\mathcal{A}$, iff for each $i \geq 1$, $\mathcal{A}$ induces a transition $\sigma_i \to \sigma_{i+1}$.*

*The semantics of an agent system characterised by a BSM $\mathcal{A}$, is a set of all runs of $\mathcal{A}$.*

Additionally, we require the non-deterministic choice of a *BSM* interpreter to fulfil the *weak fairness condition*, similar to that in [7], for all the induced runs.

**Condition 1 (weak fairness condition).** *A computation run is weakly fair iff it is not the case that an update is always yielded from some point in time on but is never selected for execution.*


## 2.3   Jazzyk

*Jazzyk* is an interpreter of the *Jazzyk* programming language implementing the computational model of the *BSM* framework. Later in this paper, we use a more readable notation mixing the syntax of *Jazzyk* with that of the *BSM* mst's introduced above. when $\phi$ then $\tau$ encodes a conditional mst $\phi \longrightarrow \tau$. Symbols ; and , stand for choice | and sequence $\circ$ operators respectively. To facilitate operator precedence, mental state transformers can be grouped into compound structures, blocks, using curly braces {...}.

To better support source code modularity and re-usability, *Jazzyk* interpreter integrates a macro preprocessor, a powerful tool for structuring and modularising and encapsulating the source code and writing code templates.

For further details on the *Jazzyk* programming language and the macro preprocessor integration with *Jazzyk* interpreter, consult [10].

## 3    Probabilistic BSMs

In the plain *BSM* framework, the syntactic construct of a mental state transformer encodes a transition function over the space of mental states of a *BSM*
(cf. Definition 4). Hence, an execution of a compound non-deterministic choice
mst amounts to a non-deterministic selection of one of its components and its
subsequent application to the current mental state of the agent. In order to
enable a finer grained control over this selection process, in this section I introduce an extension of the *BSM* framework with specifications of a probability
distributions over components of choice mst's.

The *P-BSM* formalism introduced below heavily builds on associativeness of
*BSM* composition operators of non-deterministic choice and sequence. We also
informally say that an mst $\tau$ *occurs* in a mst $\tau'$ iff $\tau'$ can be constructed from
a set of mst's $\mathcal{T}$, s.t. $\tau \in \mathcal{T}$, by using composition operators as defined by the
Definition 1.

**Definition 6 (Probabilistic BSM).** *A Probabilistic Behavioural State Ma-
chine (P-BSM)* $\mathcal{A}_p$ *is a tuple* $\mathcal{A}_p = (\mathcal{M}_1, \ldots, \mathcal{M}_n, \mathcal{P}, \Pi)$, *where* $\mathcal{A} = (\mathcal{M}_1, \ldots,$
$\mathcal{M}_n, \mathcal{P})$ *is a* BSM *and* $\Pi : \tau \mapsto P_\tau$ *is a function assigning to each non-
deterministic choice mst of the form* $\tau = \tau_1 | \cdots | \tau_k \in \mathcal{P}$ *occurring in* $\mathcal{P}$ *a discrete
probability distribution function* $P_\tau{:}\tau_i \mapsto [0,1]$, *s.t.* $\sum_{i=1}^k P_\tau(\tau_i) = 1$.

*W.l.o.g. we assume that each mst occurring in the agent program* $\mathcal{P}$ *can be
uniquely identified (e.g. by its position in the agent program).*

The probability distribution function $P_\tau$ assigns to each component of a non-
deterministic choice mst $\tau = \tau_1 | \tau_2 | \cdots | \tau_k$ a probability of its selection for appli-
cation by a *BSM* interpreter.

Note, that because of the unique identification of mst's in an agent program
$\mathcal{P}$, the function $\Pi$ assigns two distinct discrete probability distributions $P_{\tau_1}$ and
$P_{\tau_2}$ to choice mst's $\tau_1$, $\tau_2$ even when they share the syntactic form but occur as
distinct components of $\mathcal{P}$.

To distinguish from the *BSM* formalism, we call mst's occurring in a *P-BSM*
*probabilistic mental state transformers*. *BSM* mst's as defined in Section 2 will
be called *plain*.

Similarly to plain mst's, the semantic counterpart of a probabilistic mst is a prob-
abilistic update. A *probabilistic update* of a *P-BSM* $\mathcal{A}_p = (\mathcal{M}_1, \ldots, \mathcal{M}_n, \mathcal{P}, \Pi)$ is
a tuple $p{:}\rho$, where $p \in \mathbb{R}$, s.t. $p \in [0,1]$, is a probability and $\rho = (\oslash, \psi)$ is an update
from the *BSM* $\mathcal{A} = (\mathcal{M}_1, \ldots, \mathcal{M}_n, \mathcal{P})$.

The semantics of a probabilistic mental state transformer in a state $\sigma$, formally
defined by the *yields*$_p$ predicate below, is the probabilistic update set it yields
in that mental state.

**Definition 7 (yields$_p$ calculus).** *A probabilistic mental state transformer* $\tau$
*yields a probabilistic update* $p{:}\rho$ *in a state* $\sigma$, *iff yields*$_p(\tau, \sigma, p{:}\rho)$ *is derivable in
the following calculus:*

$$\frac{\top}{yields_p(\mathbf{skip},\sigma,1{:}\mathbf{skip})} \qquad \frac{\top}{yields_p(\oslash\psi,\sigma,1{:}(\oslash,\psi))} \qquad (primitive)$$

$$\frac{yields_p(\tau,\sigma,p{:}\rho),\ \sigma\models\phi}{yields_p(\phi\longrightarrow\tau,\sigma,p{:}\rho)} \qquad \frac{yields_p(\tau,\sigma,\theta,p{:}\rho),\ \sigma\not\models\phi}{yields_p(\phi\longrightarrow\tau_p,\sigma,1{:}\mathbf{skip})} \qquad (conditional)$$

$$\frac{\tau=\tau_1|\cdots|\tau_k,\ \Pi(\tau)=P_\tau,\ \forall1\leq i\leq k{:}\ yields_p(\tau_i,\sigma,p_i{:}\rho_i)}{\forall1\leq i\leq k{:}\ yields_p(\tau,\sigma,P_\tau(\tau_i)\cdot p_i{:}\rho_i)} \qquad (choice)$$

$$\frac{\tau=\tau_1\circ\cdots\circ\tau_k,\ \forall1\leq i\leq k{:}\ yields_p(\tau_i,\sigma_i,p_i{:}\rho_i)\wedge\sigma_{i+1}=\sigma_i\oplus\rho_i}{yields(\tau,\sigma_1,\prod_{i=1}^k p_i{:}\rho_1\bullet\cdots\bullet\rho_k)} \qquad (sequence)$$

The modification of the plain *BSM* *yields* calculus introduced above for primitive and conditional mst's is rather straightforward. A plain primitive mst yields the associated primitive update for which there's no probability of execution specified. A conditional mst yields probabilistic updates of its right hand side if the left hand side query condition is satisfied. It amounts to a **skip** mst otherwise. The function $\Pi$ associates a discrete probability distribution function with each non-deterministic choice mst and thus modifies the probability of application of the probabilistic updates yielded by its components accordingly. Finally, similarly to the plain *yields* calculus, a sequence of probabilistic mst's yields sequences of updates of its components, however the joint application probability equals to the conditional probability of selecting the particular sequence of updates. The following example illustrates the sequence rule of the probabilistic $yields_p$ calculus.

*Example 1.* Consider the following mst: $(0.3{:}\tau_1\,|\,0.7{:}\tau_2)\circ(0.6{:}\tau_3\,|\,0.4{:}\tau_4)$. Let's assume that for each of the component mst's $\tau_i$, we have $yields_p(\tau_i,\sigma,p_i{:}\rho_i)$ in a state $\sigma$. The plain *yields* calculus yields the following sequences of updates $\rho_1\bullet\rho_3$, $\rho_1\bullet\rho_4$, $\rho_2\bullet\rho_3$ and $\rho_2\bullet\rho_4$. The probability of selection of each of them, however, equals to the conditional probability of choosing an update from the second component of the sequence, provided that the choice from the first one was already made. I.e. the probabilistic $yields_p$ calculus results in the following sequences of probabilistic updates $0.18{:}(\rho_1\bullet\rho_3)$, $0.12{:}(\rho_1\bullet\rho_4)$, $0.42{:}(\rho_2\bullet\rho_3)$ and $0.28{:}(\rho_2\bullet\rho_4)$.

The corresponding adaptation of the mst functional semantics straightforwardly follows.

**Definition 8 (probabilistic mst functional semantics).** *Let* $\mathcal{A}_p=(\mathcal{M}_1,\ldots,$ $\mathcal{M}_n,\mathcal{P},\Pi)$ *be a P-BSM. A probabilistic mental state transformer* $\tau$ *encodes a transition function* $\mathfrak{fp}_\tau:\sigma\mapsto\{p:\rho\,|\,yields_p(\tau,\sigma,p:\rho)\}$ *over the space of mental states* $\sigma=\langle\sigma_1,\ldots,\sigma_n\rangle\in S_1\times\cdots\times S_n.$

According to the Definition 6, each mst occurring in a *P-BSM* agent program can be uniquely identified. Consequently, also each probabilistic update yielded by the program can be uniquely identified by the mst it corresponds to. The consequence is, that w.l.o.g. we can assume that even when two probabilistic updates $p_1{:}\rho_1$, $p_2{:}\rho_2$ yielded by the agent program $\mathcal{P}$ in a state $\sigma$ share their syntactic form (i.e. $p_1=p_2$ and $\rho_1,\rho_2$ encode the same plain *BSM* update) they both independently occur in the probabilistic update set $\mathfrak{fp}(\sigma)$.

The following lemma shows, that the semantics of probabilistic mst's embodied by the $yields_p$ calculus can be understood as *an encoding of a probability distribution*, or *a probabilistic policy* over updates yielded by the underlying plain mst. Moreover, it also implies that composition of probabilistic mst's maintains their nature as probability distributions.

**Lemma 1.** *Let $\mathcal{A}_p = (\mathcal{M}_1, \ldots, \mathcal{M}_n, \mathcal{P}, \Pi)$ be a P-BSM. For every mental state transformer $\tau$ occurring in $\mathcal{P}$ and a mental state $\sigma$ of $\mathcal{A}_p$, we have*

$$\sum_{p:\rho \in \mathfrak{fp}_\tau(\sigma)} p = 1 \tag{1}$$

*Proof.* Cf. Appendix A.

Finally, the semantics of a *P-BSM* agent is defined as a set of traces in the induced transition system enabled by the *P-BSM* agent program.

**Definition 9 (BSM semantics).** *A P-BSM $\mathcal{A}_p = (\mathcal{M}_1, \ldots, \mathcal{M}_n, \mathcal{P}, \Pi)$ can make a step from state $\sigma$ to a state $\sigma'$ with probability $p$, iff $\sigma' = \sigma \oplus \rho$, s.t. $p:\rho \in \mathfrak{fp}_\tau(\sigma)$. We also say, that with a probability $p$, $\mathcal{A}_p$ induces a (possibly compound) transition $\sigma \overset{p:\rho}{\rightarrow} \sigma'$.*

*A possibly infinite sequence of states $\omega = \sigma_1, \ldots, \sigma_i, \ldots$ is a run of P-BSM $\mathcal{A}_p$, iff for each $i \geq 1$, $\mathcal{A}$ induces the transition $\sigma_i \overset{p_i:\rho_i}{\rightarrow} \sigma_{i+1}$ with probability $p_i$.*

*Let $pref(\omega)$ denote the set of all finite prefixes of a possibly infinite computation run $\omega$ and $|.|$ the length of a finite run. $P(\omega) = \prod_{i=1}^{|\omega|} p_i$ is then the probability of the finite run $\omega$.*

*The semantics of an agent system characterised by a P-BSM $\mathcal{A}_p$, is a set of all runs $\omega$ of $\mathcal{A}_p$, s.t. all of their finite prefixes $\omega' \in pref(\omega)$ have probability $P(\omega') > 0$.*

Informally, the semantics of an agent system is a set of runs involving only transitions induced by updates with a non-zero selection probability.

Additionally, we require an admissible *P-BSM* interpreter to fulfil the following specialisation of the weak fairness condition, for all the induced runs.

**Condition 2 (P-BSM weak fairness condition).** *Let $\omega$ be a possibly infinite computation run of a P-BSM $\mathcal{A}_p$. Let also $freq_{p:\rho}(\omega')$ be the number of transitions induced by the update $p:\rho$ along a finite prefix of $\omega' \in pref(\omega)$.*

*We say that $\omega$ is weakly fair w.r.t. $\mathcal{A}_p$ iff for all updates $p:\rho$ we have, that if from some point on $p:\rho$ is always yielded in states along $\omega$, then*

1. *it also occurs on $\omega$ infinitely often, and*
2. *for the sequence of finite prefixes of $\omega$ ordered according to their length holds*

$$\liminf_{\substack{|\omega'| \to \infty \\ \omega' \in pref(\omega)}} \frac{freq_{p:\rho}(\omega')}{|\omega'|} = p$$

Similarly to the plain *BSM* weak fairness Condition 1, the above stated Condition 2 embodies a minimal requirement on admissible *P-BSM* interpreters. It admits only *P-BSM* interpreters which honor the intended probabilistic semantics of the non-deterministic choice selection of the *yields$_p$* calculus. The first part of the requirement is a consequence of the plain *BSM* weak fairness condition (Condition 1), while the second states that in sufficiently long computation runs, the frequency of occurrence of an always yielded probabilistic update corresponds to its selection probability in each single step.

## 4   Jazzyk(P)

*Jazzyk* is a programming language instantiating the plain *BSM* theoretical framework introduced in [10]. This section informally describes its extension *Jazzyk(P)*, an instantiation of the framework of *Probabilistic Behavioural State Machines* introduced in Section 3 above.

*Jazzyk(P)* syntax differs from that of *Jazzyk* only in specification of probability distributions over choice mst's. *Jazzyk(P)* allows for explicit labellings of choice mst members by their individual application probabilities. Consider the following labelled choice mst $p_1{:}\tau_1$ ; $p_2{:}\tau_2$ ; $p_3{:}\tau_3$ ; $p_4{:}\tau_4$ in the *Jazzyk(P)* notation. Each $p_i \in [0,1]$ denotes the probability of selection of mst $\tau_i$ by the interpreter. Furthermore, to ensure that the labelling denotes a probability distribution over $\tau_i$'s, *Jazzyk(P)* parser requires that $\sum_{i=1}^{k} p_i = 1$ for every choice mst $p_1{:}\tau_1$ ; $\dots$ ; $p_k{:}\tau_k$ occurring in the considered agent program. Similarly to *Jazzyk*, during the program interpretation phase, *Jazzyk(P)* interpreter proceeds in a top-down manner subsequently considering nested mst's from the main agent program, finally down to primitive update formulae. When the original *Jazzyk* interpreter faces a selection from a non-deterministic choice mst, it randomly selects one of them assuming a discrete uniform probability distribution. I.e., the probability of selecting from a choice mst with $k$ members is $\frac{1}{k}$ for each of them. The extended interpreter *Jazzyk(P)* respects the specified selection probabilities: it generates a random number $p \in [0,1]$ and selects $\tau_s$, s.t. $\sum_{i=1}^{s-1} p_i \leq p \leq \sum_{i=1}^{s} p_i$.

For convenience, *Jazzyk(P)* enables use of incomplete labellings. An *incompletely labelled* non-deterministic choice mst is one containing at least one member mst without an explicit probability specification such as $p_1{:}\tau_1$ ; $p_2{:}\tau_2$ ; $\tau_3$ ; $\tau_4$. In such a case, the *Jazzyk(P)* parser automatically completes the distribution by uniformly dividing the remaining probability range to unlabelled mst's. I.e., provided an incompletely labelled choice mst with $k$ members, out of which $m < k$ are labelled $(p_1{:}\tau_1$ ; $\dots$ ; $p_m{:}\tau_m$ ; $\tau_{m+1}$ ; $\cdots$ ; $\tau_k)$, it assigns probability $p = \frac{1-\sum_{i=1}^{m} p_i}{k-m}$ to the remaining mst's $\tau_{m+1}, \dots, \tau_k$.

The Listing 1 provides an example of a *Jazzyk(P)* code snippet adapted from the *Jazzbot*[1] project [6]. Consider a BDI-style virtual agent (bot) in a simulated 3D environment. The bot moves around a virtual building and searches for items

---

[1] A detailed description is also provided on the project website
http://jazzyk.sf.net/

**Listing 1.** Example of *Jazzyk(P)* syntax

```
when ⊨_bel [{ threatened }] then {
    /* ***Emergency modus operandi*** */

    /* Detect the enemy's position */
    0.7 : when ⊨_bel [{ attacker(Id) }] and ⊨_env [{ eye see Id player Pos }]
    then ⊕_map [{ positions[Id] = Pos }] ;

    /* Check the camera sensor */
    0.2 : when ⊨_env [{ eye see Id Type Pos }] then {
        ⊕_bel [{ see(Id, Type) }] ,
        ⊕_map [{ objects[Pos].addIfNotPresent(Id) }]
    }

    /* Check the body health sensor */
    when ⊨_env [{ body health X }] then ⊕_bel [{ health(X). }] ;
} else {
    /* ***Normal mode of perception*** */

    /* Check the body health sensor */
    when ⊨_env [{ body health X }] then ⊕_bel [{ health(X). }] ;

    /* Check the camera sensor */
    when ⊨_env [{ eye see Id Type Pos }] then {
        ⊕_bel [{ see(Id, Type) }] ,
        ⊕_map [{ positions[Id] = Pos }]
    }
}
```

which it picks up and delivers to a particular place in the environment. Upon encountering an unfriendly agent (attacker), it executes an emergency behaviour, such as running away until it feels safe again. The agent consists of several KR modules *bel*, *map* and *env* respectively representing its beliefs about the environment and itself, the map of the environment and an interface to its sensors and actuators, i.e. the body. The KR module *env* represents a connector to the environment and can possibly involve also other agents, or human players. The corresponding query and update operators ⊨ and ⊕ are sub-scripted with the KR module label they correspond to.

The Listing 1 provides a piece of code for perception of the bot. In the normal mode of operation, the bot in a single step queries either its camera, or its body health status sensor with the same probability of selection for each of them, i.e., 0.5. However, in the case of emergency, the bot focuses more on escaping the attacker, therefore, in order to retrieve the attacker's position, it queries the camera sensor more often (selection probability $p = 0.7$) than sensing objects around it ($p = 0.2$). Checking it's own body health is of the least importance ($p = 0.1$), however not completely negligible.

In an implemented program, however, the Listing 1 would be rewritten using the macro facility of the *Jazzyk* interpreter and reduced to a more concise code shown in the Listing 2.

**Listing 2.** Example of focusing bot's attention during emergency situations rewritten with reusable macros

```
when ⊨bel [{ threatened }] then {
    /* ***Emergency modus operandi*** */
    0.7 : DETECT_ENEMY_POSITION ;
    0.2 : SENSE_CAMERA ;
          SENSE_HEALTH
} else {
    /* ***Normal mode of perception*** */
    SENSE_HEALTH ;
    SENSE_CAMERA
}
```

## 5   Discussion

The main contribution of the presented paper is introduction of *Probabilistic Behavioural State Machines* framework with the associated agent programming language *Jazzyk(P)*. P-BSM, and in turn *Jazzyk(P)*, allow for labelling of alternatives in non-deterministic choice mental state transformers, thus providing a specification of a probability distribution over the set of enabled transitions for the next step in agent's life-cycle. Besides the, in the field of rule based agent programming languages conventional, Plotkin style operational semantics [13], the *BSM* semantics allows a functional view on mental state transformers (cf. Definition 8). In turn, the informal reading of a *P-BSM* choice mst's can be seen as a specification of the probability with which the next transition will be chosen from the function denoted by the particular member mst. In other words, *a probability of applying the member mst function to the current mental state.*

The proposed extension allows a finer grained steering of the interpreter's non-deterministic selection mechanism and has applications across several niches of methodologies for rule based agent oriented programming languages. Our analyses and first experiments in the context of the *Jazzbot* application have shown that labelling probabilistic mst's is a useful means to contextually focus agent's perception (cf. Listing 2). Similarly, the labelling technique is useful in contexts, when it is necessary to execute certain behaviours with a certain given frequency. For example, approximatelly in about every 5th step broadcast a ping message to peers of the agent's team. Finally, the technique can be used when the agent developer has an informal intuition that preferring more frequent execution of certain behaviours over others (e.g. cheaper, but less efficient over resource intensive, but rather powerful) might suffice, or even perform better in a given context. Of course writing such programs makes sense only when a rigorous analysis of the situation is impossible, or undesirable and at the same time a suboptimal performance of the agent system is acceptable.

An instance of the latter technique for modifying the main control cycle of the agent program is what I call *adjustable deliberation*. Consider the following *Jazzyk BSM* code for the main control cycle of an agent adapted from [12]:

```
PERCEIVE ; HANDLE_GOALS ; ACT
```

The macros PERCEIVE, HANDLE_GOALS and ACT encode behaviours for perception (similar to that in the Listing 1), goal commitment strategy implementation and action selection respectively. In the case of emergency, as described in the example in Section 4 above, it might be useful to slightly neglect deliberation about agent's goals, in favour of an intensive environment observation and quick reaction selection. The following reformulation of the agent's control cycle demonstrates the simple program modification:

$$\textbf{when} \models_{bel} [\{ \textit{emergency} \}] \textbf{ then } \{ \text{ PERCEIVE ; HANDLE\_GOALS ; ACT } \}$$
$$\textbf{else } \{ 0.4 : \text{PERCEIVE ; HANDLE\_GOALS ; } 0.4 : \text{ACT} \}$$

The underlying semantic model of *Behavioural State Machines* framework is a labelled transition system [11]. In consequence, the underlying semantic model of the *P-BSM* framework is a discrete probabilistic labelled transition system, i.e., a structure similar to a *Markov chain* [8]. This similarity suggest a relationship of the *P-BSM* underlying semantic structure to various types of *Markov models* (cf. e.g. [9]), however a more extensive exploration of this relationship is beyond the scope of this paper.

In the field of agent oriented programming languages, recently Hindriks et al. [5] introduced an extension of the *GOAL* language [4], where a quantitative numeric value is associated with execution of an action leading from a mental state $m$ to another mental state $m'$. I.e., a triple of a precondition $\phi$ (partially describing $m$), an action $a$ and a post-condition $\psi$ (describing $m'$) is labelled with a utility value $U(\phi, a, \psi)$. Subsequently, in each deliberation cycle, the interpreter selects the action with the highest expected future utility w.r.t. agent's goals.

The approach of Hindriks et al. focuses on estimating aggregate utility values of bounded future evolutions of the agent system, i.e., evaluating possible future courses of evolution, plans, the agent can consider, and subsequently choosing an action advancing the system evolution along the best path. The *P-BSM*, on the other hand, is concerned only with selection of the next action resulting from the bottom-up propagation of probabilistic choices through the nested structure, a decision tree, of the agent program. So, while the approach of Hindriks et al. can be seen as a step towards look-ahead like reactive planning, *P-BSM* remains a purely reactive approach to programming cognitive agents. Informally, except for the nested structuring of agent programs (the distinguishing practical feature of the *BSM* framework w.r.t. to other theoretically founded agent programming languages), the *P-BSM* framework could be emulated by the approach of Hindriks et al. with the look-ahead planning bound of the length one.

## 6   Conclusion

The main contribution of the presented paper is introduction of *Probabilistic Behavioural State Machines* framework with the associated agent programming language *Jazzyk(P)*. The proposed extension of the plain *BSM* framework is a result of practical experience with *BSM* case-studies [6] and introduces a straightforward and pragmatic, yet quite a powerful, extension of the *BSM* framework. However, the presented paper presents only first steps towards a more rigorous approach to dealing with underspecification in agent oriented programming by means of probabilistic action selection.

Underspecification of agent programs is in general inevitable. However, in situations when a suboptimal performance is tolerable, providing the agent program interpreter with a heuristics for steering its choices can lead to rapid development of more efficient and robust agent systems.

# References

1. Bordini, R.H., Dastani, M., Dix, J., El Fallah Seghrouchni, A.: Multi-Agent Programming Languages, Platforms and Applications. Multiagent Systems, Artificial Societies, and Simulated Organizations, vol. 15. Kluwer Academic Publishers, Dordrecht (2005)
2. Bordini, R.H., Hübner, J.F., Vieira, R.: Jason and the Golden Fleece of Agent-Oriented Programming. Multiagent Systems, Artificial Societies, and Simulated Organizations [1], vol. 15, ch. 1, pp. 3–37 (2005)
3. Dastani, M., van Riemsdijk, M.B., Meyer, J.-J.: Programming Multi-Agent Systems in 3APL. Multiagent Systems, Artificial Societies, and Simulated Organizations [1], vol. 15, ch. 2, pp. 39–68 (2005)
4. de Boer, F.S., Hindriks, K.V., van der Hoek, W., Meyer, J.-J.C.: A verification framework for agent programming with declarative goals. J. Applied Logic 5(2), 277–302 (2007)
5. Hindriks, K.V., Jonker, C.M., Pasman, W.: Exploring heuristic action selection in agent programming. In: Hindriks, K.V., Pokahr, A., Sardina, S. (eds.) Programming Multi-Agent Systems. LNCS (LNAI), vol. 5442, pp. 24–39. Springer, Heidelberg (2009)
6. Köster, M., Novák, P., Mainzer, D., Fuhrmann, B.: Two case studies for Jazzyk BSM. In: Proceedings of Agents for Games and Simulations, AGS 2009, AAMAS 2009 co-located workshop, pp. 31–45 (2009)
7. Manna, Z., Pnueli, A.: The temporal logic of reactive and concurrent systems. Springer-Verlag New York, Inc., New York (1992)
8. Markov, A.A.: Extension of the law of large numbers to dependent quantities (in Russian). Izvestiya Fiziko-matematicheskogo obschestva pri Kazanskom Universitete 2(15), 135–156 (1906)
9. Meyn, S.P., Tweedie, R.L.: Markov Chains and Stochastic Stability. Springer, London (1993)
10. Novák, P.: Jazzyk: A programming language for hybrid agents with heterogeneous knowledge representations. In: Hindriks, K.V., Pokahr, A., Sardina, S. (eds.) Programming Multi-Agent Systems. LNCS (LNAI), vol. 5442, pp. 72–87. Springer, Heidelberg (2009)
11. Novák, P., Jamroga, W.: Code patterns for agent-oriented programming. In: Proceedings of The Eighth International Conference on Autonomous Agents and Multi-Agent Systems, AAMAS 2009 (2009)
12. Novák, P., Köster, M.: Designing goal-oriented reactive behaviours. In: Proceedings of the 6th International Cognitive Robotics Workshop, CogRob 2008, ECCAI co-located workshop, Patras, Greece, July 21-22, pp. 24–31 (2008)
13. Plotkin, G.D.: A Structural Approach to Operational Semantics. Technical Report DAIMI FN-19, University of Aarhus (1981)

14. Pokahr, A., Braubach, L., Lamersdorf, W.: Jadex: A BDI Reasoning Engine. Multiagent Systems, Artificial Societies, and Simulated Organizations [1], vol. 15, ch. 6, pp. 149–174 (2005)
15. Rao, A.S., Georgeff, M.P.: An Abstract Architecture for Rational Agents. In: KR, pp. 439–449 (1992)
16. Winikoff, M.: JACK$^{\text{TM}}$ Intelligent Agents: An Industrial Strength Platform. Multiagent Systems, Artificial Societies, and Simulated Organizations [1], vol. 15, ch. 7, pp. 175–193 (2005)

# A    Proofs

*Proof (Proof of Lemma 1).* The proof follows by induction on nesting depth of mst's. The nesting depth of an mst is the maximal number of steps required to derive $yields_p(\tau, \sigma, p{:}\rho)$ in the $yields_p$ calculus for all $\sigma$ from $\mathcal{A}_p$ and all $p{:}\rho$ yielded by $\tau$.

$depth = 1$: Equation 1 is trivially satisfied for primitive updates from $\mathcal{A}_p$ of the form **skip** and $\oslash\psi$.

$depth = 2$: let's assume $\tau_1, \ldots, \tau_k$ are primitive mst's yielding $1{:}\rho_1, \ldots, 1{:}\rho_k$ in a state $\sigma$ respectively, and $\phi$ be a query formula. We recognise three cases:

**conditional** in the case $\sigma \models \phi$, we have $yields_p(\phi \longrightarrow \tau_1, \sigma, 1{:}\rho_1)$. Similarly for $\sigma \not\models \phi$, we have $yields_p(\phi \longrightarrow \tau_1, \sigma, 1{:}\textbf{skip})$, hence Equation 1 is satisfied in both cases.

**choice** according to Definition 7 for each $1 \leq i \leq k$ we have

$$yields_p(\tau_1| \cdots |\tau_k, \sigma, P_{\tau_1|\cdots|\tau_k}(\tau_i){:}\rho_i)$$

where $\Pi(\tau_1| \cdots |\tau_k) = P_{\tau_1|\cdots|\tau_k}$. Since $P_{\tau_1|\cdots|\tau_k}$ is a discrete probability distribution (cf. Definition 6) over the elements $\tau_1, \ldots, \tau_k$, we have

$$\sum_{1 \leq i \leq k} P_{\tau_1|\cdots|\tau_k}(\tau_i) = 1$$

hence Equation 1 is satisfied as well.

**sequence** for the sequence mst, we have $yields_p(\tau_1 \circ \cdots \circ \tau_k, \sigma, 1{:}(\rho_1 \bullet \cdots \bullet \rho_k))$, so Equation 1 is trivially satisfied again.

$depth = n$: assume Equation 1 holds for mst's of nesting depth $n-1$, we show it holds also for mst's of depth $n$. Again we assume that $\phi$ is a query formula of $\mathcal{A}_p$ and $\tau_1, \ldots, \tau_k$, are compound mst's of maximal nesting depth $n-1$ yielding sets of updates $\mathfrak{fp}_{\tau_1}(\sigma), \ldots, \mathfrak{fp}_{\tau_k}(\sigma)$ in a mental state $\sigma$ respectively. Similarly to the previous step, we recognise three cases:

**conditional** according to the derivability of $\phi$ w.r.t. $\sigma$, for the conditional mst $\phi \longrightarrow \tau_1$ we have either $\mathfrak{fp}_{\phi \longrightarrow \tau_1}(\sigma) = \mathfrak{fp}_{\tau_1}(\sigma)$, or $\mathfrak{fp}_{\phi \longrightarrow \tau_1}(\sigma) = \{1{:}\textbf{skip}\}$. For the latter case, Equation 1 is trivially satisfied and since $\tau_1$ is of maximal nesting depth $n-1$, we have $\sum_{p{:}\rho \in \mathfrak{fp}_{\phi \longrightarrow \tau_1}(\sigma)} p = \sum_{p{:}\rho \in \mathfrak{fp}_{\tau_1}(\sigma)} p = 1$ as well.

**choice** let $P_{\tau_1|\cdots|\tau_k}$ be the probability distribution function assigned to the choice mst $\tau_1|\cdots|\tau_k$ by the function $\Pi$. We have

$$\mathfrak{fp}_{\tau_1|\cdots|\tau_k}(\sigma) = \left\{p{:}\rho \mid \exists 0 \le i \le k : yields_p(\tau_i, \sigma, p_i{:}\rho) \wedge p = P_{\tau_1|\cdots|\tau_k}(\tau_i) \cdot p_i\right\}$$

Subsequently,

$$\sum_{p{:}\rho\in\mathfrak{fp}_{\tau_1|\cdots|\tau_k}(\sigma)} p = \sum_{0\le i\le k} \left(P_{\tau_1|\cdots|\tau_k}(\tau_i) \cdot \sum_{p{:}\rho\in\mathfrak{fp}_{\tau_i}(\sigma)} p\right)$$

However, because of the induction assumption that Equation 1 holds for mst's $\tau_i$ with maximal nesting depth $n-1$, for all $i$ $\sum_{p{:}\rho\in\mathfrak{fp}_{\tau_i}(\sigma)} p = 1$, and since $P_{\tau_1|\cdots|\tau_k}$ is a discrete probability distribution function, we finally arrive to

$$\sum_{p{:}\rho\in\mathfrak{fp}_{\tau_1|\cdots|\tau_k}(\sigma)} p = \sum_{0\le i\le k} P_{\tau_1|\cdots|\tau_k}(\tau_i) = 1$$

**sequence** for the sequence mst $\tau_1 \circ \cdots \circ \tau_k$, we have

$$\mathfrak{fp}_{\tau_1\circ\cdots\circ\tau_k}(\sigma) = \left\{\prod_{i=1}^{k} p_i{:}(\rho_1 \bullet \cdots \bullet \rho_k) \mid \forall 1 \le i \le k : yields_p(\tau_i, \sigma, p_i{:}\rho_i)\right\}$$

and subsequently

$$\sum_{p{:}\rho\in\mathfrak{fp}_{\tau_1\circ\cdots\circ\tau_k}(\sigma)} p = \sum_{\prod_{i=1}^{k} p_i{:}(\rho_1\bullet\cdots\bullet\rho_k)\in\mathfrak{fp}_{\tau_1\circ\cdots\circ\tau_k}(\sigma)} \prod_{i=1}^{k} p_i \qquad (2)$$

Observe, that if we fix the update sequence suffix $\rho_2 \bullet \cdots \bullet \rho_k$, the sum 2 can be rewritten as

$$\left(\sum_{p_1:\rho_1\in\mathfrak{fp}_{\tau_1}(\sigma)} p_1\right) \cdot \left(\sum_{\prod_{i=2}^{k} p_i{:}(\rho_2\bullet\cdots\bullet\rho_k)\in\mathfrak{fp}_{\tau_2\circ\cdots\circ\tau_k}(\sigma)} \prod_{i=2}^{k} p_i\right)$$

Finally, by reformulation of the sum of products 2 as a product of sums and by applying the induction assumption for the mst's $\tau_1, \ldots, \tau_k$ of nesting depth $n - 1$, we arrive to

$$\prod_{i=1}^{k} \sum_{p{:}\rho\in\mathfrak{fp}_{\tau_i}(\sigma)} p = \prod_{i=1}^{k} 1 = 1$$

Hence, Equation 1 is satisfied. $\qquad\qquad\qquad\qquad\qquad\qquad\qquad\qquad\qquad$ $\square$

# Golog Speaks the BDI Language

Sebastian Sardina[1] and Yves Lespérance[2]

[1] Department of Computer Science and IT
RMIT University,
Melbourne, Australia
`sebastian.sardina@rmit.edu.au`
[2] Department of Computer Science and Engineering
York University,
Toronto, Canada
`lesperan@cse.yorku.ca`

**Abstract.** In this paper, we relate two of the most well developed approaches to agent-oriented programming, namely, BDI (Belief-Desire-Intention) style programming and "Golog-like" high-level programming. In particular, we show how "Golog-like" programming languages can be used to develop BDI-style agent systems. The contribution of this paper is twofold. First, it demonstrates how *practical* agent systems can be developed using high-level languages like Golog or IndiGolog. Second, it provides BDI languages a clear classical-logic-based semantics and a powerful logical foundation for incorporating new reasoning capabilities not present in typical BDI systems.

## 1   Introduction

BDI (Belief-Desire-Intention) agent programming languages and platforms (e.g., PRS [13], AgentSpeak and Jason [23,3], Jack [5], and JADEX [21]) and the situation calculus-based Golog high-level programming language and its successors (e.g., ConGolog [8], IndiGolog [27,9], and FLUX [29]) are two of the most well developed approaches within the agent-oriented programming paradigm. In this paper, we analyze the relationship between these two families of languages and show that BDI agent programming languages are closely related to IndiGolog, a situation calculus based programming language supporting online execution of programs in dynamic environments, sensing actions to acquire information from the environment, and exogenous events.

BDI agent programming languages were conceived as a simplified and operationalized version of the BDI (Belief, Desire, Intention) model of agency, which is rooted in philosophical work such as Bratman's [4] theory of practical reasoning and Dennett's theory of intentional systems [10]. Practical work in the area has sought to develop programming languages that incorporate a simplified BDI semantics basis that has a computational interpretation. An important feature of BDI-style programming languages and platforms is their interleaved account of sensing, deliberation, and execution [22,25]. In BDI systems, *abstract plans* written by programmers are combined and executed in real-time. By executing as they reason, BDI agents reduce the likelihood that decisions will be made on the basis of outdated beliefs and remain responsive

L. Braubach, J.-P. Briot, and J. Thangarajah (Eds.): ProMAS 2009, LNAI 5919, pp. 82–99, 2010.

to the environment by making adjustments in the steps chosen as they proceed. Because of this, BDI agent programming languages are well suited to implementing systems that need to operate in "soft" real-time scenarios [19,2,1]. Unlike in classical planning-based architectures, *execution* happens at each step. The assumption is that the careful crafting of plans' preconditions to ensure the selection of appropriate plans at execution time, together with a built-in mechanism for retrying alternative options, will usually ensure that a successful execution is found, even in the context of a changing environment.

In contrast to this, high-level programming languages in the Golog line aim for a middle ground between classical planning and normal programming. The idea is that the programmer may write a *sketchy* non-deterministic program involving domain specific actions and test conditions and that the interpreter will reason about these and search for a valid execution. The semantics of these languages is defined on top of the *situation calculus*, a popular predicate logic framework for reasoning about action [20,26]. The interpreter for the language uses an action theory representing the agent's beliefs about the state of the environment and the preconditions and effects of the actions to find a provably correct execution of the program. By controlling the amount of nondeterminism in the program, the high-level program execution task can be made as hard as classical planning or as easy as deterministic program execution. In IndiGolog, this framework is generalized to allow the programmer to control planning/lookahead and support on-line execution and sensing the environment.

In this paper, we show how a BDI agent can be built within the IndiGolog situation calculus-based programming framework. More concretely, we describe how to translate an agent programmed in a typical BDI programming language into a high-level IndiGolog program with an associated situation calculus action theory, such that *(i)* their ultimate behavior coincide; and *(ii)* the original structure of the propositional attitudes (beliefs, intentions, goals, etc.) of the BDI agent and the model of execution are preserved in the IndiGolog translation. We first do this (Section 3) for what we call the *core* engine of BDI systems, namely, the reactive context-sensitive expansion of events/goals. After this, in Section 4, we show how to accommodate more sophisticated BDI reasoning mechanisms such as goal failure recovery. Before presenting these results, in Section 2, we give a brief overview of BDI programming languages and Golog-related programming languages. The paper ends with a short discussion in Section 5, where we mention some potential advantages of programming BDI agents in the situation calculus, in particular, various reasoning about action techniques that IndiGolog BDI agents could incorporate.

## 2   Preliminaries

### 2.1   BDI Programming

BDI agent systems were developed as a way of enabling *abstract plans* written by programmers to be combined and used in real-time, in a way that is both flexible and robust. A BDI system responds to *events*, the inputs to the system, by selecting a plan from the *plan library*, and placing it into the *intention base*, thus committing to the plan for responding to the event/goal in question. The execution of this plan-strategy may, in turn, post new subgoal events to be achieved. The plan library stands for a collection of pre-defined *hierarchical plans* indexed by goals (i.e., events) and representing the standard operations in the domain. Figure 1 depicts a typical BDI-style architecture.

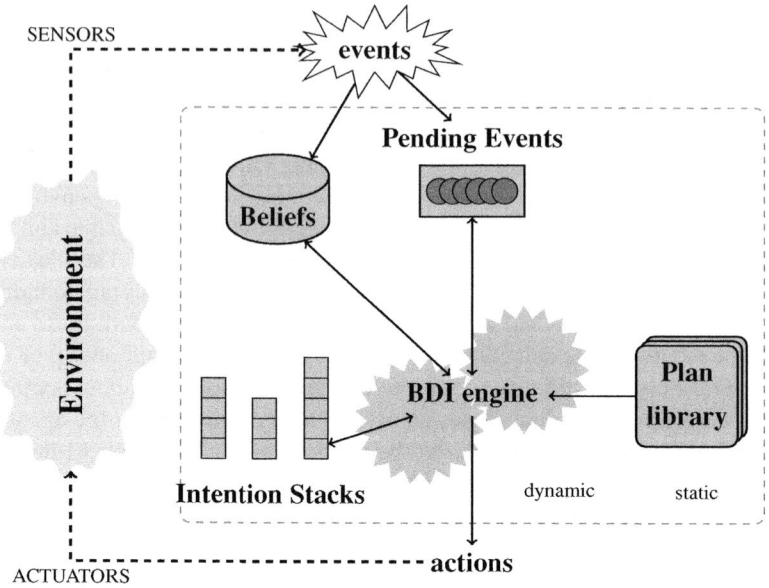

**Fig. 1.** A typical BDI-style architecture

There are a number of agent programming languages and development platforms in the BDI tradition, such as PRS [13], AgentSpeak and Jason [23,3], Jack [5], JADEX [21], and 3APL/2APL [15,7]. Our discussion is based on the CAN family of BDI languages [30,28] (Conceptual Agent Notation), which are AgentSpeak-like languages with a semantics capturing the common essence of typical BDI systems.

A BDI agent configuration (or simply a BDI agent) $\Upsilon$ is a tuple $\langle \Pi, \mathcal{B}, \mathcal{A}, \Gamma \rangle$, where $\mathcal{B}$ stands for the agent's current beliefs about the world, generally a set of atoms, $\Pi$ is the (static) plan-library, $\mathcal{A}$ is the sequence of actions executed so far, and $\Gamma$ is the multi-set of intentions the agent is currently pursuing. The *plan library* contains plan rules of the form $e : \psi \leftarrow P$, where $e$ is an event/goal that triggers the plan, $\psi$ is the context for which the plan may be applied (i.e., the precondition of the rule), and $P$ is the body of the plan rule—$P$ *is a reasonable strategy in order to resolve the event/goal $e$ when condition $\psi$ is believed to hold*. The *plan-body* $P$ is a program built from primitive actions $A$ that the agent can execute directly (e.g., $drive(loc1, loc3)$), operations to add $+b$ and delete $-b$ beliefs, tests for conditions $?\phi$, and (internal) subgoaling event posting $!e$ (e.g., $!Travel(mel, yyz)$). Complex plan bodies are built with the usual sequence ; and concurrency $\|$ constructs. There are also a number of auxiliary constructs internally used when assigning semantics to programs: the empty (terminating) program *nil*; the construct $P_1 \rhd P_2$, which tries to execute $P_1$, falling back to $P_2$ if $P_1$ is not executable; and $(\!|\psi_1 : P_1, \ldots, \psi_n : P_n|\!)$, which encodes a set of alternative guarded plans. Lastly, the *intention base* $\Gamma$ contains the current, partially instantiated, plan-body programs that the agent has already committed to for handling some events—since $\Gamma$ is a multi-set it may contain a program more than once.

As with most BDI agent programming languages, the Plotkin-style operational semantics of CAN closely follows Rao and Georgeff's abstract interpreter for intelligent rational agents [25]: *(i)* incorporate any pending external events; *(ii)* select an intention and execute a step; and *(iii)* update the set of goals and intentions. A *transition relation* $C \longrightarrow C'$, on so-called *configurations* is defined by a set of *derivation rules* and specifies that executing configuration $C$ a *single step* yields configuration $C'$. A *derivation rule* consists of a, possibly empty, set of premises, typically involving the existence of transitions together with some auxiliary conditions, and a single transition conclusion derivable from these premises. Two transition relations are used to define the semantics of the CAN language. The first transition relation $\longrightarrow$ defines what it means to execute a single intention and is defined in terms of *intention-level* configurations of the form $\langle \Pi, \mathcal{B}, \mathcal{A}, P \rangle$ consisting of the agent's plan-library $\Pi$ and belief base $\mathcal{B}$, the actions $\mathcal{A}$ executed so far, and the program $P$ being executed. The second transition relation $\Longrightarrow$ is defined in terms of the first and characterizes what it means to execute a whole agent.

So, the following are some of the intention-level derivation rules for the language:[1]

$$\frac{\Delta = \{\psi : P \mid e : \psi \leftarrow P \in \Pi\}}{\langle \Pi, \mathcal{B}, \mathcal{A}, !e \rangle \longrightarrow \langle \Pi, \mathcal{B}, \mathcal{A}, (\!|\Delta|\!)\rangle} \; Ev \qquad \frac{\langle \Pi, \mathcal{B}, \mathcal{A}, P_1 \rangle \longrightarrow \langle \Pi, \mathcal{B}', \mathcal{A}', P_1' \rangle}{\langle \Pi, \mathcal{B}, \mathcal{A}, P_1 \triangleright P_2 \rangle \longrightarrow \langle \Pi, \mathcal{B}', \mathcal{A}', P_1' \triangleright P_2 \rangle} \; \triangleright$$

$$\frac{\mathcal{B} \models \phi\theta}{\langle \mathcal{B}, \mathcal{A}, ?\phi \rangle \longrightarrow \langle \mathcal{B}, \mathcal{A}, nil \rangle} \; ? \qquad \frac{\psi : P \in \Delta \quad \mathcal{B} \models \psi\theta}{\langle \Pi, \mathcal{B}, \mathcal{A}, (\!|\Delta|\!)\rangle \longrightarrow \langle \Pi, \mathcal{B}, \mathcal{A}, P\theta \triangleright (\!|\Delta \setminus \{\psi : P\}|\!)\rangle} \; Sel$$

Derivation rule $Ev$ captures the first stage in the plan selection process for a (pending) event/goal $e$, in which the agent collects, from the plan library, the set $(\!|\Delta|\!)$ of the so-called *"relevant"* (guarded) plans that may be used to resolve the pending event. Such set is later used by rules $Sel$ and $\triangleright$ to commit to and execute, respectively, an *applicable* strategy/plan $P$ (one whose condition $\psi$ is believed true). Notice in rule $Sel$ how the remaining non-selected plans are kept as backup plans as the second program in the $\triangleright$ construct. Finally, rule $?$ accounts for transitions over a basic test program.

On top of these intention-level derivation rules, the set of agent-level derivation rules are defined. Basically, an agent transition involves either assimilating external events from the environment or executing an active intention. The set of external events $\mathcal{E}$ stands for those external events that were "sensed" by the agent, and it may include external achievement events of the form $!e$ as well as belief update events of the form $+b$ and $-b$. Also, in the rules below, the following auxiliary function is used to represent the set of achievement events caused by belief changes: $\Omega(\mathcal{B}, \mathcal{B}') = \{!b^- \mid \mathcal{B} \models b, \mathcal{B}' \not\models b\} \cup \{!b^+ \mid \mathcal{B} \not\models b, \mathcal{B}' \models b\}$.

$$\frac{\mathcal{E} \text{ is a set of external events} \quad \mathcal{B}' = (\mathcal{B} \setminus \{b \mid -b \in \mathcal{E}\}) \cup \{b \mid +b \in \mathcal{E}\}}{\langle \Pi, \mathcal{B}, \mathcal{A}, \Gamma \rangle \Longrightarrow \langle \Pi, \mathcal{B}', \mathcal{A}, \Gamma \uplus \{!e \mid !e \in \mathcal{E}\} \uplus \Omega(\mathcal{B}, \mathcal{B}')\rangle} \; A_{ext}$$

$$\frac{P \in \Gamma \quad \langle \Pi, \mathcal{B}, \mathcal{A}, P \rangle \longrightarrow \langle \Pi, \mathcal{B}', \mathcal{A}', P' \rangle}{\langle \Pi, \mathcal{B}, \mathcal{A}, \Gamma \rangle \Longrightarrow \langle \Pi, \mathcal{B}', \mathcal{A}', (\Gamma \setminus \{P\}) \uplus \{P'\} \uplus \Omega(\mathcal{B}, \mathcal{B}')\rangle} \; A_{exec}$$

---

[1] Configurations must also include a variable substitution $\theta$ for keeping track of all bindings done so far during the execution of a plan-body. For legibility, we keep substitutions implicit in places where they need to be carried across multiple rules (e.g., in rule $?$).

Rule $A_{ext}$ assimilates a set of external events, including achievements events of the form $!e$, as well as belief update events of the form $+b$ and $-b$, after which both belief and intention bases of the agent may be updated. Note that, by means of auxiliary function $\Omega$, a new (achievement) event of the form $!b^+$ or $!b^-$ is posted for each belief $b$ that changes due to an external belief update; such an event may in turn trigger some new behavior.

Rule $A_{exec}$ states that the agent may evolve one step if an active intention $P$ can be advanced one step with remaining intention $P'$ being left to execute. In such a case, the intention base is updated by replacing $P$ with $P'$ and including the belief update events produced by potential changes in the belief base. Observe that the intention base is a *multi-set*, which means that it may contain several occurrences of the same intention.

Relative to the above derivation rules, one can formally define the meaning of an agent as its possible execution traces. (See [30,28] for the complete semantics.)

**Definition 1 (BDI Execution).** *A BDI execution $E$ of an agent $\Upsilon_0 = \langle \Pi, \mathcal{B}_0, \mathcal{A}_0, \Gamma_0 \rangle$ is a, possibly infinite, sequence of agent configurations $\Upsilon_0 \cdot \Upsilon_1 \cdot \ldots \cdot \Upsilon_n \cdot \ldots$ such that $\Upsilon_i \Longrightarrow \Upsilon_{i+1}$, for all $i \geq 0$.*

## 2.2 High-Level Programming in Golog

The *situation calculus* [20,26] is a logical language specifically designed for representing dynamically changing worlds in which all changes are the result of named *actions* The constant $S_0$ is used to denote the initial situation where no actions have yet been performed. Sequences of actions are built using the function symbol *do*: $do(a, s)$ denotes the successor situation resulting from performing action $a$ in situation $s$. Relations whose truth values vary from situation to situation are called *fluents*, and are denoted by predicate symbols taking a situation term as their last argument (e.g., $Holding(x, s)$). A special predicate $Poss(a, s)$ is used to state that action $a$ is executable in $s$.

Within this language, we can formulate action theories describing how the world changes as the result of the available actions. For example, a *basic action theory* [26] includes domain-independent foundational axioms to describe the structure of situations, one successor state axiom per fluent (capturing the effects and non-effects of actions), one precondition axiom per action (specifying when the action is executable), and initial state axioms describing what is true initially (i.e., what is true in the initial situation $S_0$).

On top of situation calculus action theories, logic-based programming languages can be defined, which, in addition to the primitive actions, allow the definition of complex actions. Golog [18], the first situation calculus-based agent programming language, provides all the usual control structures (e.g., sequence, iteration, conditional, etc.) plus some *nondeterministic constructs*. These nondeterministic constructs allow the loose specification of programs by leaving "*gaps*" that ought to be resolved by the reasoner/planner or executor. ConGolog [8] extends Golog to support concurrency. To provide an intuitive overview of the language, consider the following nondeterministic program for an agent that goes to work in the morning:[2]

---

[2] We thank Ryan Kelly and Adrian Pearce for allowing us to re-use their example.

**proc** $goToWork$
   $ringAlarm; (hitSnooze; ringAlarm)^*; turnOffAlarm;$
   $(\pi food)[Edible(food)?; eat(food)];$
   $(haveShower \parallel brushTeeth);$
   $(driveToUniversity \mid trainToUniversity);$
   $(Time < 11 : 00)?$
**endProc**

While this high-level program provides a general strategy for getting up and going to work, it is underspecified, and many details, such as what to eat and how to travel to work, are left open. Program $\delta_1 \mid \delta_2$ nondeterministically chooses between programs $\delta_1$ and $\delta_2$, $\pi x. \delta(x)$ executes program $\delta(x)$ for *some* legal binding for variable $x$, and $\delta^*$ performs $\delta$ zero or more times. Concurrency is supported by the following three constructs: $(\delta_1 \| \delta_2)$ expresses the concurrent execution (interpreted as interleaving) of programs $\delta_1$ and $\delta_2$; $\delta_1 \rangle\rangle \delta_2$ expresses the concurrent execution of $\delta_1$ and $\delta_2$ with $\delta_1$ having higher priority; and $\delta^{\|}$ executes $\delta$ zero or more times concurrently. Note that a concurrent process may become (temporarily) blocked when it reaches a test/wait action $\phi$? whose condition $\phi$ is false, or a primitive action whose preconditions are false. Test/wait actions can also be used to control which nondeterministic branches can be executed, e.g. $[(\phi?; \delta_1) \mid (\neg\phi?; \delta_2)]$, and to constrain the value of a nondeterministically bound variable, e.g., $\pi x.[\phi(x)?; \delta(x)]$. Finally, the language also accommodates the standard if-then-elses, while loops, and recursive procedures.

Finding a legal execution of a high-level program is at the core of the whole approach. Originally, Golog and ConGolog programs were intended to be executed *offline*, that is, a complete execution was obtained before committing even to the first action. However, IndiGolog [27,9], the latest language within the Golog family, provides a formal logic-based account of interleaved planning, sensing, and action by executing programs *online* and using a specialized new construct $\Sigma(\delta)$, the *search operator*, to perform local offline planning when required.

Roughly speaking, an *online* execution of a program finds a next possible action, executes it in the real world, then obtains sensing results and observed exogenous actions, and repeats the cycle until the program's execution is completed.

Formally, an online execution is a sequence of so-called online configuration of the form $(\delta, \sigma)$, where $\delta$ is a high-level program and $\sigma$ is a history (see [9] for its formal definition). A history contains the sequence of actions executed so far as well as the sensing information obtained. Online executions are characterized in terms of the following two predicates [8]: $Final(\delta, s)$ holds if program $\delta$ may legally terminate in situation $s$; and $Trans(\delta, s, \delta', s')$ holds if a single step of program $\delta$ in situation $s$ may lead to situation $s'$ with $\delta'$ remaining to be executed. In the next section, we will generalize the notion of online execution to suit our purposes.

## 3  BDI Programming in IndiGolog

Programming a BDI agent in the situation calculus amounts to developing a special basic action theory and a special IndiGolog high-level agent program to be executed with it. From now on, let $\Upsilon = \langle \Pi, \mathcal{B}, \mathcal{A}, \Gamma \rangle$ be the BDI agent to program in IndiGolog.

## 3.1   The BDI Basic Action Theory

We start by showing how to obtain an action theory $\mathcal{D}^{\Upsilon}$ for our agent $\Upsilon$. We assume that $\Upsilon$ is stated over a first-order language $\mathcal{L}_{BDI}$ containing finitely many belief and event atomic relations, namely, $b_1(\boldsymbol{x_1}), \ldots, b_n(\boldsymbol{x_n})$ and $e_1(\boldsymbol{x_1}), \ldots, e_m(\boldsymbol{x_n})$.

Let us then define what the fluents and actions available in the situation calculus language $\mathcal{L}_{sitCalc}$ are. First, for every belief atomic predicate $b(\boldsymbol{x})$ in $\mathcal{L}_{BDI}$, the language $\mathcal{L}_{sitCalc}$ includes a relational fluent $b(\boldsymbol{x}, s)$ together with two primitive actions $add_b(\boldsymbol{x})$ and $del_b(\boldsymbol{x})$ which are meant to change the fluent's truth value. Second, for each achievement event type $e(\boldsymbol{x})$ in the domain, there is a corresponding action term $ach_e(\boldsymbol{x})$ in $\mathcal{L}_{sitCalc}$. Finally, for every action atom $A(\boldsymbol{x})$ in $\mathcal{L}_{BDI}$, there is a corresponding action function $A(\boldsymbol{x})$ in $\mathcal{L}_{sitCalc}$.

In addition, the language $\mathcal{L}_{sitCalc}$ shall include one auxiliary distinguished fluent and two actions to model external event handling. Fluent $PendingEv(s)$ stands for the multi-set of events that are "pending" and need to be handled, either belief update or achievement events. This fluent is affected by two actions. Whereas action $post(e)$ indicates the external posting of event $e$; action $serve(e)$ indicates that (pending) event $e$ has been selected and is being handled. In both actions, argument $e$ is of sort action.

Let us now construct the basic action theory $\mathcal{D}^{\Upsilon}$ corresponding to a BDI agent $\Upsilon = \langle \Pi, \mathcal{B}, \mathcal{A}, \Gamma \rangle$, as follows:

1. The initial description in $\mathcal{D}^{\Upsilon}$ is defined in the following way:

$$\mathcal{D}^{\Upsilon}_{S_0} = \bigcup_{i=1}^{n} \{\forall \boldsymbol{x}.b_i(\boldsymbol{x}, S_0) \equiv \boldsymbol{x} = \boldsymbol{t}_i^1 \vee \ldots \vee \boldsymbol{x} = \boldsymbol{t}_i^{k_i}\} \cup$$
$$\{\forall a.Exog(a) \equiv (\exists a')a = post(a')\},$$

   where for every $i \in \{1, \ldots, n\}$, $\mathcal{B} \models b_i(\boldsymbol{x}) \equiv [\boldsymbol{x} = \boldsymbol{t}_i^1 \vee \ldots \vee \boldsymbol{x} = \boldsymbol{t}_i^{k_i}]$, for some $k_i \geq 0$—$b_i(\boldsymbol{t}_i^1), \ldots, b_i(\boldsymbol{t}_i^{k_i})$ are all the true belief atoms in $\mathcal{B}$ with respect to belief relation $b_i$ (each $\boldsymbol{t}_i^j$ is a vector of ground terms).

2. The following precondition axioms, for every fluent $b(\boldsymbol{x})$ and action type $A(\boldsymbol{x})$:

$$Poss(serve(a), s) \equiv (a \in PendingEv(s)) \qquad Poss(A(\boldsymbol{x}), s) \equiv \text{True}$$
$$Poss(add_b(\boldsymbol{x}), s) \equiv Poss(del_b(\boldsymbol{x}), s) \equiv \text{True} \qquad Poss(post(a), s) \equiv \text{True}$$

3. For every domain fluent $b(\boldsymbol{x}, s)$, $\mathcal{D}^{\Upsilon}$ includes the following successor state axiom:

$$b(\boldsymbol{x}, do(a, s)) \equiv$$
$$a = add_b(\boldsymbol{x}) \vee a = post(add_b(\boldsymbol{x})) \vee b(\boldsymbol{x}, s) \wedge (a \neq del_b(\boldsymbol{x}) \wedge a \neq post(del_b(\boldsymbol{x})).$$

   That is, the truth-value of fluent $b$ is affected only by actions $add_b$ and $del_b$, either internally executed or externally sensed from the environment.

   More importantly, action theory $\mathcal{D}^{\Upsilon}$ includes a successor state axiom for fluent $PendingEv(do(a, s))$ specifying how the multi-set of pending events changes:

$PendingEv(do(a, s)) = v \equiv [\gamma(a, v, s) \vee PendingEv(s) = v \wedge \neg \exists v'.\gamma(a, v', s)];$

where:

$\gamma(a, v, s) \overset{\text{def}}{=} ( \bigvee_{i=1}^{n} [\gamma_i^+(a, v, s) \vee \gamma_i^-(a, v, s)] \vee \bigvee_{i=1}^{m} [\gamma_i^e(a, v, s)] \vee \\ \qquad \exists a'.a = serve(a') \wedge v = PendingEv(s) \setminus \{a'\});$

$\gamma_i^+(a, v, s) \overset{\text{def}}{=} \\ \exists \boldsymbol{x}. a \in \{add_{b_i}(\boldsymbol{x}), post(add_{b_i}(\boldsymbol{x}))\} \wedge \neg b_i(\boldsymbol{x}) \wedge v = PendingEv(s) \uplus \{add_{b_i}(\boldsymbol{x})\};$

$\gamma_i^-(a, v, s) \overset{\text{def}}{=} \\ \exists \boldsymbol{x}. a \in \{del_{b_i}(\boldsymbol{x}), post(del_{b_i}(\boldsymbol{x}))\} \wedge b_i(\boldsymbol{x}) \wedge v = PendingEv(s) \uplus \{del_{b_i}(\boldsymbol{x})\};$

$\gamma_i^e(a, v, s) \overset{\text{def}}{=} \exists \boldsymbol{x}. a = post(ach_{e_i}(\boldsymbol{x})) \wedge v = PendingEv(s) \uplus \{ach_{e_i}(\boldsymbol{x})\}.$

That is, an actual change in the belief of an atom, either due to the execution of some intention or an external event, automatically produces a corresponding pending belief update event. Moreover, an external achievement event $ach_e(\boldsymbol{x})$ becomes pending when sensed. On the other hand, an event $e$ ceases to be pending when action $serve(e)$ is executed.

4. Theory $\mathcal{D}^\Upsilon$ includes unique name axioms for all actions in $\mathcal{L}_{sitCalc}$, as well as the standard domain-independent foundational axioms for the situation calculus ([26]).

This concludes the construction of the BDI basic action theory $\mathcal{D}^\Upsilon$.

## 3.2   The BDI Agent Program

Let us now construct the IndiGolog BDI agent program $\delta^\Upsilon$ that is meant to execute relative to the BDI action theory $\mathcal{D}^\Upsilon$. We start by showing how to inductively transform a BDI plan-body program $P$ into an IndiGolog program $\delta_P$, namely (remember that plan-bodies programs are used to build BDI plans in the plan library):

$$\delta_P = \begin{cases} P & \text{if } P = A \mid nil \\ \phi? & \text{if } P = ?\phi \\ add_b(t) & \text{if } P = +b(t) \\ del_b(t) & \text{if } P = -b(t) \\ handle(ach_e(t)) & \text{if } P = !e(t) \\ (\delta_{P_1}; \delta_{P_2}) & \text{if } P = (P_1; P_2) \\ \delta_{P_1} & \text{if } P = P_1 \triangleright P_2 \\ achieve_e(\boldsymbol{x}\theta) & \text{if } P = (\!|\Delta|\!) \text{ and } \Delta \subseteq \{\psi\theta : P\theta \mid e : \psi \leftarrow P \in \Pi\}, \text{ for} \\ & \quad \text{some } \theta \text{ (partially) binding the parameters of event } e(\boldsymbol{x}). \end{cases}$$

Notice that achievement events $!e$ occurring in a plan are handled via simple plan invocation, by invoking procedure $handle$. Also, for now, the translation just ignores the second program in $P_1 \triangleright P_2$, as the version of CAN we consider in this section does not try $P_2$ when $P_1$ happens to fail. We shall revisit this later in Section 4. Finally, when the BDI program is a set of (relevant) alternatives of the form $(\!|\Delta|\!)$ for some event $e$, we map it to a procedure call that will basically amount to a non-deterministic choice among all such alternatives (see below).

Next, we describe how to transform the BDI plans in the agent's plan library. To that end, suppose that $e(x)$ is an event in the BDI language $\mathcal{L}_{BDI}$ such with the following $n \geq 0$ plans in $\Pi$ ($v_t$ denotes all the distinct free variables in the terms $t$):

$$e(t_i) : \psi_i(v_{t_i}, y_i) \leftarrow P_i(v_{t_i}, y_i, z_i), \text{ where } i \in \{1, \ldots, n\}.$$

Then, we build the following high-level Golog procedure with $n$ non-deterministic choices (i.e., as many as plan-rules for the event):

> **proc** $achieve_e(x)$
> $\quad |_{i \in \{1,\ldots,n\}} [(\pi v_{t_i}, y_i, z_i).(x = t_i \wedge \psi_i(v_{t_i}, y_i))?; \delta_{P_i}(v_{t_i}, y_i, z_i)]$
> **endProc**

Roughly speaking, executing $achieve_e(x)$ involves nondeterministically choosing among the $n$ available options in the plan library for event $e$. See that the first test statement in each option amounts to checking the relevance and applicability of the option. Thus, the execution of $achieve_e(x)$ is bound to *block* if no option is relevant or applicable. In particular, the procedure will *always* block if the agent $\Upsilon$ has no plan to handle the event in question—that is, if $n = 0$, the corresponding Golog procedure is simply ?(False).

Let $\Delta_{\Pi}$ denote the set of Golog procedures as above, one per event in the BDI language, together with the following procedure:

> **proc** $handle(a)$
> $\quad |_{i=1}^{n} [(\exists x_i.a = add_{b_i}(x_i))?; achieve_{b_i^+}(x_i)] \mid$
> $\quad |_{i=1}^{n} [(\exists x_i.a = del_{b_i}(x_i))?; achieve_{b_i^-}(x_i)] \mid$
> $\quad |_{i=1}^{m} [(\exists x_i.a = ach_{e_i}(x_i))?; achieve_{e_i}(x_i)]$
> **endProc**

That is, when $a$ is a legal event (belief update or achievement goal), procedure $handle(a)$ calls the appropriate procedure that is meant to *resolve* the event. Observe that this program contains two nondeterministic programs per belief atom in the domain (one to handle its addition and one to handle its deletion from the belief base), plus one nondeterministic program per achievement event in the domain.

Finally, we define the top-level IndiGolog BDI agent program as follows:

$$\delta^{\Upsilon} \stackrel{\text{def}}{=} \Delta_{\Pi}; [\delta_{env} \| (\delta_{\Gamma} \| \delta_{BDI})]; (\neg \exists e \, PendingEv(e))?, \tag{1}$$

where (assuming that $\Gamma = \{P_1, \ldots, P_n\}$):

$$\delta_{\Gamma} \stackrel{\text{def}}{=} \delta_{P_1} \| \cdots \| \delta_{P_n}; \quad \delta_{env} \stackrel{\text{def}}{=} (\pi a.Exog(a)?; a)^*; \quad \delta_{BDI} \stackrel{\text{def}}{=} [\pi a.serve(a); handle(a)]^{\|}.$$

The set of programs $\Delta_{\Pi}$ provides the environment encoding the BDI plan library. Program $\delta_{\Gamma}$ accounts for all current intentions in $\Upsilon$; if $\Gamma = \emptyset$, then $\delta_{\Gamma} = nil$. In turn, program $\delta_{env}$ models the external environment, which can perform zero, one, or more actions of the form $post(a)$, representing an external achievement event goal ($a = ach_e(t)$) or a belief update event ($a = add_b(t)$ or $a = del_b(t)$).

The most interesting part of $\delta^T$ is indeed the ConGolog program $\delta_{BDI}$, which implements (part of) the BDI execution cycle. More concretely, $\delta_{BDI}$ is responsible for selecting an external event and *spawning* a new "intention" concurrent thread for handling it. To that end, $\delta_{BDI}$ picks an event $a$ (e.g., $add_{At}(23, 32)$ or $achieve_{moveTo}(0, 0)$) to be served and executes action *serve*($a$). Observe that an event can be served only if it is currently pending (see action precondition for action *serve*($a$) in Subsection 3.1). After the action *serve*($a$) has been successfully executed, the selected event $a$ is actually handled, by calling procedure *handle*($a$) defined in $\Delta_\Pi$. More importantly, this is done in a "new" concurrent thread, so that program $\delta_{BDI}$ is still able to serve and handle other pending events. The use of concurrent iteration to spawn a new intention from the "main BDI thread" is inspired from the server example application in [8].

Note that $\Delta_\Pi$ and $\delta_\Gamma$ are domain dependent, i.e., they are built relative to a particular BDI agent $T$, whereas programs $\delta_{BDI}$ and $\delta_{env}$ are independent of the BDI agent being encoded. Observe also that the whole high-level program $\delta^T$ may terminate only when no more events are pending.

From now on, let $\mathcal{G}^T = \langle \mathcal{D}^T, \delta^T, \mathcal{A} \rangle$ denote the IndiGolog agent for BDI agent $T$.

### 3.3   LC-Online Executions

Once we have a BDI IndiGolog program $\mathcal{G}^T$ on hand, we should be able to execute it and obtain the same behavior and outputs as with the original BDI agent. Unfortunately, we cannot execute $\mathcal{G}^T$ *online*, as defined in [9], as such executions may commit too early to free variables in a program—online executions are sequences of *ground* online configurations. For example, program $\pi x.turnOffAlarm; Edible(x)?; eat(x)$ may do a transition by execution the primitive action *turnOffAlarm* and instantiating $x$ to *Clock*, yielding remaining program *Edible(Clock)?; eat(Clock)*, which is bound to fail as the object picked is not edible. In fact, as no constraints are imposed on $x$ in the first transition, any binding for it would be legal.

What we need, instead, is an account of execution that commits to free variables only when necessary. To that end, we generalize the online execution notion from [9,27] to what we call *least-committed* online executions. Below, we use $end[\sigma]$ to denote the situation term corresponding to the history $\sigma$; and $Axioms[\mathcal{D}, \sigma]$ to denote the complete set of axioms in the IndiGolog theory, which includes the action theory $\mathcal{D}$ for the domain, the sensing results gathered so far in history $\sigma$, and all axioms for *Trans* and *Final*. So, we first define two meta-theoretic versions of relations *Trans* and *Final* as follows:

$$mTrans(\delta(\boldsymbol{x}, \boldsymbol{y}), \sigma, \delta'(\boldsymbol{x}, \boldsymbol{z}), \sigma') \overset{\text{def}}{=}$$
$$Axioms[\mathcal{D}, \sigma] \models \exists \boldsymbol{y} \forall \boldsymbol{x}, \boldsymbol{z}.Trans(\delta(\boldsymbol{x}, \boldsymbol{y}), end[\sigma], \delta'(\boldsymbol{x}, \boldsymbol{z}), end[\sigma']);$$

$$mFinal(\delta(\boldsymbol{x}, \boldsymbol{y}), \sigma) \overset{\text{def}}{=} Axioms[\mathcal{D}, \sigma] \models \exists \boldsymbol{x}.Final(\delta(\boldsymbol{x}), end[\sigma]).$$

Here, $\delta(\boldsymbol{x})$ means that the vector of variables $\boldsymbol{x}$ contains *all* the free variables mentioned in the program; different variables vectors are assumed disjoint. Thus, $\boldsymbol{x}$ are the free variables in $\delta$ that are still free in $\delta'$; $\boldsymbol{y}$ are the free variables in $\delta$ that have been instantiated and are not present in $\delta'$; and $\boldsymbol{z}$ are the new free variables in $\delta'$ that did not appear in $\delta$.

We can then define least-committed executions as follows.

**Definition 2 (LC-Online Execution).** *A least-committed online (lc-online) execution of an* IndiGolog *program* $\delta$ *starting from a history* $\sigma$ *is a, possibly infinite, sequence of configurations* $(\delta_0 = \delta, \sigma_0 = \sigma), (\delta_1, \sigma_1), \ldots$ *such that for every* $i \geq 0$:

1. *m Trans*$(\delta_i, \sigma_i, \delta_{i+1}, \sigma_{i+1})$ *holds; and*
2. *for all* $\delta'$ *such that m Trans*$(\delta_i, \sigma_i, \delta', \sigma_{i+1})$ *and* $\delta_{i+1} = \delta'\theta$ *for some substitution* $\theta$*, there exists* $\theta'$ *such that* $\delta' = \delta_{i+1}\theta'$.

*A finite lc-online execution* $(\delta_0, \sigma_0), \ldots, (\delta_n, \sigma_n)$ *is terminating iff m Final*$(\delta_n, \sigma_n)$ *or for all* $\delta', \sigma'$ *m Trans*$(\delta_n, \sigma_n, \delta', \sigma')$ *does not hold.*

We notice that, as expected, it can be shown that an lc-online execution stands for all its ground online instances as defined in [9]. However, by executing programs in a least committed way, we avoid premature binding of variables and eliminate some executions where the program is bound to fail.

### 3.4  BDI/IndiGolog Bisimulation

We are now ready to provide the main results of the paper. Namely, we show that given any BDI execution of an agent, there exists a matching execution of the corresponding IndiGolog agent, and vice-versa. In addition, the correspondence in the internal structure of the agents is always maintained throughout the executions.

We start by characterizing when a BDI agent and an IndiGolog agent configuration "match." To that end, we shall use relation $\Upsilon \approx \mathcal{G}$, which, intuitively, holds if a BDI agent $\Upsilon$ and an IndiGolog agent $\mathcal{G}$ represent the same (BDI) agent system. Formally, relation $\langle \Pi, \mathcal{B}, \mathcal{A}, \Gamma \rangle \approx \langle \mathcal{D}, \delta, \sigma \rangle$ holds iff

1. $\delta = \Delta_\Pi; [\delta_{env} \| (\delta_{\Gamma'} \| \delta_{BDI})]; ?(\neg\exists e \, PendingEv(e))$, for some $\Gamma' \subseteq \Gamma$ such that $\Gamma = \Gamma' \uplus \{a \mid Axioms[\mathcal{D}, \sigma] \models a \in PendingEv(end[\sigma])\}$;
2. $\mathcal{A}$ and $\sigma$ contain the same sequence of *domain* actions;
3. for every ground belief atom $b$: $\mathcal{B} \models b$ iff $Axioms[\mathcal{D}, \sigma] \models b[end[\sigma]]$;
4. $\mathcal{D} = \mathcal{D}^{\Upsilon'}$, for some $\Upsilon' = \langle \Pi, \mathcal{B}', \mathcal{A}, \Gamma \rangle$.

The first condition states that the IndiGolog program is of the form shown in equation (1) above (see Section 3.2), but where some active intentions may still be "pending." In other words, some intentions in $\Gamma$ that have not yet started execution may not show up yet as concurrent processes in $\delta$, but they are implicitly represented as "pending" in fluent $PendingEv(s)$. The second requirement states that both agents have performed the same sequence of domain primitive actions, that is, actions other than the internal ones $serve(a)$, $post(a)$, $add_b(x)$, and $del_b(x)$. The third condition requires both agents to coincide on what they *currently* believe. Observe that the *initial* beliefs of the IndiGolog agent do not necessarily need to coincide with those of the BDI agent, as long as the *current* beliefs do (i.e., the beliefs that hold after history $\sigma$); in fact the BDI agent configuration does not specify what it believed initially, while the IndiGolog agent's action theory does. Lastly, the IndiGolog agent executes relative to a basic action theory whose dynamics are as described in Section 3.1.

First of all, it is possible to show that the encoding of initial BDI agents, that is agents that have not yet performed any action, into IndiGolog agents described above is in the $\approx$ relation with the original BDI agent.

**Theorem 1.** *Let $\Upsilon$ be an initial BDI agent (that is, $\mathcal{A} = \epsilon$). Then, $\Upsilon \approx \langle \mathcal{D}^\Upsilon, \delta^\Upsilon, \mathcal{A} \rangle$.*

The importance of a BDI agent and an IndiGolog agent being in the $\approx$ relation is that their respective transitions can then always be simulated by the other type of agent To demonstrate that, we first show that any BDI transition can be replicated by the corresponding IndiGolog agent. Observe that IndiGolog may need several transitions to replicate the BDI transition when it comes to assimilating external events; whereas BDI agents incorporate sets of external events in a single transition, the IndiGolog agent incorporates one event per transition. Also, IndiGolog agents ought to execute the special action $serve(a)$ to start handling external achievement events.

**Theorem 2.** *Let $\Upsilon$ be a BDI agent and $\langle \mathcal{D}, \delta, \sigma \rangle$ an IndiGolog agent such that $\Upsilon \approx \langle \mathcal{D}, \delta, \sigma \rangle$. If $\Upsilon \implies \Upsilon'$, then there exists a program $\delta'$ and a history $\sigma'$ such that $m\,Trans^*(\delta, \sigma, \delta', \sigma')$ holds relative to action theory $\mathcal{D}$, and $\Upsilon' \approx \langle \mathcal{D}, \delta', \sigma' \rangle$.*

Furthermore, in the other direction, any step in a BDI IndiGolog execution can always be "mimicked" by the corresponding BDI agent.

**Theorem 3.** *Let $\Upsilon$ and $\langle \mathcal{D}, \delta, \sigma \rangle$ be a BDI and an IndiGolog agents, respectively, such that $\Upsilon \approx \langle \mathcal{D}, \delta, \sigma \rangle$. Suppose that $m\,Trans(\delta, \sigma, \delta', \sigma')$ holds relative to action theory $\mathcal{D}$, for some IndiGolog program $\delta'$ and history $\sigma'$. Then, either $\Upsilon \approx \langle \mathcal{D}, \delta', \sigma' \rangle$ or there exists a BDI agent $\Upsilon'$ such that $\Upsilon \implies \Upsilon'$ and $\Upsilon' \approx \langle \mathcal{D}, \delta', \sigma' \rangle$.*

So, when the IndiGolog agent performs a transition it remains "equivalent" to the BDI agent or to some evolution of the BDI agent. The former case applies only when the transition in question involved the execution of a $serve(a)$ action to translate a pending event into a concurrent process.

Putting both theorems together, our encoding allows IndiGolog to bisimulate BDI agents.

## 4 BDI Failure Handling

Since BDI systems are meant to operate in dynamic settings, plans that were supposed to work may fail due to changes in the environment. Indeed, a plan may fail because a test condition $?\phi$ is not believed true, an action cannot be executed, or a sub-goal event does not have any applicable plans. The BDI language we have discussed so far has no strategy towards failed plans or intentions, once an intention cannot evolve, it simply remains in the intention base *blocked*. In this section, we discuss how BDI programming languages typically address plan/intention failure and show how the above IndiGolog encoding can be extended accordingly. In particular, we show how agents can *abandon* failed intentions and *recover* from problematic plans by trying alternative options.

Before getting into technical details, we shall first introduce a new construct into the IndiGolog language. In "Golog-like" languages, a program that is *blocked* may not be dropped for the sake of another program. To overcome this, we introduce the construct

$\delta_1 \rhd \delta_2$ with the intending meaning that $\delta_1$ should be executed, falling back to $\delta_2$ if $\delta_1$ becomes blocked:[3]

$$Trans(\delta_1 \rhd \delta_2, s, \delta', s') \equiv (\exists\gamma.Trans(\delta_1, s, \gamma, s') \wedge \delta' = \gamma \rhd \delta_2) \vee$$
$$\neg\exists\gamma, s''.Trans(\delta_1, s, \gamma, s'') \wedge Trans(\delta_2, s, \delta', s');$$

$$Final(\delta_1 \rhd \delta_2, s, \delta', s') \equiv Final(\delta_1, s) \vee \neg\exists\gamma, s''.Trans(\delta_1, s, \gamma, s'') \wedge Final(\delta_2, s).$$

### 4.1 Dropping Impossible Intentions

It is generally accepted that intentions that cannot execute further may simply be *dropped* by the agent — rational agents should not pursue intentions/goals that are deemed impossible [24,6]. This is indeed the behavior of AgentSpeak agents.[4]

The BDI language of Section 2.1 can be easily extended to provide such an intention-dropping facility, by just adding the following agent-level operational rule:

$$\frac{P \in \Gamma \quad \langle \Pi, \mathcal{B}, \mathcal{A}, P \rangle \not\longmapsto}{\langle \Pi, \mathcal{B}, \mathcal{A}, \Gamma \rangle \Longrightarrow \langle \Pi, \mathcal{B}, \mathcal{A}, \Gamma \setminus \{P\} \rangle} A_{clean}$$

That is, an agent may choose to just drop an intention from its intention base if it cannot execute further in the current mental state. To mimic this behavior in our BDI IndiGolog formalization, we slightly modify the domain-independent program $\delta_{BDI}$ as follows:

$$\delta_{BDI} \overset{\text{def}}{=} [\pi a.serve(a); (handle(a) \rhd (\texttt{True})?)]^{\|}.$$

Here, a pending event is handled within the scope of a $\rhd$, which basically allows the intention thread to simply terminate if it becomes blocked. Notice that, as with BDI languages, for procedure $handle(a)$ to be blocked, every sub-goal event triggered by the handling of $a$ (represented in the IndiGolog program as simple procedure calls) ought to be blocked. Observe also that in this approach, only the main program corresponding to a top-level event may be dropped, not lower-level instrumental subgoals.

### 4.2 BDI Goal Failure Recovery

Merely dropping a whole intention when it becomes *blocked* provides a rather weak level of commitment to goals. The failure of a plan should not be equated to the failure of its parent goal, as there could be alternative ways to achieve the latter. For example, suppose an agent has the goal to quench her thirst, and in the service of this goal, she adopts the subgoal of buying a can of soda [28]. However, upon arrival at the store, she realizes that all the cans of soda are sold out. Fortunately though, the shop has bottles of water. In this situation, it is irrational for the agent to drop the whole goal of quenching her thirst just because soda is not available. Yet this is what an AgentSpeak agent would do. Similarly, we do not expect the agent to fanatically insist on her subgoal and just

---

[3] One could easily extend these definitions to only allow dropping a blocked $\delta_1$ under given conditions; this could be used to implement "time outs" or allow blocking for synchronization.

[4] There has been work on more sophisticated treatments of plan failure in extensions of AgentSpeak; see for instance [3].

wait indefinitely for soda to be delivered. What we expect is the agent to merely drop her commitment to buy soda and adopt the alternative subgoal of buying a bottle of water, thereby achieving the *main* goal.

As a matter of fact, one of the typical features of implemented BDI languages is that of plan-goal failure recovery: if a plan happens to fail for a goal, usually due to unexpected changes in the environment, another plan is tried to achieve the goal. If no alternative strategy is available, then the goal is deemed failed and failure is propagated to higher-level motivating goals, and so on. This mechanism thus provides a stronger level of *commitment to goals*, by decoupling plan failure from goal failure.

To accommodate this approach to failure recovery, we further extend the BDI language of Section 2.1, by providing the following additional derivation rule for "try" construct $\triangleright$:

$$\frac{\langle \Pi, \mathcal{B}, \mathcal{A}, P_1 \rangle \not\longmapsto \quad \langle \Pi, \mathcal{B}', \mathcal{A}', P_2' \rangle \longrightarrow \langle \Pi, \mathcal{B}', \mathcal{A}', P_2' \rangle}{\langle \Pi, \mathcal{B}, \mathcal{A}, P_1 \triangleright P_2 \rangle \longrightarrow \langle \Pi, \mathcal{B}', \mathcal{A}', P_2' \rangle} \triangleright_f$$

That is, if the current strategy $P_1$ is *blocked* but the alternative backup program $P_2$ is able to evolve, then it is legal to drop $P_1$ and switch to $P_2$. Observe that due to derivation rules $Ev$ and $Sel$, $P_2 = (\!|\Delta|\!)$ will encode the set of *relevant* plans that have not yet been tried for the event being addressed. From now on, let the CAN language refer to our extended BDI language, with both new derivation rules $A_{clean}$ and $\triangleright_f$ for failure included.

Hence, due to the interaction between derivation rules $Ev$, $Sel$ and $\triangleright_f$, a CAN BDI agent executes a program $P_1 \triangleright (\!|\Delta|\!)$ in order to resolve an goal event $!e$. When the current strategy $P_1$ being pursued is not able to make a step, the agent may check the set of alternatives $(\!|\Delta|\!)$ in the hope of finding another option $P_2$ for addressing $e$. If one is found, the agent may opt to abandon its strategy $P_1$ and continue with $P_2$. (Details can be found in [30,28].)

Let us now describe how to replicate this failure recovery behavior within our IndiGolog framework of Section 3. For simplicity, we shall assume that, as with actions, only *ground* posting of subgoal events are allowed in the BDI language. This means that all variables $x$ in an event posting $!e(x)$ are considered *inputs* to the event. If an event is meant to return data, it must do so by using of the belief base. To support failure recovery, we slightly modify how plans in the plan library $\Pi$ are converted into ConGolog procedures. Specifically, for each event $e(x)$, we define the following procedure (and make procedure $achieve_e(x)$ simply call $achieve'_e(x, [1, \ldots, 1])$):

**proc** $achieve'_e(x, w)$    // $w$ is an $n$-long boolean vector
$|_{i \in \{1,\ldots,n\}} [(\pi v_{t_i}, y_i, z_i).(x = t \land \psi_i(v_t, y) \land w = 1)?; \delta_{P_i}(v_{t_i}, y_i, z_i) \triangleright \Phi_i(x, w)]$
**endProc**

where $\Phi_i(x, w) \stackrel{\text{def}}{=} achieve'_e(x, [w_1, \ldots, w_{i-1}, 0, w_{i+1}, \ldots, w_n])$.

The boolean vector $w$ has one component per plan rule in the library for the event in question; its $i$-th component $w_i$ states whether the $i$-th plan in $\Pi$ is *available* for selection. Condition $(x = t \land \psi_i(v_t, y) \land w = 1)$ checks whether event $e(x)$ is relevant, applicable, and available. Program $\Phi_i$ determines the *recovery strategy*, in this case, recursively calling the procedure to achieve the event, but removing the current plan from consideration (by setting its component in $w$ to 0). Due to the semantics of $\triangleright$, recovery would only be triggered if procedure $achieve'_e(x, w)$ may execute one step, which implies that there is indeed an available plan that is relevant and applicable for the event.

It turns out that these are the only modifications to the encoding of Section 3 required to mimic the behavior of CAN agents with failure handling in the IndiGolog high-level language.

**Theorem 4.** *Theorems 2 and 3 hold for CAN agents that drop impossible intentions and perform failure recovery under the extended translations into IndiGolog agents.*[5]

More interestingly, the proposed translation can be adapted to accommodate several alternative accounts of execution and failure recovery. For example, goal failure recovery can be disallowed for an event by just taking $\Phi_i(x, w) \stackrel{\text{def}}{=} ?(\texttt{False})$ above. Similarly, a framework under which *any* plan may be (re)tried for achieving a goal event, regardless of previous (failed) executions, is obtained by taking $\Phi_i(x, w) \stackrel{\text{def}}{=} achieve_e(x)$. In this case, the event is "fully" re-posted within the intention.

The key point here is that, due to the fact that the BDI execution and recovery model is represented in our BDI IndiGolog at the *object* level, one can go even further and design more sophisticated accounts of execution and failure recovery for BDI agents. It is straightforward, for instance, to model the kind of goal failure recovery originally proposed for AgentSpeak, in which the system would automatically post a distinguished *failure goal* (denoted $!-g$); the programmer may then choose to provide handling plan could, for example, carry out some clean-up tasks and even re-post the failed event [23,3]. This type of behavior can be easily achieved by taking $\Phi_i(x, w) \stackrel{\text{def}}{=} ach_{fail\_e}(x); ?(\texttt{False})$, and allowing the programmer to provide plan rules in the library for handling the special event $fail\_e(x)$. Notice that the event is *posted* so it would eventually create a new intention all-together; the current plan would then immediately be blocked/failed.

# 5   Discussion

In this paper, we have shown how one can effectively program BDI-style agent systems in the situation calculus-based IndiGolog high-level programming language. The benefits of this are many. First, we gain a better understanding of the common features of BDI agent programming languages and "Golog-like" high-level programming languages, as well as of what is specific to each type of language, and what is required to reproduce BDI languages in the latter. We also get a new classical-logic situation calculus-based semantics for BDI agent programming languages. This opens many avenues for enhancing the BDI programming paradigm with reasoning capabilities, for instance, model-based belief update capabilities, lookahead planning capabilities,

---

[5] Note that for this to go through, we have to extend the translation $\delta_P$ (Section 3.2) of programs of the form $(\!|\Delta|\!)$ to set the bit vector $w$ in $achieve_e(x.w)$ properly (i.e., to 1 iff the alternative is in the $(\!|\Delta|\!)$).

plan/goal achievement monitoring capabilities, etc. In fact, the situation calculus and basic action theories provide a rich and and well-studied logical framework for specifying the belief update and planning part of agent programming languages.

It might be said that our bisimulation results are not very surprising, as both BDI languages and IndiGolog are universal programming languages. However, the simplicity and modularity of our encoding shows that the relationship between BDI languages and IndiGolog is actually fairly close. Representing a BDI-style plan library (including the association between a plan and the event/goal it addresses) in IndiGolog is quite straightforward: each plan becomes an alternative in an achievement procedure associated with the event/goal; event-directed plan invocation can be done by calling the event's achievement procedure. The key feature that is missing, BDI-style event-directed plan triggering, can in fact be added by incorporating into the IndiGolog program an "event server" that calls the event's achievement procedure; such a server can easily be programmed using IndiGolog's concurrent iteration construct. We also show how the simple BDI language approach to belief update can be modeled in the situation calculus, using action theories with a simple type of successor state axiom and $add_{b_i}$ and $del_{b_i}$ actions. This then gives us a nice framework for defining more sophisticated belief update approaches. As well, we have shown that failure recovery mechanisms can be added to IndiGolog by introducing constructs such as the "try" construct $\triangleright$, very much as has been done in some BDI-languages.

One could also argue that the approach we follow decreases the "separation of concerns" in that both the agent program and the generic BDI execution engine are encoded into a single IndiGolog high-level program, meaning that the agent program and the BDI interpreter are no longer separated. To avoid this, one could develop an alternative account where one gives a situation calculus semantics for the BDI execution cycle at the meta-level, by re-defining what a BDI-IndiGolog agent is and what counts as an "online" execution for such agents. In this paper, however, we intended to keep the IndiGolog framework as intact as possible. Also, by encoding the BDI engine in a logical/object language (as an IndiGolog program), one can formally express (and prove) properties of programs and of the programming language in the (situation calculus) object language. Nonetheless, the alternative approach is of interest and we are in fact working on it.

There has only been limited work on relating "Golog-like" and BDI programming languages. Hindriks et al. [16] show that ConGolog can be bisimulated by the agent language 3APL under some conditions, which include the agent having complete knowledge. In [14], it is also shown that AgentSpeak can be encoded into 3APL. Our results, thus, are complementary, in showing the inverse relationship.

Also related is the work of Gabaldon [12] on encoding Hierarchical Task Network (HTN) libraries in ConGolog. There are similarities between our work and his in the way procedural knowledge is encoded in ConGolog. This is is not surprising, as HTN planning systems and BDI agents have many similarities [11]. But note that in HTNs, and hence in Gabaldon's translation, the objective is *planning* and not reactive execution. We on the other hand, focus on capturing the typical execution regime of BDI agent systems, rather than on performing lookahead planning to synthesize a solution. As a result, we address issues such as external events and plan failure that do not arise in HTN planning.

Finally, we note that in this work we have mostly focused on the core features of BDI systems, and have not dealt with more advanced features present in some more recent versions of BDI systems. For instance, the full CAN [30,28] language as well as 2APL [7] and Jason [3,17] provide, in some way or other, support for so-called *declarative goals*, goals which go beyond "events" by decoupling goal success/failure from plan success/failure. However, the way such advanced features have been added to different BDI languages is not always uniform. More work is needed to handle those advanced features in an encoding of BDI programming into IndiGolog.

**Acknowledgments.** We thank the reviewers for their interesting comments. This work was supported by Agent Oriented Software and the Australian Research Council (grant LP0882234) and the National Science and Engineering Research Council of Canada.

# References

1. Belecheanu, R.A., Munroe, S., Luck, M., Payne, T., Miller, T., McBurney, P., Pechoucek, M.: Commercial applications of agents: Lessons, experiences and challenges. In: Proceedings of Autonomous Agents and Multi-Agent Systems (AAMAS), pp. 1549–1555 (2006)
2. Benfield, S.S., Hendrickson, J., Galanti, D.: Making a strong business case for multiagent technology. In: Proceedings of Autonomous Agents and Multi-Agent Systems (AAMAS), pp. 10–15 (2006)
3. Bordini, R.H., Hübner, J.F., Wooldridge, M.: Programming Multi-agent Systems in AgentSpeak Using Jason. Wiley Series in Agent Technology. Wiley, Chichester (2007)
4. Bratman, M.E.: Intentions, Plans, and Practical Reason. Harvard University Press, Cambridge (1987)
5. Busetta, P., Rönnquist, R., Hodgson, A., Lucas, A.: JACK intelligent agents: Components for intelligent agents in Java. AgentLink Newsletter 2, 2–5 (1999)
6. Cohen, P.R., Levesque, H.J.: Intention is choice with commitment. Artificial Intelligence Journal 42, 213–261 (1990)
7. Dastani, M.: 2APL: A practical agent programming language. Autonomous Agents and Multi-Agent Systems 16(3), 214–248 (2008)
8. De Giacomo, G., Lespérance, Y., Levesque, H.J.: ConGolog, a concurrent programming language based on the situation calculus. Artificial Intelligence Journal 121(1–2), 109–169 (2000)
9. De Giacomo, G., Lespérance, Y., Levesque, H.J., Sardina, S.: IndiGolog: A high-level programming language for embedded reasoning agents. In: Bordini, R.H., Dastani, M., Dix, J., Fallah-Seghrouchni, A.E. (eds.) Multi-Agent Programming: Languages, Platforms and Applications, ch. 2, pp. 31–72. Springer, Heidelberg (2009)
10. Dennett, D.: The Intentional Stance. The MIT Press, Cambridge (1987)
11. Dix, J., Muñoz-Avila, H., Nau, D.S., Zhang, L.: IMPACTing SHOP: Putting an AI planner into a multi-agent environment. Annals of Mathematics and Artificial Intelligence 37(4), 381–407 (2003)
12. Gabaldon, A.: Programming hierarchical task networks in the situation calculus. In: Proc. of AIPS 2002 Workshop on On-line Planning and Scheduling, Toulouse, France (April 2002)
13. Georgeff, M.P., Ingrand, F.F.: Decision making in an embedded reasoning system. In: Proceedings of the International Joint Conference on Artificial Intelligence (IJCAI), Detroit, USA, pp. 972–978 (1989)

14. Hindriks, K.V., de Boer, F.S., van der Hoek, W., Meyer, J.-J.: A formal semantics for an abstract agent programming language. In: Proceedings of the International Workshop on Agent Theories, Architectures, and Languages (ATAL), pp. 215–229 (1998)

15. Hindriks, K.V., de Boer, F.S., van der Hoek, W., Meyer, J.-J.: Agent programming in 3APL. Autonomous Agents and Multi-Agent Systems 2, 357–401 (1999)

16. Hindriks, K.V., Lespérance, Y., Levesque, H.J.: An embedding of ConGolog in 3APL. In: Proceedings of the European Conference in Artificial Intelligence (ECAI), pp. 558–562 (2000)

17. Hübner, J.F., Bordini, R.H., Wooldridge, M.: Programming declarative goals using plan patterns. In: Baldoni, M., Endriss, U. (eds.) DALT 2006. LNCS (LNAI), vol. 4327, pp. 123–140. Springer, Heidelberg (2006)

18. Levesque, H.J., Reiter, R., Lespérance, Y., Lin, F., Scherl, R.B.: GOLOG: A logic programming language for dynamic domains. Journal of Logic Programming 31, 59–84 (1997)

19. Ljungberg, M., Lucas, A.: The OASIS air-traffic management system. In: Proceedings of the Pacific Rim International Conference on Artificial Intelligence, PRICAI (1992)

20. McCarthy, J., Hayes, P.J.: Some philosophical problems from the standpoint of artificial intelligence. Machine Intelligence 4, 463–502 (1969)

21. Pokahr, A., Braubach, L., Lamersdorf, W.: JADEX: Implementing a BDI-infrastructure for JADE agents. EXP - in search of innovation (Special Issue on JADE) 3(3), 76–85 (2003)

22. Pollack, M.E.: The uses of plans. Artificial Intelligence Journal 57(1), 43–68 (1992)

23. Rao, A.S.: Agentspeak(L): BDI agents speak out in a logical computable language. In: Velde, W.V., Perram, J.W. (eds.) MAAMAW 1996. LNCS, vol. 1038, pp. 42–55. Springer, Heidelberg (1996)

24. Rao, A.S., Georgeff, M.P.: Modeling rational agents within a BDI-architecture. In: Proceedings of Principles of Knowledge Representation and Reasoning (KR), pp. 473–484 (1991)

25. Rao, A.S., Georgeff, M.P.: An abstract architecture for rational agents. In: Proceedings of Principles of Knowledge Representation and Reasoning (KR), pp. 438–449 (1992)

26. Reiter, R.: Knowledge in Action. Logical Foundations for Specifying and Implementing Dynamical Systems. The MIT Press, Cambridge (2001)

27. Sardina, S., De Giacomo, G., Lespérance, Y., Levesque, H.J.: On the semantics of deliberation in IndiGolog – From theory to implementation. Annals of Mathematics and Artificial Intelligence 41(2–4), 259–299 (2004)

28. Sardina, S., Padgham, L.: Goals in the context of BDI plan failure and planning. In: Durfee, E.H., Yokoo, M., Huhns, M.N., Shehory, O. (eds.) Proceedings of Autonomous Agents and Multi-Agent Systems (AAMAS), pp. 16–23 (2007)

29. Thielscher, M.: FLUX: A logic programming method for reasoning agents. Theory and Practice of Logic Programming 5(4–5), 533–565 (2005); Special Issue of Theory and Practice of Logic Programming on Constraint Handling Rules

30. Winikoff, M., Padgham, L., Harland, J., Thangarajah, J.: Declarative & procedural goals in intelligent agent systems. In: Proceedings of Principles of Knowledge Representation and Reasoning (KR), pp. 470–481 (2002)

# A Middleware for Modeling
# Organizations and Roles in Jade

Matteo Baldoni[1], Guido Boella[1], Valerio Genovese[1],
Andrea Mugnaini[1], Roberto Grenna[1], and Leendert van der Torre[2]

[1] Dipartimento di Informatica, Università degli Studi di Torino, Italy
{baldoni,guido,grenna}@di.unito.it,
{mugnaini81,valerio.click}@gmail.com
[2] Computer Science and Communications, University of Luxembourg, Luxembourg
leon.vandertorre@uni.lu

**Abstract.** Organizations and roles are often seen as mental constructs, good to
be used during the design phase in Multi Agent Systems, but they have also been
considered as first class citizens in MAS, when objective coordination is needed.
Roles facilitate the coordination of agents inside an organization, and they give
new abilities in the context of organizations, called powers, to the agents which
satisfy the necessary requirements to play them. No general purpose programming languages for multiagent systems offer primitives to program organizations
and roles as instances existing at runtime, so, in this paper, we propose our extension of the Jade framework, with Java primitives to program organizations structured in roles, and to enable agents to play roles in organizations. We provide
classes and protocols which enable an agent to enact a new role in an organization, to interact with the role by invoking the execution of powers, and to receive
new goals to be fulfilled. Roles and organizations can be on a different platform
with respect to the role players, and communication is protocol-based. Since they
can have complex behaviours, they are implemented by extending the Jade agent
class. Our aim is to give to programmers a middle tier, built on the Jade platform,
useful to solve with minimal implementative effort many coordination problems,
and to offer a first, implicit, management of norms and sanctions.

## 1 Introduction

Roles facilitate the coordination of agents inside an organization, giving new abilities in
the context of organizations, called powers, to the agents which satisfy the requirements
necessary to play them. Organizations and roles are often seen as mental constructs,
good to be used during the design phase in MAS, but they have also been considered as
first class citizens in multiagent systems [13], when objective coordination is needed.
No general purpose programming language for multiagent systems offers primitives to
program organizations and roles as instances existing at runtime yet.

So, this paper answers the following research questions:

- How to introduce organizations and roles in a general purpose framework for pro-
  gramming multiagent systems?
- Which are the primitives to be added for programming organizations and roles?
- How is it possible to restructure roles at runtime?

L. Braubach, J.-P. Briot, and J. Thangarajah (Eds.): ProMAS 2009, LNAI 5919, pp. 100–117, 2010.

Our aim is to give to programmers a middle tier, built on the Jade platform, useful to solve coordination problems with minimal implementative effort. Our proposal extends of the Jade multiagent system framework, with primitives to program, in Java, organizations that are structured in roles, and for enabling agents to play roles in organizations. As ontological model of organizations and roles we rely on [8] which merges two different and complementary views or roles, providing a high-level logical specification.

To pass from the logical specification to the design and implementation of a framework for programming multiagent systems, we provide classes and protocols which enable an agent to enact a new role in an organization, to interact with the role by invoking the execution of powers (as intended in OO programming [11], see Section 2.5), and to receive new goals to be fulfilled. Since roles and organizations can be on a different platform with respect to the role player they need to communicate. Communication is based on protocols. Complex behaviours are implemented by extending the Jade agent class.

In this paper we do not consider the possibility to have BDI agents yet, although both the ontological model (see [11]) and the Jade framework allow such extension. However, we give some hints on the usefulness of introducing BDI into our proposal. This issue will be faced in future work.

The paper is organized as follows. First, Section 2 summarizes the model of organizations and roles we take inspiration from, and we give a short description of our concept of "role", "organization", "power". Section 2.6 describes an example of a typical MAS situation that motivates our proposal; Section 3 describes how our model is realized introducing new packages in Jade; Section 4 discusses a possible powerJade solution to a practical problem (the manager-bidder one), and Section 5 finishes this paper with related work and conclusions.

## 2  The Model of Organizations and Roles

Since we speak about organizations and roles, we need to define both, and to refer to a formalized ontological model. In the following subsections we introduce the notions of *role* and *organization*, based on previous work ([5]), then we give two different (but complementary) views about roles (see [11] and [14]), we introduce a unified model, and define a well-founded meta-model. Last, we explain the notions "*power*", "*capability*", and "*requirement*".

### 2.1  Our Definition for Organizations and Roles

In ontology and knowledge representation (like [9], [10], [23], and [25]), we can find a quite complete analysis for organizational roles. Our intention is to introduce a notion of role which is well founded, on which there is a wide agreement and which is justified independently from the practical problems we want to solve using it. We use a metaphor directly taken from organizational management. An organization (or, more generally, an institution) is not an "object" which can be manipulated from the outside but rather it belongs to the social reality, and all the interactions with it can be performed only via the roles it offers ([12]). The utility of roles is not only for modeling domains including institutions and organizations, because we can consider every "object" as an institution or an organization offering different ways for interacting with it. Each way is offered by a different role. So, *our roles are based on an organizational metaphor.*

## 2.2   The Ontological Model for the Organization

In [11] an ontological analysis shows the following properties for roles:

- *Foundation*: a role instance has always to be associated to an instance of the organization to which it belongs, and to an instance of the player of the role;
- *Definitional dependence*: the role definition depends the one of the organization it belongs to;
- *Institutional powers*: the operations defined into the role can access to the state of the organization, and to the states of the other roles of the organization too;
- *Prerequisites*: to play a role, it is necessary to satisfy some requirements, i.e. the player must be able to do actions which can be used in the role's execution.

Also the model in [11] is focused on the definition of the structure of organizations, based on their ontological status, which is only partly different from the one of agents or objects. On the one hand, roles do not exist as independent entities, since they are linked to organizations. Thus, they are not components like objects. Moreover, organizations and roles are not autonomous and act via role players. On the other hand, organizations and roles are descriptions of complex behaviours: in the real world, organizations are considered legal entities, so they can even act like agents, albeit via their representative playing roles. So, they share some properties with agents, and, in some respects, can be modeled using similar primitives.

## 2.3   The Model for the Role Dynamics

In [14] Dastani et al. propose a model, which focuses on role dynamics, rather than on their structure; four operations to deal with role dynamics are defined: *enact* and *de-act*, which mean that an agent respectively starts/ends occupying (playing) a role in a system, and *activate* and *deactivate*, which respectively mean that an agent starts executing actions (operations) belonging to the role or suspends their execution. Although it is possible to have an agent with multiple roles enacted simultaneously, only one role can be *active* at the same time: specifically, when an agent performs a power, in that moment it is playing only one role .

## 2.4   The Unified Model

Using the distinction of Omicini et al. [26], we use the model presented in [11] as an objective coordination mechanism, in a similar way as, for example, artifacts do: organizations are first class entities of the MAS rather than a mental construction which agents use to coordinate themselves. However, this model leaves unspecified how, given a role, its player will behave. For this reason, we merged it with [14], and solved the problem of formally defining the dynamics of roles, by identifying the actions that can be done in a *open system*, so that agents can enter and leave. Organizations are not simple mental constructions, roles are not only abstractions used at design time, and players are not isolated agents: they are all agents interacting with the one anothers. A logical specification of this integrated model can be found in [8].

Also considering what we can find in [7] about mental attitudes, we can summarize some points of the model:

- Roles are instances with associated beliefs and goals attributed to them. These mental attitudes are public.
- The public beliefs and goals attributed to roles are changed by speech acts executed either by the role or by other roles. The former case accounts for the addition of preconditions and of the intention to achieve the rational effect of a speech act, the latter accounts for the case of commands or other speech acts presupposing a hierarchy of authority among roles.
- The agents execute speech acts via their roles.

This model has been applied to provide a semantics to both FIPA and Social Commitment approaches to agent communication languages, and this semantics overcomes the problem of the unverifiability of private mental attitudes of agents. The implementation of this model is shown in Section 3.

### 2.5 "Powers" and "Capabilities"/"Requirements" in Our View

We know that roles work as "interfaces" between organizations and agents, and they give so called "powers" to agents. A power can extend agents abilities, allowing them to operate inside the organization and inside the state of the other roles. An example of such powers, called "institutional powers" in [22], is the signature of a director which counts as the commitment of the entire institution.

The powers added to the players, by means of the roles, can be different for each role and, thus, represent different affordances offered by the organization to other agents in order allow them to interact with it [4].

Powers are invoked by players on their roles, but they are executed by the roles, since they own both state and behaviour.

For what concerns the "requirements", we consider them as *needed capabilities* that a candidate player must have to be able to play a particular role. An example of "capability" can be the ability for a bank employee to log into the software of his/her bank.

### 2.6 An Example

The usefulness of the above proposal, that brought to the development of powerJade, introduced in the next section, can be seen by an example. The scenario we consider involves two organizations: a bank, and a software house. Bob is a programmer in a software house. The software house management requires him to own a bank account, in order to directly deposit his salary on it. Bob goes to the bank, where the employee, George, gives him some forms to fill. Once Bob has finished filling in the forms, George inputs the data on a terminal, creating a new account, which needs to be activated. George forwards the activation request to his director, Bill, who is the only person in the bank, who can activate an account. Once the account is activated, Bob will be a new bank customer.

Years later Bob, who in the meantime became a project manager, decides to buy a little house. He has to obtain a loan, and the bank director informs him that for having a loan, his wage packet is needed. Bob asks to the management of the software house for his wage packet, and brings it to Bill. After some days (and other filled forms), the bank gives Bob the loan and he can finally buy his new house.

Each organization *offers* some roles, which have to be *played* by some agents, called, for this reason, *players*. In the bank, Bob plays the *customer* role, while George plays the *employee* one, and Bill the *director* role. Since Bob interacts with both organizations, he has to play a role also inside the software house: he enters as a *programmer*, but after some years he changes it, becoming a *project manager*. As a bank customer, Bob has some *powers*: to open an account, to transfer money on it, to request a loan. As a simple employee, George has only the power to create Bob's account, but the account activation is to be done by Bill, the director. The activation is done by means of a specific request from George to Bill, who has a specific *responsability*. For loan request, the director has to examine Bob's account, and ask him for his wage packet. Another of Bob's powers is to ask for his wage packet. Speaking about personal capabilities, we can imagine that Bill, in order to access the bank procedures, he is allowed to execute, must fill a login page with his ID and password; the same happens to George, and for Bob, in the moment in which he accesses his account using Internet. However, Bob has also another capability, that is *requested* when he plays the programmer role (but the same happens for the project manager one): to give his login name and password for entering the enterprise IT system. Finally, the director is required to have more complex capabilities, like evaluating the solvency of a client requesting a loan.

## 3   PowerJade

The main idea of our work is to offer to programmers a complete middle tier with the primitives for implementing organizations, roles, and players in Jade (see Figure 1), giving a declarative model based on Finite State Automaton (FSM), which is modifiable also at run-time. We called this middleware *powerJade*, remembering the importance of powers in the interaction between roles and organizations. The powerJade conceptual model is inspired to *open systems*: participants can enter the system and leave it whenever they want. For granting this condition, and for managing the (possibly) continuous operations for enacting, deacting, dactivating, and deactivating roles (in an asynchronous and dynamic way), many protocols have been implemented. Another starting point was the re-use of the software structure already implemented in powerJava [5], based on an intensive use of so-called *inner classes*.

In order to give an implementation based on the conceptual model we discussed in Section 2.4, not only the three subclasses of the Jade `Agent` class (`Organization`, `Role`, and `Player`) have been realized (they will be described in Sections 3.1, 3.2, 3.3), but also classes for other important concepts, like `Power`, and `Requirement` were implemented (and shown in Sections 3.2, 3.3). For representing the dynamics of the roles, we also implemented all the needed communication protocols, that will be described in Section 3.4.

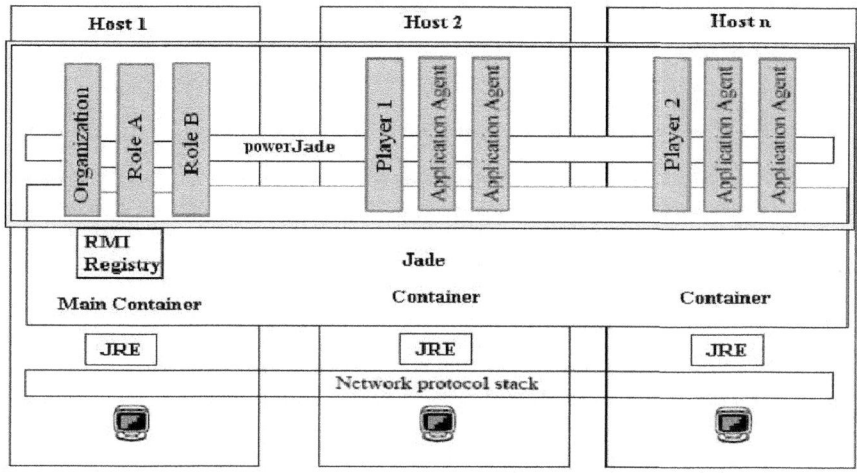

**Fig. 1.** The Jade architecture and the powerJade middle tier

It can sound strange that we implemented `Organization`, `Role`, and `Player` as subclasses of the Jade `Agent` class. We adopted this solution for taking advantage of the possibility for agents in Jade to communicate by mean of FIPA messages. The only agent having the full autonomy is the `Player`: it can decide whether enacting a role, or activating/deactivating it, and also to deact it. The `Role`, instead, has a very limited autonomy, due, for example, to hierarchical motivation (but, however, it's always the `Player` which decides...). The `Organization`, we would like to extend our middleware giving an organization the opportunity to play a role inside another one, like in the real world. This consideration also answers the question: what is the advantage of programming roles and organizations as instances? More details can be found in [8,5,3,6], where we started from a theoretical well-formed model for organizations and roles applied it to object-oriented programming (with the language powerJava), then to multiagent systems, to the web world (currently under implementation).

`Organization`, `Role`, and `Player` have similar structures: they contain a finite state machine behaviour instance which manages the interaction at the level of the new middle tier by means of suitable protocols for communication.

To implement each protocol in Jade two further FSMBehaviour are necessary, one for each of the interacting partners; for example, the enactment protocol between the organization and the player requires two FSMBehaviours, one in the organization and one in the player.

## 3.1   The `Organization` Class

The `Organization` class is structured as in Figure 2. The `OrgManagerBehaviour` is a finite state machine behaviour created inside the `setup()` method of `Organization`. It operates in parallel with other behaviours created by the programmer of the organization, and allows the organization to interact

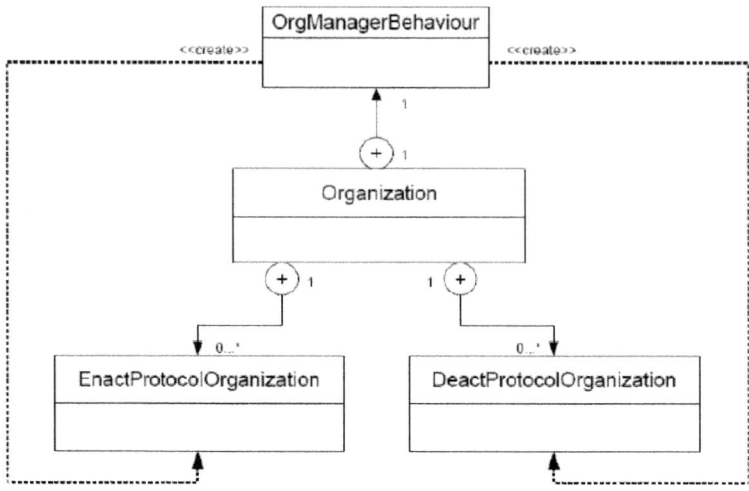

**Fig. 2.** The Organization diagram

via the middle tier. Its task is to manage the enact and deact requests done by the players. At each iteration, the OrgManagerBehaviour looks for any message having the *ORGANIZATION_PROTOCOL* and the performative *ACLMessage.Request*. EnactProtocolOrganization and DeactProtocolOrganization are the counterparts of the respective protocols inside the players which realize the interaction between organizations and players: instances of these two classes are created by the OrgManagerBehaviour when needed.

When the OrgManagerBehaviour detects a message to manage, it extracts the sender's AID, and the type of request. In case of an *Enact* request (and whether all the controls described on Subsection 3.4 about the *Enact* protocol succeeded), a new instance of EnactProtocolOrganization behaviour is created, and added to the queue of behaviours to be executed. The same happens (with a new instance of the DeactProtocolOrganization behaviour) if a *Deact* request has been done, while if the controls related to the requested protocol do not succeed, the iteration terminates, and the OrgManagerBehaviour its cycle. In the behavioural part of this class, programmers can add a "normative" control on the players' good intentions, and manage the possibility of discovering lies before enacting the role, or immediately after having enacted it. Primitives implementing these controls are ongoing work.

### 3.2   The Role Class

As described in [3], the Role class is an Agent subclass, but also an Organization *inner class*. Using this solution, each role can access the internal state of the organization, and the internal state of other roles too. Like the Organization class has the OrgManagerBehaviour, the Role has the RoleManagerBehaviour, a finite state machine behaviour created inside the setup() method of Role. Its task is to manage the commands (messages) coming from the player: a power invocation, an *Activate*, or a *Deactivate*.

Inside the role, an instance of the `PowerManager` class is present. The `PowerManager` is a `FSMBehaviour` subclass, and it has the whole list of the powers of the role (linked as states of the FSM). It is composed as follows:

- a first state, the `ManagerPowerState`, that must understand which power has been invoked;
- a final state, the `ResultManager`, that has to return the power result to its caller;
- a self-created and linked state for each power implemented by the role programmer.

All the transitions between states are added at run-time to the FSM, respecting the code written by the programmer.

**The Powers.** Powers are a fundamental part of our middleware. They can be invoked by a player on the active role, and they represent the possibility of action for that role inside the organization. For coherence with the Jade framework and to exploit the scheduling facility, powers are implemented as behaviours, taking also advantage from their more declarative nature with respect to methods.

Sometimes, a power execution needs some requirements to be completed; this is a sort of remote method call dealt by our middleware, since requirements are player's actions. In our example, George, as a bank employee, has the *power* of creating a bank account for a customer; to exercise this power, George as player has to input his credentials: the login and the password.

The problem to be solved is that requirements invocations must be transparent to the role programmer, who should be relieved from dealing the message exchange with the player.

We modeled the class `Power` as a `FSMBehaviour` subclass, where the complete finite state machine is automatically constructed from a declarative specification containing the component behaviours to be executed by the role and the name of the requirements to be executed by the player; in this way, we can manage the request for any requirement as a particular state of the FSM. When a requirement is invoked, a `RequestRequirementState` (that is another subclass of `FSMBehaviour`) is automatically added in the correct point invoking the required requirement by means of a protocol: the programmer has only to specify the requirement name.

The complexity of this kind of interaction is shown in Figure 3. The great balloon indicating one of the powers for that particular role contains the final state machine obtained writing the following code:

```
addState(new myState1("S1", "R1", "E1"));
addState(new myState2("S2"));
```

where *S1* and *S2* are names of possibly complex behaviours implemented by the role programmer which will be instanced and added to the finite state machine representing the power, *R1* is the requirement, and *E1* is a behaviour for managing errors. Analyzing the structure of the power, we can see that the execution of *S1* is followed by a macro-state (that is a `FSMBehaviour`), managing the request for a requirement, automatically created by the `addState()` method. This state will send the player the request for the needed requirement, waiting for the answer. If the answer is positive, the transition to the next state of the power is done (or to the ResultManager, if needed); otherwise, the error is managed (if possible), or the power is aborted. The ErrorManager is a particular state that allows to manage all the possible kinds of error, including the case of a player lying about its requirements).

Error management is done via the middle tier. We can detect two kinds of possible errors: (i) *accidental* ones, and (ii) *voluntary* ones. Typical cases of (i) are "practical" problems (i.e. network too busy and timeout expired), or the ones linked to a bad working player or to programming problem; those indicated as (ii) are related to an incorrect (malicious) behaviour of the player, e.g. when an agent lies about its requirements during a protocol enactment, pretending to own them, while this is not the truth. The latter case of error management allows the organization and the programmer a first, rough, implicit, normative and sanctioning mechanism: if the player, for any reason, shows a lack of requirements, it could be obliged to the deact protocol w.r.t. that particular role, or it can be "marked" with a negative score, that could mean a lower trust level exercised from the organization on it.

An advantage given by using a declarative mechanism like behaviours (we can use instructions to add or remove states to a FSMBehaviour) for modeling powers is that new powers can be dynamically added or removed from the role. It is sufficient to add or remove (at run-time) transactions linking the power to the ManagerPowerState which is a FSMBehaviour too.

This mechanism can be used to model both dynamics of roles in organizational change or access restrictions. In the former case we can model situations like the power of the director to give the employee the power of giving loans. In the latter case, we can model security restrictions by removing powers from roles, thus avoiding the situation where first a power is invoked and then aborted after controlling an access control list.

### 3.3   The Player Class

Analogously to Organization and Role, also the Player class is an Agent subclass. Like in the other two cases, we have a PlayerManagerBehaviour, a FSM-Behaviour managing all the possible messages that the player can receive. The player is the only agent that is totally autonomous. It contains other behaviours, created by the agent programmer, which are scheduled in parallel with the manager behaviour and it can obviously also interact with other agents, not involved in any organization, but it's constrained to interact with any kind of organization using a role offered by the organization itself. Any activity, communication, or action that both the agents could do without passing through their roles will not have effects on the internal state of the organization at all. Only the player can use all the four protocols described in Subsection 2.3: *Enact* and *Deact* with the organization, *Activate* and *Deactivate* with the role.

It is important to notice that, as we discuss in Subsection 3.4, only the Player is able to start the *Enact* protocol, which can be refused by the Organization, but it has the absolute control on activation and deactivation of the roles (once enacted). A role can be deacted because the Player wants to deact it (e.g., a clerk who leaves for a new job), or because the Organization forces the deacting (the same clerk can be fired).

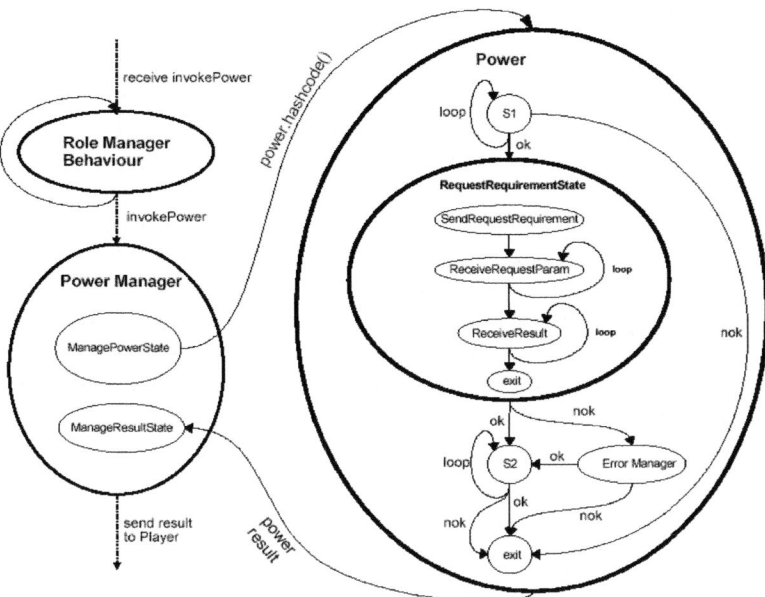

**Fig. 3.** Power management

While the role has to manage powers, the player deals with requirements: this is done by a `RequirementManager`.

The `Player` class offers some methods. They can be used in programming the other behaviours of the agent when it is necessary to change the state of role playing or to invoke powers. We assume invocations of powers to be asynchronous via the `invokePower` method from any behaviour implemented by the programmer. The call informs the `PlayerManagerBehaviour` which the interaction with the role has started and returns a call id which is used to receive the correct return value in the same behaviour. It is left to the programmer how to manage the necessity of blocking the behaviour till an answer is returned, with the usual *block* instruction of JADE. This solution is coherent with the standard message exchange of JADE and allows to avoid the use of more sophisticated behaviours based on threads. The behaviour can then consult the `PlayerManagerBehaviour` to get the return value of the power.

The player, once having invoked a power, i.e., for messages o requests from the active role. When the role needs some requirements, the `PlayerManagerBehaviour` passes the control to the `RequirementManager`, which executes all the tasks which are needed.

It's important to notice that a player can always grow w.r.t. its capabilities/requirements.

A player can know organizations and roles on the platform by using the *Yellow Pages* mechanism, that is a basic JADE feature.

**The Requirements.** Requirements are, for a player, a subset of the behaviours representing its capabilities, and, in some sense, the plans for achieving the personal goals of the agent. By playing a role, an agent can achieve multiple goals (i.e., the goals achievable invoking a power), but, in a general case, the execution of requirements may be necessary during the invocation of a power. Referring to our bank example, George can achieve many goals through its employee role (i.e., create a new account), but to do it, it is necessary for him to log in inside the bank IT system. Seen as a requirement, its log in capability denotes "attitude", "possibility" of playing the employee role.

During the enact protocol, the organization sends (see Section 3.4) the agent, willing to play one of its roles, the list of requirements to be fulfilled. As we said, the candidate player could lie (e.g., telling that it is able to fulfill some requirement), however, the organization and the programmer have the possibility to check the truth of the candidate player's answer before it begins to play the role, not enacting it, or deacting immediately after the enact. Also this kind of choice has been done to grant the highest degree of freedom.

### 3.4   Communication Protocols

In this Section, an example of a complex communication between a player, an organization, and a role is shown. We have to make some preliminary considerations, about communication. Each protocol is split in two, specular, but complementary behaviours, one for each actor. In fact, if we consider a communication, two "roles" may be seen: an initiator, which is the object sending the first message, and a responder, which can never begin a communication. For example, when a player wants to play a role inside an organization, an `EnactProtocolPlayer` instance is created. The player is the initiator, and a request for a role is done from its new behaviour to the `OrgManagerBehaviour`, which instantiates an `EnactProtocolOrganization` behaviour. This behaviour will manage the request, sending to the `EnactProtocolPlayer` an `Inform` containing the list of the requirements needed to play the requested role.

The `EnactProtocolPlayer` evaluates the list, answering to the organization whether it agrees (notice that the player programmer could implement a behaviour that always answers in a positive way, that sounds like a lie). Only after receiving the agreement, the `EnactProtocolOrganization` creates a `RoleManager` instance, and sends the AID of the role just created to the player. The protocol ends with the update of the player's internal state.

Since the instance of a role, once created, is not yet activated, when the player wants to "use" a role, has to activate it. Only one role at a time is active, while the others, for which the agent finished successfully the enactment protocol, are deactivated. The activation protocol moves from the player to the role instance. The player creates an `ActivateProtocolPlayer`, which sends a message to the role, calling for the activation. This message produces a change into the internal state of the role, which answers with an `inform` telling its agreement.

Once the role has been activated, the player can proceed with a power invocation. As discussed in [3], this is not the only way in which player and role can communicate. We consider it, because it can require a complex interaction, beginning from the `invoke`

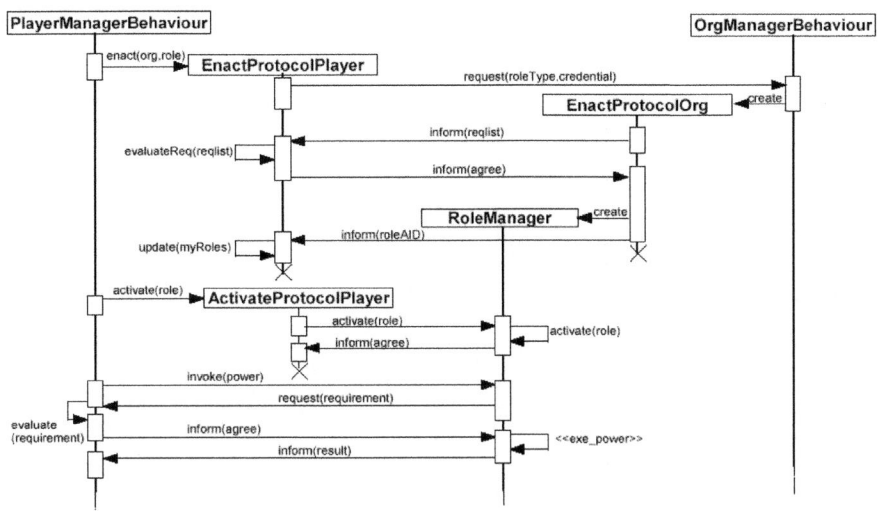

**Fig. 4.** The Sequence Diagram for a complex communication

done by the player on a power of the role. As we shown in Subsection 3.2, the power management can involve the request to the player for the execution of one or more requirements. In this case, the role sends a `request` with the list of requirements to be fulfilled. The player, since autonomous, can evaluate the opportunity to execute the requirement(s), and take the result(s) to the role (using an `inform`, waiting for the execution of the power and for receiving the `inform` with the result. A particular case, not visible in Figure 4, is the one in which the player, for any reason, does not execute the requirements. This "bad" interaction will finish with an automatic deactment of the role.

## 4   The CNP Scenario in PowerJade

In Section 2.6, we discussed the bank example, trying to focus on roles' powers, players' requirements, responsibility calls, and all that has a place in our middleware. In this Section, we show a more technical example: the Contract Net Protocol (CNP), or manager-bidder problem. In the left part of Figure 5, the inside of a player is shown, with its `Player Manager`, and its `RequirementManager` too.

Attached to the `RequirementManager`, we see two possible requirements: they can be requested by a role, in this case, the M_CNP, which is shown in the right part of the same Figure. The double rounded states are the ones created at run-time for the power called *CNP*. By figure 6 we try to explain a little part of the interactions between the player playing the manager role, and its role.

Our scenario considers an agent executing one of its behaviours. When a task is to be executed, but the agent cannot do it because it does not have the right capabilities. The only solution is to find someone able to execute the task. The agent knows that there is an organization that offers the CNP by means of its roles. The agent contacts

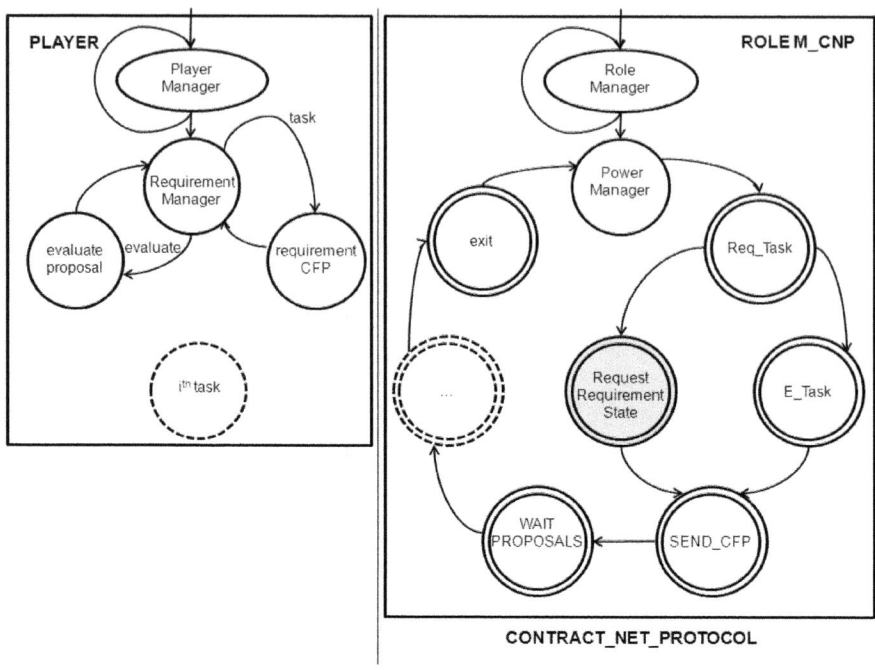

**Fig. 5.** Player and Manager role for the CNP example. The player is the candidate to play the Manager role in the CNP. The interaction after a successfully enactment is shown in Figure 6.

the organization, starting the enact protocol for the role of manager in the CNP M_CNP. The organization sends the list of requirements to be fulfilled, composed by the "task" requirement (that is the ability to send a task for a call for proposal operation), and the "evaluate" task (that is the ability to evaluate the various bidders' proposals, choosing the best one). The candidate player owns the requirements, so the role is created. When the player executes once again the behaviour containing the previously not executable task, an invokePower is executed, calling for the power with name *CNP* (the bold arc labeled with letter *a*, starting from the state with label *1* in the left part and arriving in the right part of Figure 6, to the RoleManager, which has label *2*).

The RoleManager passes the control to the PowerManager (label *3*), which finds the appropriate power in its list, and begins its execution (the first state is the one with label *4*). The first step is the call for the task which will be evaluated by bidders, but the task is known only by the player of the role, so a request for a requirement is done (label *5*). This means, a message is sent to the player, calling for the execution of a requirement (in this case, "task"). The dotted arc with label *b* simulates this message, which is received and managed by the PlayerManager (label *6*, which passes the control to the RequirementManager (*7*). Once the requirement identified, the correct state is reached (label *8*). After the execution, the control is passed again to the RequirementManager (label *9*), which passes, through an appropriate message, the result(s) to the role's RequestRequirementState (simulated by the dotted

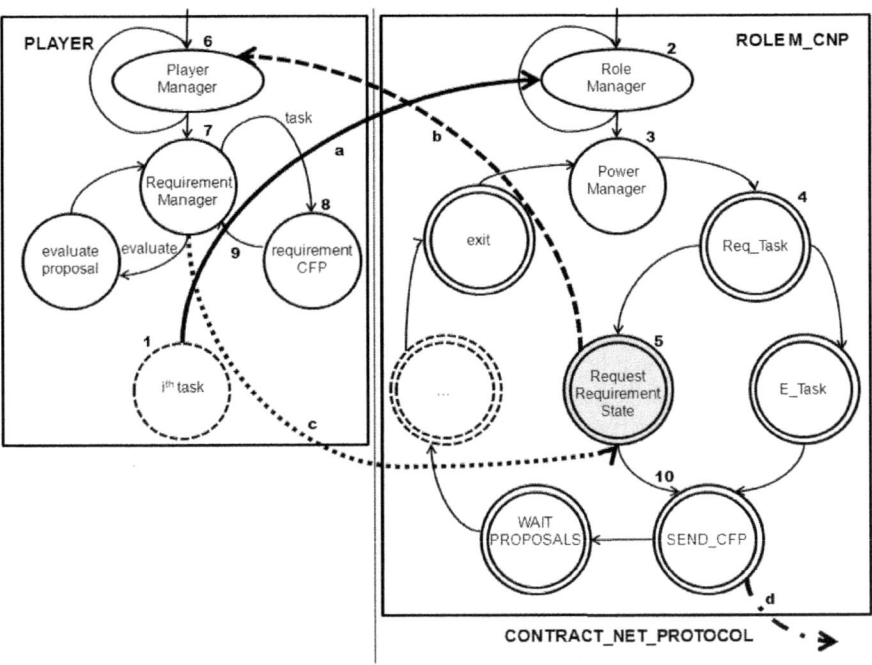

**Fig. 6.** The various interactions between player and role. The double circled states inside the role M_CNP are the ones composing the ContractNet power.

arc with label *c*). Supposing that a valid result has been returned, the power execution goes on, arriving (label *10*) to the SEND_CFP state, that provides the call for proposal to any bidder known inside the organization (dotted arc with label *4*, we assume that some agents already enacted the bidder role), going directly to add the appropriate behaviour to the PowerManager of the B_CNP instances found. The bidder roles will send messages back to the manager role, after requesting to their players the requirement to specify or not a price for the task to be delegated (with a process that is quite the same of the one just described).

The complex interaction between players and their roles, and between role and role, is executed *without* players to know the CNP dynamics, since all the complexity has been introduced in the roles. For the player playing the manager role, and for the ones playing the bidder role, the organization is a kind of black box; roles are the "wizards" managing the communication logics, and opportunely calling operations to be done by the players (that are absolutely *autonomous*: they are the only agents able to take decisions).

## 5   Related and Future Works, and Conclusions

In this paper we introduce organizations and roles as new classes in the Jade framework which are supported by a middle tier offering to agents the possibility to enact roles, invoke powers and to coordinate inside an organization. The framework is based on a set of FSMBehaviours which realize the middle tier by means of managers keeping track of the state of interaction and protocols to make the various entities communicate with each other. Powers offered by roles to players have a declarative nature that does not only make them easier to be programmed, but allows the organization to dynamically add and remove powers so to have a restructuring of the roles.

Speaking about organizations and roles, we can find very different approaches and results: models like the one in [17], applications modeling organizations or institutions like in [26], software engineering methods using organizational concepts like roles (GAIA, in [32]). GAIA is a general methodology which can be applied to a wide range of MAS, but also deals with social (macro) level, and agent (micro) level. Under the GAIA vision, a MAS can be modeled as a computational organization composed by many interactive roles. Regarding the analysis of organizations, in [30] can be found what is called the perspective of computational organization theory and artificial intelligence, in which organizations are basically described at the role, and group, composed of roles, levels.

Under the point of view of programming languages, an example is 3APL [31]. 3APL is a programming language developed for implementing cognitive agents and also for programming constructs for implementing cognitive agents and provides programming constructs for implementing agents' beliefs, goals, basic capabilities (e.g., beliefs update, etc.), and a set of practical reasoning rules for updating or revising agents' goals, but it has not primitives for modeling organizations and roles. Another language is the Normative Multi-Agent Programming Language in [29], which is more oriented to model the institutional structure composed by obligations, more than the organizational structure composed by roles. ISLANDER [15], is a tool for the definition and verification of agent mediated electronic institutions. The declarative textual language of ISLANDER can be used for specifying the institution components, and a graphical editor is also available. The definition of organizations as electronic institutions is done mainly in terms of norms and rules.

Speaking about frameworks, MetateM is a multi-agent framework using a language in which each agent is programmed using a set of (augmented) temporal logic specifications of the behaviour it should adopt. The behaviour is generated by the direct execution of the specifications. The framework is based on the notion of group, and is BDI oriented. Even if the language is not general purpose, the idea of groups can be considered similar to the one of roles. Moise [19] is an organizational model that helps the developer to cope with the agent-centered and the organizational-centered approaches. The MOISE model is structured along three levels: the individual level (in which, for each agent, the definition of its responsibilities is given), the agency level (which specifies aggregations of agents in large structures), and the society level (which defines global structures and interconnections of the agents, and their relations with each other). SMoise+ [21] (which ensures that agents will follow the organizational constraints, is suitable for open systems, and supports for reorganisation) and J-MOISE+ [20] (which is more oriented to programming *how* agents play roles in organizations) are framework based on the MOISE model, but seem to be limited for programming organizations. MadKit [18] is a modular and scalable multiagent platform written in Java. It's built upon the AGR (Agent/Group/Role) organizational model: agents are situated in groups and play roles. It allows high heterogeneity in agent architectures and communication languages, and various customizations, but seems to be also limited in programming organizations.

With respect to organizational structures, Holonic MAS [28] present particular pyramidal organizations in which agents of a layer (under the same coordinator, also known as the holon's *head*) are able to communicate and to negotiate directly between them [1]. Any holon that is part of a whole is thought to contribute to achieving the goals of this superior whole. Apart from the head, each holon consist of a (possibly empty) set of other agents, called body agents. Roles and groups can express quite naturally in Holonic structures, under the previously described perspective.

Looking at agent platforms, there are two other—other than JADE—which can be considered relevant in this context. JACK Intelligent Agents [2] support organizational structures through the Team Mode, where goals can be delegated to team members. JADEX [27] presents another interesting platform for the implementation of organizations, even if it does not currently have organizational structures.

The authors of [24] make a very similar proposal to powerJade. However, they do not propose a middle tier supported by a set of managers and behaviours making all the communication transparent to agent programmers. The approach relies mostly on the extension of agents through behaviours and represents Roles as components on an ontology, while in our approach roles are implemented as agents. Further decoupling is provided by brokering between organizations and players; a state machine permits precise monitoring of the state of the roles.

The normative part of our work is to be improved, since, at the moment, only a kind of "implicit" one is present. It can be seen, for example, in the constraints which make possible to play a role only if some requirements are respected. We are also considering possible merge with Jess (in order to use an engine for goals processing), and Jason, and some works using defeasible logic [16], in order to obtain the BDI part which is not present at this moment. We are also applying our model to the web, in order to use roles and organizations, and to improve the concept of *session*, introducing a typed, and permanent, session.

# References

1. Adam, E., Mandiau, R.: Roles and hierarchy in multi-agent organizations. In: Pěchouček, M., Petta, P., Varga, L.Z. (eds.) CEEMAS 2005. LNCS (LNAI), vol. 3690, pp. 539–542. Springer, Heidelberg (2005)
2. AOS. JACK Intelligent Agents, The Agent Oriented Software Group (AOS) (2006), http://www.agent-software.com/shared/home/
3. Baldoni, M., Boella, G., Genovese, V., Grenna, R., van der Torre, L.: How to Program Organizations and Roles in the JADE Framework. In: Bergmann, R., Lindemann, G., Kirn, S., Pěchouček, M. (eds.) MATES 2008. LNCS (LNAI), vol. 5244, pp. 25–36. Springer, Heidelberg (2008)
4. Baldoni, M., Boella, G., van der Torre, L.: Modelling the interaction between objects: Roles as affordances. In: Lang, J., Lin, F., Wang, J. (eds.) KSEM 2006. LNCS (LNAI), vol. 4092, pp. 42–54. Springer, Heidelberg (2006)

5. Baldoni, M., Boella, G., van der Torre, L.: Interaction between Objects in powerJava. Journal of Object Technology 6(2), 7–12 (2007)
6. Boella, G., Cerisara, A., Grenna, R.: Roles in building web applications using java. In: Procs. of RAOOL 2009, ECOOP 2009 - Genova (2009)
7. Boella, G., Damiano, R., Hulstijn, J., van der Torre, L.: ACL semantics between social commitments and mental attitudes. In: Dignum, F.P.M., van Eijk, R.M., Flores, R. (eds.) AC 2005. LNCS (LNAI), vol. 3859, pp. 30–44. Springer, Heidelberg (2006)
8. Boella, G., Genovese, V., Grenna, R., der Torre, L.: Roles in coordination and in agent deliberation: A merger of concepts. In: PRIMA 2007 (2007)
9. Boella, G., van der Torre, L.: An agent oriented ontology of social reality. In: Procs. of Formal Ontologies in Information Systems (FOIS 2004), Amsterdam, pp. 199–209. IOS (2004)
10. Boella, G., van der Torre, L.: The ontological properties of social roles: Definitional dependence, powers and roles playing roles. In: Procs. of LOAIT workshop at ICAIL 2005 (2005)
11. Boella, G., van der Torre, L.: Organizations as socially constructed agents in the agent oriented paradigm. In: Gleizes, M.-P., Omicini, A., Zambonelli, F. (eds.) ESAW 2004. LNCS (LNAI), vol. 3451, pp. 1–13. Springer, Heidelberg (2005)
12. Boella, G., van der Torre, L.: A foundational ontology of organizations and roles. In: Baldoni, M., Endriss, U. (eds.) DALT 2006. LNCS (LNAI), vol. 4327, pp. 78–88. Springer, Heidelberg (2006)
13. Colman, A., Han, J.: Roles, players and adaptable organizations. Applied Ontology (2007)
14. Dastani, M., van Riemsdijk, B., Hulstijn, J., Dignum, F., Meyer, J.-J.: Enacting and deacting roles in agent programming. In: Odell, J.J., Giorgini, P., Müller, J.P. (eds.) AOSE 2004. LNCS, vol. 3382, pp. 189–204. Springer, Heidelberg (2005)
15. Esteva, M., de la Cruz, D., Sierra, C.: ISLANDER: an electronic institutions editor. In: AAMAS, pp. 1045–1052. ACM, New York (2002)
16. Governatori, G., Maher, M.J., Antoniou, G., Billington, D.: Argumentation semantics for defeasible logic, p. 675 (2004)
17. Grossi, D., Dignum, F., Dastani, M., Royakkers, L.: Foundations of organizational structures in multiagent systems. In: Procs. of AAMAS 2005, pp. 690–697 (2005)
18. Gutknecht, O., Ferber, J.: The madkit agent platform architecture. In: Agents Workshop on Infrastructure for Multi-Agent Systems, pp. 48–55 (2000)
19. Hannoun, M., Boissier, O., Sichman, J.S., Sayettat, C.: Moise: An organizational model for multi-agent systems. In: IBERAMIA-SBIA, pp. 156–165 (2000)
20. Huebner, J.F.: J-Moise$^+$ programming organizational agents with Moise$^+$ and Jason (2007), http://moise.sourceforge.net/doc/tfg-eumas07-slides.pdf
21. Huebner, J.F., Sichman, J.S., Boissier, O.: S-moise+: A middleware for developing organised multi-agent systems. In: Boissier, O., Padget, J., Dignum, V., Lindemann, G., Matson, E., Ossowski, S., Sichman, J.S., Vázquez-Salceda, J. (eds.) ANIREM 2005 and OOOP 2005. LNCS (LNAI), vol. 3913, pp. 64–78. Springer, Heidelberg (2006)
22. Jones, A., Sergot, M.: A formal characterisation of institutionalised power. Journal of IGPL 3, 427–443 (1996)
23. Loebe, F.: Abstract vs. social roles - a refined top-level ontological analysis. In: Procs. of AAAI Fall Symposium Roles 2005, pp. 93–100. AAAI Press, Menlo Park (2005)
24. Madrigal-Mora, C., León-Soto, E., Fischer, K.: Implementing Organisations in JADE. In: Bergmann, R., Lindemann, G., Kirn, S., Pěchouček, M. (eds.) MATES 2008. LNCS (LNAI), vol. 5244, pp. 135–146. Springer, Heidelberg (2008)
25. Masolo, C., Vieu, L., Bottazzi, E., Catenacci, C., Ferrario, R., Gangemi, A., Guarino, N.: Social roles and their descriptions. In: Procs. of Conference on the Principles of Knowledge Representation and Reasoning (KR 2004), pp. 267–277. AAAI Press, Menlo Park (2004)

26. Omicini, A., Ricci, A., Viroli, M.: An algebraic approach for modelling organisation, roles and contexts in MAS. Applicable Algebra in Engineering, Communication and Computing 16(2-3), 151–178 (2005)
27. Pokahr, A., Braubach, L., Lamersdorf, W.: Jadex: Implementing a bdi-infrastructure for jade agents. EXP 3(3), 76–85 (2003)
28. Schillo, M., Fischer, K.: A taxonomy of autonomy in multiagent organisation. In: Nickles, M., Rovatsos, M., Weiss, G. (eds.) AUTONOMY 2003. LNCS (LNAI), vol. 2969, pp. 68–82. Springer, Heidelberg (2004)
29. Tinnemeier, N., Dastani, M., Meyer, J.-J.C.: Orwell's nightmare for agents? programming multi-agent organisations. In: Hindriks, K.V., Pokahr, A., Sardina, S. (eds.) PROMAS 2008. LNCS, vol. 5442, pp. 56–71. Springer, Heidelberg (2009)
30. van den Broek, E.L., Jonker, C.M., Sharpanskykh, A., Treur, J., Yolum, P.: Formal modeling and analysis of organizations. In: AAMAS Workshops, pp. 18–34 (2005)
31. van der Hoek, W., Hindriks, K., de Boer, F., Meyer, J.-J.C.: Agent programming in 3APL. Autonomous Agents and Multi-Agent Systems 2(4), 357–401 (1999)
32. Zambonelli, F., Jennings, N., Wooldridge, M.: Developing multiagent systems: The Gaia methodology. IEEE Transactions of Software Engineering and Methodology 12(3), 317–370 (2003)

# An Open Architecture for Service-Oriented Virtual Organizations

Adriana Giret, Vicente Julián, Miguel Rebollo, Estefanía Argente,
Carlos Carrascosa, and Vincente Botti

Dept. Sistemas Informáticos y Computación
Universidad Politécnica de Valencia
Camino de Vera s/n
46022 - Valencia, Spain
{agiret,vinglada,mrebollo,eargente,carrasco,vbotti}@dsic.upv.es

**Abstract.** Recent technological advances in open systems have imposed
new needs on multi-agent systems. Nowadays, open systems require open
autonomous scenarios in which heterogeneous entities (agents or services)
interact to fulfill the system goals. The main contribution of this paper is
the definition of an open architecture and computational model for large-
scale open multi-agent systems based on a service-oriented approach.
This work requires a high-level design of all features and needs for systems of this kind. The new proposed architecture, called THOMAS, is
specifically addressed for the design of virtual organizations. A simplified
example for the management of a travel agency system, which shows the
features of the proposal, is also included.

## 1  Introduction

The technological advances of recent years have defined the "new society", in
which a multi-agent system participates as an open environment in which het-
erogeneos entities (agents and services) interact. This new environment needs
to meet several requirements such as: distribution, constant evolution, flexibility to allow members enter or exit the society, appropriate management of the
organizational structure that defines the society, multi-device agent execution
including devices with limited resources, and so on. All these requirements define a set of features that can be addressed through the open system paradigm
and virtual organizations.

Regarding organizations, this paradigm has been conceived as an encouraging
solution for managing coordination and controlling agent behavior, specially in
open multi-agent systems [12]. Organization modeling not only allows describing structural composition (i.e. roles, agent groups, interaction patterns, role
relationships) and functional behavior (i.e. agent tasks, plans or services), but
also normative regulations for controlling agent behavior, dynamic entry/exit of
components and dynamic formation of agent groups.

Over recent years several works have appeared trying to solve the problem
of integrating the multi-agent system paradigm and the service-oriented computing paradigm. By integrating these two technologies it is possible to model

L. Braubach, J.-P. Briot, and J. Thangarajah (Eds.): ProMAS 2009, LNAI 5919, pp. 118–132, 2010.

autonomous and heterogeneous computational entities in dynamic and open environments. Such entities may be reactive, proactive and have the ability to communicate in a flexible way with other entities [29]. The *Agent and Web Services Interoperability* (AWSI) IEEE FIPA Working Group[1] proposes to create links, as a gateway, between the two approaches. In this paper, it is defined a new open multi-agent system architecture consisting of a related set of modules that are suitable for the development of systems applied in environments such as those raised above. This new architecture is called THOMAS (Me*TH*ods, Techniques and Tools for *O*pen *M*ulti-*A*gent *S*ystems). The proposed solution tries to communicate agents and web services in a transparent, but independent, way, going beyond related works, raising a total integration of both technologies. So agents can offer and invoke services in a transparent way to other agents or entities, as well as external entities can interact with THOMAS agents through the use of the offered services.

This paper is structured as follows: Section 2 presents the proposed architecture model. The description of the services offered by the THOMAS main components are described in Sections 3 and 4. Section 5 shows a simplified example of a travel agency in which the overall functioning of the THOMAS architecture can be observed. In Section 6, a prototype of THOMAS is overviewed. Section 7 presents a discussion on the features of the proposal related with state of the art works. Finally, the conclusions are presented.

## 2   THOMAS Architecture

THOMAS architecture basically consists of a set of modular services. Though THOMAS feeds initially on the FIPA architecture, it expands its capabilities to deal with organizations, and to boost up its services abilities. In this way, a new module in charge of managing organizations has been introduced into the architecture, along with a redefinition of the FIPA *Directory Facilitator* that is able to deal with services in a more elaborated way, following *Service Oriented Architectures* guidelines. As it has been stated before, services are very important in this architecture. In fact, agents have access to the THOMAS infrastructure through a range of services included on different modules or components. The main components of THOMAS are the following (Figure 1):

- *Service Facilitator* (SF), it offers simple and complex services to the active agents and organizations. Basically, its functionality is like a yellow page service and a service descriptor in charge of providing a green page service. The detailed description of this module is presented in Section 3.
- *Organization Management System* (OMS), it is mainly responsible of the management of the organizations and their entities. Thus, it allows creation and management of any organization. The OMS is described in Section 4.
- *Platform Kernel* (PK), it maintains basic management services for an agent platform. The PK represents any FIPA compliant platform. In this way,

---

[1] http://www.fipa.org/subgroups/AWSI-WG.html

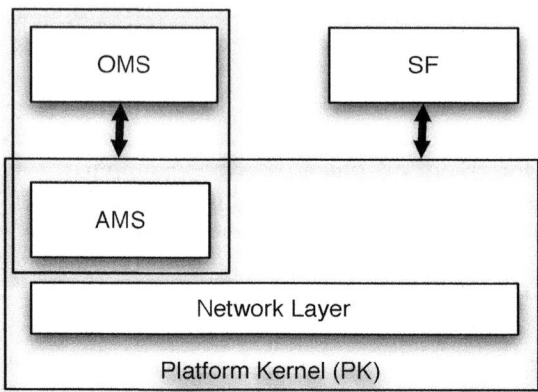

**Fig. 1.** THOMAS Architecture

THOMAS can be configured to work with any agent platform which implements the FIPA AMS and the FIPA communication network layer.

The following sections describe, in a deeper detail, the main components of the THOMAS architecture.

## 3   Service Facilitator

The Service Facilitator (SF) is a mechanism and support by which organizations and agents can offer and discover services. The SF provides a place in which the autonomous entities can register service descriptions as directory entries.

The SF acts as a gateway to access the THOMAS platform. It manages this access transparently, by means of security techniques and access rights management. The SF can find services searching for a given service profile or searching by the goals that can be fulfilled when executing the service. This is done using the matchmaking and service composition mechanisms that are provided by the SF. The SF also acts as a yellow pages manager and in this way it can find which entities provide a given service.

A service represents an interaction of two entities, which are modeled as communications among independent processes. Regarding service description, keywords or semantic annotations can be used. Languages as OWL-S[18], WSMO[25], SAWSDL[9] or WSDL-S[7] are the most used ones to describe services.

Furthermore, a service offers some capabilities, each of which enables fulfilling a given goal. Services are characterized by their inputs, outputs, preconditions and effects. Furthermore, there could be additional parameters in a service description, which are independent of the service functionality (non-functional parameters), such as quality of service, deadlines and security protocols. Taking into account that THOMAS works with semantic services, another important data is the ontology used in the service. Thus, when the service description is accessed, any entity will have all needed information in order to interact with the service and make an application that can use this service. Such a description can also be employed for pre-compiled services, in which the process model of the service is composed of the sequence of the elementary services that will be executed, instead of the internal processes of this service.

A service can be supplied by more than one provider in the system. In this way, a service has an associated list of providers. All providers can offer exact copies of the service, that is, they share a common implementation of the service. Or they may share only the interface and each provider may implement the service in a different way. This is easily achieved in THOMAS because the general service profile is separated from the service process.

A service is defined as a tuple $<sID, goal, prof, proc, ground, ont>$ where:

- $sID$ is an unique service identifier.
- $goal$ is a logical formula that describes the final purpose of the service, composed by a set of abstract concepts provided in the system's design. It provides a first abstraction level for service search and composition.
- $prof$ is the service profile that describes the service in terms of its IOPEs (Inputs, Outputs, Preconditions and Effects) and non-functional attributes, in a readable way for those agents that are searching information. Preconditions and effects (or postconditions) are also logical formulas.
- $proc$ specifies how to call a service and what happens when it is executed.
- $ground$ specifies in detail how an agent can access the service. A grounding specifies a communication protocol, the message formats, the contact port and other specific details of the service.
- $ont$ is the ontology that gives meaning to all the elements of the service. OWL-DL is the chosen language.

In THOMAS, services are described in OWL-S, which has been extended with goals and roles (client/provider) descriptions. The SF component also allows traditional OWL-S description for services, but in this case the service postcondition (or effect) is also employed as the service goal.

The tuple defined above for service specification is implemented in two parts: the *abstract service*, general for all providers; and the *concrete service*, with the implementation details. In this way, services are stored inside the system split into these two parts: the *service profile* (that represents the abstract service specification) and a set of *service processes specifications* (that detail the concrete service). Thus, in THOMAS services are implemented as the following tuple:

$<ServiceID, Providers, ServGoal, ServProfile>$
$Providers ::= <ProvIDList, ServImpID, ServProcess, ServGround>$ $^+$
$ProvIDList ::= ProviderID^+$

where:

**Table 1.** SF Services

| Service | Description |
|---|---|
| *Registration* | |
| **RegisterProfile**(?p:Profile, ?g:Goal) | Creates a new service description (*profile*) |
| **RegisterProcess**(?s:ID, ?pr:Process, ?gr:Grounding, ?prov:ID) | Creates a particular implementation (*process*) for a service |
| **ModifyProfile**(?s:ID, ?p:Profile, ?g:Goal) | Modifies an existing service profile |
| **ModifyProcess**(?sImp:ID, ?pr:Process, ?gr:Grounding) | Modifies an existing service process |
| **DeregisterProfile**(?s:ID) | Removes a service description |
| *Affordability* | |
| **AddProvider**(?sImp:ID, ?prov:ID) | Adds a new provider to an existing service process |
| **RemoveProvider**(?sImp:ID, ?prov:ID) | Removes a provider from a service process |
| *Discovery* | |
| **SearchService**(?pu:ServPurpose) | Searches a service (or a composition of services) that satisfies the user requirements |
| **GetProfile**(?s:ID) | Gets the description (profile) of an specific service |
| **GetProcess**(?sImp:ID) | Gets the implementation (process) of an specific service |

- *Providers* is a set of tuples composed of a *Providers identifier list* (ProvIDList), the service process model specification (*ServProcess*), and its particular instantiation (*ServGround*).
- *ProvIDList* maintains a list of service provider identifiers.

The SF supplies a set of standard services to manage the services provided by organizations or individual agents. These services can also be used by the rest of THOMAS components to advertise their own services. SF services can be classified in three types:

- *Registration*: for adding, modifying and removing services from the SF directory.
- *Affordability*: for managing the relation between providers and their services.
- *Discovery*: for searching and composing services as an answer to user requirements. Their functionality is so complex that they can be delegated to a specialized component.

The complete relation of the SF services can be found in Table 1.

The architecture does not provide with any special support for ontology management. Ontologies are taken into consideration in the service description itself, following the OWL-S specification and allowing the use of ontological concepts as the IOPEs of the services. Agents are responsible of dealing with the ontologies.

## 4   Organization Management System

The *Organization Management System (OMS)* is in charge of the organization life-cycle management, including specification and administration of both the structural components of the organization (roles, units and norms) and its execution components (participant agents and roles they play).

Organizations are structured by means of *organizational units* (OUs), which represent groups of entities (agents or other units), that are related in order to pursue a common goal. These OUs have an internal structure (i.e. hierarchical, team, plain), which imposes restrictions on agent relationships and control (ex. supervision or information relationships). OUs can also be seen as virtual meeting points because agents can dynamically enter and leave them by means of adopting (or leaving) roles inside. Roles represent all required functionality needed in order to achieve the unit goal. They might also have associated norms for controlling role actions. Agents can dynamically adopt roles inside units, so a control for role adoption is needed. Finally, services represent some functionality that agents offer to other entities, independently of the concrete agent that makes use of them.

The OMS keeps record on which are the Organizational Units of the system, the roles defined in each unit and their attributes, the entities participating inside each OU and the roles that they enact through time. Moreover, the OMS also stores which are the norms defined in the system. Regarding roles, the role attributes are: *accessibility*, that indicates whether a role can be adopted by an agent on demand; *visibility*, that indicates whether agents can obtain information from this role on demand; *position*, that indicates whether it is a supervisor, subordinate or simple member of the unit; and *inheritance*, that indicates which is its parent role, establishing a hierarchy of roles.

The OMS offers a set of services for organization life-cycle management, classified in (Table 2): (i) structural services, which modify the structural and normative organization specification; (ii) informative services, that provide information of the current state of the organization; and (iii) dynamic (role-management) services, which allow managing dynamic entry/exit of agents and role adoption.

The **structural services** deal with adding/deleting norms (*RegisterNorm, DeregisterNorm*), adding/deleting roles (*RegisterRole, DeregisterRole*) and creating new organizational units or deleting them (*RegisterUnit, DeregisterUnit*).

The **informative services** give specific information of the current state of the organization, detailing which are the roles defined in an OU (*InformUnitRoles*), the roles played by an agent (*InformAgentRoles*), the specific members that participate inside an OU (*InformMembers*), the number of members of an OU (*InformQuantity*), its internal structure (*InformUnit*), and the services and norms related with a specific role (*InformRoleProfiles, InformRoleNorms*).

The **dynamic services** allow defining how agents can adopt roles inside OUs (*AcquireRole, LeaveRole*) or how agents can be forced to leave a specific role (*Expulse*), normally due to sanctions.

By means of the publication of the *structural services*, the OMS allows the modification of some aspects related to the organization structure, functionality or normativity at execution time. For example, a specific agent of the organization can be allowed to add new norms, roles or units during system execution. These types of services should be restricted to the internal roles of the system, which have a level of permission high enough to these kinds of operations (i.e. supervisor role). Moreover, these services might not be published in the SF in some specific applications

Table 2. OMS Services

| Service | Description |
|---|---|
| *Structural Services* | |
| **RegisterRole**(?Role:ID, ?Unit:ID, ?Attr:Attributes) | Creates a new role within a unit, with specific attributes (visibility, accessibility, position, inheritance) |
| **RegisterNorm**(?Norm:ID, ?Role:ID, ?Content: NormContent, ?Issuer:ID, ?Defender:ID, ?Promoter:ID) | Includes a new norm within a unit, indicating its content (deontic value, conditions, actions and associated sanctions or rewards) |
| **RegisterUnit**(?Unit:ID, ?UnitType:Type, ?UnitGoal:Goal, [?UnitParent:ID]) | Creates a new unit within a specific organization, indicating its structure (type), goal and its parent inside the organization hierarchy |
| **DeregisterRole**(?Role:ID, ?Unit:ID) | Removes a specific role description from a unit |
| **DeregisterNorm**(?Norm:ID) | Removes a specific norm description |
| **DeregisterUnit**(?Unit:ID, [?UnitParent:ID]) | Removes a unit from an organization |
| *Informative Services* | |
| **InformAgentRole**(?Agent:ID) | Indicates roles adopted by an agent |
| **InformMembers**(?Unit:ID, [?Role:ID]) | Indicates entities that are members of a specific unit. Optionally, indicates only members playing the specific role inside that unit. |
| **QuantityMembers**(?Unit:ID, [?Role:ID]) | Provides the number of current members of a specific unit. Optionally, indicates only the number of members playing the specific role inside the unit |
| **InformUnit**(?Unit:ID) | Provides unit description |
| **InformUnitRoles**(?Unit:ID) | Indicates which roles are the ones defined within a specific unit |
| **InformRoleProfiles**(?Role:ID) | Indicates all profiles associated to a specific role |
| **InformRoleNorms**(?Role:ID) | Provides all norms addressed to a specific role |
| *Dynamic Services* | |
| **RegisterAgentRole**(?Agent:ID, ?Role:ID, ?Unit:ID) | Creates a new <*entity, unit, role*> relationship. Private OMS service. |
| **DeregisterAgentRole**(?Agent:ID, ?Role:ID, ?Unit:ID) | Removes a specific <*entity, unit, role*> relation. Private OMS service. |
| **AcquireRole**(?Unit:ID, ?Role:ID) | Requests the adoption of a specific role within a unit |
| **LeaveRole**(?Unit:ID, ?Role:ID) | Requests to leave a role |
| **Expulse**(?Agent:ID, ?Unit:ID, ?Role:ID) | Forces an agent to leave a specific role |

in which the system structure must not be dynamically modified. The *information services* might also be restricted to some internal roles of the system, as they provide with specific information of all the components of the organization.

The OMS offers a set of basic services for dynamical role adoption and the entry/exit of unit members, which are not directly accessible to agents, but are combined through compound services. The *basic services* for role adoption are *RegisterAgentRole* (that creates a new <*entity, unit, role*> relationship) and *DeregisterAgentRole* (that removes a specific <*entity, unit, role*> relationship). The OMS also offers a set of compound services that can be used by agents for adopting roles, leaving them and applying sanctions. These *compound services* are *AcquireRole*, *LeaveRole* and *Expulse*, detailed in Table 2. Publishing these services enables external agents to participate inside the system.

To sum up, the OMS is responsible for managing the life-cycle of the organizations. Thus, it includes services for defining structural components of organizations, i.e. roles, units and norms. These structural components could be dynamically modified over the lifetime of the organization. Moreover, it includes services for creating new organizations (i.e. creating new units), admitting new members within those organizations (i.e. acquiring roles) and member resigning (i.e. expulsing or leaving roles).

# 5  A Simplified Usage Sample

In order to illustrate the usage of the THOMAS architecture, a simplified case-study for making flight and hotel arrangements is used (a more complete specification can be downloaded from the project's web-page[2]). This is a well known example that has been modeled by means of electronic institutions in previous works [11,38]. The *Travel Agency* example is an application that facilitates the interconnection between clients (individuals, companies, travel agencies) and providers (hotel chains, airlines); delimiting services that each one can request or offer. The system controls which services must be provided by each agent. Internal functionality of these services is responsibility of provider agents. However, the system imposes some restrictions about service profiles, service requesting orders and service results.

The *Travel Agency* case-study has been modelled as a THOMAS organization composed of different agents that implement travel agency services. The *TravelAgency* unit is formed by two organizational units (*HotelUnit* and *FlightUnit*) which represent groups of agents, dedicated to hotels or flights, respectively. The *Customer* role requests system services and it is specialized into *HotelCustomer* and *FlightCustomer*. Similarly, the *Provider* role is in charge of performing services (hotel or flight search services) and it is also specialized into *HotelProvider* and *FlightProvider*. The *TravelAgency* unit offers a *SearchTravel* service, which is internally specialized into *SearchHotel* and *SearchFlight*. The visibility of these services is limited to the members of the *TravelAgency* unit.

The scenario depicted in Figure 2 shows the set of service calls for registering new agents as service clients inside the *TravelAgency* organization. A new client agent C1, already registered in the THOMAS platform, requests *SearchService* to SF for finding services of its interest (message 1). As a result, C1 obtains *SearchTravel* service identifier and a ranking value (message 2). Then, C1 employs *GetProfile* (message 3), which specifies that service clients must play *Customer* role inside the *TravelAgency* (message 4). Therefore, C1 must adopt the *Customer* role for demanding this service, requesting *AcquireRole* to OMS (messages 5 and 6).

Once C1 plays this customer role, it employs *GetProcess* service to know who are the service providers and how this service can be requested (message 7). However, there are none providers for the general *SearchTravel* service (message 8). Inside the *TravelAgency* unit, C1 requests *SearchService* again (message 9). In this case, SF returns *SearchFlight* and *SearchHotel* services because both services are accessible from the *TravelAgency* organization. Then C1 demands the profile of *SearchHotel* service (using *GetProfile*, message 11), since this service is more appropriated to its needs. Taking into account the *SearchHotel* profile (message 12), C1 requests adopting *HotelCustomer* role inside *HotelUnit*, demading the *AcquireRole* service to the OMS (messages 13 and14). The OMS checks all restrictions (ex. role compatibility, norms related to the requested role) and registers the <*C1,HotelUnit, HotelCustomer*> relationship.

---

[2] http://www.dsic.upv.es/users/ia/sma/tools/Thomas

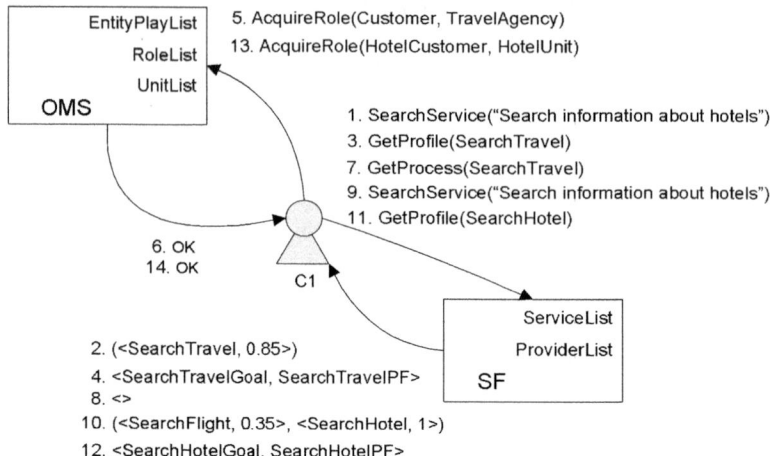

EntityPlayList
RoleList
UnitList
OMS

5. AcquireRole(Customer, TravelAgency)
13. AcquireRole(HotelCustomer, HotelUnit)

1. SearchService("Search information about hotels")
3. GetProfile(SearchTravel)
7. GetProcess(SearchTravel)
9. SearchService("Search information about hotels")
11. GetProfile(SearchHotel)

6. OK
14. OK

C1

ServiceList
ProviderList
SF

2. (<SearchTravel, 0.85>)
4. <SearchTravelGoal, SearchTravelPF>
8. <>
10. (<SearchFlight, 0.35>, <SearchHotel, 1>)
12. <SearchHotelGoal, SearchHotelPF>

**Fig. 2.** A client registering scenario of a Travel Agency system

## 6    The THOMAS Framework: A Prototype

Nowadays, a new agent platform based on the above described THOMAS abstract architecture is available. But, as this abstract architecture has been designed to work making use of any FIPA-compliant platform (as the Platform Kernel of the architecture) a new idea has arisen: the THOMAS Framework. This framework is composed by the OMS and SF modules of the abstract architecture, and its purpose is to try to obtain a product wholly independent of any internal agent platform, and as such, that is fully addressed for open systems. This framework is based upon the idea that no internal agent exists, and the architecture services are offered as web services. In this way, only the OMS and the SF are composing such framework (avoiding the use of the PK due to the lack of internal agents to control). Thus, the THOMAS framework (Figure 3) allows any agent to create a virtual organization with the structure and norms he wants, along with the demanding and offering services that he needs. The framework is in charge of the management of this organization structure, norms and life cycle, on one hand. On the other hand, it also controls the visibility of the offered and demanded services and the fulfillment of the conditions to use them. But, as it is fully addressed to open systems, the framework does not control the involved agents life-cycle, being all of them external to it.

The first version of this framework, v0.1, is available for download in the project's web-page. It implements the whole set of services described in the abstract architecture, with a basic support for norm management. This version has been used to check the feasibility of this approach with several examples using JADE and SPADE [16] agents.

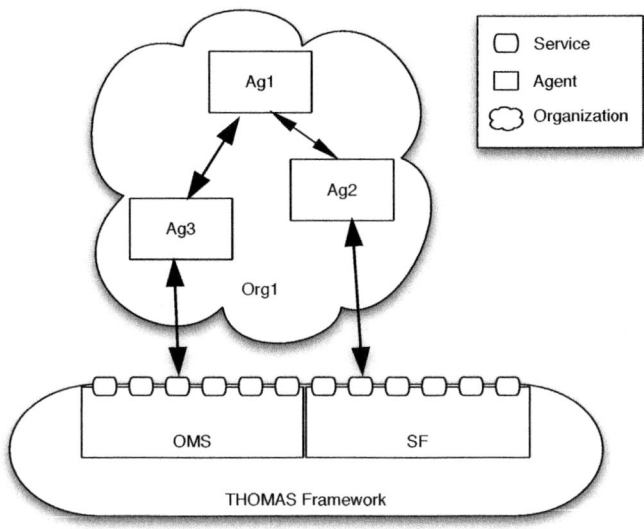

**Fig. 3.** THOMAS Framework

# 7   Discussion and Related Works

In previous sections an abstract architecture for the development of open MAS
has been proposed. This proposal aims to instigate the total integration of two
promising technologies, that is, multi-agent systems and service-oriented computing as the foundation of such virtual organizations. Both technologies try
to deal with the same kind of environments formed by loose-coupled, flexible,
persistent and distributed tasks [30]. Traditional web services, or even semantic
web services, might be a valid solution when point-to-point integration of static-
binded services is needed. But they are clearly not good enough for working
in a changing environment, in which new services appear, have to be discov-
ered and composed or adapted to different ontologies. The nature of agents,
as intelligent and flexible entities with auto-organizative capabilities, facilitates
automatic service discovery and composition. The vision of agents and organizations as service-provider entities is not new. The main effort in the integration
of agents and web services is directed at masking services for redirection, aggre-
gation, integration or administration purposes [23].

We can identify two approaches in previous related works: (i) direct integration of web services and agents by means of message exchange and (ii) the
consideration of agents as matchmakers for service discovering and composition.
Works related with the former are the *Web Service Integration Gateway Service*
(WSIG) architecture [24] and *AgentWeb Gateway* [37] which are based on the
idea of using an intermediary entity between agents and web services. Another
examples are *WSDL2JADE* [40] and *WS2JADE* [34] which provide agents with

an interface for communicating directly with web services. Finally, *Web Service Agent Integration*[3] (WSAI) solves the problem in the opposite way by allowing web service clients to use agent services.

The latter approach is represented by works such as [6], which complements the existing methods by considering the types of interactions and roles that services can be used in. Other approaches, such as [36], use the objective experience data of agents in order to evaluate their expectations from a service provider and make decisions using their own criteria and mental state. [39] presents a brokering protocol which consists of two complex reasoning tasks: discovery and mediation. Negotiation protocols are other mechanisms normally used. In this case, participant agents negotiate about the properties of the services they request and provide to bind agreements and contracts with each other [10]. Our proposal goes beyond because agents can offer and invoke services in a transparent way from other agents, virtual organizations or entities, and external entities can interact with agents by using the offered services.

Regarding organizational concepts in an open MAS system, we consider an agent organization as a social entity composed of a specific number of members which accomplish several distinct tasks or functions. These members are structured following some specific topology and communication interrelationship in order to achieve the main aim of the organization [3]. Agent organizations assume the existence of global goals, outside of the objectives of any individual agent, and they exist independently of agents [12].

Organizations have been usefully employed as a paradigm for developing agent systems [4,20]. One of the advantages of the organization development is that systems are modeled with a high level of abstraction, so the conceptual gap between real world and models is reduced. Also, these systems provide facilities to implement open systems and heterogeneous member participation [33].

Research into MAS organizations has ranged from basic organizational concepts, such as groups, communities, roles, functions [31,41,19,35,21]; organizational modeling [27,14,19,15]; Human Organization Theory [22,2]; structural topologies [26,3]; to normative research, including norms internal representation [32], deontic logics [13,5] and institutional approaches [17]. Our work presents an approach covering all the life-cycle management of an agent organization through the use of the OMS entity, which is in charge of specifying and administrating all the structural and dynamic components of an agent organization.

Finally, another key problem for open MAS development is the existence of real agent platforms that support organizational concepts. Over the last few years, many agent platforms and agent architectures have been proposed. A detailed comparison of these platforms, focusing on organizational concepts, can be found in [1]. Despite the large number of agent platforms in existence, the majority are lacking in the management of virtual organizations for dynamic, open and large-scale environments. Designers must implement nearly all of the organizational features by themselves, namely organization representation, control mechanisms, organization descriptions, AMS and DF extensions, communication layer, monitoring,

---

[3] http://www.agentcities.org/rec/00006/actf-rec-00006a.pdf

organization modeling support and organizational API. These features are briefly explained as follows.

With respect to *organization representation*, a possible solution is that agents have an explicit representation of the organization which has been defined. This paper deals with this approach as S-Moise+ [28] and AMELI (EI platform) [17]. They have an explicit representation of the organization and both have similar architectures. Another feature well supported by *AMELI* and *S-Moise+* are *control mechanisms* that ensure the satisfaction of the organizational constraints. The organization should have an available *description* in a standard language. This allows external and internal agents to get specific information about the organization at run-time. This feature is not only useful in open systems, but also when considering a reorganization process. A good example of organization specification can be found in the *S-Moise+* platform.

One of the main lacks in current agent platforms is the *AMS and DF extension*. The AMS should have information on the existing organizations and their members. The DF should publish the services offered by agents individually and the services offered by organizations. Another important features are: the *communication layer*, as the kind of communication layer used in communicative acts is a very important feature; the *system monitoring*, i.e. the platform should offer a mechanism for monitoring the states of agents and organizations; the *modeling concepts support*, as the platform and the programming language should cover all of the concepts related to the virtual organization. For example, which types of topologies are defined within the platform, which kind of norms are modeled, etc. Not all platforms have a complete modeling concept support. For example *AMELI* is focused on the management of rules and norms but does not support the definition of complex topologies. *Jack Teams* platform allows the creation of composed "Teams" but it does not take into account other topologies.

Finally, the platform should offer an *organizational API* that makes it possible to create, destroy and modify organizations; consult and modify the organization description; add, query and delete agents of an organization; send messages to a whole organization, etc [3,8]. Our proposal includes a platform fully addressed for open systems which has in mind all these factors trying to obtain a framework wholly independent of any internal agent platform.

# 8   Conclusions

The main contribution of this paper is the definition of an open architecture for large scale open multi-agent systems based on a service-oriented approach. As the previous mentioned discussion has shown, there exists a current research interest in the integration of agents and services, agents being complex entities that can handle the problem of service discovery and composition in dynamic and changing open environments. Moreover, current agent approaches are not organized into plain societies, but into structured organizations that enclose the real world with the society representation and ease the development of open and heterogeneous systems. Current agent architectures and platforms must integrate these concepts to allow designers to employ higher abstractions when modeling and implementing these complex systems. All of these concerns are gathered in the previously presented THOMAS proposal.

The framework presented in this paper is a particular implementation of THOMAS abstract architecture, in which the OMS and the SF modules are implemented as centralized entities. Nevertheless, the THOMAS approach may be implemented in a distributed fashion, with federated OMS and SF entities. This is an ongoing work we are developing in order to deal with large-scale open real case studies with full distribution of OMS and SF services.

Moreover, there is a new idea of providing a platform-independent set of services in a framework to manage virtual organizations for open systems that has been implemented and is available for downloading in the project's web-page.

## Acknowledgments

This work has been partially funded by TIN2008-04446, TIN2006-14630-C03-01, PROMETEO/2008/051, and GVPRE/2008/070 projects and CONSOLIDER-INGENIO 2010 under grant CSD2007-00022.

## References

1. Argente, E., Giret, A., Valero, S., Julian, V., Botti, V.: Survey of MAS Methods and Platforms focusing on organizational concepts. In: Vitria, J., Radeva, P., Aguilo, I. (eds.) Recent Advances in Artificial Intelligence Research and Development. Frontiers in Artificial Intelligence and Applications, pp. 309–316 (2004)
2. Argente, E., Julian, V., Botti, V.: Multi-agent system development based on organizations. Electronic Notes in Theoretical Computer Science 150, 55–71 (2006)
3. Argente, E., Palanca, J., Aranda, G., Julian, V., Botti, V., García-Fornes, A., Espinosa, A.: Supporting agent organizations. In: Burkhard, H.-D., Lindemann, G., Verbrugge, R., Varga, L.Z. (eds.) CEEMAS 2007. LNCS (LNAI), vol. 4696, pp. 236–245. Springer, Heidelberg (2007)
4. Boissier, O., Padget, J., Dignum, V., Lindemann, G., Matson, E., Ossowski, S., Sichman, J., Vazquez-Salceda, J.: ANIREM 2005 and OOOP 2005. LNCS (LNAI), vol. 3913, pp. 25–26. Springer, Heidelberg (2006)
5. Broersen, J., Dignum, F., Dignum, V., Meyer, J.: Designing a deontic logic for deadlines. In: Lomuscio, A., Nute, D. (eds.) DEON 2004. LNCS (LNAI), vol. 3065, pp. 43–56. Springer, Heidelberg (2004)
6. Caceres, C., Fernandez, A., Ossowski, S., Vasirani, M.: Role-based service description and discovery. In: International Joint Conference on Autonomous Agents and Multi-Agent Systems (2006)
7. W. W. W. Consortium. Web service semantics - wsdl-s, http://www.w3.org/Submission/WSDL-S/
8. Criado, N., Argente, E., Julian, V., Botti, V.: Organizational services for spade agent platform. In: Proc. 6th International Workshop on Practical Applications on Agents and Multi-Agent Systems, IWPAAMS 2007 (2007)
9. Martin, M.P.D., Wagner, M.: Towards semantic annotations of web services: Owl-s from the sawsdl perspective (2007)

10. Dang, J., Hungs, M.: Concurrent multiple-issue negotiation for internet-based services. IEEE Internet Computing 10(6), 42–49 (2006)
11. Dignum, F., Dignum, V., Thangarajah, J., Padgham, L., Winikoff, M.: Open Agent Systems? In: Luck, M., Padgham, L. (eds.) Agent-Oriented Software Engineering VIII. LNCS, vol. 4951, pp. 73–87. Springer, Heidelberg (2008)
12. Dignum, V., Dignum, F.: A landscape of agent systems for the real world. Technical report 44-cs-2006-061, Institute of Information and Computing Sciences, Utrecht University (2006)
13. Dignum, V., Dignum, F.: A logic for agent organization. In: Proc. FAMAS@Agents 2007 (2007)
14. Dignum, V., Meyer, J., Weigand, H., Dignum, F.: An organization-oriented model for agent societies. In: Lindemann, G., Moldt, D., Paolucci, M. (eds.) RASTA 2002. LNCS (LNAI), vol. 2934, pp. 31–50. Springer, Heidelberg (2004)
15. Dignum, V., Vazquez-Salceda, J., Dignum, F.: Omni: Introducing social structure, norms and ontologies into agent organizations. In: Bordini, R.H., Dastani, M.M., Dix, J., El Fallah Seghrouchni, A. (eds.) PROMAS 2004. LNCS (LNAI), vol. 3346, pp. 181–198. Springer, Heidelberg (2005)
16. Escrivà, M., Palanca, J., Aranda, G., García-Fornes, A., Julian, V., Botti, V.: A jabber-based multi-agent system platform. In: Proc. of AAMAS 2006, pp. 1282–1284 (2006)
17. Esteva, M., Rodriguez-Aguilar, J., Sierra, C., Arcos, J., Garcia, P.: On the Formal Specification of Electronic Institutions. In: Sierra, C., Dignum, F.P.M. (eds.) AgentLink 2000. LNCS (LNAI), vol. 1991, pp. 126–147. Springer, Heidelberg (2001)
18. Martin, D., et al.: Owl-s: Semantic markup for web services (2004), http://www.w3.org/Submission/2004/OWL-S
19. Ferber, J., Gutknecht, O.: A meta-model for the analysis and design of organizations in multi-agent systems. In: Proceedings of the Third International Conference on Multi-Agent Systems (ICMAS 1998), pp. 128–135. IEEE Computer Society, Los Alamitos (1998)
20. Ferber, J., Gutknecht, O., Michel, F.: From Agents to Organizations: an Organizational View of Multi-Agent Systems. In: Giorgini, P., Müller, J.P., Odell, J.J. (eds.) AOSE 2003. LNCS, vol. 2935, pp. 214–230. Springer, Heidelberg (2004)
21. Gasser, L.: Perspective on Organizations in Multi-Agent Systems, pp. 1–16. Springer, Heidelberg (2001)
22. Giorgini, P., Kolp, M., Mylopoulos, J.: Multi-agent architectures as organizational structures. Autonomous Agents and Multi-Agent Systems 13(1), 3–25 (2006)
23. Greenwood, D., Calisti, M.: Engineering web service - agent integration. In: IEEE International Conference on Systems, Man and Cybernetics, vol. 2, pp. 1918–1925 (2004)
24. Greenwood, D., Lyell, M., Mallya, A., Suguri, H.: The IEEE FIPA approach to integrating software agents and web services. In: AAMAS 2007: Proceedings of the 6th international joint conference on Autonomous agents and multiagent systems, pp. 1–7. ACM, New York (2007)
25. Lausen, A.P.H., Roman, D.: Web service modeling ontology (wsmo) (2005), http://www.w3.org/Submission/WSMO/
26. Horling, B., Lesser, V.: A survey of multiagent organizational paradigms. The Knowledge Engineering Review 19, 281–316 (2004)
27. Horling, B., Lesser, V.: Using ODML to Model Multi-Agent Organizations. In: IAT 2005: Proceedings of the IEEE/WIC/ACM International Conference on Intelligent Agent Technology (2005)

28. Hubner, J., Sichman, J., Boissier, O.: S-Moise+: A middleware for developing organised multi-agent systems. In: Boissier, O., Padget, J., Dignum, V., Lindemann, G., Matson, E., Ossowski, S., Sichman, J.S., Vázquez-Salceda, J. (eds.) ANIREM 2005 and OOOP 2005. LNCS (LNAI), vol. 3913, pp. 64–78. Springer, Heidelberg (2006)
29. Huhns, M., Singh, M.: Reseach directions for service-oriented multiagent systems. IEEE Internet Computing, Service-Oriented Computing Track 9(1) (2005)
30. Huhns, M., Singh, M.: Service-oriented computing: Key concepts and principles. IEEE Internet Computing, Service-Oriented Computing Track 9(1) (2005)
31. Jennings, N.R., Wooldridge, M.: Agent-oriented software engineering. In: Handbook of Agent Technology (2002)
32. Lopez, F., Luck, M., d'Inverno, M.: A normative framework for agent-based systems. Computational and Mathematical Organization Theory 12, 227–250 (2006)
33. Mao, X., Yu, E.: Organizational and social concepts in agent oriented software engineering. In: Odell, J.J., Giorgini, P., Müller, J.P. (eds.) AOSE 2004. LNCS, vol. 3382, pp. 184–202. Springer, Heidelberg (2005)
34. Nguyen, T., Kowalczyk, R.: Ws2jade: Integrating web service with jade agents. Technical Report SUTICT-TR2005.03, Centre for Intelligent Agents and Multi-Agent Systems, Swinburne University of Technology (2005)
35. Odell, J., Nodine, M., Levy, R.: A Metamodel for Agents, Roles, and Groups. In: Odell, J.J., Giorgini, P., Müller, J.P. (eds.) AOSE 2004. LNCS, vol. 3382, pp. 78–92. Springer, Heidelberg (2005)
36. Sensoy, M., Pembe, C., Zirtiloglu, H., Yolum, P., Bener, A.: Experience-based service provider selection in agent-mediated e-comerce. In: Engineering Applications of Artificial Intelligence, vol. 3, pp. 325–335 (2007)
37. Shafiq, M.O., Ali, A., Ahmad, H.F., Suguri, H.: Agentweb gateway - a middleware for dynamic integration of multi agent system and web services framework. In: 14th IEEE International Workshops on Enabling Technologies (WETICE 2005), Linköping, Sweden, June 13-15, pp. 267–270. IEEE Computer Society, Los Alamitos (2005)
38. Sierra, C., Thangarajah, J., Padgham, L., Winikoff, M.: Designing Institutional Multi-Agent System. In: Padgham, L., Zambonelli, F. (eds.) AOSE VII / AOSE 2006. LNCS, vol. 4405, pp. 84–103. Springer, Heidelberg (2007)
39. Sycara, K., Paolucci, M., Soudry, J., Srinivasan, N.: Dynamic discovery and coordination of agent-based semantic web services. IEEE Internet Computing 8(3), 66–73 (2004)
40. Varga, L.Z., Hajnal, Á.: Engineering web service invocations from agent systems. In: Mařík, V., Müller, J.P., Pěchouček, M. (eds.) CEEMAS 2003. LNCS (LNAI), vol. 2691, pp. 626–635. Springer, Heidelberg (2003)
41. Zambonelli, F., Parunak, H.: From design to intention: Signs of a revolution. In: Proc. 1st Int. Joint Conference on Autonomous Agents and MultiAgent Systems, pp. 455–456 (2002)

# Formalising the Environment in MAS Programming: A Formal Model for Artifact-Based Environments

Alessandro Ricci, Mirko Viroli, and Michele Piunti

DEIS, Alma Mater Studiorum – Università di Bologna
via Venezia 52, 47023 Cesena, Italy
{a.ricci,mirko.viroli,michele.piunti}@unibo.it

**Abstract.** Although the role of *environment* in designing and engineering Multi-Agent Systems (MAS) has been largely acknowledged and explored in literature, no formal model has been developed so far to rigorously define the main features of environment in the context of MAS *programming*, in particular to be integrated and exploited with existing agent programming languages/frameworks and related formalisations. Accordingly, in this paper we present a formalisation of a general-purpose model for environment programming, based on the notion of *artifact* as introduced in the A&A meta-model and implemented by the CArtAgO framework. Although based on the A&A meta-model, we argue that the model can be useful to understand and analyse aspects that are important for environment programming in general.

## 1  Introduction

*Environment programming* in Multi-Agent System (MAS) accounts for considering the computational environment where agents are situated a *first-class abstraction* that can be used in MAS design and programming [6]. The background idea is that the environment can be an effective place where to encapsulate functionalities for MAS, in particular those that concern the management of agent interactions and coordination [12]. This turns out to be useful for defining and enacting into the environment strategies for MAS coordination, organisation, and security—the interested readers can find in [13] a survey of works endorsing this viewpoint[1].

By adopting this viewpoint, a main issue concerns the availability of general-purpose computational models, languages and frameworks to program the environment as part of the MAS, integrated with agent programming. This would allow MAS developers to use the agent abstraction to program those parts of the systems that are responsible to accomplish tasks with a certain level of autonomy, pro-activeness and reactivity, and use environmental abstractions to program those parts of the system that are functional to agents, i.e. that provide some kind of functionality that can be exploited by agents to do their works. A straightforward metaphor comes from human cooperative environments, which contain *tools* properly designed to be exploited by humans to achieve

---

[1] This sums up the the results of three years of E4MAS (Environment for Multi-Agent System) workshop, held at AAMAS from 2004 to 2006.

L. Braubach, J.-P. Briot, and J. Thangarajah (Eds.): ProMAS 2009, LNAI 5919, pp. 133–150, 2010.
© Springer-Verlag Berlin Heidelberg 2010

their individual and cooperative tasks. In MAS, CArtAgO [6] framework originally introduced this perspective. Another framework that promotes a similar viewpoint is GOLEM [3].

Besides implementations, the availability of abstract models describing in a rigorous way the main features and properties of such environments becomes essential to understand how they could be suitably integrated with agent programming languages and frameworks, and what are the properties of the resulting MAS programming model in the overall. Existing formalisations – accounted in Section 6 – have not been devised for being exploited in the context of MAS programming and to be easily integrated with agent programming languages and related formalisations.

Accordingly, in this paper we present a formalisation of a general-purpose model for environment programming, based on the notion of *artifact* as introduced by the A&A (Agents and Artifacts) meta-model [5] and implemented by CArtAgO framework. Although based on the A&A meta-model, we believe that the model is useful to understand aspects that characterise any general-purpose environment model used in MAS programming. These aspects include *(a)* agent-environment interaction model, in particular the action and perception model adopted, which greatly impacts on the functionalities related to agent coordination that can be encapsulated in the environment; *(b)* environment computational behaviour, which impacts on the type of computational works that can be embedded inside the environment, and *(c)* environment topology and distribution, which impacts on the overall MAS distribution.

The remainder of the paper is organized as follows: in Section 2 we provide a brief overview of the basic concepts and features of artifact-based environments, identifying the essential elements that we will include in the abstract formal model. After that, in the two following sections we describe the model by first defining the structures involved (Section 3) and then their dynamics (Section 4). Then, in Section 5 we outline some basic properties and features of artifact-based environments and environment programming in general. Finally, in Section 6 we provide an overview of related works and in Section 7 concluding remarks.

## 2   Basic Concepts

### 2.1   Environment Programming with Artifacts

The approach considered in this paper is based on the A&A (Agents and Artifacts) meta-model [5,7] and related CArtAgO framework/infrastructure [6,8]. In A&A, a programmable environment for a MAS is conceived as set of distributed *workspaces*, each one representing a locality containing a dynamic set of computational entities called *artifacts*. From the agent viewpoint, artifacts are *first-class entities* of their world, representing resources and tools that they can dynamically instantiate, share and use to support individual and collective activities. From the MAS designer/programmer viewpoint, artifacts are *first-class abstractions* to shape the environment, defining the type of functional bricks that agents will exploit at runtime, providing functionalities, for instance, to mediate and empower agent interaction and coordination, or wrap external resources. On the topology side, workspaces can be used to structure and organise the overall MAS; agents can work simultaneously in multiple workspaces, which can be distributed among different nodes of the network.

In order to be used by agents, artifacts expose a *usage interface* listing a set of *operations* that agents can execute so as to exploit artifact functionalities. Operation execution can be composed by a single computational step or being a process involving multiple steps. Besides operations, artifacts can have a set of *observable properties*, that are attributes that can be observed by agents as environment percepts (without to need ot executing operations). The value of an observable property can change dynamically, as result of operations execution. By executing an operation an artifact can generate *signals*, i.e. observable events – not persistent, as in the case of observable properties – which can be perceived by agents *observing* the artifact. So, differently from the interaction models based on agent communication languages and speech-act theories, the interaction model defining agent-artifact interaction is based on *use* and *observation*: agents use artifacts by acting on their usage interface so as to execute operations, and by perceiving observable events generated by artifact and observable properties that constitute artifact observable state. Then, artifacts can be *linked* (connected) together by agents, so as to create complex artifacts as a composition of simpler ones. To this end, an artifact may have a *link interface*, exposing operations that can be triggered by artifacts linked to it. Finally, an artifact can be equipped with a *manual*, i.e. a machine-readable document describing what are functionalities provided by artifact and how to exploit them.

In the overall the artifact abstraction reminds the object (class) abstraction in Object-Oriented Programming, re-conceptualised and extended with further features as so as to be exploited in agent-oriented programs at the agent level of abstraction.

## 2.2 CArtAgO API

CArtAgO (Common Artifact infrastructure for Agent Open environment) is a framework and infrastructure providing *(a)* a set of Java-based API to program artifacts and run artifact-based environments and *(b)* an agent API on the agent side, including a basic set of actions for creating and interacting with artifacts, and for managing and joining workspace. The API can be exploited by existing agent programming languages/frameworks to leverage CArtAgO environments.

Just to have a taste of the API, here we report a very simple example, composed by two agents – programmed using the *Jason* platform [2], so based on the AgentSpeak(L) language – working with a shared *counter* artifact. The counter artifact (see Fig. 1) has a single observable property, count, and a single operation inc that increments the property and also generates a tick signal. The Java-based artifact definition is shown in Fig. 1, on the right—the full explanation of the API is beyond the scope of this paper: the interested reader can find it in [6,8], along with more complex examples that fully exploit artifact features.

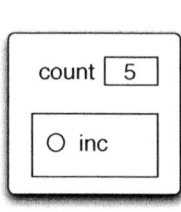

```
import alice.cartago.*;

public class Counter extends Artifact {

    void init(){
        defineObsProperty("count",0);
    }

    @OPERATION void inc(){
        int count = getObsProperty("count").intValue();
        updateObsProperty("count",count+1);
        signal("tick");
    }
}
```

**Fig. 1.** Definition of a simple artifact functioning as counter using CArtAgO API

```
// user agent                          // observer agent

// initial goal                        // initial goal
!create_and_use.                       !discover_and_observe.

// plans                               // plans
+!create_and_use : true <-             +!discover_and_observe : true <-
  cartago.makeArtifact("counter","Counter",C);  cartago.lookupArtifact("counter",C).
  cartago.use(C,inc);                    cartago.focus(C).
  cartago.use(C,inc);
  cartago.observeProperty(C,count(V));  +tick [source("counter")] : true <-
  cartago.use(console,                    cartago.use(console,println("tick. ").
    println("Final count value: ", V)).
                                        +count(V) [artifact("counter")] : true <-
                                          cartago.use(console,println("count:  ",V)).
```

**Fig. 2.** Two *Jason* agents sharing and working with the counter: a user agent creating and using the counter (on the left), an observer agent locating and observing the artifact (on the right)

The AgentSpeak(L) source code of the two simple agents sharing and working with the counter artifact is reported in Fig. 2[2]. The first agent (Fig. 2, left) simply creates a Counter artifact called counter and interacts with it by executing twice the

---

[2] An agent program in *Jason* is defined by an initial set of beliefs, representing agent's initial knowledge about the world, a set of goals, and a set of plans that the agent can dynamically instantiate and execute to achieve such goals. Agent plans are described by rules of the type Event : Context <- Body (the syntax is Prolog like), where Event represents the specific event triggering the plan – examples are the addition of a new belief (+b), a goal (+!g), the perception of an observable event generated by an artifact (+ev [source(?Art)]), the perception of an update of an artifact observable property, (+p [artifact(?Art)]). The plan context is a logic formula on the belief base – a belief formula – asserting the conditions under which the plan can be executed. The plan body includes basic actions to create subgoals to be achieved (!g), to update agent inner state – such as adding a new belief +b – and to work with artifacts (provided by the integration with CArtAgO). CArtAgO actions – which are prefixed by "cartago." – include use, to execute an operation on an artifact, focus, to start observing a specific artifact, makeArtifact to create a new artifact, and lookupArtifact to get artifact unique identifier given its name.

inc operation and finally printing on the `console` artifact[3] the value of the observable property `count`, retrieved by means of the `observeProperty` action. The agent has an initial goal `create_and_use`. A plan to achieve the goal is specified, which is triggered by the `+!create_and_use` goal addition event. The second agent (Fig. 2, right) acts as a pure observer, first locating and then focussing the `counter` artifact so as to be aware of signals that the artifact generates (tick in this case) and of the changes to the observable properties (count in this case). By focussing an artifact, observable properties are mapped into beliefs of the agent, annotated with `source(percept)` annotation, which are automatically updated as soon as the value of observable properties changes. Also signals are mapped onto beliefs, annotated with `source(ArtName)`. As soon as the agent perceives a new value for the `count` observable property, it prints a message about the new value on standard output by exploiting the `console` artifact. A message is printed also as soon as the agent perceive a signal, `tick` in this case.

### 2.3   Defining an Abstract Formal Model

Our interest in this paper is to define an abstract model including those core aspects that are necessary to explain and rigorously define mechanisms and features for MAS programming that result from programming the environment. To this end, we formalise a single workspace, focussing on two basic aspects: the agent-environment *interaction model*, i.e. how agents use the environment, which means in our case how agents act upon artifacts to execute operations and perceive their observable properties and events; the environment *computational model*, which means how the computational behaviour of artifacts works and what are the related properties useful for MAS programming. In the model we will not include the manual since it is not necessary to define these two aspects.

We chose a formalisation based on state transition systems. We model a workspace as a transition system $(W, \longrightarrow)$, where $W$ is the set of states representing all the possible configurations of that a workspace can assume, and $\longrightarrow \subseteq W \times W$ is a binary relation over $W$, describing how the workspace evolves from configuration to configuration, given the computational behaviour of agents and the environment. We use the infix notation $w \longrightarrow w'$ to denote that $(w, w') \in \longrightarrow$.

This formalisation is used mainly to capture the essential structures involved in the two aspects mentioned above and their dynamics, on the one side abstracting from the concrete implementation (CArtAgO technology in this case and related bridges with agent platforms), and, on the other side, including all those aspects that – we argue – are essential for environment programming in practice.

## 3   Structures

We first describe the structure of the states of the transition systems, which correspond to workspace configurations. In the following, we use symbols starting with an uppercase to denote sets.

---

[3] An instance of `console` artifact is available in each workspace and it is useful to print messages to standard output.

**Definition 1** *(Workspace configuration).* A workspace configuration is represented by a tuple

$$\langle Ag, Ar, Om \rangle$$

where $Ag$ is a set of agents, $Ar$ is a set of artifacts, $Om$ is the *observability* map, tracking who (agent) is observing what (artifact).

**Definition 2** *(agent configuration).* An agent configuration $ag \in Ag$ is represented by a tuple:

$$\langle ag_{id}, ag_s, Ev, ag_{pr} \rangle$$

where $ag_{id}$ is the agent unique identifier, $ag_s$ is the agent internal state – here we abstract from its specific structure – $Ev$ is ordered set of environment events collected in current agent execution cycle (described in Section 4), and finally $ag_{pr}$ defines the agent computational behaviour—we refer to it as "agent program" even if it includes aspects that concern both the program and the architecture of the agent.

Environment events $ev \in Ev$ are represented by tuples $\langle ev_t, ev_v \rangle$ with information about the type of the event and the value. The possible types are:

- action completed or failed – $ev_t \in \{\text{action\_completed}, \text{action\_failed}\}$, $ev_v = \langle ac, ac_{fb} \rangle$ carrying information about the action that has completed/failed and an action *feedback*, i.e. information resulting from action execution;
- new observable property observed (event generated when a new artifact property is observable to the agent) – $ev_t = \text{new\_prop}$, $ev_v = \langle ar_{id}, p_n, p_v \rangle$ including the identifier of the artifact, the name of the observable property and its value;
- observable property updated (event generated every time a property currently observed by the agent changes its value) – $ev_t = \text{prop\_updated}$, $ev_v = \langle ar_{id}, p_n, p_v \rangle$ including the identifier of the artifact, the name of the observable property and its new value;
- property no more observed (event generated when an artifact property is not more observable to the agent) – $ev_t = \text{prop\_nomore\_obs}$, $ev_v = \langle ar_{id}, p_n \rangle$ including the identifier of the artifact and the name of the observable property;
- signal generated by an artifact – $ev_t = \text{signal}$, $ev_v = \langle ar_{id}, s \rangle$ including the identifier of the artifact and the signal $s = \langle s_t, s_v \rangle$, including information about the type and value of the signal.

The agent program is modelled as a function:

$$ag_{pr} : \text{Ags} \times \text{Ev} \rightarrow \text{Ags} \times (\text{Ac} \cup \bot)$$

which, given the current state of the agent $ag_s \in \text{Ags}$ and current event set $Ev \in \text{Ev}$, computes the new state of the agent $ag'_{st} \in \text{Ags}$ and the action to do $ac \in \text{Ac} \cup \bot$. The value $ac = \bot$ is used to represent those situations in which no action is chosen.

**Remark.** Actions are not modelled as single events – as typically happens in agent programming language – but as a sequence of events (causing atomic transitions inside the system), the first when the action is done and start its execution, and the last concerning action completion (or failure).

**Definition 3** *(artifact configuration).*  An artifact configuration $ar \in Ar$ is represented by a tuple:

$$\langle ar_{id}, I, P, V, Li, O, Li_{req}, ar_{pr} \rangle$$

Besides the artifact identifier $ar_{id}$, the configuration includes the main elements that characterise artifacts as environmental abstractions:

- *Interface for agent action:* $I$ is the usage interface, listing the (dynamic) set of operations that can be currently executed by the artifact. Elements $op_{req} \in I$ include both the name of the operation and the parameters.
- *Observable state:* $P$ is the set of the observable properties, represented by tuples $\langle p_n, p_v \rangle$ keeping track of the name and current value of the property.
- *Inner (non-observable) state:* $V$ is the set of inner variables of the artifact, represented by tuples $\langle v_n, v_v \rangle$ including the name and current value of a state variable.
- *Ongoing operations:* $O$ is the set of operations in execution inside the artifact, represented by tuples $\langle op_{id}, op_{req}, tag_\perp \rangle \in O$ including an identifier of the operation, the request that triggered the operation, and a tag (possibly not defined, i.e. $\perp$) specified by the agent that executed the operation to mark the events generated by the operation execution (this aspect will be clarified later on).
- *Link structures:* $Li$ is the link interface, i.e. a set of operations that can be linked (triggered) by other artifacts, $Li_{req}$ is a set of linked operations currently requested on this artifact.
- *Computational behaviour:* $ar_{pr}$ is the artifact program defining artifact computational behaviour. The program is actually represented by a single partial function:

$$ar_{pr}(op_{id}, op_{req}, I, P, V) : (I', P', V', Li', S, OR, LR, op_{cs}) \cup \perp$$

The function defines the computation behaviour of operation steps of the artifact, i.e. the atomic computations composing the execution of an operation.

Given an operation request $op_{req}$ identified by the operation identifier $op_{id}$, current usage interface $I$, current observable state $P$ and non-observable state $V$, the function defines the value of the new usage interface $I'$, observable state $P'$, non-observable state $V'$, the new link interface $Li'$, the set of signals $S$ possibly generated by the step execution, the set of new operation requests $OR$ specifying further operations to execute inside the artifact as a result of step execution, the set of link operation requests $LR$ to trigger the execution of other operations in other artifacts, and the operation completion state $op_{cs}$, indicating if the operation has completed or not.

Signals $s \in S$ are represented by tuples $\langle s_t, s_v \rangle$, including information about the type of the signal and its value.

Link operation requests $l_r \in LR$ are represented by tuples $\langle ar_{id}, op_{req} \rangle$, keeping track of the target artifact identifier and the (link) operation to be triggered.

The completion state $op_{cs}$ is represented by a tuple $\langle op_s, op_{res} \rangle$, where $op_s \in$ {op_completed, op_ongoing, op_failed} and $op_{res}$ is an operation feedback (which can be not defined, i.e. $\perp$), used as action feedback for the action (use in this case) that triggered the execution of the operation.

As an example of artifact configuration, an extended version of the counter artifact described in Section 2 is considered here. The extension accounts for considering two further operations in the usage interface, namely start and stop, to start and stop a counting process inside the artifact, and updating the count observable property only when stop is executed. The extended version of the artifact can be formalised as follows:

$$counter\_artifact = \langle counter, \{inc, start\}, \{\langle count, 0 \rangle\}, \emptyset, \emptyset, \emptyset, \emptyset, counter_{pr} \rangle$$

where the artifact program counter$_{pr}$ is defined as follows:

counter$_{pr}(op_{id}, inc, \{start, inc\}, \{\langle count, v \rangle\}, \emptyset) =$
  $(\{start, inc\}, \{\langle count, v+1 \rangle\}, \emptyset, \emptyset, \{tick\}, \emptyset, \emptyset, \langle op\_completed, \bot \rangle)$

counter$_{pr}(op_{id}, start, \{start, inc\}, \{\langle count, v \rangle\}, \emptyset) =$
  $(\{stop\}, \{\langle count, v \rangle\}, \{\langle i, 0 \rangle, \langle stopped, false \rangle\}, \emptyset, \{started\}, \{counting\}, \emptyset, \langle op\_completed, \bot \rangle)$

counter$_{pr}(op_{id}, counting, I, P, \{\langle i, x \rangle, \langle stopped, false \rangle\}) =$
  $(I, P, \{\langle i, x+1 \rangle, \langle stopped, false \rangle\}, \emptyset, \emptyset, \emptyset, \emptyset, \langle op\_ongoing, \bot \rangle)$

counter$_{pr}(op_{id}, counting, I, P, \{\langle i, x \rangle, \langle stopped, true \rangle\}) = (I, P, \emptyset, \emptyset, \emptyset, \emptyset, \emptyset, \langle op\_completed, \bot \rangle)$

counter$_{pr}(op_{id}, stop, \{stop\}, \{\langle count, v \rangle\}, \{\langle i, x \rangle, \langle stopped, false \rangle\}) =$
  $(\{inc, started\}, \{\langle count, v+x \rangle\}, \{\langle i, x \rangle, \langle stopped, true \rangle\}, \emptyset, \{stopped\}, \emptyset, \emptyset, \langle op\_completed, \bot \rangle)$

counter$_{pr}(\ldots) = \bot$ otherwise.

A brief explanation follows. An inc request triggers the execution of an operation which completes in one step, updating the count observable property and generating a tick signal. A start request changes the usage interface so as to include only a stop operation, sets up an internal variable i to keep track of the number of iterations done and a flag stopped, initially set to false, and generates a started signal, completing in one step. Also this operation completes in one step, however instantiating a new counting operation request. Then, the counting operation request causes the repeated execution of an operation step which increments the internal variable. Such a process terminates as soon as a stop operation is executed, which completes in one step by setting the flag stopped, generating a stopped signal. In that case, the couting operation completes, clearing the set of internal variables.

To conclude the description of the structures involved in a workspace configuration $\langle Ag, Ar, Om \rangle$, the elements of the observability map $Om$ are tuples $\langle ag_{id}, ar_{id}, filter_f \rangle$, keeping track of the identifier of the observer agent, the identifier of the observed artifact, and a filtering function $filter_f$ (described in detail later on) that specifies the possible kinds of events that the observer agent is interested in.

## 4   Dynamics

Once defined the general shape of a workspace configuration, we now describe the main transition rules that define how the configuration evolves. First we describe the transitions affecting agent configuration, then those affecting artifact one. To make the description more understandable, in the definition of the transition rules we include only those structures that are actually changed by the transition, sometimes splitting the description of the overall effect of a transition in multiple rules, in particular when the transition affects multiple structures of the workspace configuration. Also, for lack of space, we omit the description of those transitions that are related to failures.

## 4.1 Agent Execution Cycle

**Definition 4** *(agent execution cycle)*. Being $\langle ag_{id}, ag_s, Ev, ag_{pr} \rangle$ the configuration of an agent $ag \in Ag$, then:

$$\frac{ag_{pr}(ag_s, Ev) = (ag'_s, ac_\perp)}{\langle ag_{id}, ag_s, Ev, ag_{pr} \rangle \longrightarrow \langle ag_{id}, ag'_s, Ev', ag_{pr} \rangle}$$

that is, being $(ag'_s, ac_\perp)$ the new state and action computed by the agent program in current state $ag_s$ and current event set $Ev$, the configuration of the agent changes according to the agent program: $Ev'$ represents the set of events that are generated with the transition, depending on the specific action $ac_\perp$ done—this is detailed in next subsection. If the action is $\perp$ – that means no action chosen – then $Ev'$ is $\emptyset$.

## 4.2 Environment Operations

The computational behaviour of the environment is given by the operations executed inside artifacts. An operation inside an artifact can be triggered in three ways described in the following: *(a)* by the action of agents; *(b)* by other operations in execution inside the same artifact; *(c)* by the link of other artifacts.

**Agent Action.** To act upon the environment the action

$$\mathsf{use}(ar_{id}, op_{req}, tag_\perp, align_f \cup \perp)$$

is provided. The action triggers the execution of an operation $op_{req}$ on the target artifact $ar_{id}$, possibly specifying a symbolic tag to mark the events generated by the operation execution and an *alignment* condition function $align_f$. The alignment condition function $align_f : P \rightarrow \{true, false\}$ defines the condition on the observable state of the artifact that the agent expects to be true when the operation is actually triggered. Specifying $\perp$ in this case means an alignment function which is true for every value of the observable properties.

The semantics of action execution is that the action completes (fails) when the requested operation completes (fails), using the operation feedback as action feedback. Independently from the completion or failure of the operation, during operation (action) execution the artifact may generate observable events that the agent can perceive, eventually marked by the specified tag.

On the artifact side, the transition of a use action causes the synchronous execution of an operation step (the first step of the operation). If the operation has a single step, then the operation and the use action complete in a single transition and the set of generated events $Ev'$ defined in Definition 4 includes the event about action completion. Otherwise the operation (and action) will be eventually completed by the execution of an operation step in the future. Formally:

**Definition 5** *(use action).* Being $\langle ag_{id}, ag_s, Ev, ag_{pr} \rangle \in Ag$ the configuration of the agent doing the use action, $\langle ar_{id}, I, P, V, Li, O, Li_{req}, ar_{pr} \rangle \in Ar$ the configuration of the target artifact, and being $ac = \mathsf{use}(ar_{id}, op_{req}, align_f, tag_\perp)$ the action selected, then:

$$\frac{op_{req} \in I \quad align_f(P) = true \quad ar_{pr}(op_{id}, op_{req}, I, P, V) = (I', P', V', Li', S, OR, LR, op_{cs})}{\langle ar_{id}, I, P, V, Li, O, Li_{req}, ar_{pr} \rangle \longrightarrow \langle ar_{id}, I', P', V', Li, O', Li_{req}, ar_{pr} \rangle}$$

The transition is triggered only if the operation requested is part of the usage interface and the align function is satisfied. In that case the set on going operations $O$ is extended $O' = O \cup O_{new}$ with a (possibly empty) set of new operations to execute. If the operation does not complete in a single step ($op_{cs}$ is ongoing) $O_{new}$ includes a new element $\langle op_{id}, op_{req}, tag_\perp \rangle$ about the operation in execution, being $op_{id}$ a fresh operation identifier. $O_{new}$ includes also a new element $\langle op'_{id}, op'_{req}, \perp \rangle$ for each $op'_{req} \in OR$, that is for each new operation triggered by the artifact itself.

On the agent side, the set of events $Ev'$ used to update the agent configuration is the summation of two contributions $Ev' = Ev_{act} \cup Ev_{obs}$, related respectively to action completion events and observable events generated by the artifact. The first set is not empty only if the operation completed or failed, the second set is not empty if the agent is among the observers of the artifact. More precisely, being $ac = \mathsf{use}(ar_{id}, op_{req}, align_f \cup \perp)$, then:

$$Ev_{act} = \begin{cases} \emptyset & : \quad op_{cs} = \langle \mathsf{op\_ongoing}, \perp \rangle \\ \{\langle \mathsf{action\_completed}, \langle ac, op_{res} \rangle \rangle\} & : \quad op_{cs} = \langle \mathsf{op\_completed}, op_{res} \rangle \\ \{\langle \mathsf{action\_failed}, \langle ac, op_{res} \rangle \rangle\} & : \quad op_{cs} = \langle \mathsf{op\_failed}, op_{res} \rangle \end{cases}$$

$$Ev_{obs} = \begin{cases} Ev_{prop} \cup Ev_{sig} & : \quad \exists \langle ag_{id}, ar_{id}, filter_f \rangle \in Om \\ \emptyset & : \quad otherwise \end{cases}$$

$Ev_{prop}$ is a set of events $ev$ of type new_prop for each new property $\langle p_n, p_v \rangle$ observable to the agent (according to $P$ and $P'$ sets), update_prop for each observable property whose value has been changed by the step execution, prop_nomore_obs for each property which is not more observable to the agent. The set of events is filtered by the filter function $filter_f$—that is, the set contains only those events $ev$ such that $filter_f(ev)$ is true (the filter is specified by the focus action, described later on in this section). $Ev_{sig}$ is a set of events of type signal, one for each signal $\langle s_t, s_v \rangle$ included in the set of signal $S$ generated by the step, again filtered by the filter function $filter_f$.

Along with the configuration of the agent that executed the operation, the transition updates also the event set $Ev$ of all the other agents currently observing the artifact. Formally, for each $\langle ag'_{id}, ag_s, Ev, ag_{pr} \rangle \in Ag$ – where $ag'_{id} \neq ag_{id}$, being $ag_{id}$ the identifier of the agent that executed the operation – such that it exists $\langle ag'_{id}, ar_{id}, tag \rangle \in Om$, then:

$$\langle ag'_{id}, ag_s, Ev, ag_{pr} \rangle \longrightarrow \langle ag'_{id}, ag_s, Ev \cup Ev_{obs}, ag_{pr} \rangle$$

where $Ev_{obs}$ is a set of events defined as above.

**Remarks.** *(a)* The tag specified as a parameter of use can be exploited on the observation side to select only those percepts that have been generated by a specific artifact, in the context of a specific operation execution. *(b)*The alignment condition function is necessary when there is the need to enforce consistency between the environment state expected by the agent acting upon the environment and its actual state when such action take place.

Finally, the (possibly empty) set of link operation requests $LR$ generated by the step execution of the artifact are notified to linked artifacts. Formally, for each $\langle ar'_{id}, op_{req} \rangle \in LR$, $ar'_{id} \neq ar_{id}$, the transition changes the configuration of the target $ar'_{id}$ artifact by adding a new link operation request $op_{req}$ to the $Li_{req}$ set:

$$\langle ar'_{id}, I, P, V, Li, O, Li_{req}, ar_{pr} \rangle \longrightarrow \langle ar'_{id}, I, P, V, Li, O, Li'_{req}, ar_{pr} \rangle$$

where $Li'_{req} = Li_{req} \cup \{op_{req}\}$.

**Internal Operations.** An operation executed by an agent can trigger the execution of new independent operations inside the same artifact—as an example, consider the counting operation triggered by the start operation in the counter artifact shown in Section 3. So, either being triggered by an agent or as an internal operation, an operation step is executed as soon as the ongoing operation set in the artifact configuration is not empty and the artifact program $ar_{pr}$ for that request – given the current state of the artifact – yield to a new valid configuration $\neq \perp$. Formally:

**Definition 6** *(artifact step execution).* Being $\langle ar_{id}, I, P, V, Li, O, Li_{req}, ar_{pr} \rangle \in Ar$ an artifact in the workspace, such that

$$\frac{\langle op_{id}, op_{req}, tag_\perp \rangle \in O \quad ar_{pr}(op_{id}, op_{req}, I, P, V) = (I', P', V', Li', S, OR, LR, op_{cs}) \neq \perp}{\langle ar_{id}, I, P, V, Li, O, Li_{req}, ar_{pr} \rangle \longrightarrow \langle ar_{id}, I', P', V', Li, O', Li_{req}, ar_{pr} \rangle}$$

where $O' = (O \setminus O_{req}) \cup O_{new}$, being

$$O_{req} = \begin{cases} \emptyset & : \quad op_{cs} = \langle \text{op\_ongoing}, \perp \rangle \\ \{\langle op_{id}, op_{req}, tag_\perp \rangle\} & : \quad \textit{otherwise} \end{cases}$$

That is, the operation request that triggered the step is removed if the operation has completed. $O_{new}$ is a set including a new element $\langle op'_{id}, op'_{req}, \perp \rangle$, being $op'_{id}$ fresh operation identifier, for each $op'_{req} \in OR$, i.e. for each new operation triggered by the artifact itself.

As in the use action case, the execution of a step by the artifact may cause the update of both the event set $Ev$ of agents observing the artifact and of the link request set $Li$ of the artifact linked referenced in $LR$. So, for each $\langle ag'_{id}, ag_s, Ev, ag_{pr} \rangle \in Ag$ – where $ag'_{id} \neq ag_{id}$, being $ag_{id}$ the identifier of the agent that executed the operation – such that it exists $\langle ag'_{id}, ar_{id}, tag \rangle \in Om$, and , then:

$$\langle ag'_{id}, ag_s, Ev, ag_{pr} \rangle \longrightarrow \langle ag'_{id}, ag_s, Ev \cup Ev_{obs}, ag_{pr} \rangle$$

where $Ev_{obs}$ is defined as in Def. 5. For each $\langle ar'_{id}, op_{req} \rangle \in LR$, $ar'_{id} \neq ar_{id}$, the configuration of the target $ar'_{id}$ artifact is updated by adding a new link operation request $op_{req}$ to the $Li_{req}$ set:

$$\langle ar'_{id}, I, P, V, Li, O, Li_{req}, ar_{pr} \rangle \longrightarrow \langle ar'_{id}, I, P, V, Li, O, Li'_{req}, ar_{pr} \rangle$$

where $Li'_{req} = Li_{req} \cup \{op_{req}\}$.

**Artifact Link.** Finally, a step is executed also in the case that the set of link operation requests $Li_{req}$ is not empty, to serve operations triggered by other artifacts.

**Definition 7** *(artifact link execution).* Being $\langle ar_{id}, ar_n, I, P, V, Li, O, Li_{req} \rangle$ the configuration of an artifact, being $op_{req} \in Li_{req}$ a link operation request, then:

$$\frac{op_{req} \in Li \quad ar_{pr}(op_{id}, op_{req}, I, P, V) = (I', P', V', Li', S, OR, LR, op_{cs}) \neq \perp}{\langle ar_{id}, I, P, V, Li, O, Li_{req}, ar_{pr} \rangle \longrightarrow \langle ar_{id}, I', P', V', Li, O', Li'_{req}, ar_{pr} \rangle}$$

where $Li'_{req} = Li_{req} \setminus \{op_{req}\}$. Analogously to previous rules, the execution of a step by the artifact causes the update of both the event set $Ev$ of agents observing the artifact and of the link request set $Li$ of the artifact linked referenced in $LR$ (transitions not reported).

## 4.3   Environment Observation

Environment observation concerns two main aspects: *(a)* agent capability to *select* which parts of the environment to perceive, in order to focus only on specific artifacts; *(b)* agent capability to synchronously read the value of an observable property of an artifact.

The first capability is provided by the focus($ar_{id}, filter_f$) action, where $ar_{id}$ is the identifier of the artifact to observe and $filter_f$ is a boolean function $filter_f :$ Ev $\longrightarrow$ {*true, false*} representing a filtering condition on events—an event is collected only if the filter on the event is true. Formally:

**Definition 8** *(focus action).* Being the agent configuration $\langle ag_{id}, ag_s, Ev, ag_{pr} \rangle \in Ag$, the artifact configuration $\langle ar_{id}, I, P, V, Li, O, Li_{req}, ar_{pr} \rangle \in Ar$, $Om$ the observability map, and being $ac =$ focus($ar_{id}, filter_f$) the action to do, then:

$$Om \longrightarrow Om'$$

where $Om' = Om \cup \{\langle ag_{id}, ar_{id}, filter_f \rangle\}$. On the agent side:

$$Ev' = \{\langle \text{action\_completed}, \langle \text{focus}(ar_{id}, filter_f), \perp \rangle \rangle\} \cup Ev_{newprop}$$

where $Ev_{newprop}$ is a set of events of type new\_prop, one for each observable property $\langle p_n, p_v \rangle \in P$ (i.e. the set of events includes an event related to the completion of the action and the set of events about the new set of observable properties observed).

Dually to focus, the stopFocus($ar_{id}$) action stops getting events related to a specific artifact. This is modelled by a transition rule removing the element from the observability map:

**Definition 9** *(stop-focus action).* Being the agent configuration $\langle ag_{id}, ag_s, Ev, ag_{pr} \rangle \in Ag$, the artifact configuration $\langle ar_{id}, I, P, V, Li, O, Li_{req}, ar_{pr} \rangle \in Ar$, $Om$ the observability map, and being $ac =$ focus($ar_{id}, filter_f$) then:

$$\frac{\langle ag_{id}, ar_{id}, filter_f \rangle \in Om}{Om \longrightarrow Om'}$$

where $Om' = Om \setminus \{\langle ag_{id}, ar_{id}, filter_f \rangle\}$. On the agent side

$$Ev' = \{\langle action\_completed, \langle stopFocus(ar_{id}), \bot \rangle \rangle\} \cup Ev_{prop}$$

where $Ev_{prop}$ is a set of events $ev$ of type prop_nomore_obs, one for each observable property $\langle p_n, p_v \rangle \in P$ (i.e. the set of events includes an event related to the completion of the action and the set of events about the set of properties no more observable).

Finally, the capability to synchronously read the value of an observable property is provided by the observeProp action, which simply retrieves the value of the observable property as action feedback:

**Definition 10** *(observe property action).*    Being    the    artifact    configuration $\langle ar_{id}, I, P, V, Li, O, Li_{req}, ar_{pr} \rangle \in Ar$, being the agent configuration $\langle ag_{id}, ag_s, Ev, ag_{pr} \rangle \in Ag$, and being $ac = observeProp(ar_{id}, p_n)$ the action to do such that $\langle p_n, p_v \rangle \in P$, then the action completes in the same transition and the action feedback is the value of the observable property $p_v$: $Ev' = \{\langle action\_completed, \langle observeProp(ar_{id}, ar_n), p_v \rangle \rangle\}$.

**Remark.** Actions related to environment observation do not alter artifact configurations. observeProp action in particular does not change any structure of the environment configuration.

## 4.4   Environment Management

Besides use and observation, specific actions are provided to change the structure of the environment, by dynamically creating and disposing artifacts.

The dynamic instantiation of a new artifact is realised by the makeArtifact action. In this abstract model all the information needed to create the artifact are specified as parameters of the action. Formally:

**Definition 11** *(artifact instantiation action).*   Being $\langle ag_{id}, ag_s, Ev, ag_{pr} \rangle \in Ag$ the configuration of the agent, and being $ac = makeArtifact(ar_{id}, I_0, P_0, V_0, Li_0, ar_{pr})$ the action to do, where $ar_{id}$ the identifier of the artifact to be created, $I_0$, $P_0$, $V_0$, $Li_0$ and $ar_{pr}$ the initial value of the usage interface, the observable property set, the non-observable state set, the link interface set and $ar_{pr}$ the artifact program, then:

$$\frac{\nexists \langle ar_{id}, \ldots \rangle \in Ar}{Ar \longrightarrow Ar'}$$

where $Ar' = Ar \cup \{\langle ar_{id}, I_0, P_0, V_0, Li_0, \emptyset, \emptyset, ar_{pr} \rangle\}$. That is, the new artifact is added only if no artifact with the same identifier exists. On the agent side: $Ev' = \{\langle action\_completed, \langle makeArtifact(ar_{id}, I_0, P_0, V_0, Li_0, ar_{pr}), \bot \rangle \rangle\}$

Artifact disposal is realised by means of a disposeArtifact($ar_{id}$) action, described by the following rule:

**Definition 12** *(artifact dispose action).*   Being $\langle ag_{id}, ag_s, Ev, ag_{pr} \rangle \in Ag$ the configuration of the agent, and being $ac = disposeArtifact(ar_{id})$ the action to do, where $ar_{id}$ the identifier of the artifact to be removed, then:

$$\frac{\langle ar_{id}, I, P, V, Li, O, Li_{req}, ar_{pr} \rangle \in Ar}{Ar \longrightarrow Ar'}$$

where $Ar' = Ar \setminus \{\langle ar_{id}, I, P, V, Li, O, Li_{req}, ar_{pr}\rangle\}$. On the agent side: $Ev' = \{\langle \mathsf{action\_completed}, \langle \mathsf{disposeArtifact}(ar_{id}), \bot\rangle\rangle\}$.

# 5   Features

The abstract model is useful to understand and analyse the features that artifact-based environments have for environment programming and – more generally – for programming MAS. In this section we consider some main ones, mainly concerned to agent coordination.

## 5.1   Mutual Exclusion

By definition the environment is shared among agents and then it can be naturally exploited for enabling (and ruling) the access to shared resources. A main problem in this case is to avoid *interferences* that can occur when multiple agents access and change the same part of the environment concurrently. The artifact model provides a native support for mutual exclusion, that can be exploited by environment programmers.

**Proposition 1.** *Being N agents that concurrently access a resource R modelled as an artifact providing operations op composed by a single-step. Then, the access is guaranteed to be mutually exclusive and no interference can occur.*

This directly derives from definitions 5, 6 and 7, i.e. the transitions related to the execution of an artifact operation step.

## 5.2   Synchronisation

A basic coordination problem is synchronisation, i.e. enforcing an order in agent actions execution. In MAS the problem is classically solved by means of message-based communication protocols. Environment programming allows for alternative solutions.

**Proposition 2.** *Being N agents that need to achieve a synchronisation point. Then, it exists an environment that solves the problem minimising the number of agent actions required.*

The problem can be solved by a *barrier* artifact, exposing a usage interface with a single operation, synch. The operation, once triggered, completes only when the number of times that the operation has been triggered is equal to the number of agents. The formal definition of the barrier artifact follows:

$$barrier\_artifact = \langle \mathsf{barrier}, \{\mathsf{synch}\}, \{\langle \mathsf{n}, 0\rangle, \langle \mathsf{max}, \mathsf{m}\rangle\}, \{\langle \mathsf{reqs}, \emptyset\rangle\}, \emptyset, \emptyset, \emptyset, \mathsf{barrier_{pr}}\rangle$$

where m is an integer specifying the number of participant agents. The artifact program $\mathsf{barrier_{pr}}$ is defined as follows:

$\mathsf{barrier_{pr}}(op_{id}, \mathsf{synch}, \{\mathsf{synch}\}, \{\langle \mathsf{n}, N\rangle, \langle \mathsf{max}, \mathsf{m}\rangle\}, \{\langle \mathsf{reqs}, R\rangle\}) =$
$\quad (\{\mathsf{synch}\}, \{\langle \mathsf{n}, N+1\rangle, \langle \mathsf{max}, \mathsf{m}\rangle\}, \{\langle \mathsf{reqs}, R \cup \{op_{id}\}\rangle\}, \emptyset, \emptyset, \emptyset, \emptyset, \langle \mathsf{op\_ongoing}, \bot\rangle),$
$\quad$ if $N < \mathsf{m} - 1$ and $op_{id} \notin R$

$\text{barrier}_{\text{pr}}(op_{id}, \text{synch}, \{\text{synch}\}, \{\langle n, N \rangle, \langle \text{max}, m \rangle\}, \{\langle \text{reqs}, R \cup \{op_{id}\} \rangle\}) =$
    $(\{\text{synch}\}, \{\langle n, N+1 \rangle, \langle \text{max}, m \rangle\}, \{\langle \text{reqs}, R \rangle\}, \emptyset, \emptyset, \emptyset, \emptyset, \langle \text{op\_completed}, \bot \rangle), \text{ if } N = m-1$
$\text{barrier}_{\text{pr}}(\ldots) = \bot \text{ otherwise.}$

The internal variable reqs is used to keep track of the set of pending synch operations, which have not been completed yet. The observable property n is used to count the number of agents that achieved the barrier, and as soon as such number achieves the number of participants m – stored in max – the operation synch completes. By exploiting the barrier, each agent needs to perform a single use(barrier,synch) action to synchronize with the other agents, so $N$ actions in the overall.

### 5.3 Event-Driven Observation

The observation mechanism ensures that agents observing an artifact will eventually perceive all the values (changes) that artifact observable properties will assume. Let's define as *agent logical time* the number of execution cycles completed since its creation. Then:

**Proposition 3.** *Being $ag_{id}$ an agent focussing an artifact $ar_{id}$ with an observable property $\langle p_n, p_v \rangle$. If the value of the property is changed to $p'_v$ when the agent logical time is $t$, then the agent will eventually perceive the change at time $t+1$.*

This follows from the transition rules related to the execution of a step by the artifact (def. 5, 6, 7): the change generated by the execution of a step generates an event that is added to the event set of the agent, and that will be perceived then by the agent in next execution cycle. Actually this property would not be guaranteed by assuming a perception model not event-driven but state-driven, i.e. where percepts are snapshots about the current state of the environment.

### 5.4 Information Sharing

The observation mechanism provided by artifact-based environments can be effectively exploited for *information sharing* among the agents.

**Proposition 4.** *Being N agents that need to share the knowledge about the content v of some information item p, possibly updating the content when needed. The problem can be solved by designing a proper environment that makes it possible to avoid message exchanges among the agents and that minimises the number of actions requested to agents to access and to update the shared information.*

In this case the problem can be solved by a single artifact kb with an observable property reporting the value of the information item, and a usage interface with a single set operation to update the value. The formal definition of the kb artifact follows:

$$kb\_artifact = \langle kb, \{\text{set}\}, \{\langle \text{info}, v \rangle\}, \emptyset, \emptyset, \emptyset, \emptyset, kb_{\text{pr}} \rangle$$

where the artifact program $kb_{\text{pr}}$ is defined as follows:

$kb_{\text{pr}}(op_{id}, \text{set}(v'), \{\text{set}\}, \{\langle \text{info}, v \rangle\}, \emptyset) = (\{\text{set}\}, \{\langle \text{info}, v' \rangle\}, \emptyset, \emptyset, \emptyset, \emptyset, \emptyset, \langle \text{op\_completed}, \bot \rangle)$
$kb_{\text{pr}}(\ldots) = \bot \text{ otherwise.}$

On the one side, by focussing on the artifact every agent is aware of the actual value of the information item as soon as it changes – so no action are requested to know the value. On the other side, to change the value a single use(kb, set($NewValue$)) agent action is needed.

## 6  Related Work

As mentioned in the introduction, several models and frameworks have been proposed in literature for designing and developing environments in MAS in recent years. Actually, here we focus only on related works that concern specifically *formal models* of the environment.

A classical AI-oriented formalisation of the notion of environment is provided by the *task environment* model [15], where the environment is described as a triple $Env = \langle E, e_0, \tau \rangle$: $E$ is a set of environment states, $e_0 \in E$ is an initial state, and $\tau$ is a state transformer function $E \times A \rightarrow E$, computing the new state of the environment given an agent action $a \in A$. This simple model is effective for studying agent strategies in doing tasks inside the environment, but too abstract and simple for the purpose of environment programming, since it does not directly capture aspects such as the concurrent work of multiple agents in the same environment, environment observability, environment processes. These aspects are taken into the account instead in the seminal work of Ferber and Müller [4] and then in the work of Weyns and Holvoet in [10], which is actually an extension of [4].

In Ferber and Müller model, the overall system dynamics in decomposed in two parts, the dynamics of the environment and the dynamics of the agents situated in the environment. MAS evolution is described as the transformation of a *dynamical state*, defined as a tuple consisting of the state of the environment and the set of *influences* simultaneously produced in the environment. Influences come from inside the agents and are attempts to modify the course of events in the world. *Reactions*, which result in state changes, are produced by the environment by combining influences of all agents, given the local state of the environment and the laws of the world. A *Cycle* function is used to formally define this evolution. An extension of this action model is adopted by Weyns and Holvoet in [10], where a complete formalisation of a general abstract *architecture for situated MAS* is presented. In this architecture each agent is situated in his local context that he is able to perceive and in which he can act. The model deals with three main aspects: (a) the actions of agents in the environment, (b) ongoing activities in the environment, and (c) the interactions between agents and ongoing activities through the environment. Main features of the model include *regional synchronisation*, which makes it possible to avoid the need of a global synchronizer used in Ferber and Müller's approach (that results in a synchronous evolution of the MAS), and the support for *active perception* [14], which enables an agent to direct its perception at the most relevant aspects of the environment according to its current task, facilitating situation awareness.

The work presented in this paper shares many points with the work of Weyns and Hoelvet (and Ferber and Müller), such as the perspective on the environment as a first-class abstraction of the MAS, and the kind of problems considered—setting up an abstract rigorous model that is able to deal with the three aspects mentioned above. Differently from these works, our approach is explicitly oriented to MAS *programming*, in particular to devise a programming and computational model for the environment to be integrated with agent programming languages. The perspective adopted in Weyns and Hoelvet work is intentionally oriented to an *architectural* level. The main elements of the abstract model concern the functional modules that are needed to provide the functionalities that are meant to be encapsulated in the environment: interaction, communication, synchronisation and data-processing, observation and data-processing, translation [11]. So, by adopting this approach, from a MAS programmer viewpoint the environment is single abstraction, whose design/programming means devising the overall set of actions and percepts at the interface, and then defining environment behaviour by designing/programming its functional modules, according to the specific problem to solve (system to build).

In our case instead a general-purpose programming model is explicitly defined, based on the notion of artifact as a first-class abstraction for MAS developers and a first-class entity for agents of the MAS. The artifact programming model defines the basic set of features and mechanisms that can be used on the one side by MAS programmers to shape the environment of the MAS, by defining specific kinds of artifact based on the basic model, and on the other side by agents, to dynamically construct, use and adapt their environment. So the environment is not conceive as a single block, but as a dynamic composition of artifacts—organised in localities called workspaces. It's worth noting that a similar modularisation appears in a recent work of Ferber and colleagues [9], where a generic notion of *object* is used. The different perspective is evident also in the formalisation, which is not based (in our case) on global functions like *React*, *Apply*, *Compose*, *Collect* as in [10], or like *React* and *Exec* in [4], but on structures representing artifacts and their dynamics ($ar_{pr}$ function).

Finally, even if not directly related to MAS engineering, the *Lifeworld* abstract model introduced by Agre and Horswill in [1] is a main related work of ours. In contrast to traditional AI models for environment – such as task environments – Agre and Horswill recognise the importance of properly modelling agent-environment *interactions*, including also the *conventions* and *invariants* maintained in the environment by agents throughout their activity. Following [1], a lifeworld is a description of an environment in terms of the customary ways of structuring the activities that take place within it – the conventional uses of tools and materials, the "loop invariants" that are maintained within it by conventional activities, and so on. Lifeworlds typically contain *artifacts* such as tools that have been specifically evolved to support those activities, arranged in the world in ways that simplify life and reduce the cognitive burden on individuals. Our approach is based on the same perspective, in our case applied not to the analysis of physical environments but to the design and engineering of computational (virtual) environments for software MAS. However, the formal approach presented in [1] models these environments as state machines, with actions mapping states to state and the behavior of agents as policies mapping states to actions. So, the formalisation abstracts from aspects that are of primary importance when taking a programming/engineering perspective, analogously to the task environment model.

## 7   Concluding Remarks

In this paper we presented a formalisation of artifact-based environments, as a general-purpose model for programming environments is MAS based on the notion of artifact, implemented by the CArtAgO framework. Even if based on the A&A meta-model, the abstract model deals with aspects that we believe are important – more generally – for any general-purpose environment model to be used in MAS programming. Future works will be devoted to a deeper and more systematic investigations of the formal properties of environments programmed with this model and their impact on the properties of the MAS in general.

# References

1. Agre, P., Horswill, I.: Lifeworld analysis. Journal of Artificial Intelligence Reserach 6, 111–145 (1997)
2. Bordini, R., Hübner, J., Wooldridge, M.: Programming Multi-Agent Systems in AgentSpeak Using Jason. John Wiley & Sons, Ltd., Chichester (2007)
3. Bromuri, S., Stathis, K.: Situating Cognitive Agents in GOLEM. In: Weyns, D., Brueckner, S.A., Demazeau, Y. (eds.) EEMMAS 2007. LNCS (LNAI), vol. 5049, pp. 115–134. Springer, Heidelberg (2008)
4. Ferber, J., Müller, J.-P.: Influences and reaction: a model of situated multi-agent systems. In: Proc. of the 2nd Int. Conf. on Multi-Agent Systems (ICMAS 1996). AAAI, Menlo Park (1996)
5. Omicini, A., Ricci, A., Viroli, M.: Artifacts in the A&A meta-model for multi-agent systems. Autonomous Agents and Multi-Agent Systems 17(3) (December 2008)
6. Ricci, A., Piunti, M., Viroli, M., Omicini, A.: Environment programming in CArtAgo. In: Bordini, R.H., Dastani, M., Dix, J., El Fallah-Seghrouchni, A. (eds.) Multi-Agent Programming: Languages, Platforms and Applications, vol. 2. Springer, Heidelberg (2009)
7. Ricci, A., Viroli, M., Omicini, A.: The A&A programming model and technology for developing agent environments in MAS. In: Dastani, M.M., El Fallah Seghrouchni, A., Ricci, A., Winikoff, M. (eds.) ProMAS 2007. LNCS (LNAI), vol. 4908, pp. 91–109. Springer, Heidelberg (2008)
8. Ricci, A., Viroli, M., Omicini, A.: CArtAgO: A framework for prototyping artifact-based environments in MAS. In: Weyns, D., Van Dyke Parunak, H., Michel, F. (eds.) E4MAS 2006. LNCS (LNAI), vol. 4389, pp. 67–86. Springer, Heidelberg (2007)
9. Stratulat, T., Ferber, J., Tranier, J.: MASQ: towards an integral approach to interaction. In: Sierra, C., Castelfranchi, C., Decker, K.S., Sichman, J.S. (eds.) AAMAS (2), pp. 813–820, IFAAMAS (2009)
10. Weyns, D., Holvoet, T.: Formal model for situated multiagent systems. Fundamenta Informaticae 63(2–3), 125–158 (2004)
11. Weyns, D., Holvoet, T.: A reference architecture for situated multiagent systems. In: Weyns, D., Van Dyke Parunak, H., Michel, F. (eds.) E4MAS 2006. LNCS (LNAI), vol. 4389, pp. 1–40. Springer, Heidelberg (2007)
12. Weyns, D., Omicini, A., Odell, J.J.: Environment as a first-class abstraction in multi-agent systems. Autonomous Agents and Multi-Agent Systems 14(1), 5–30 (2007); Special Issue on Environments for Multi-agent Systems
13. Weyns, D., Parunak, H.V.D. (eds.): Journal of Autonomous Agents and Multi-Agent Systems. Special Issue: Environment for Multi-Agent Systems, vol. 14(1). Springer, Netherlands (2007)
14. Weyns, D., Steegmans, E., Holvoet, T.: Towards active perception in situated multi-agent systems. Applied Artificial Intelligence 18(9-10), 867–883 (2004)
15. Wooldridge, M.: An Introduction to Multi-Agent Systems. John Wiley & Sons, Ltd., Chichester (2002)

# Debugging BDI-Based Multi-Agent Programs

Mehdi Dastani, Jaap Brandsema, Amco Dubel, and John-Jules Ch. Meyer

Utrecht University
The Netherlands
{mehdi,jj}@cs.uu.nl, jaap_b82@hotmail.com, amco@orais.org

**Abstract.** The development of multi-agent programs requires debugging tools and techniques to find and resolve possible defects in such programs. This paper focuses on BDI-based multi-agent programs, discusses some existing debugging approaches that are developed for specific BDI-based multi-agent programming languages, and proposes a generic and systematic approach for debugging BDI-based multi-agent programs. The proposal consists of an assertion language to specify cognitive and temporal behavior of multi-agent programs and a set of debugging tools. The assertions can be assigned to the debugging tools which will be activated as soon as the execution of a multi-agent program satisfies the assertion.

## 1 Introduction

Debugging is the art of finding and resolving errors or possible defects, also called bugs, in a computer program. In the context of this paper we divide bugs into three categories: syntax bugs, semantic bugs (logical and concurrent bugs), or design bugs. Design bugs arise before the actual programming and are based on erroneous design of software programs. In contrast to design bugs, both syntax and semantic bugs arise during programming and are related to the actual code of the program. Although syntax bugs are (most of the time) simple typos, which can easily be detected by the program parser (compiler), semantic bugs are, as the name implies, mistakes at the semantic level. Because they often depend on the intention of the developer they can rarely be detected automatically by the program parsers. Therefore, special tools are needed to detect semantic bugs. The ease of the debugging experience is largely dependent on the quality of these debugging tools and the ability of the developer to work with these tools.

A promising approach to develop computer programs for complex and concurrent applications are multi-agent systems. In order to implement multi-agent systems, various agent-oriented programming languages and development tools have been proposed [2]. These agent-oriented programming languages facilitate the implementation of individual agents and their interactions. A special class of these programming languages aims at programming BDI-based multi-agent systems, i.e., multi-agent systems in which individual agents are programmed in terms of cognitive concepts such as beliefs, events, goals, plans, and reasoning rules [18,13,3,7].

L. Braubach, J.-P. Briot, and J. Thangarajah (Eds.): ProMAS 2009, LNAI 5919, pp. 151–169, 2010.
© Springer-Verlag Berlin Heidelberg 2010

Despite numerous proposals for BDI-based multi-agent programming languages, there has been little attention on building effective debugging tools for *BDI-based* agent-oriented programs. The existing debugging tools for BDI-based programs enable the observation of program execution traces (the sequence of program states generated by the program's execution) [5,13,6,7,3] and browsing through these execution traces, allowing to run multi-agent programs in different execution modes by for example using breakpoints and assertions [5,7,3,13], observing the message exchange between agents and checking the conformance of agents' interactions with a specific communication protocol [4,17,13,5,14,15]. Although most proposals are claimed to be applicable to other BDI-based multi-agent programming languages, they are presented for a specific multi-agent platform and the corresponding multi-agent programming language. In these proposals, debugging multi-agent aspects of such programs are mainly concerned with the interaction between individual agents and the exchanged messages. Finally, the temporal aspects of multi-agent program execution traces are only considered in a limited way and not fully exploited for debugging purposes.

In this paper, we focus on the semantic bugs in BDI-based multi-agent programs and propose a generic approach for debugging such programs. Our proposal extends previous approaches by debugging the *interaction* between implemented agents, not only in terms of the exchanged messages, but also in terms of the relations between their internal states.[1] Moreover, we propose a set of debugging constructs that illustrate how a developer can debug both *cognitive* and *temporal* aspects of the execution traces of multi-agent programs. For example, we show that the debugging constructs allow a developer to log specific parts of the cognitive state of individual agent programs (e.g., log the beliefs, events, goals, or plans) from the moment that specific condition holds, stop the execution of multi-agent programs whenever a specific cognitive condition holds, or check whether an execution trace of a multi-agent program (a sequence of cognitive states) satisfies a specific (cognitive / temporal) property. In general, we propose a set of debugging actions/tools and an assertion language. The expressions of the assertion language are assigned to the proposed actions/tools such that they are performed/activated when their associated assertions hold during the execution of multi-agent programs. Our approach does not assume a specific representation for the internals of individual agents and can be applied to any BDI-based multi-agent programming language. We only assume that the state of individual BDI-based agents consists of cognitive components such as beliefs, goals, and plans without assuming how these components are represented.

The structure of this paper is as follows. In section 2, we discuss some related works on debugging multi-agent programs, and in section 3, we present our generic vision on multi-agent programs and their semantics. Based on this vision, our approach for debugging multi-agent programs is presented in section 4. The paper concludes with some comments and future works.

---

[1] A developer/debugger of a multi-agent program is assumed to have access to the multi-agent program code and therefore to the internal state of those programs.

## 2    Background and Related Work

A well-known technique often used for debugging single sequential and concurrent programs is a *breakpoint*. A breakpoint is a marker that can be placed in the program's code. Breakpoints can be used to control the program's execution. When the marker is reached program execution is halted. Breakpoints can be either conditional or unconditional. Unconditional breakpoints halt the program execution when the breakpoint marker is reached. Conditional breakpoints only halt the program execution when the marker is reached and some extra condition is fulfilled. Another (similar) functionality, that can be used to re-synchronize program executions, is called a process barrier breakpoint. Process barrier breakpoints are much like normal breakpoints. The difference is they halt the processes that reached the barrier point until the last process reaches the barrier point. A different debugging technique used for traditional programming practices is called the *watch*. The watch is a window used to monitor variables' values. Most watch windows also allow the developer to type in a variable name and if the variable exists the watch will show the variable's value. In the IDEs of most high-level programming languages the watch is only available when the program's execution is halted. Other traditional debugging techniques are logging and visualization. Logging allows a developer to write some particular variable's value or some statement to a logging window or a file. Visualization is particularly helpful in the analysis and fine tuning of concurrent systems. Most relevant in light of our research is the ability to visualize the message queue.

These traditional debugging techniques have inspired many agent researchers to develop debugging frameworks for multi-agent programs. An example of such a framework, proposed by Collier [5], is designed for Agent Factory and its corresponding AFAPL (Agent Factory Agent Programming Language). In this approach, debugging can be done both at compile time and at run time. At compile time, syntax errors as well as reference to non-existing files, the definition of belief terms, and the declaration of actions and plans are checked. Run time debugging focuses on semantic bugs such as sending wrong messages and the internal working of individual agents. The run time debugging is done by a debugging tool called *AFAPL Debugger*. This tool provides a number of views of an agent system, among which, a view that enables to inspect and trace an agent's internal state, and to start, stop, and step through the execution of the agent program. Beside these standard functionalities, this view enables to highlight the interplay between different mental attitudes of one individual agent, to check the performance of an agent with respect to the execution of perceptors and actuators, and to increase the level of control over granularity of the step operation using breakpoints. Using this extended view tool, one can inspect beliefs that are generated by a perceptor, the current primary commitments of the agent, and a list of all messages sent/received by the agent. The views can be filtered to, for example, focus on the beliefs generated by a single preceptor. Other views present information about services that are deployed on the agent platform and the previous runs (histories) of the agent system.

Sudeikat [16] presents an assertion based debugging mechanism for the Jadex platform and its corresponding programming language. In this approach, assertions statements can be annotated to the BDI elements (e.g., beliefs, goals, plans) of an individual agent program. Assertions specify relations between BDI concepts or the invariant properties of the execution of an agent program. Assertion statements, which evaluate to boolean values, are arbitrary Java statement executed by the underlying Jadex assertion mechanism. When an assertion is evaluated to false, a warning is generated to inform the developer about the agent and the element where the assertion evaluated to false. The execution of the Java statements is triggered by the Jadex BDI reasoning events. They also propose a three dimensional graph of the overall communication structure of the multi-agent system. Finally, they propose run time monitoring of exchanged messages in order to detect possible violation with respect to a given communication protocol.

An important aspect of debugging multi-agent programs is related to message exchanges between individual agents. In many existing approaches, e.g., [1,7,3,13], message exchanges are logged and presented by means of different visualization techniques. In [4], Botía and his colleagues use traditional data mining techniques to visualize the logged (FIPA) exchanged messages. This approach creates two main types of graphs: an agent communication graph, and a clustered graph where agents are clustered based on similar communication activity or cooperation activity. In another work [17], Vigueras and Botía propose the use of causality graphs to track causality amongst messages sent by individual agents. The causality graph is created from conversations that are previously logged. The ordering of the messages is done by using a logical vector clock.

Yet another approach to debug a multi-agent program based on comparing the actual behavior of the program with the desired behavior is proposed by Lam [6]. In this paper, a tracing method and tracer tool are proposed. The tracing method captures dynamic runtime data by logging actual agent behavior. The data is logged by introducing logging statements into the agent program. The captured data is used to create behavioral models of the agents' activities in terms of agent concepts (e.g. beliefs, goals, and intentions). These models can be used to compare the actual behaviour of the models with the expected agent behaviour, to identify bugs in the agent's program. Currently the comparision has to be made manually, since no specification for expected agent behavior has been developed yet. The tracer tool creates relational graphs which can be used to manually verify the initial design diagrams.

The techniques mentioned above are helpful when errors manifest themselves directly to the developer or user. However, errors in a program do not always manifest themselves directly. For mission and industrial critical systems it is necessary to extensively test the program before deploying it. This testing should remove as many bugs (and possible defects) as possible. However, it is infeasible to test every single situation the program could be in. A testing approach proposed for multi-agent programs is proposed by Poutakidis and his colleagues [14,15].

# 3    Programming Multi-Agent Systems

A multi-agent program comprises a set of individual agent programs possibly together with the specification of organizational structures and laws that should be respected during their executions. In order to keep our approach generic, we do not make any assumption about organizational structures and laws. Without losing generality, we assume that a multi-agent program looks like the following program.

```
Agents:        cleaner   :   cleaner.prog    1
               explorer  :   explorer.prog   3
Environment:   gridworld
```

This program declares one cleaner agent and three explorer agents. It also indicates that the agents can perform actions in a grid-like environment, called gridworld. We assume that the agents are implemented to cooperate to remove bombs placed in the gridworld.[2] We further assume that the goal of the explorer agent is to explore the environment to find the bombs that are placed in that environment. When a bomb is found, the explorer agent communicates the location of the bomb to the cleaner agent who has to dismantle the bomb.

An individual BDI-based agent can be programmed by specifying its initial (cognitive) state/configuration in terms of beliefs (information), events (observation), goals (objectives), plans (means), and reasoning rules (for generating plans). In programming terminology, these ingredients can be considered as (cognitive) data structures specifying the (initial) state/configuration of the agent program. Without losing generality and committing to a specific knowledge representation scheme, we assume in the rest of the paper a BDI-based agent programming language that provides (cognitive) data structures to represent the initial cognitive state/configuration of each individual agent.

The execution of a BDI-based multi-agent program is the concurrent executions of all individual agent programs. The execution of each individual agent program is based on a cyclic process called *deliberation cycle* (sense-reason-act cycle). Each iteration of this process starts with sensing the environment (i.e., receive events and messages), reasoning based on its state (i.e., update beliefs and goals based on events and messages, and generate plans to either achieve goals or to react to events), and performing actions (i.e., perform actions of the generated plans). An execution of a multi-agent program generates a trace of the program (a sequence of multi-agent program states). Each state in such a trace consists of the states of all individual cognitive agents, i.e., it consists of beliefs, events, goals, plans of all individual agents. It is important to note that similar BDI ingredients and deliberation cycle are used in existing BDI-based programming languages such as Jason [3], 2APL [7], Jadex [13], and Jack [18].

In this paper, the concurrent execution of different individual agent programs is assumed to follow the interleaving execution model, i.e., two individual agent

---

[2] It should be noted that the declaration of agents can also be done by means of loading agent programs in a multi-agent platform such that there is no need for a specific multi-agent program.

programs cannot be executed at the same time. Note that this assumption does not pose any problem for multi-agent programs running on one single platform because in such cases individual agent programs are executed in the interleaving mode. However, if individual agent programs are executed on different platforms, then one should investigate if and how these different execution threads can be merged into one single multi-agent program thread. In this paper, we consider only the interleaving executions of individual agent programs.

In the following, we assume that an execution of a multi-agent program starts with the initial state of the declared agents (specified by the individual agent programs) and generates a sequence of states based on a deliberation cycle (i.e., sense, reason and act cycle). Formally, a state of a multi-agent program is a tuple $\langle A_1, \ldots, A_n, \chi \rangle$, where $A_i = \langle i, \sigma, \gamma, \Pi, \xi \rangle$ denotes the state of individual agent $i$ (with beliefs $\sigma$, goals $\gamma$, plans $\Pi$, and events $\xi$) and $\chi$ denotes the environment in which agents' actions can be performed. An execution of a multi-agent program is then a sequence $s_0, s_1, \ldots$, where $s_0 = \langle A_1^0, \ldots, A_n^0, \chi^0 \rangle$ is the initial state specified by a multi-agent program, and state $s_n$ is reached by means of a deliberation action (update beliefs, generate/execute plans, process events) performed by one of the agents in state $s_{n-1}$.

For example, the multi-agent program mentioned above specifies the initial state $\langle cleaner, explorer_1, explorer_2, explorer_3, gridworld \rangle$. The state of the cleaner agent is $cleaner = \langle c, \sigma_c, \gamma_c, \Pi_c, \xi_c \rangle$, where $\sigma_c$ represents the beliefs of the cleaner agent (initially specified by `cleaner.prog`), $\gamma_c$ represents its goal base, $\Pi_c$ represents its plan base, and $\xi_c$ represents its event base. The beliefs can be a set of propositions, a set of objects, or any other data structure that can represent facts. The exact nature of beliefs depends on the programming constructs provided by the programming language. Note that $\Pi$ is a set of plans (also called plan instances) each consists of domain actions, e.g., $\Pi = \{goto(2,3); pickup()$ , $sense(bombs)\}$ consists of two plans; the first plan indicates that the agent should move to location $(2,3)$ followed by a picking up (a bomb) action, and the second plan indicates that the agent should sense the world to find some bombs. The state of other agents are similar. The *gridworld* is assumed to be an specification of the state of the `gridworld` environment.

## 4    Debugging Multi-Agent Programs

Given an execution of a multi-agent program, one may want to check if an implemented agent[3] will drop a specific goal when it is achieved, when two or more agents will have the same beliefs, whether the number of agents is suited for the environment (e.g. it is useless to have a dozen explorers on a small area, or many explorers when there is only one cleaner that cannot keep up with them.), whether the protocol is suited for the given task (e.g. there might be a lot of overhead because facts are not shared, and therefore, needlessly rediscovered), whether important beliefs are shared and adopted, or rejected, once they are

---

[3] In the following, we write 'agents' and 'implemented agents' interchangeably since we focus on programs that implement agents.

received. We may also want to check if unreliable sources of information are ignored, whether the actions of one agent are rational to take based on the knowledge of other agents, or if sent messages are received by the recipient. This can, for example, be used to locate deadlocks where one more agents keep waiting for a message to be sent.

Ideally one would specify a *cognitive* and *temporal* property by means of an assertion and use it in two different debugging modes. In one debugging mode, called *continuous mode*, one may want to execute a multi-agent program and get notified when the assertion evaluates to true *during its execution*. In the second debugging mode, called *post mortem*, one may want to execute a multi-agent program, stop it after some execution steps, and check if the assertion evaluates to true for the performed execution. For both debugging modes, the assertions are evaluated in the *initial state* of the multi-agent program *execution trace generated thusfar*. For the post mortem debugging mode, the generated execution trace thusfar is the trace generated from the start of the program execution until the execution is stopped. However, for the continuous debugging mode, the assertions are evaluated after each execution step and with respect to the execution trace generated thusfar, i.e., the execution trace generated from the start of the program execution until the last execution step. This is because during a program execution a trace is modified and extended after each execution step. It should be noted that subsequent execution steps generate new program states and therefore new traces.

In the continuous debugging mode, the evaluation of an assertion *during* the execution of a multi-agent program means a continuous evaluation of the assertion on its evolving execution trace as it develops by consecutive execution steps. This continuous evaluation of the assertion can be used to halt the program execution as soon as a trace is generated which satisfies the assertion. It is important to know that assertions are evaluated in the initial state of the execution trace such that the trace properties should be specified as temporal assertions. A developer of multi-agent programs is assumed to know these aspects of our debugging framework in order to debug such programs effectively. Similar ideas are proposed in Jadex [13].

In the following, we introduce an assertion language, called MDL (multi-agent description language), to specify the *cognitive* and *temporal* behavior (i.e., execution traces) of the BDI-based multi-agent programs. The MDL description language is taken to be a variant of LTL (Linear Temporal Logic) because execution traces of multi-agent programs, which are used to debug[4] such programs, are assumed to be linear traces. Note that this assumption is realistic as the interpreter

---

[4] In contrast to debugging that analyzes one linear execution trace of a program, other verification techniques such as model checking and theorem proving analyze all possible execution traces of a program at once. Therefore, variants of CTL (Computation Tree Logic) are used for model-checking and theorem proving of programs. It is important to emphasize that model-checking and theorem proving can therefore be used to prove the correctness of programs, while debugging can only be used to find possible defects of programs (as displayed in particular runs).

of most (multi-agent) programs performs one execution step at a time and thereby generates a linear trace. A MDL assertion is evaluated on the (finite) execution trace of a multi-agent program and can activate a debugging tool when it is evaluated to true. The debugging tools are inspired by traditional debugging tools, extended with the functionality to verify a multi-agent program execution trace. One example of such a debugging tool is a multi-agent version of the breakpoint. The breakpoint can halt the execution of a single agent program, a group of agent programs or the complete multi-agent program. This multi-agent version of the breakpoint can also have a MDL assertion as a condition, making it a conditional breakpoint.

## 4.1   Syntax of Assertion Language

In this section, we present the syntax of the MDL written in EBNF notation. An expression of this language describes a property of a multi-agent program execution and can be used as assertions based on which debugging actions/tools will be performed/activated. In the following, $\langle group\_id \rangle$ is a group identifier (uncapitalized string), $\langle agent\_id \rangle$ an agent identifier (uncapitalized string), $\langle query\_name \rangle$ a property description name (a reference to an assertion used in the definition of macros; see later on for a discussion on macros), $\langle Var \rangle$ a variable (Variables are capitalized strings), $[all]$ indicates the group of all agents, and $\langle agent\_var \rangle$ an agent identifier, a group identifier, or a variable. In order not to make any assumption about the exact representation of an agent's beliefs, goals, events, and plans, we assume $Bquery$, $Gquery$, $Equery$, and $Pquery$ to denote an agent's Beliefs, Goals, Events, and Plans, respectively. This makes it possible to apply this assertion language to other BDI-based multi-agent programming languages.

| $\langle group\_def \rangle$ | $::=$ " [" $\langle group\_id \rangle$ "]" " $=$ " $\langle agent\_list \rangle$ |
|---|---|
| $\langle agent\_list \rangle$ | $::=$ " [" $\langle agent\_id \rangle$ ( "," $\langle agent\_id \rangle$) $*$ "]" |
| $\langle mdl\_pd \rangle$ | $::=$ $\langle query\_name \rangle$ "{" $\langle mdl\_query \rangle$ "}" |
| $\langle mdl\_query \rangle$ | $::=$ "{" $\langle mdl\_query \rangle$ "}" |
| | $\mid \langle agent\_var \rangle$ "@Beliefs (" $\langle Bquery \rangle$ ")" |
| | $\mid \langle agent\_var \rangle$ "@Goals (" $\langle Gquery \rangle$ ")" |
| | $\mid \langle agent\_var \rangle$ "@Plans (" $\langle Pquery \rangle$ ")" |
| | $\mid \langle agent\_var \rangle$ "@Events (" $\langle Equery \rangle$ ")" |
| | $\mid \langle UnOp \rangle \langle mdl\_query \rangle$ |
| | $\mid \langle mdl\_query \rangle \langle BinOp \rangle \langle mdl\_query \rangle$ |
| | $\mid$ "?" $\langle query\_name \rangle$ |
| $\langle BinOp \rangle$ | $::=$ "and" $\mid$ "or" $\mid$ "implies" $\mid$ "until" |
| $\langle UnOp \rangle$ | $::=$ "not" $\mid$ "next" $\mid$ "eventually" $\mid$ "always" |
| $\langle agent\_var \rangle$ | $::=$ $\langle Var \rangle \mid \langle agent\_id \rangle \mid \langle group\_id \rangle \mid$ "[all]" |

Note that $\langle mdl\_pd \rangle$ is an assertion that describes the (temporal and cognitive) behavior of a multi-agent program execution. In order to illustrate the use of this assertion language, we present a number of examples in which logic-based representation are used to express an agent's beliefs, goals, events, and plans. For example, bomb(2,3) (read as *there is a bomb at position (2,3)*) and clean(gridworld) and carry(bomb) (read as *the gridworld is clean and the agent carries a bomb*) are used to represent an agent's beliefs or goals, event(bombAt(3,4)) (read as *it is perceived that a bomb is at position (3,4)*) or message(explorer, inform, bombAt(2,3)) (read as *a message is received from explorer informing there is a bomb at position (2,3)*) are used to represent an agent's events and messages, and goto(X, Y); dropBomb(X',Y') (read as *go first to position (X,Y) and then drop the bomb that is originally found at position (X',Y')*) are used to represent an agent's plan.

In order to specify that either all agents believe that there is a bomb at position 2,3 (i.e., bomb(2,3)) or all agents believe that there is no bomb at that position (i.e. not bomb(2,3)), we can use the following assertion.

[all]@Beliefs( bomb(2,3) ) or [all]@Beliefs( not bomb(2,3) )

Since assertions in our framework are always evaluated in the initial state of the program execution trace (and thus specified by the multi-agent program), the above assertion will evaluate to true if it holds in the initial state. Therefore, if this assertion is evaluated to true in a program execution trace, then it will evaluate to true for the rest of the program execution. Note that if this assertion should hold in all states of the program execution, then it should be put in the scope of the 'always' operator. Moreover, if the assertion should hold in the last state of the program execution, then it should be put in the scope of the 'eventually' operator.

We can generalize the above assertion by assigning a name to it and parameterizing the specific beliefs (in this case bomb(X,Y)). This generalization allows us to define an assertion as a macro that can be used to define more complex assertions. For example, consider the following generalization (macro) that holds in a state of a multi-agent program if and only if either all agents believe the given belief $\phi$ or all agents do not believe $\phi$.

isSharedBelief($\phi$) { [all]@Beliefs( $\phi$ ) or [all]@Beliefs( not $\phi$ ) }

Note that isSharedBelief($\phi$) can now be used (e.g., in other assertions) to check whether or not $\phi$ is a shared belief. In general, one can use the following abstract scheme to name an MDL assertion. Parameters Var1, Var2, and Var3 are assumed to be used in the MDL assertion.

name( Var1, Var2, Var3, ...) { MDL assertion }

The following example demonstrates the use of macros. To use a MDL assertion inside another one, the macro's names should be preceded by a "?" mark. We now define a cell as detected when agents agree on the content of that cell. We define detectedArea(R) as follows.

detectedArea(X, Y) { ?isSharedBelief( bomb(X,Y) ) }

The next example shows a MDL assertion that can be used to verify whether the `gridworld` will eventually be clean if an agent has the goal to clean it. In particular, the assertion states that if an agent `A` has the goal to clean the `gridworld` then eventually that agent `A` will believe that the `gridworld` is clean.

```
cleanEnvironment(A) {
  A@Goals(clean(gridworld)) implies eventually A@Beliefs(clean(gridworld))
}
```

It is important to note that if this assertion evaluates to false for an execution thusfar, it may *not* continue to be false for the rest of the execution. This is due to the evaluation of the `eventually` operator in the context of finite traces. In particular, if the above assertion evaluates to false for a finite program execution trace, then it may not evaluate to false for a suffix of that trace. One particular use of the eventually operator is therefore to check and stop the execution of a multi-agent program when it reaches a state with a specific property.

The following MDL assertion states that an agent `A` will not unintentionally drop the bomb that it carries. More specifically, the assertion states that if an agent believes to carry a bomb, then the agent will believe to carry the bomb until it has a plan to drop the bomb. In this example, `dropBomb(_,_)` is assumed to be a plan to drop a bomb at any position. The two underscore parameters indicate that the positions where the bomb should be dropped do not matter such that `dropBomb(_,_)` holds for the agent `A` if `A` has a plan to drop a bomb at any position. It is implicitly assumed that all plans will be successfully executed.

```
doesNotLoseBomb(A) {
   always ( A@Beliefs(carry(bomb))
            implies
            ( A@Beliefs(carry(bomb)) until A@Plans(dropBomb(_,_)))))
}
```

## 4.2  Semantics

The semantics of the MDL language describe how an assertion is evaluated against a trace of a BDI-based multi-agent program. In the context of debugging, we consider *finite traces* generated by partial execution of multi-agent programs (a partial execution of a program starts in the initial state of the program and stops after a finite number of deliberation steps). A finite trace is a finite sequence of multi-agent program states in which the state of each agent is a tuple consisting of beliefs, goals, events, and plans. In the following, we write $\sigma_i$ to denote the belief base $\sigma$ of individual agent $i$. Similar notation will be used for goal base, plan base, and event base.

**Definition 1.** *Let* $s = \langle A_1, \ldots, A_n, \chi \rangle$ *be a state (configuration) of a multi-agent program, and* $A_i = \langle i, \sigma_i, \gamma_i, \Pi_i, \xi_i \rangle$ *be the state of the individual agent* $i$. *The assignment functions* $V_b$, $V_g$, $V_e$, *and* $V_p$ *determine the beliefs, goals, events, and plans of an individual agent in a state of a multi-agent program. These assignment function are defined as follows:* $V_b(i, s) = \sigma_i$, $V_g(i, s) = \gamma_i$, $V_p(i, s) = \Pi_i$, *and* $V_e(i, s) = \xi_i$.

An arbitrary MDL assertion can be evaluated with respect to a finite multi-agent program trace that is resulted by a partial execution of a multi-agent program. In the following, we use $t$ to denote a finite trace, $|t|$ to indicate the length of the trace $t$ (a natural number; a trace consists of 1 or more states), $st$ to indicate a trace starting with state $s$ followed by the trace $t$, $|st| = 1 + |t|$, and functions $head$ and $tail$, defined as follows: $head(st) = s$, $head(t) = t$ if $|t| = 1$, $tail(st) = t$ and $tail(t)$ is undefined if $|t| \leq 1$ ($tail$ is a partial function). Moreover, given a finite trace $t = s_1 s_2 \ldots s_n$, we write $t_i$ to indicate the suffix trace $s_i \ldots s_n$.

**Definition 2.** *Let $t = s_1 s_2 \ldots s_n$ be a finite trace of a multi-agent program such that $|t| \geq 1$. The satisfaction of MDL expressions by the trace $t$ is defined as follows:*

$t \models \texttt{i@Beliefs}(\phi) \Leftrightarrow \phi \in V_b(i, head(t))$
$t \models \texttt{i@Goals}(\phi) \Leftrightarrow \phi \in V_g(i, head(t))$
$t \models \texttt{i@Plans}(\phi) \Leftrightarrow \phi \in V_p(i, head(t))$
$t \models \texttt{i@Events}(\phi) \Leftrightarrow \phi \in V_e(i, head(t))$
$t \models \phi \texttt{ and } \psi \Leftrightarrow t \models \phi \ \ and \ \ t \models \psi$
$t \models \phi \texttt{ or } \psi \Leftrightarrow t \models \phi \ \ or \ \ t \models \psi$
$t \models \phi \texttt{ implies } \psi \Leftrightarrow t \models \phi \ \ implies \ \ t \models \psi$
$t \models \texttt{not } \phi \Leftrightarrow t \not\models \phi$
$t \models \texttt{next } \phi \Leftrightarrow tail(t) \models \phi \ and \ |t| > 1$
$t \models \texttt{eventually } \phi \Leftrightarrow \exists i \leq |t| \ \ (t_i \models \phi)$
$t \models \texttt{always } \phi \Leftrightarrow \forall i \leq |t| \ \ (t_i \models \phi)$
$t \models \phi \texttt{ until } \psi \Leftrightarrow \exists i \leq |t| \ \ (t_i \models \psi \ and \ \forall j < i \ \ (t_j \models \phi))$

Based on this definition of MDL assertions, we have implemented some debugging tools that are activated and updated when their corresponding MDL assertion holds in a partial execution of a multi-agent program. These debugging tools are described in the next section. It should be noted that this definition of the satisfaction relation can behave different than the standards definition of satisfaction relation of LTL which is defined on infinite traces. For example, some LTL properties such as $\neg\texttt{next}\phi = \texttt{next}\neg\phi$ are valid only for infinite traces. However, the validity of such properties is not relevant for our debugging framework as debugging is only concerned with the execution thusfar and therefore with finite traces.

### 4.3   Multi-Agent Debugging Tools

This section presents a set of Multi-Agent Debugging Tools (MADTs) to illustrate how the assertion language can be used to debug multi-agent programs. In order to use the debugging tools, markers are placed in the multi-agent programs to denote under which conditions which debugging tool should be activated. A marker consists of a (optional) MDL assertion and a debugging tool. The MDL assertion of a marker specifies the condition under which the debugging tool of the marker should be activated. In particular, if the MDL assertion of a marker evaluates to true for a given finite trace/partial execution of a multi-agent program, then the debugging tool of the marker will be activated. When

the assertion of a marker is empty (i.e., not specified), then the associated debugging tool will be activated as soon as the multi-agent program is executed.
Besides a MDL assertion, a marker can also have a group parameter. This group
parameter specifies which agents the debugging tool operates on. The general
syntax of a marker is defined as follows:

$\langle marker \rangle$     ::= "MADT(" $\langle madt \rangle$ [", " $\langle mdl\_query \rangle$][", @" $\langle group \rangle$] ")"

$\langle group \rangle$     ::= "[" $\langle group\_id \rangle$ "]" | $\langle agent\_list \rangle$

The semantics of these marker as well as the use of parameters in the markers are
explained informally. The markers that are included in a multi-agent program
are assumed to be processed by the interpreter of the corresponding multi-agent
programming language. In particular, the execution of a multi-agent program
by the interpreter will generate consecutive states of a multi-agent program and,
thereby, generating a trace. At each step of the trace generation (i.e., at each
step where a new state is generated) the interpreter evaluates the assertion of the
specified markers in the initial state of the finite trace (according to the definition
of the satisfaction relation; see definition 2) and activates the corresponding
debugging tools if the assertions are evaluated to true. This means that the
trace of a multi-agent program is verified after every change in the trace. This
mode of processing markers corresponds to the *continuous debugging mode* and
does not stop the execution of the multi-agent program; markers are processed
*during* the execution of the program. In the *post mortem debugging mode*, where
a multi-agent program is executed and stopped after some deliberation steps, the
markers are processed based on the finite trace generated by the partial execution
of the program. It is important to note again that assertions are always evaluated
in the initial state of traces as we aim at debugging the (temporal) behavior of
multi-agent programs and thus their execution traces from the initial state. The
following example illustrates the use of a marker in a multi-agent program:

```
Agents:        cleaner   :  cleaner.prog    1
               explorer  :  explorer.prog   3
Environment:   gridworld

Markers:       MADT(breakpoint_madt, eventually cleaner@Beliefs(bomb(_,_)) )
```

This marker, which is placed in the multi-agent program, activates a breakpoint as soon as the cleaner agent believes that there is a bomb in a cell of
the `gridworld`. It is important to note that if no MDL assertion is given in a
specified marker, then the associated debugging tool will be activated after each
update of the trace. Removing the specified MDL expression from the above-
mentioned marker means that the execution of the multi-agent program will be
stopped after each trace update. This results in a kind of stepping execution
mode. Also note that if no group parameter is given in the marker, the "[all]"
group is used by default.

In the rest of this section, we illustrate the use of a set of debugging tools
that have shown to be effective in debugging software systems. Examples of
debugging tools are breakpoint, logging, state overview, or message list. The

behavior of these debugging tools in the context of markers are explained in the rest of this section. The proposed set of debugging tools is by no means exhaustive and can be extended with other debugging tools. We thus do neither propose new debugging tools nor evaluate their effectiveness. The focus of this paper is a framework for using (existing) debugging tools to check cognitive and temporal behavior of multi-agent program. Our approach is generic in the sense that a debugging tool can be associated with an assertion by means of a marker and that markers can be used in two debugging modes.

**Breakpoint.** The breakpoints for multi-agent programs are similar to breakpoints used in concurrent programs. They can be used to pause the execution of a single agent program, a specific group of agent programs, or the execution of the entire multi-agent program. Once the execution of a program is paused, a developer can inspect and browse through the program execution trace generated so far (including the program state in which the program execution is paused). The developer can then continue the program execution in a stepping mode to generate consecutive program states. It is important to note that an attempt to further execute the program continuously (not in stepping mode) pauses immediately since the assertion associated to the breakpoint will be evaluated in the initial state of an extension of the same trace. In general, if an assertion evaluates to true in a state of a trace, then it will evaluate to true in the same state of any extension of that trace.

The example below demonstrates the use of a conditional breakpoint on the agents `explorer1` and `explorer2`. The developer wants to pause both agents as soon as agent `cleaner` has the plan to go to cell (5, 5).

```
MADT(breakpoint_madt,
     eventually cleaner@Plans(goto(5, 5)), @[explorer1, explorer2])
```

Note that it is possible to use the cognitive state of more than one agent as the break condition. The next example demonstrates how a developer can get an indication about whether the number of explorer and cleaner agents are suitable for a certain scenario. In fact, if there are not enough cleaners to remove bombs, or when all explorers are located at the same area, then all explorers will find the same bomb.

```
MADT(breakpoint_madt, eventually [explorers]@Beliefs(bomb(X,Y)))
```

The breakpoint tool is set to pause the execution of all agents, once all agents that are part of the "explorers" group have the belief that a bomb is located at one and the same cell (X,Y). If instead of X and Y the underscore parameters (i.e., _) are used, then the execution will be paused if the explorers agents have the belief that a bomb is located at a position, though not necessarily the same position. Note that it does not need to indicate explicitly to pause the execution of *all* agents. The breakpoint is useful in conjunction with the watch tool to investigate the mental state of the agent. Other agent debugging approaches, e.g., [5], propose a similar concept for breakpoints, but for a single BDI-based agent program. Also, Jason [3] allows annotations in plan labels to associate extra information to a plan. One standard plan annotation is called a breakpoint. If the debug mode is used and the agent executes a plan that has a breakpoint annotation, execution pauses and the control is given to the developer, who can then use the step and run buttons to carry on the execution. Note that in contrast with other approaches, the condition in our approach may contain logic and temporal aspects.

**Watch.** The watch can display the current mental state of one or more agents. Furthermore, the watch allows the developer to query any of the agents' bases. The developer can, for example, use the watch to check if a belief follows from the belief base. It is also possible to use a MDL assertion in the watch; if the assertion evaluates to *true*, the watch will show the substitution found. The watch tool can also be used to visualize which agents have shared or conflicting beliefs. The watch tool is regularly used in conjunction with a conditional breakpoint. Once the breakpoint is hit, the watch tool can be used to observe the mental state of one or more agents. In general, the watch tool should be updated unconditionally and for all agents in the system. Adding MADT(watch_madt) to a multi-agent program will activate the watch on every update of its execution trace. In Jason [3], a similar tool is introduced which is called the mind inspector. This mind inspector, however, can only be used to observe the mental state of individual agents. Jadex [13] offers a similar tool called the BDI-inspector which allows visualization and modification of internal BDI-concepts of individual agents.

**Logging.** Logging is done by the usage of probes which, unlike breakpoints, do not halt the multi-agent program execution. When a probe is activated it writes the current state of a multi-agent program, or a part of it, to a log screen or a file (depending on the type of probe). Using a probe without a MDL assertion and without a group specification is very common and can be done by adding MADT(probe_madt) in multi-agent programs. The probe will be activated on every update of the program trace such that it keeps a log of all multi-agent program states. The next example saves the state of the multi-agent program when the cleaner agent aims at dropping a bomb at a position and there is an agent who believes there is a bomb at that position. The same parameters X and Y are used to ensure that these positions are the same.

```
MADT(probe_madt,
     eventually(cleaner@Plans(dropBomb(X,Y)) and A@Beliefs(bomb(X,Y)))
)
```

It is important to note that in the continuous debugging mode the assertion part of the marker will be evaluated in the initial state of a finite program trace and after each execution step. This means that the probe_madt will be activated directly after an execution step that generates a trace on which the assertion evaluates to true. A developer can thus use such expressions (of the form eventually$\phi$) in order to be notified at once and as soon as the program execution satisfies it. Once this expression evaluates to true, the developer should know that any continuation of the program execution will evaluates it to true.

Thus, from a developer's perspective, properties specified by expressions of the form `eventually`$\phi$ can be used to get notified (or stop the execution) only once and as soon as it is satisfied. Similar work is done in Jadex [16] where a logging agent is introduced to allow collection and viewing of logged messages from Jadex agents. It should be noted that the probes in our approach offer the added functionality of filtering on a cognitive condition of *one ore more agents.*

**Message-list.** Another visualization tool is the message-list, which is one of the simplest forms of visualization. The message-list keeps track of the messages sent between agents, by placing them in a list. This list can be sorted on each of the elements of the messages. For example, sorting the messages on the "sender" element can help finding a specific message send by a known agent. Besides ordering, the list can also be filtered. For example, we could filter on "Senders" and only show the message from the sender with the name "cleaner". To update the message-list on every update of the trace, we can place the marker `MADT(message_list_madt)` in the multi-agent program. Another use of the message-list could be to show only the messages from within a certain group, e.g., `MADT(message_list_madt, @[explorers])` can be used to view the messages exchanged between the members of the explorers group. Finally, in our proposal one can also filter exchanged messages based on conditions on the mental states of individual agents. For example, in the context of our gridworld example, one can filter useless messages, i.e., messages whose content are known facts. Note that exchanging too many useless messages is a sign of non-effective communication. The example below triggers the message list when an agent `A`, who believes there is a bomb at coordinates `X,Y`, receives a message about this fact from another agent `S`.

```
MADT(message_list_madt,
    eventually(A@Beliefs(bomb(X,Y)) and A@Messages(S,P,bombAt(X,Y)))
)
```

All existing agent programming platforms offer a similar tool to visualize exchanged messages. The main difference with our approach is the ability to log when certain cognitive conditions hold.

**Causal tree.** The causal tree tool shows each message and how it relates to other messages in a tree form. The hierarchy of the tree is based on the relation between messages (replies become branches of the message they reply to). Messages on the same hierarchical level, of the same branch, are ordered chronologically. The advantage of the causal tree (over the message-list) is that it is easier to spot communication errors. When, for example, a reply is placed out of context (not in relation with its cause) this implies there are communication errors. The causal tree also provides an easy overview to see if replies are sent when required. The causal tree tool can be used by adding the marker `MADT(causal_tree_madt)` to multi-agent programs. Another example could be to set the group parameter and only display message from a certain group, e.g., `MADT(causal_tree_madt, @[explorers])`.

**Sequence diagram.** The sequence diagram is a commonly used diagram in the Unified Modeling Language (UML) or its corresponding agent version (AUML). An instantiation of a sequence diagram can be used to give a clear overview of (a specific part of) the communication in a multi-agent program. They can help to find irregularities in the communication between agents. The sequence diagram tool can be used by adding the marker MADT(sequence_diagram_madt) to multi-agent programs. This example updates the sequence diagram on every update of the trace. Another example could be to use the group parameter and only update the sequence diagram for the agents in a certain group, e.g., MADT(sequence_diagram_madt, @[cleaner, explorer2]). Adding this marker to our multi-agent program will show the communication between the agents "cleaner" and "explorer2". The sequence diagram tool is useful in conjunction with a conditional breakpoint and the stepwise execution mode where the diagram can be constructed step by step. The sequence diagram is also useful in conjunction with the probe. The probe can be used to display detailed information about the messages. Similar tools are proposed in some other approaches, e.g., the sniffer agent in [1]. However, we believe that the sequence diagram tool in our approach is more effective since it can be used for specific parts of agent communication.

**Visualization.** Sometimes the fact that a message is sent is more important than the actual contents of the message. This is, for example, the case when a strict hierarchy forbids certain agents to communicate. In other cases it can be important to know how much communication takes place between agents. For such situations the *dynamic agent communication* tool is a valuable add-on. This tool shows all the agents and represents the communication between the agents by lines. When agents have more communication overhead the line width increase in size and the agents are clustered closer together. This visualization tool, which can be triggered by adding the marker MADT(dynamic_agent_madt) to multi-agent program, is shown on the left side of figure 1. Another visualization tool is the static group tool, which shows specific agent groups, as illustrated on the right side of figure 1. The line between the groups indicates the (amount) of communication overhead between the groups. In addition the developer can "jump into" a group and graphically view the agents and the communication between them. If two groups show an unusual amount of communication overhead the developer can jump into the group and locate the source of the problem. The marker to activate the static group tool can be specified as follow:

```
MADT(static_group_madt, @[explorers])
MADT(static_group_madt, @[cleaners])
```

The above markers update the tool on every change of the multi-agent program trace. According to these markers, the groups "explorers" and "cleaners" will be visualized. Generally it is most valuable to have a visualization of all communication between agents. However, to pinpoint the exact problem in a communication protocol it can be an invaluable addition to use a condition, which filters the messages that are shown. As discussed in the related works section, other approaches (e.g., [4]) offers similar tools.

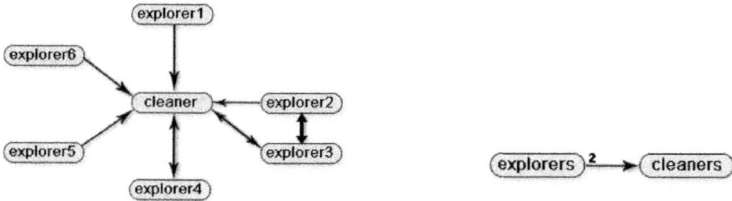

**Fig. 1.** The dynamic agent communication tool (left) and the static group tool (right)

## 5    Conclusion

In this paper, we briefly discussed existing debugging approaches for multi-agent programs and presented a generic approach for debugging BDI-based multi-agent programs. Our approach is generic as it does not assume any specific representation for the internals of individual agents as well as the content of their exchanged messages. The proposed approach is based on an assertion language to express cognitive and temporal properties of the executions of multi-agent programs. The expressions of the assertion language can be used to trigger debugging tools such as breakpoints, watches, probes, and different visualization tools to examine and debug communication between individual agents. Since the assertion language is abstract, it can be applied to arbitrary BDI-based multi-agent programming languages.

We have already applied this debugging approach to 2APL [7] platform by modifying its corresponding interpreter to process debugging markers in a continuous mode. The 2APL interpreter evaluates the expressions of the assertion language based on the partial execution trace of the multi-agent programs. We have also implemented the proposed debugging tools that are discussed in this paper for the 2APL platform. The parser of 2APL is modified to analyze the markers included in the multi-agent program file. This implementation of 2APL is the official 2APL distribution that can be downloaded from http://www.cs.uu.nl/2apl/. It should be noted that the examples discussed in this paper are already implemented in 2APL and the provided analysis is based on our implementation results.

We plan to extend the debugging mechanism of 2APL implementation such that debugging markers can be processed both in continuous and post mortem modes. We also plan to extend the MDL language by including constructs related to the external environments of a multi-agent program. In this way, one can specify properties that relates agent states to the state of the external environments. Moreover, we plan to extend our debugging framework with the society aspects that may be involved in multi-agent programming languages [12]. Recent developments in multi-agent programming languages[9,10,11,8] have proposed specific programming constructs enabling the implementation of social concepts such as norms, roles, obligations, and sanctions. Debugging such multi-agent programs requires therefore specific debugging constructs to specify properties related to the social aspects and facilitate finding and resolving defects involved in such programs. It should be noted that the presented debugging framework assumes all agents are developed on one single platform such that their executions for debugging purposes are not distributed on different platforms. One important challenge and a future work on debugging multi-agent systems remains the debugging of multi-agent programs that run simultaneously on different platforms. We believe that testing is an indispensable part of evaluating multi-agent programs and plan to follow the existing approaches on *testing* multi-agent programs and integrate them in our proposed debugging approach. In this way, we may generate a set of critical test traces and start debugging them in post mortem mode.

# References

1. Bellifemine, F., Bergenti, F., Caire, G., Poggi, A.: JADE - a java agent development framework. In: Multi-Agent Programming: Languages, Platforms and Applications. Kluwer, Dordrecht (2005)
2. Bordini, R.H., Dastani, M., Dix, J., El Fallah Seghrouchni, A.: Multi-Agent Programming: Languages, Platforms and Applications. Springer, Berlin (2005)
3. Bordini, R.H., Wooldridge, M., Hübner, J.F.: Programming Multi-Agent Systems in AgentSpeak using Jason. John Wiley & Sons, Chichester (2007)
4. Botía, J.A., Hernansáez, J.M., Gómez-Skarmeta, A.F.: On the application of clustering techniques to support debugging large-scale multi-agent systems. In: Bordini, R.H., Dastani, M.M., Dix, J., El Fallah Seghrouchni, A. (eds.) PROMAS 2006. LNCS (LNAI), vol. 4411, pp. 217–227. Springer, Heidelberg (2007)
5. Collier, R.: Debugging agents in agent factory. In: Bordini, R.H., Dastani, M.M., Dix, J., El Fallah Seghrouchni, A. (eds.) PROMAS 2006. LNCS (LNAI), vol. 4411, pp. 229–248. Springer, Heidelberg (2007)
6. Barber, K.S., Lam, D.N.: Debugging agent behavior in an implemented agent system. In: Bordini, R.H., Dastani, M.M., Dix, J., El Fallah Seghrouchni, A. (eds.) PROMAS 2004. LNCS (LNAI), vol. 3346, pp. 104–125. Springer, Heidelberg (2005)
7. Dastani, M.: 2APL: A practical agent programming language. Autonomous Agents and Multi-Agent Systems 16(3), 214–248 (2008)
8. Dastani, M., Tinnemeier, N.A.M., Meyer, J.-J.C.: A programming language for normative multi-agent systems. In: Dignum, V. (ed.) Multi-Agent Systems: Semantics and Dynamics of Organizational Models, ch. 16. IGI Global (2008)
9. Esteva, M., Rodríguez-Aguilar, J.A., Rosell, B., Arcos, J.L.: Ameli: An agent-based middleware for electronic institutions. In: Proc. of AAMAS 2004, New York, US (2004)
10. Garcia-Camino, A., Noriega, P., Rodriguez-Aguilar, J.A.: Implementing norms in electronic institutions. In: Proc. of AAMAS 2005, pp. 667–673. ACM, New York (2005)
11. Hubner, J.F., Sichman, J.S., Boissier, O.: Developing organised multiagent systems using the moise+ model: programming issues at the system and agent levels. Int. J. Agent-Oriented Softw. Eng. 1(3/4), 370–395 (2007)
12. Nwana, H.S., Ndumu, D.T., Lee, L.C., Collis, J.C.: ZEUS. a toolkit for building distributed multi-agent systems. Applied Artificial Intelligence Journal 13(1), 129–185 (1999)

13. Pokahr, A., Braubach, L., Lamersdorf, W.: Jadex: A BDI reasoning engine. In: Multi-Agent Programming: Languages, Platforms and Applications. Kluwer, Dordrecht (2005)
14. Poutakidis, D., Padgham, L., Winikoff, M.: Debugging multi-agent systems using design artifacts: The case of interaction protocols. In: Proceedings of AAMAS 2002, pp. 960–967 (2002)
15. Poutakidis, D., Padgham, L., Winikoff, M.: An exploration of bugs and debugging in multi-agent systems. In: Proceedings of the 14th International Symposium on Methodologies for Intelligent Systems (ISMIS), pp. 628–632. ACM Press, New York (2003)
16. Sudeikat, J., Braubach, L., Pokahr, A., Lamersdorf, W., Renz, W.: Validation of BDI agents. In: Bordini, R.H., Dastani, M.M., Dix, J., El Fallah Seghrouchni, A. (eds.) PROMAS 2006. LNCS (LNAI), vol. 4411, pp. 185–200. Springer, Heidelberg (2007)
17. Vigueras, G., Botía, J.A.: Tracking causality by visualization of multi-agent interactions using causality graphs. In: Dastani, M.M., El Fallah Seghrouchni, A., Ricci, A., Winikoff, M. (eds.) ProMAS 2007. LNCS (LNAI), vol. 4908, pp. 190–204. Springer, Heidelberg (2008)
18. Winikoff, M.: JACK$^{TM}$ intelligent agents: An industrial strength platform. In: Multi-Agent Programming: Languages, Platforms and Applications. Kluwer, Dordrecht (2005)

# Space-Time Diagram Generation for Profiling Multi Agent Systems

Dinh Doan Van Bien, David Lillis, and Rem W. Collier

School of Computer Science and Informatics
University College Dublin
dinh@doanvanbien.com, {david.lillis,rem.collier}@ucd.ie

**Abstract.** Advances in Agent Oriented Software Engineering have focused on the provision of frameworks and toolkits to aid in the creation of Multi Agent Systems (MASs). However, despite the need to address the inherent complexity of such systems, little progress has been made in the development of tools to allow for the debugging and understanding of their inner workings.

This paper introduces a novel performance analysis system, named AgentSpotter, which facilitates such analysis. AgentSpotter was developed by mapping conventional profiling concepts to the domain of MASs. We outline its integration into the Agent Factory multi agent framework.

## 1 Introduction

Recent developments in the area of Multi Agent Systems (MASs) have been concerned with bridging the gap between theory and practice, by allowing concrete implementations of theoretical foundations to be built and deployed. However, the dearth of agent-specific development and debugging tools remains a significant obstacle to MASs being adopted in industry on a large scale.

While some simple debugging and logging tools exist for MAS analysis, these tend not to aid in reasoning about large-scale system when viewed at the high agent-oriented abstraction level. Such tools typically allow for traditional debugging actions such as state stepping and breakpoint insertion.

One popular performance analysis technique is known as *profiling*. Profiling is based on the observation that the majority of the execution time of a program can be attributed to a small number of *bottlenecks* (or *hot spots*). By improving the efficiency of these portions of a program, overall performance can be dramatically improved. Profiling was initially introduced by Donald E. Knuth in an empirical study conducted on FORTRAN programs [1]. Since then, the technique has been successfully applied to a variety of languages, platforms and architectures.

The aim of this paper is to apply the principles of traditional profiling systems in a multi agent environment, so as to facilitate the developers of MASs in debugging their applications by gaining a better understanding of where the bottlenecks exist and performance penalties are incurred.

L. Braubach, J.-P. Briot, and J. Thangarajah (Eds.): ProMAS 2009, LNAI 5919, pp. 170–184, 2010.

This paper is organised as follows: Section 2 provides a brief overview of existing tools aimed at aiding in the analysis of MASs. In Section 3, we introduce the AgentSpotter profiling system, with particular focus on outlining a conceptual model for generic MAS profiling. A concrete implementation of this work, aimed at the Agent Factory MAS framework, is outlined in Section 4. Section 5 presents the space-time diagram produced by AgentSpotter in more detail, with an evaluation of its usefulness given in Section 6. Finally, Section 7 presents our conclusions and ideas for future work.

## 2   Related Work

In designing a profiler for MASs, the features that tend to be present in traditional profilers for non-MAS applications must be identified. It is also necessary to examine those debugging and analysis tools that already exist for MASs.

The motivation behind the use of profiling on computer applications is clearly outlined in Knuth's observation that "less than 4% of a program accounts for more than half of its running time" [1]. This statement implies that a developer can achieve substantial increases in performance by identifying and improving those parts of the program that account for the majority of the execution time. The key aim of profilers is to identify these bottlenecks.

Another observation leading to the widespread adoption of profilers as debugging tools is that there frequently exists a mismatch between the actual run-time behaviour of a system and the programmers' mental map of what they expect this behaviour to be. Profilers are useful in enlightening developers to particular aspects of their programs that they may not otherwise have considered.

A traditional profiler typically consists of two logical parts. Firstly, an *instrumentation apparatus* is directly weaved into the program under study or run side-by-side to gather and record execution data. Secondly, a *post-processing system* uses this data to generate meaningful performance analysis listings or visualisations.

In the traditional software engineering community, historical profilers such as gprof [2] or performance analysis APIs like ATOM [3] and the Java Virtual Machine Tool Interface (JVMTI) [4] have made performance analysis more accessible for researchers and software engineers. However, the MAS community does not yet have general access to these types of tools.

Unique amongst all of the mainstream MAS development platforms, Cougaar is alone in integrating a performance measurement infrastructure directly into the system architecture [5]. Although this is not applicable to other platforms, it does provide a good insight into the features that MAS developers could reasonably expect from any performance measurement application. The principal characteristics of this structure are as follows:

- Primary data channels consist of raw polling sensors at the heart of the system execution engine that gather simple low-impact data elements such as counters and event sensors.
- Secondary channels provide more elaborate information, such as summaries of the state of individual components and history analysis that stores performance data over lengthy running times.

- Computer-level metrics provide data on such items as CPU load, network load and memory usage.
- The message transport service gathers data on messages flowing through it.
- An extension mechanism based on servlets allows the addition of visualisation plugins that bind to the performance metrics data source.
- The service that is charged with gathering these metrics is designed so as to have no impact on system performance when not in use.

Other analysis tools exist for aiding the development of MASs. However, these tend to be narrower in their focus, concentrating only on specific aspects of debugging MASs and typically being only applicable to a specific agent platform. The Agent Factory Debugger [6] is an example of a tool that is typical of most multi agent frameworks. Its principal function is inspecting the status and mental state of an individual agent: its goals, beliefs, commitments and the messages it has exchanged with other agents. Tools such as this give limited information about the interaction between agents and the consequences of these interactions.

The Brahms toolkit features an AgentViewer that allows developers to view along a time line the actions that particular agents have taken, so as to enable them to verify that the conceptual model of the MAS is reflected in reality [7]. An administrator tool for the LS/TS agent platform provides some high-level system monitoring information, such as overall memory consumption and data on the size of the agent population [8]. Another type of agent debugging tool is the ACLAnalyzer that has been developed for the JADE platform [9]. Rather than concentrating on individual agents, it is intended to analyse agent interaction in order to see how the community of agents interacts and is organised. In addition to visualising the number and size of messages sent between specific agents, it also employs clustering in order to identify cliques in the agent community.

These latter tools are focused mostly on identifying what actions an agent is carrying out, together with identifying the reasons why such actions are taken (in response to the agents' own belief set or as a result of receiving communication from other agents).

## 3   AgentSpotter Overview

The overriding objective of AgentSpotter is to map the traditional concepts of profiling to agent-oriented concepts so as to build a profiler tool for MAS developers. It could be argued that most mainstream agent toolkits are written in Java, hence the existing profiling tools for the Java programming language are appropriate for the analysis of such platforms and their agents. However, to do so would necessitate the mapping of low-level method profiles to high-level agent-specific behaviour. Thus, tools aimed specifically at Java operate at an inappropriate conceptual level to be of use in agent analysis. Although it may be useful to incorporate some Object-Oriented metrics into an MAS profiling tool, the focus of this paper is on the agent-specific metrics that are appropriate.

Ideally, MASs should be capable of managing their own performance and identifying their own bottlenecks which hamper system efficiency, and indeed

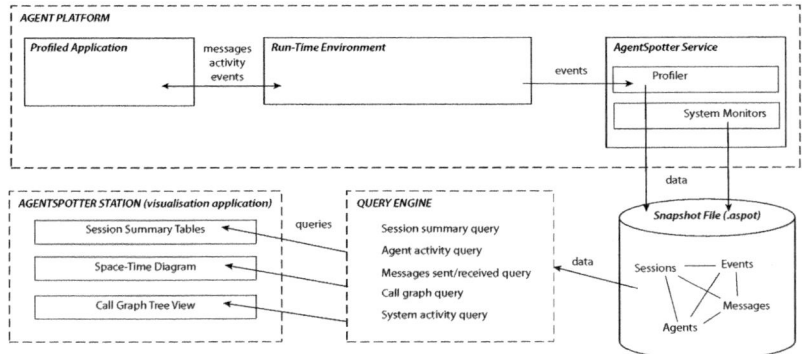

**Fig. 1.** AgentSpotter abstract architecture

much work is being undertaken towards this goal [10]. However, until this aim is realised, the provision of analysis tools aimed at aiding human developers identify issues with their systems remains of paramount importance.

This section outlines the abstract infrastructure of the AgentSpotter system, which is capable of being integrated into any agent platform. An analysis of the integration of AgentSpotter into a specific agent platform (namely Agent Factory) is contained in Section 4.

The AgentSpotter abstract architecture is displayed in Figure 1, using the following graphical conventions:

- Top-level architectural units are enclosed in dashed lines and are titled in slanted capital letters, e.g. ⌐ _ _ _ _ _ _ _ _ _ _ _ _ _ _ _ _ _ _ _ _ _ ┐ | *AGENT PLATFORM* |
- Self-contained software packages are enclosed in solid lines e.g | Profiler |
- Logical software modules (groups of packages) are titled using slanted capitalised names e.g. | *AgentSpotter Service* |

- Arrows denote data or processing interactions e.g.    queries ⟶

At the highest level, the *AgentSpotter Service* should communicate with the *Run-Time Environment* to capture the profiling data from a *Profiled Application* running inside an *Agent Platform*. The captured data should be stored into a *Snapshot File* which would then be processed by a *Query Engine* to generate the input data for *AgentSpotter Station*, the visualisation application.

The AgentSpotter profiler monitors performance events generated by the Agent Platform's Run-Time Environment. These include such events as agent management events, messaging and other platform service activity. Additionally, the AgentSpotter service may employ system monitors to record performance information such as CPU load, memory usage or network throughput. This provides a general context for the event-based information.

The event data and other information collected by the AgentSpotter profile is stored in a *snapshot file*, which contains the results of a single uninterrupted data capture session. This snapshot contains a series of raw instrumentation data. Because large MASs may generate potentially hundreds of events per second, it is necessary to introduce a *Query Engine* that is capable of extracting summaries and other information and make it available to visualisation tools in a transparent manner. Ideally, this should be through a data manipulation language such as SQL so as to facilitate the specification of rich and complex queries.

The final component of the abstract architecture is the *AgentSpotter Station*, which is the visualisation tool that summarises the information gathered from the Query Engine in a visual form. The principal focus of this paper is the Space-Time Diagram, which is presented in Section 5.

When profiling any application, it is important to identify the appropriate execution unit for profiling (e.g. in the context of object-oriented programming, this would typically be an object or a method). For profiling a MAS, we believe that the appropriate execution units are individual agents.

At the *agent level*, when considering only the autonomous computational entity abstracted away from the interaction with its peers, the focus is on responsiveness. It is obvious that the main influence on the responsiveness of an agent is the amount of computation it requires to carry out the set of tasks required to meet its design objectives. Agreeing with the BT researchers in [11], we make a further distinction based on the *rationality level* of the agent architecture. For reactive agents, this set of tasks includes only purely reactive behaviour, which is similar to the behaviour of a traditional process. For deliberative agents that implement a reasoning system, the computational cost of the reasoning activity must be considered separately from the actual task execution. Based on this analysis, the minimum information provided by the system should include:

- **Agent description:** name, role, type (deliberative or reactive) of the agent.
- **Cumulative activity:** cumulative computation time used by the agent.
- **Perception time:** perception time used by a deliberative agent.
- **Action time:** task execution time used by a deliberative agent.
- **Reasoning time:** reasoning time used by a deliberative agent.
- **% session activity:** percentage of the global session computation time used by the agent.
- **Number of iterations:** number of non-zero duration iterations used by the agent.
- **Total number of messages sent and received:** total number of ACL messages exchanged by the agent.

Additionally, a number of global statistics should also be maintained:

- **Total duration:** session run-time recorded.
- **Total activity:** amount of computation time recorded over the session.
- **Total number of messages:** number of messages sent or received by agents on the platform being profiled.
- **Average number of active agents per second:** This gives an idea of the level of concurrency in the application.

**Table 1.** Benchmark application flat profile

| Total Session Time | 18:50.691 |
|---|---|
| Total Activity | 10:29.164 |
| Messages Sent | 1206 |
| Messages Received | 1206 |
| Time Slice Duration | 1000 ms |

| Agent | $T > 0$ iterations | $T > 100\%$ overload | Activity mm:ss.ms | % Session activity | $Max(T)$ ss.ms | $Average(T)$ ss.ms | Msg. sent | Msg. rec. |
|---|---|---|---|---|---|---|---|---|
| agent001 | 338 | 22 | 1:08.564 | 10.90 | 3.740 | 0.202 | 6 | 57 |
| agent009 | 365 | 21 | 1:04.257 | 10.21 | 3.425 | 0.176 | 13 | 77 |
| agent004 | 349 | 22 | 1:01.529 | 9.78 | 3.235 | 0.176 | 10 | 69 |
| agent014 | 284 | 14 | 46.413 | 7.38 | 3.148 | 0.163 | 2 | 36 |
| agent003 | 401 | 13 | 43.881 | 6.97 | 3.323 | 0.109 | 12 | 76 |
| agent006 | 361 | 12 | 40.141 | 6.38 | 3.279 | 0.111 | 12 | 73 |
| agent005 | 367 | 12 | 34.903 | 5.55 | 3.325 | 0.095 | 17 | 76 |
| agent013 | 301 | 9 | 34.716 | 5.52 | 3.190 | 0.115 | 14 | 71 |
| agent007 | 378 | 11 | 31.864 | 5.06 | 3.356 | 0.084 | 21 | 71 |
| agent008 | 357 | 7 | 30.850 | 4.90 | 3.201 | 0.086 | 14 | 72 |
| agent010 | 330 | 8 | 30.280 | 4.81 | 3.147 | 0.091 | 21 | 81 |
| agent015 | 285 | 9 | 29.382 | 4.67 | 3.257 | 0.103 | 4 | 42 |
| agent002 | 348 | 8 | 23.196 | 3.69 | 3.147 | 0.066 | 9 | 70 |
| agent011 | 357 | 5 | 19.363 | 3.08 | 3.095 | 0.054 | 4 | 39 |
| agent012 | 225 | 3 | 13.172 | 2.09 | 3.049 | 0.058 | 9 | 41 |
| master2 | 901 | 0 | 6.681 | 1.06 | 0.183 | 0.007 | 504 | 86 |
| master1 | 873 | 0 | 6.485 | 1.03 | 0.227 | 0.007 | 514 | 82 |
| agent024 | 46 | 2 | 6.281 | 1.00 | 3.045 | 0.136 | 3 | 7 |
| agent019 | 31 | 1 | 4.449 | 0.71 | 3.014 | 0.143 | 0 | 5 |
| agent026 | 42 | 1 | 4.400 | 0.70 | 3.084 | 0.104 | 0 | 4 |
| agent030 | 26 | 1 | 4.002 | 0.64 | 3.132 | 0.153 | 2 | 8 |
| agent017 | 46 | 1 | 3.811 | 0.61 | 3.031 | 0.082 | 0 | 3 |
| agent025 | 40 | 1 | 3.767 | 0.60 | 3.006 | 0.094 | 0 | 3 |
| agent027 | 31 | 1 | 3.694 | 0.59 | 3.103 | 0.119 | 0 | 2 |
| agent018 | 38 | 1 | 3.384 | 0.54 | 3.044 | 0.089 | 2 | 7 |
| agent020 | 39 | 0 | 1.762 | 0.28 | 0.547 | 0.045 | 0 | 3 |
| agent022 | 47 | 0 | 1.523 | 0.24 | 0.559 | 0.032 | 5 | 13 |
| agent021 | 32 | 0 | 1.300 | 0.21 | 0.555 | 0.040 | 2 | 7 |
| agent016 | 219 | 0 | 1.194 | 0.19 | 0.555 | 0.005 | 2 | 6 |
| agent029 | 38 | 0 | 1.039 | 0.17 | 0.550 | 0.027 | 2 | 8 |
| agent028 | 45 | 0 | 0.749 | 0.12 | 0.546 | 0.016 | 1 | 4 |
| agent032 | 34 | 0 | 0.749 | 0.12 | 0.561 | 0.022 | 1 | 4 |
| agent031 | 36 | 0 | 0.742 | 0.12 | 0.545 | 0.020 | 0 | 2 |
| agent023 | 40 | 0 | 0.598 | 0.10 | 0.543 | 0.014 | 0 | 1 |
| agent033 | 30 | 0 | 0.043 | 0.01 | 0.003 | 0.001 | 0 | 0 |

Following the convention of traditional profiling tools, we describe this information as a *flat profile*. AgentSpotter displays this by means of a JTable (provided by Java's Swing interface tools). An example of how the information is presented is given in Table 1. This is not necessarily an exhaustive list of every piece of information a developer may desire for identifying problems with a system, however we believe that other metrics (such as memory consumption) are not as crucial for the purposes of profiling the application.

## 4    Agent Factory Integration

Following the definition of the abstract architecture outlined above, a concrete (i.e. platform-specific) implementation was created for Agent Factory. Agent Factory is a cohesive framework that supports a structured approach to the development of agent-oriented applications [12]. This implementation is illustrated in Figure 2, which uses the same graphical conventions as Figure 1.

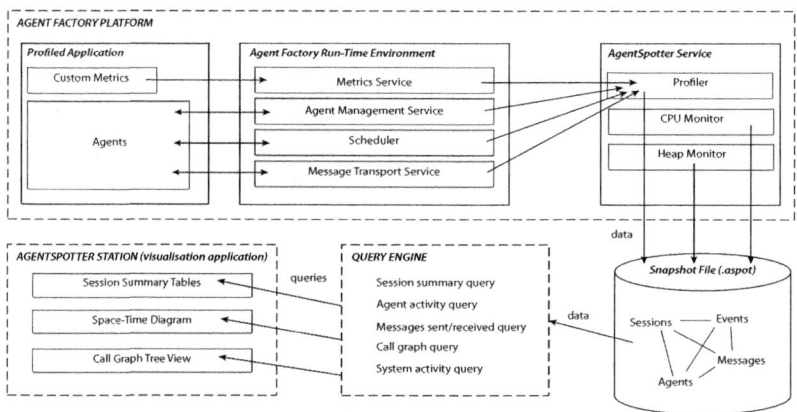

**Fig. 2.** AgentSpotter concrete architecture

To create a concrete implementation, only the platform-specific details must change, as the mechanisms required to monitor events vary from one agent platform to another. In contrast, the AgentSpotter file processing and visualisation components (shown in the lower part of Figure 2) are identical to those in the abstract architecture (Figure 1). Thus, when implementing AgentSpotter for a new type of agent platform, only the AgentSpotter Service that is coupled directly with the platform needs to be reprogrammed. Provided this service creates snapshot files in a consistent way, the Query Engine need not differentiate between agent platforms. AgentSpotter snapshot files are actually transportable single-file databases managed by the public domain *SQLite Database Engine* [13]. As a result, profiling data is stored as queryable relational database tables.

Within the Agent Factory Run-Time Environment, there are three specific subsystems that generate events of interest in agent profiling, and as such are

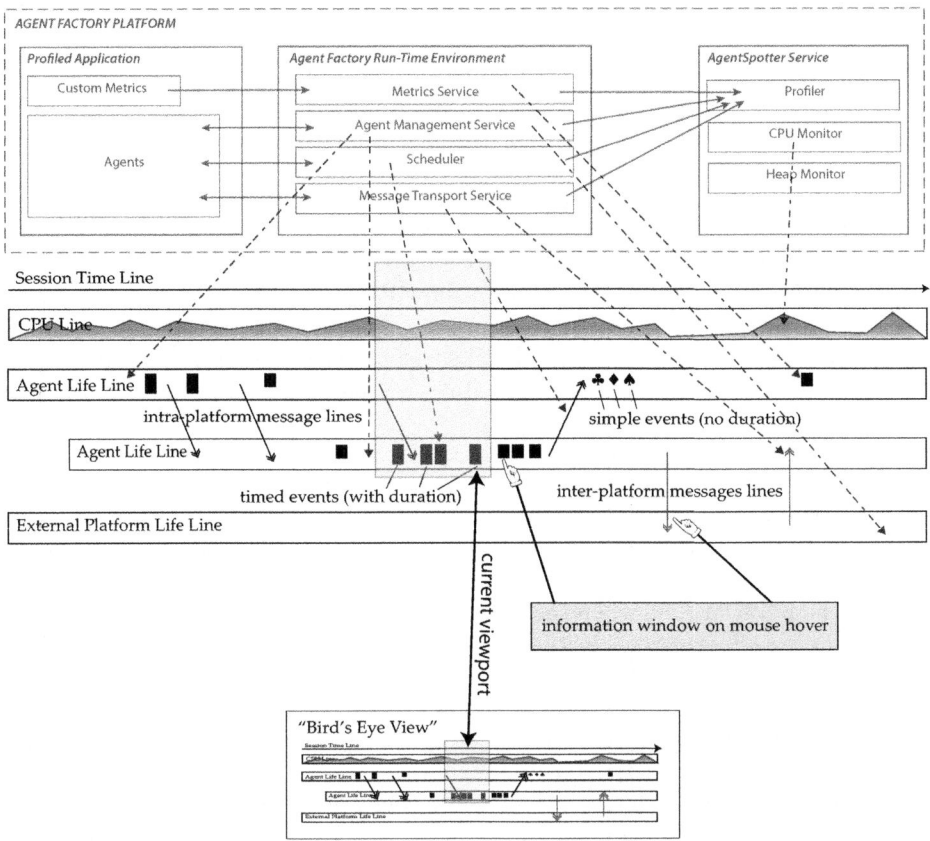

**Fig. 3.** AgentSpotter Space-Time Diagram specification annotated with AgentSpotter for Agent Factory infrastructure links (see Figure 2)

recorded by the AgentSpotter service. First, the *Agent Management Service* is responsible for creating, destroying, starting, stopping and suspending agents. It generates events corresponding to each of these actions, which are recorded in the snapshot file. The *Scheduler* is charged with scheduling which agents are permitted to execute at particular times and generates events based on this. Finally, the *Message Transport Service* records the sending and receipt of FIPA messages by agents.

## 5    Space-Time Diagram

In Section 3, we outlined the minimum amount of information that should be made available by an agent profiler. However, this information can be presented merely by the creation of a simple table. We believe that proper visualisation tools will be far more useful to a developer in understanding a MAS. This section introduces the Space-Time Diagram, which is at the core of the AgentSpotter Station visualisation application. The aim of this diagram is to give as much detail and context as possible about the performance of the MAS to the developer. The user may pan the view around and zoom in and out so as to reveal hidden details or focus on minute details.

The *Session Time Line* represents the running time of the application being profiled. Regardless of the position and scale of the current viewport, this time line remains visible to provide temporal context to the section being viewed and also to allow a developer to move to various points in the session.

The *CPU Line* is a graphical plot of the CPU load of the host system during the session. A vertical gradient going from green (low CPU usage) to red (high CPU usage) provides a quick graphical sense of system load. A popup information window reveals the exact usage statistics once the mouse is hovered over the line.

Perhaps the most important feature of the space-time diagram is the *Agent Time Lines*. Each of these display all the performance and communication events that occur for a single agent during a profiling session. A number of visual features are available to the developer so as to gain greater understanding of the status and performance of the system. For instance, an agent time line begins only at the point in time when the agent is created. This facilitates the developer in viewing the fluctuations in the agent population. Another simple visual aid is that a time line's caption (i.e. the name of the associated agent) is always visible, regardless of what position along the line a developer has scrolled to. Visual clutter may also be reduced by temporarily hiding certain time lines that are not of interest at a particular point in time.

The time line also changes colour to distinguish busier agents from the rest of the community. Darker lines indicate agents that have consumed a greater proportion of the system's CPU time. In a situation where system performance has been poor, this will allow a developer to quickly identify candidate agents for debugging, if they are consuming more resources than is appropriate or expected.

The default ordering of the time lines shares this aim. The time lines are in descending order of total computation time, again visually notifying the developer of those agents consuming more processing resources. However, a developer may alter this default order by dragging time lines into different positions, perhaps to group lines with particularly interesting interactions.

In addition to this simple information, the main purpose of the time line is to show events performed by an agent that are likely to be of interest from a performance point of view. These *performance events* are divided into two categories. *Simple performance events* are those that have a time stamp only. These are shown by means of standard icons (such as an envelope icon to denote that a message was received by the agent).

The other category of performance events are *timed performance events*. These events are typically actions being performed by an agent. A basic timed performance event displays as a rectangle with a fixed height and a width proportional to its duration. More elaborate event representations can be implemented. For

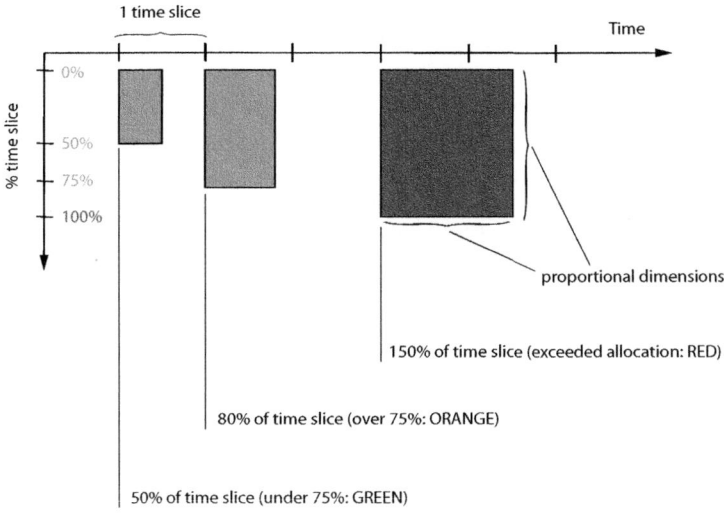

**Fig. 4.** Agent Factory agent activity representation in the Space-Time Diagram

example, in the context of Agent Factory's time slice based scheduler, we have represented the concept of time slice overshoots i.e. when an agent has overused its time slice allocation.

An example of how these timed events are represented is given in Figure 4. Each agent has a particular time slice within which it is expected to perform all of its actions in a particular iteration. Agents exceeding their time slice may prevent or delay other agents from accessing CPU. As a visual aid to identifying when this situation occurs, timing events are represented by coloured rectangles. The size of these rectangles is proportional to the duration of the event and the percentage of the allocated timeslice used. The colour code also indicates how the agent has used its available time. A green rectangle indicates that the agent has used anything up to 75% of the time available. From 75% to 100%, an orange rectangle indicates that the agent may require further analysis from the developer to avoid the danger of exceeding the time slice. Finally, whenever an agent exceeds its time, a red rectangle is used. It must be acknowledged that as a result of different approaches to scheduling agent platforms, timed performance events may not be available to a specific AgentSpotter implementation. When this arises, all events will be recorded as simple performance events.

Communication between agents is shown by lines linking the appropriate agent timelines. These include arrows to indicate the direction of the communication. Hovering the mouse pointer over such a line causes a popup window to display the FIPA headers and content of the message. There is also a distinction made between messages passed between agents housed on the same agent platform (intra-platform) and those passed between agents on different platforms (inter-platform). Since agents on other platforms will not have an agent time line, an *external platform life line* is drawn for each other platform with which agents communicate. Rather than linking with individual agent time lines, communications with these platforms are drawn directly to the external platform life line.

The combination of these communication lines and the performance event indicators are very useful in identifying the causes of agent activity. Given the inherently social nature of MASs, it is very common for agent activity to be motivated by communication. For example, an agent may be requested to perform a task by some other agent. Alternatively, an agent may receive a piece of information from another agent that it requires in order to perform a task to which it has previously committed as a result of its own goals and plans.

Providing such detailed visualisation of a MAS requires a substantial amount of screen space. The basic features of zooming and panning are complemented by the provision of a "bird's eye view", which displays a zoomed-out overview of the entire session. This allows the user to quickly move the current viewport to focus on a particular point in time during the session, as illustrated in Figure 3.

# 6   Evaluation

Having outlined the required features of AgentSpotter, along with details of its implementation, it is necessary to demonstrate how it can be utilised on a running MAS. To this end, a specialist benchmark application was developed that will allow the features of the AgentSpotter application to be shown.

## 6.1   Specification

The aim of the benchmark application is to perform all the activities necessary for AgentSpotter to display its features. The requirements for the application can be summarised as follows:

- **Load history:** a normally distributed random load history should be generated so that we can get an idea of a "normal" profile which can be contrasted with "abnormal" profiles where, for example, a single agent is monopolising all the load, or the load is spread equally among all agents.
- **Agent population:** the number of active agents should be changeable dynamically to simulate process escalation.
- **Interactions:** in addition to direct interactions, the application should exercise some task delegation scenarios. The idea is to generate multiple hops messaging scenarios and see their impact on performance.
- **Messages:** agents should generate a steady flow of messages with occasional bursts of intense communication.
- **Performance events:** all three performance behaviours described in Section 3 should be represented, i.e. green ($t \leq 50\%$ time slice), orange ($50\% \leq t \leq 75\%$ time slice), and red ($t > 100\%$).

These requirements were satisfied by creating a MAS with overseer agents that request worker agents to execute small, medium or large tasks. Worker agents that have been recently overloaded will simply refuse to carry out the tasks (in a real application they would inform requester about their refusal). From time to time, overseer agents would request agents to delegate some tasks. In this case, worker agents will behave as overseers just for one iteration. A simple interface allows the user to start and pause the process, along with the ability to set the number of active worker agents.

## 6.2 Evaluation Scenario and Objective

The following simple scenario was played out in order to generate a flat profile and space-time diagram.

1. Start the session with 12 worker agents and 2 overseer agents.
2. After 10 minutes add 15 worker agents to spread the load.
3. After 4 further minutes, suspend the process for 20 seconds.
4. At this point, reduce the number of worker agents to 12.
5. Run for 5 minutes more and then stop the session.

## 6.3 Flat profile

The resulting flat profile of this test is reproduced in Table 1. For the reader's convenience, the maximum value for each column is identified by an enclosing box. Overseer agents are called "master1" and "master2". The worker agents are called "agent" followed by a number e.g. "agent007".

Firstly, the benchmark appears to make a good job of producing a load history following a normal distribution.

Secondly, we can draw the following conclusions from a quick study of Table 1:

– The most active agents in terms of number of iterations are the overseer agents, "master1" and "master2", however in terms of CPU load and overload, three worker agents are topping the list with 30% of the total activity: "agent001", "agent009", and "agent003".
– The agents with the highest CPU load also display a high number of time slice overshoots, and a high average time slice duration.
– As expected, the overseer agents were very busy exchanging messages with the workers. However, it seems that messaging is not CPU intensive. This possibly results from the way in which message sending is implemented, with the CPU load indicated here corresponding to the scheduling of a message for sending, rather than the actual sending of the message. It may be necessary to attach a specialist monitor to the Message Transport Service to gain full information about the impact of sending messages. This causes the activity percentage of the overseer agents to be very low, at only 1%.

In this instance, the flat profile lends evidence to the notion that the actual behaviour of the system matches the design principles on which it was built.

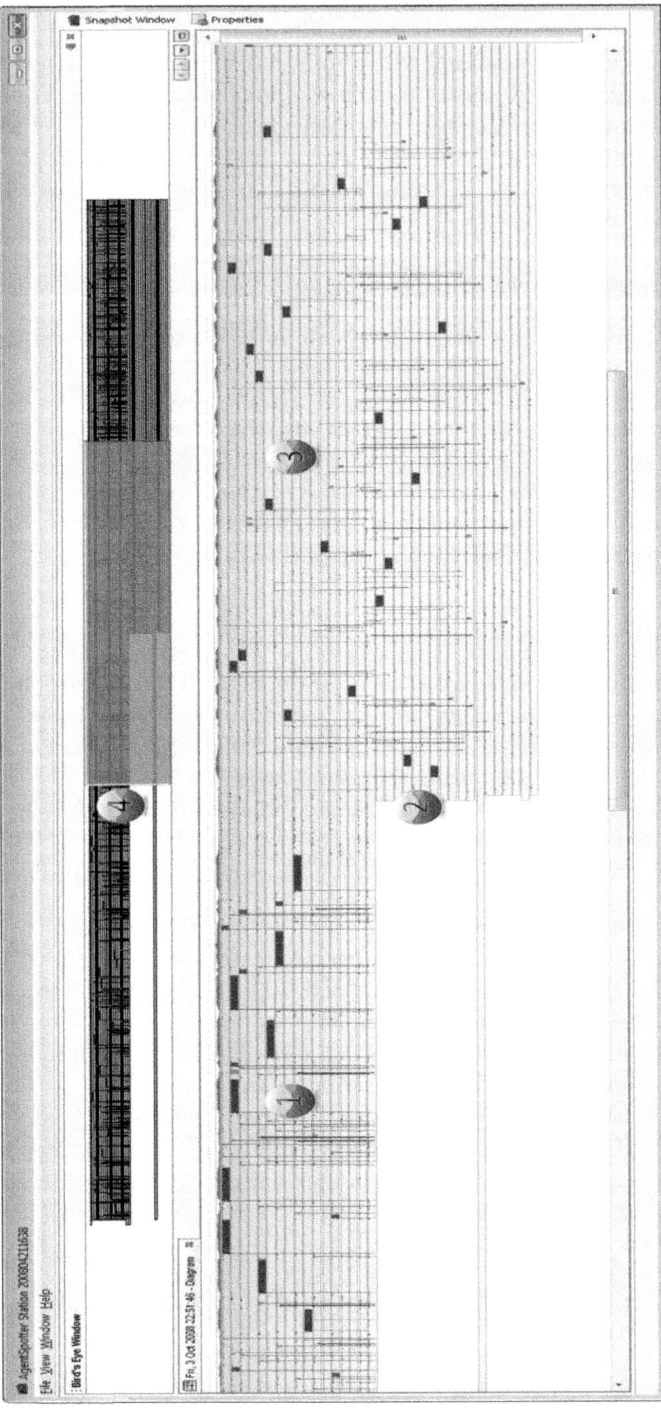

**Fig. 5.** Benchmark application sample space-time diagram (18 minute long session)

## 6.4   Space-Time Diagram

The space-time diagram for this session is shown in Figure 5. The individual agent time lines can clearly be seen as horizontal bars in the main window of the application. Within these, rectangular boxes represent processing tasks being carried out by each agent. The vertical lines between the time lines represent messages being passed between agents. For this simple scenario, only a single agent platform was used, meaning that there are no external platform time lines to indicate messages travelling to and from other agent platforms. A number of points of interest are labelled on the diagram. These can be described as follows:

- This portion of the diagram shows what happens when the initial 12 workers are active. The large red rectangles illustrate the time-consuming tasks ordered by the overseers. As mentioned in Section 5, these are also identifiable by their size, which increases proportionally to the processing time taken. These blocks never overlap because of the way Agent Factory schedules agents (i.e. agents are given access to the CPU sequentially). It is also noteworthy that the Agent Factory scheduler does not preempt agents that have exceeded their time allocation. The red rectangles also come in bursts, because both overseers send the same order to the same worker at the same time. This was revealed by zooming into what initially appeared to be a single message line. At a high magnification level, there were in fact two messages lines within a few microseconds interval to the same worker.
- At this point, 15 more workers are added to the system, following a slight pause that is indicated by the temporary absence of message lines. The agent time lines for the additional agents only begin at this point, clearly indicating an increase in the agent population.
- This third portion shows the impact of the new workers. The red blocks are still present, but they are better spread among the agents, with the new agents taking some of the load from their predecessors.
- The Bird's Eye View reveals the bigger picture, and reminds us that we are looking only at one third of the overall session.

# 7   Conclusions and Future Work

Currently, the only concrete implementation of AgentSpotter is for the Agent Factory platform. As noted in Section 3, only the data capture apparatus should require a separate implementation for another platform. It is intended to develop such an implementation for other platforms, such as JADE [14].

The most obvious source of improvement for the AgentSpotter application is the addition of extra information above that which is already available. For instance, the performance of additional system services should be recorded, and more details should be collected about agents' performance events, such as the distribution of an agent's execution time among its sensors, actuators, reasoning engine and other components. Finally, the AgentSpotter application currently supports only one agent platform at any given time. The capability to visualise multiple platforms concurrently would be desirable.

# References

1. Knuth, D.E.: An empirical study of FORTRAN programs. j-SPE 1(2), 105–133 (1971)
2. Graham, S.L., Kessler, P.B., Mckusick, M.K.: Gprof: A call graph execution profiler. SIGPLAN Not 17(6), 120–126 (1982)
3. Srivastava, A., Eustace, A.: Atom: a system for building customized program analysis tools. In: PLDI 1994: Proceedings of the ACM SIGPLAN 1994 conference on Programming language design and implementation, pp. 196–205. ACM, New York (1994)
4. Sun Microsystems, Inc. JVM Tool Interface (JVMTI), Version 1.0 (2004), http://java.sun.com/j2se/1.5.0/docs/guide/jvmti/ (accessed August 4, 2008)
5. Helsinger, A., Thome, M., Wright, T., Technol, B., Cambridge, M.: Cougaar: a scalable, distributed multi-agent architecture. In: IEEE International Conference on Systems, Man and Cybernetics, 2004, vol. 2 (2004)
6. Collier, R.: Debugging Agents in Agent Factory. In: Bordini, R.H., Dastani, M.M., Dix, J., El Fallah Seghrouchni, A. (eds.) PROMAS 2006. LNCS (LNAI), vol. 4411, pp. 229–248. Springer, Heidelberg (2007)
7. Seah, C., Sierhuis, M., Clancey, W., Cognition, M.: Multi-agent modeling and simulation approach for design and analysis of MER mission operations. In: Proceedings of 2005 International conference on human-computer interface advances for modeling and simulation (SIMCHI 2005), pp. 73–78 (2005)
8. Rimassa, G., Calisti, M., Kernland, M.E.: Living Systems®Technology Suite. In: Software Agent-Based Applications, Platforms and Development Kits. Whitestein Series in Software Agent Technologies and Autonomic Computing, pp. 73–93. Birkhäuser, Basel (2005)
9. Botia, J., Hernansaez, J., Skarmeta, F.: Towards an Approach for Debugging MAS Through the Analysis of ACL Messages. In: Lindemann, G., Denzinger, J., Timm, I.J., Unland, R. (eds.) MATES 2004. LNCS (LNAI), vol. 3187, pp. 301–312. Springer, Heidelberg (2004)
10. Horn, P.: Autonomic Computing: IBM's Perspective on the State of Information Technology. IBM TJ Watson Labs, NY (October 15, 2001)
11. Lee, L.C., Nwana, H.S., Ndumu, D.T., Wilde, P.D.: The stability, scalability and performance of multi-agent systems. BT Technology Journal 16(3), 94–103 (1998)
12. Collier, R., O'Hare, G., Lowen, T., Rooney, C.: Beyond Prototyping in the Factory of Agents. In: Multi-Agent Systems and Application III: 3rd International Central and Eastern European Conference on Multi-Agent Systems, Ceemas 2003 Proceedings, Prague, Czech Republic, June 16-18 (2003)
13. Hwaci: Web site for the SQLite Database Engine (2008), http://www.sqlite.org/ (accessed October, 2008)
14. Bellifemine, F., Poggi, A., Rimassa, G.: JADE–A FIPA-compliant agent framework. In: Proceedings of PAAM, vol. 99, pp. 97–108 (1999)

# Infrastructure for Forensic Analysis of Multi-Agent Based Simulations*

Emilio Serrano, Juan A. Botia, and Jose M. Cadenas

University of Murcia, Murcia, Spain
{emilioserra,juanbot,jcadenas}@um.es

**Abstract.** The Multi Agent Systems (MAS) theory has methodical approaches to analyze, understand and debug the social level of agents. This paper aims to argue that technologies for the analysis of MAS can be used in the field of Multi-agent based simulation (MABS). In particular, *forensic analysis* is proposed. It is explained the creation of an infrastructure for forensic analysis to assist the analysis of any model independently of its scope and framework of development. To achieve this genericity, the proposal is based in the use of Aspect Oriented Programming (AOP). In addition, it is given the key ideas used in the implementation of this infrastructure on the MABS platform MASON, giving a great power of analysis to this framework.

## 1 Introduction

*Multi-agent based simulation*, MABS, is used in more and more scientific domains [8]: sociology, biology, physics, chemistry, ecology, economy, etc. where it is progressively replacing previous simulation techniques. It is due to its ability to model very heterogeneous "individuals", starting from simple entities to more complex one. Its versatility makes MABS one of the most favorite and interesting support for the simulation of complex systems [8].

Fishwick [9] defines computer simulation as the discipline of designing a model of a system, executing the model on a computer, and analyzing the execution output. We think that the task of testing the social level of the agents, in the analysis task, is one of the most important things about these simulations. Analyzing these systems as a society refers to check if some properties are accomplished during the life time of the society [10], this is to analyze the macro-social perspective. Although there are several works about the analysis of MABS[19,3], researchers are generally more interested in model design [8]. We consider necessary the development of methodical proposals for the task of analyzing the MABS because with a bad model execution or a bad execution analysis, even the best model may not provide reliable and useful results.

---

* This research work is supported by the Spanish Ministry of Education and Science in the scope of the Research Project "Análisis, Estudio y Desarrollo de Sistemas Inteligentes y Servicios Telemáticos" through the Fundación Séneca within the Program "Generación del Conocimiento Científico de Excelencia".

L. Draubach, J.-P. Briot, and J. Thangarajah (Eds.): ProMAS 2009, LNAI 5919, pp. 185–200, 2010.
© Springer-Verlag Berlin Heidelberg 2010

As already mentioned, the scope of MABS is increasing. In addition to the increasing of application domains of MABS, it have also proliferated lots of MABS frameworks for their development. The web of the Open Agent Based Modeling Consortium[1] lists 17 of these frameworks, including: MASON [13], Repast [4] and NetLogo [1]. Because simulations analysis is an unavoidable task, all platforms provide means to this task. In the section of related work there are some of these proposals. The first and obvious desirable feature in these frameworks would be the compatibility between platforms (which is not offered). It is obvious that the more developers use a technology to debug systems, the more cases are studied with that technology. Then this technology can be improved easier because it receives feedback from the developers. Therefore, genericity in technologies for analysis and debugging is an important factor to consider. The second point which make us look for new proposals is that even in the early stages of analysis, data collection, is often required specific knowledge about how the model under review has been programmed. The basic roles in the development of a MABS are: (1) *thematicians* (experts in a particular domain), (2) *computer scientists* (needed to actually build the programs), and (3) *modellers* (people in charge of the tasks of design, building, execution and analysis) [8]. The technical skills in computer sciences are very different from the knowledge of the specific domain of the model which usually is required for the responsible for the analysis (modellers) and the responsible for the use of the results obtained from the analysis (thematicians). The ideal is to have an infrastructure for the analysis of any model and abstracted of the specific programming.

The immediate question is whether it is possible to automate or at least assist the process of analyzing a MABS regardless of the specific application domain and the way in which it was programmed. It seems difficult to find properties in common, for example, inside a model about biology and one about economy. Herbert Simon explains how patterns often appear between different complex systems [24]. For example, it explains how the complexity often takes the form of hierarchy in the sense that the complex systems are composed by subsystems which are composed of subsystems and so on. Automating, or at least assisting, the process of discovering these social structures in any model is a powerful tool. In the case of discovering hierarchies, for example, results permit to scale the analysis of a complex system in a "divide and conquer" approach. In the field of Multi Agent Systems have been proposed methods to discover hierarchies in systems independently of the specific application domain [23].

The field of *Multi Agent Systems* (MAS) is complementary in several aspects to MABS [5]. The MAS theory has methodical approaches to analyze, understand and debug the social level of agents. This paper aims to argue that technologies for the analysis of MAS can be used in the field of MABS. In particular, *forensic analysis* is proposed. Forensic analysis is the process of understanding, re-creating, and analyzing arbitrary events that have occurred previously [16]. This technology has already been used successfully to debug MAS in a social level [22]. This paper explains how to create an infrastructure for forensic analysis to be used for any

---

[1] OpenABM Consortium website: http://www.openabm.org/

platform and model for each platform. This infrastructure also supports the use of representations and Intelligent data analysis that help to analyze and understand the MABS in the same way as with the MAS.

Next section treat related works and introduces the main approaches to analyze and debug systems in the fields of MABS and MAS. Then, section 3 explains how to create an infrastructure for forensic analysis of MABS providing it with flexibility over the model and platform. Section 4 details the key ideas in the implementation of forensic analysis for MASON. Section 5 shows the use of the ideas exposed in this paper for a MABS. Finally, conclusions and future work are given.

## 2   Related Works

To a greater or lesser extent, forensic analysis is present in any MABS platforms because the analysis of the simulations is an essential task. MASON [13] is criticized for providing limited facilities for such purposes [18]. It allows developers to save properties of an agent or model in a text file, but you cannot do something as simple as saving the value of two properties in the same file. On the other hand, MASON allows developers to save a whole execution as checkpoints to re-launch simulations later. However, you cannot access to previous states in the stored simulation. On the opposite side is NetLogo [1], praised for its ability to record a great variety of events in simulations [18]. In particular, NetLogo allows a special execution which logs the simulation in a xml file. Specifically, there are 8 loggers available for different types of events: *globals* (a global variable changes), *greens* (elements of the interface change), *code* (NetLogo code is compiled), *widgets* (widgets added/removed from the interface), *buttons* (pressed or released), *speed-slider* (changes), *turtles* (die or are born), *links* (die or are born). Surprisingly, little information is given about the agents ("turtles" on NetLogo), only when they are born or they die. It is also surprising that the most revealing element of the NetLogo interface, plots, are not stored as event using the logger *greens*. These shortcomings are compensated by allowing the export of plots or the simulated world to spreadsheets. Having different approaches to log events on the same platform complicates things. In addition, these approaches are often too rigid and hardly allow configuration. About Repast [4] is said that it is the most complete platform [18] and it is really the most powerful in the analysis task because it provides the best collecting of events. Although Repast delegates several external tools for analysis, which means all the tools have to be known, the data collecting is always performed by "Datasets". The datasets can be constructed as a series of values that are obtained from calls to methods of the agents (or formulas composed of these calls). The problem is that this proposal requires a deep knowledge about the specific programming of the model being developed because the user has to distinguish between methods that make reference to relevant properties and methods that are merely irrelevant for the analysis. That is a trivial task in simple models with simple code, but in complex models may be complicated. As mentioned in the introduction, the problem of these approaches is that in the first place they have not been concerned about the compatibility between platforms. This compatibility allows studying the task of analysis itself and independently of the platform in which the models are programmed. The other major problem, most pronounced in Repast, is that the collection of data often requires specific knowledge of how the model was programmed. This means that the researcher in charge of the analysis should know the details of the model programming.

Simulations typically generate huge amounts of data. Thus, the analysis of simulations is a complex issue. Although there are several works dealing with the analysis of MABS [19,3], they often start with a record of events that they take as trivial. On the other hand, the MAS theory has literature that aims to provide general solutions for the event log and subsequent analysis. In this way, Serrano et al. [22] details the creation of an infrastructure for the forensic analysis which is flexible about the used MAS platform and which do not require deep knowledge of the specific system programming. The term "forensic analysis" (understanding, re-creating, and analyzing arbitrary events that have occurred previously [16]) is typically used in the field of intrusion detection[20]. Forensic analysis is often the basis of most proposals about debugging in MAS and it is often accompanied by understandable data representations. There are works which analyze the behavior of the agents groups with *Petri nets* [6], *AUML diagrams* [17], extensions of the *propositional dynamic logic* [15], *statecharts* [11], *dooley graphs* [14], etc. In general, the more possibilities of automation in analysis is having by the representations, the more complicated are these representations to be developed and understood by humans. These papers illustrate different infrastructures for forensic analysis in MAS which can be used in MABS. However, the objective of the analysis in these work is the understanding of the agents in their group level, not the social level which is interesting in MABS.

Beyond the group level, the field of MAS has researched the analysis of the social level of agents, which is intimately related to the analysis of MABS. Analyzing a MAS as a society refers to check if some properties are accomplished during the life time of the society [10]. The scope of such properties is the whole system, not individual or group components. The fundamental difference in the social level of MAS with their group level is that emergent properties can appear without being specified in the design. This is especially interesting for MABS [5]. It has been of interest, for example, to detect emergent behaviors in agents societies which were not included in the specification of a group of agents in the MAS design [7]. There are works which combine forensic analysis, graphs theory, and data mining to achieve simple representations of the agent society. Later, these representations can be used to discover undesired or emergent behaviors in the systems. In this way, Serrano et al. [23] have detailed the creation of graphs that reflect the collaborative cores of agents or similarity among members of the agent society. These representations are obtained independently of the specific system, the MAS platform and without requiring programming skills to be generated or understood. This type of representation can help to analyze the behavior of the system, understand it, debug it and even to identify emergent behaviors. Remondino et al. [19] also use data mining technologies (for example clustering and association rules) in order to assist the analysis of MABS. However, a discussion about the first step, the event log, is necessary. This recorded information makes the data mining powerful. This paper presents a basic forensic analysis infrastructure which can be used as basis of the assisted or automatic analysis for MABS.

## 3   Debugging MABS with Forensic Analysis

### 3.1   Proposal of Infrastructure for Forensic Analysis

The analysis of MAS in the agent level, the study of specific agents in the system without cover groups of agents, is not very different from traditional software debugging. However, most approaches to debug a MAS in its group level, the study of specific agent groups in the system without covering the whole of society, are based on the forensic analysis [16]. This is necessary because it is not as interesting the analysis of a specific execution as the overall analysis of a significant group of executions of the system. This is because the frequent presence of randomness makes irrelevant the result of a concrete execution in isolation. Works on the analysis of MABS also transmit this idea analyzing great quantities of executions [19]. A fundamental reason for the use of forensic analysis appears in the analysis of the social level of agents: detecting behaviors that have not previously been defined, as emergent behaviors. Because of the possibility of these unpredictable behaviors which make impossible define preconditions and post conditions to validate the system, most conventional approaches for the analysis, testing and debugging are ineffective. The resulting database of forensic analysis supports technologies for discovering not explicit knowledge, such as exploratory data mining, which can assist the analysis of MABS to find no predefined behaviors.

As seen in related work, the proposals for the event log provided by the frameworks are often aimed at that specific framework or a specific model and knowledge about the programming of the model is required. Serrano et al. [22] details the creation of an infrastructure for forensic analysis in MAS that can be reused for MABS. This proposal provides flexibility over the specific developed system and development platform. Besides, users of the analyzer do not need to know the details of the system implementation. The key idea is to capture interesting elements of a simulation and store them in a relational database (RDB) to allow making queries and creating simplified representations of the stored data. These representations and queries assist the analysis process. Figure 1 shows the analyzer that records data in a RDB and a developer consulting that RDB and studying representations to analyze MABS. To make the shift of this forensic analysis from the MAS to MABS, the immediate question is which elements are interesting to register in a MABS.

The related works section explains the approaches of some MABS platforms to collect the execution data. The most similar event to a common element to register for all MABS in these approaches was the creation of agents by the

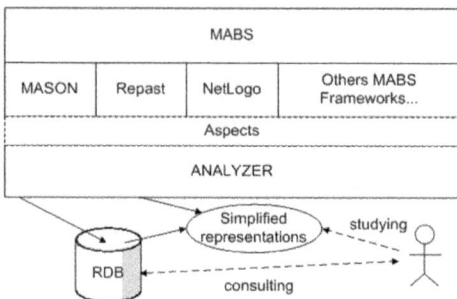

**Fig. 1.** Proposal of the paper

logger "turtles" in Netlogo. In fact, it is not even required in all MABS that the agents are located in a simulated world after creating them. It is really difficult to find common elements in the broad domain of application of MABS. Therefore, platforms usually require the programmer of the models to collect relevant information. However, the developer can use any framework and develop any model, but he is always going to use the facilities that the framework offers. In this way, elements that always appear are displays, for example, *"inspectors"* in MASON or *"monitors"* in NetLogo. These displays show certain properties of the model in general or the agents in particular selected by the programmer. Any type of interesting event can also be stored, with independence of the underlying platform or model. The ideal is to store these information in an RDB, which is a powerful tool of querying and can assist analysis of MABS permitting to make consultations and supporting exploratory data mining. As seen above, this proposal allows each domain to have its own taxonomy of events instead of imposing one. Therefore, it is the responsibility of the modeler to determine events of interest in the model and the programmer must simply use the facilities of the framework to show these events in the simulation.

### 3.2    Implementing the Infrastructure

To capture an interesting event within the simulation first the point in the code of the platform or model in which the event occurs must be located. Then, the event must be stored in this point. It could be thought that it is trivial programming calls to RDB or model into the platform to include the necessary code to store the events. This classic approach presents a major problem: this code would serve only for the specific model or the specific version of the platform. With the number of frameworks, and their continuous changes, this implementation would have a expensive maintenance. In addition, the registration code would be dispersed throughout the model or platform code. Therefore, every change in the code of forensic analysis would be very expensive because it should be replicated in practically any platform or model. The solution in this proposal is the use of *Aspect oriented programming (AOP)* [12]. AOP can isolate the aspect of register a MABS execution in certain classes which are called *"aspects"*. Then, the aspects can be programmed or modified separately and in a modular manner. Aspects are programmed to capture interesting events in models implemented in some platform. If the platform is upgraded, it only has to be recompiled to include the aspects. If the strategy of forensic analysis changes, then the only thing to change is the set of aspects used (without changing the model or the platform code). The cost of maintenance is greatly reduced because the code related to the forensic analysis is centralized in a few aspects. The only restriction is the availability of the of the MABS platform source code for the necessary recompilation of the whole distribution including the aspects. Furthermore, although it is not necessary to change the points of interest in the source code where events occur, such source code should be understandable in order to allow the programmer locating these points and including the necessary aspects there.

The execution of the code in the aspects is not fixed but depends on the flow of the program. First the aspects are defined in an isolated way. Later, the platform and the model are compiled with the aspects. Finally the code in which a new behavior must be added (platform and model) can be executed with the new behavior (aspects). This new behavior, in this case, is the event log. Aspects will be executed where they are needed depending on the powerful regular expressions which are used to define them. The next section shows examples of the aspects definition and points in the flow of the program where they are executed.

Figure 1 shows how AOP is the layer that joins a MABS platform with the analyzer. Even the programming language of the platform is not a limitation either. AspectJ for Java is the most popular AOP language. However, there are AOP languages for the major programming languages and paradigms: object-oriented programming (AspectJ for Java, AspectS for Smalltalk, AspectC++ for C++, etc), imperative programming (AspectC for C, Cobble for Cobol, the aspect module for Perl, etc), logic programming (Whirl for Prolog) and functional programming (AspectL for Lisp). Obviously, it is possible that the developer cannot find an AOP language for his favorite programming language (especially if it is too new or unpopular). With little pieces of code located isolated in a few areas and the freedom to choose the programming language, the goal of not being limited to a particular MABS platform is satisfactorily achieved. Moreover, as we have seen, the maintaining cost the infrastructure for the forensic analysis is reduced using AOP and this cost might be, as in any software, the most expensive part of its life cycle.

One interesting question is whether the infrastructure for forensic analysis used in a framework can be reused by others. There is a clear equivalence of the elements and concepts of a platform in others frameworks, a famous comparison of MABS platforms [18] even published a table in that regard. For example, the "Graphical display" concept is an inspector in MASON, a monitor in NetLogo and a probe in Repast. Using this concept, it can be registered for the forensic analysis those elements which the developers of the modelers considered relevant to the analysis. The forensic analysis can also be expanded with other concepts, such as the "agent location" (field in MASON, world in NetLogo and space in Repast) to analyze the positions of the agents at each time step, although that concept not necessarily is going to appear in all models. Besides, if the developers did not add displays of the agent locations, it would indicates the irrelevance of this concept in the analysis phase. With a clear equivalence of the fundamental concepts of MABS platforms and a code of forensic analysis isolated in aspects, reprogramming the aspects for other platforms is easy. In general and as noted above, the only restrictions are that the MABS frameworks have to be open source software to use AOP and a source code in a language with an AOP language associated. Figure 1 shows how the analyzer can be used on different platforms. With the flexibility provided by this proposal, we hope this work will be useful for the MABS community independently of the specific preferences for programming.

### 3.3   Considerations on MABS Frameworks Heterogenicity

Forensic analysis is suitable for any MABS platform, as stated in section 3.2, portability of forensic analysis between MABS platforms is an idea that always has been in our research. However, usefulness and simplicity of forensic analysis may vary from one platform to another. MASON [13], Repast [4] and NetLogo [1] were considered for the first implementations, although as noted in the introduction, simply in the web of the Open Agent Based Modeling Consortium are listed 17 frameworks. There are several papers where MABS platforms are compared. Railsback et al. [18] do not dare to recommend one platform over another, but they give conclusions on each of the frameworks. It is indicated that NetLogo is the most usable, Mason is the fastest platform and Repast is the most complete.

NetLogo cannot implement the proposal of this paper because it does not have the source code necessary for the inclusion of aspects available. So it was quickly discarded. There is also a feature of both NetLogo and Repast which makes MASON a little more compatible with the forensic analysis, the totally deterministic reproduction of the experiments. NetLogo and Repast do not provide methods to reproduce the order in which an action is executed on a list of agents. In a forensic analysis, after detecting anomalies at certain points in certain simulations, the user should be able to re-execute the simulations in these points to find out what happened. However, this trial and error approach is less effective if experiments are not totally reproducible. For this reason, we chose Mason for the first implementation of forensic analysis as a proof of concept. Other comparisons are more determined, Berryman [2] concludes that the best platform is Repast. Repast, an open source framework with a large community of developers, is undoubtedly the ideal candidate to implement the infrastructure for forensic analysis after MASON.

## 4   SAM, Social Analyzer for MASON

As noted above, the analysis phase of MABS has been traditionally performed in an exploratory and intuitive manner [8]. One of the weaknesses of MABS platforms in general including MASON, is that they offer few facilities to monitor and debug the simulated models [18]. MASON offers the possibility of fixing inspectors in individual properties (of the model or of the agents) to be monitored / recorded / modified from the simulation. However, many other options as views and records of the artificial society as a whole are needed for debugging a large-scale society of agents. In order to cope with this deficiencies, SAM (social analyzer for MASON) has been created. This section introduces the key ideas used in the implementation of SAM, an infrastructure for forensic analysis in MASON using AOP.

Before discussing the code of specific aspects of forensic analysis is necessary to explain what is an aspect. In very basic terms, the essential concepts to understand the AOP are join point, pointcut, advice and aspect. A *join point* is a point in the control flow of a program. It includes all the actions that comprise a method call, starting after all arguments are evaluated up to and including return (either normally or by throwing an exception). A *Pointcut* is a set of join points. Poincuts pick out certain join points in the program flow, but they cannot do anything apart. Whenever the program execution reaches one of the join points described in the pointcut, a piece of code associated with the pointcut is executed. These pieces of code are the advices and they must be used to actually implement additional behavior to existing software. An *Advice* brings together a pointcut (to pick out join points) and a body of code (to run at each of those join points). The combination of the pointcut and the advice is termed an *aspect*. Now, some MASON concepts have to be explained to program useful aspects in this framework.

To program the aspects in MASON, the first step is to define the interesting join points for the forensic analysis. As stated, we are interested in what the developer of a simulation chose to be shown in the MASON simulation. This is the concept of *inspector* in MASON and fortunately its location in the MASON code is clear. Any method that starts with "get" in the code of an agent (implements the *Steppable* interface) or a model (implements *SimState*) returns a property that is displayed when this agent or model respectively is being inspected. Now, aspects to add the record behavior to MASON must be programmed.

The following *pointcuts* pick out the join points where an inspector is called to show a property.

```
pointcut modelInspector(SimState model):
  target(model) && call(public get*());
pointcut agentInspector(Steppable agent):
  target(agent) && call(public get*());
```

The "target" pointcut picks out each join point where the target object (the object on which a method is called or a field is accessed) is an instance of a particular type, SimState or Steppable in these cases. And ``call(public get*())'' picks out all call join points to public methods where the method name starts with the characters "get".

In the same way, we can define pointcuts for the time of creating agents in the model which, as seen in the previous section, is one of the few elements common to all MABS.

```
pointcut newModel: call(SimState+.new());
pointcut newAgent: call(Steppable+.new());
```

These pointcuts picks out all constructor call join points where an instance of any subtype of a SimState or Steppable, respectively, is constructed. Once pointcuts are defined, we need now to specify the functionality for each; this is what is called advices. Their structure would be like this

```
after (SimState model) returning (Object r):
  modelInspector(model){
      /*mySniffingCode...*/
  }
after (Agent agent) returning (Object r):
  agentInspector(agent){
      /*mySniffingCode...*/
  }
```

in which we define an advice just after calling a model inspector and just after calling a agent inspector, respectively.

In the body of code, calls to some RDB can be made to store information about the object returned by the inspector (defined in aspect as the variable ''r''), about the model itself (defined as the variable ''model'') or on the agent (defined as the variable ''agent''). Similarly, advices for the moments of creating models or agents can be defined with the following structure.

```
after(): newModel{
  /*mySniffingCode...*/
}
after(): newAgent{
  /*mySniffingCode...*/
}
```

in which we define an advice just after creating a new model and just after creating a new agent, respectively. Notice that, due to the use of powerful regular expressions allowed by the AOP, we can define pointcuts for any model or framework with a few lines of code. To illustrate this flexibility by way of example, we can define the following pointcuts

```
pointcut myMasonClasses():
  within(SimState) || within(Steppable);
pointcut myMasonConstructor():
  myMasonClasses() && execution(new(..));
pointcut myMasonMethod():
  myMasonClasses() && execution(* *(..));
```

which pick out each method and constructor which is called by the classes SimState and Steppable of MASON.

It can be seen as the code for forensic analysis is simple and flexible. Besides all this code is in a only class aspect, isolated from the model or platform code, facilitating its maintenance. Moreover, the dependence on the framework is minimal, only a few lines of code shown in this section. Once this basic analysis has be covered, it can be captured anything of interest for forensic analysis. In any case, having all properties inspected and logged in an RDB gives a powerful capacity of analysis to MASON, allowing SQL queries like averages, standard deviations, number of different values in a property, etc. Besides the analyser supports intelligent data analysis technologies and understandable representations which can be very useful to assists the analysis of MABS.

## 5   Application to a MABS for Design of Inmotic Environments

Ubiksim[2] is a MABS to develop inmotic applications. The basic idea is that this simulation can be used to design and test inmotic applications where actual tests are too expensive, impractical or involve too many of users [21]. The simulation allows testing the effect of inmotic applications in an artificial society. In turn, the results obtained from the tests are used to improve the application changing the implemented strategies. The use of simulations allows test scenarios which would be impossible or too dangerous in real life. Moreover, the simulations allow performing large amounts of tests in a short time and getting all the data required for the study of inmotic applications.

Ubiksim has been applied, for example, in the design of emergency management strategies in a real building, the European Center of Business and Innovation (CEEIM)[3] at the University of Murcia. With this purpose, it simulates: a building, workers, fires and of course inmotic devices (fire and RFID based location sensors and visual displays). The figure 2 shows the display of a floor (left) and the zoom with the main elements of the simulation (right).

Two inmotic applications were developed in Ubiksim for a first approximation, these are explained bellow. (1) The *EvilApplication* allows an emergency without the use of inmotic devices. It is "evil" because this application deactivates the actuators and the agents must evacuate using their own criteria. However, an agent is going to flee if it sees a fire or other agent escaping. (2) The *SimpleApplication* is an initial proposal for inmotic application. The activated sensors are used to calculate the direction and distance from the fire. Then, an optimal escape path is suggested to the agents by a visual display. These calculations are repeated in each unit of time and the results change when new sensors are activated and the application knows more about the distance/direction of the fire. Furthermore, when the first sensor is activated, all the actuators in the building are activated as a visual alarm.

---

[2] Ubiksim website: http://ubiksim.sourceforge.net
[3] CEEIM website: http://www.ceeim.es/

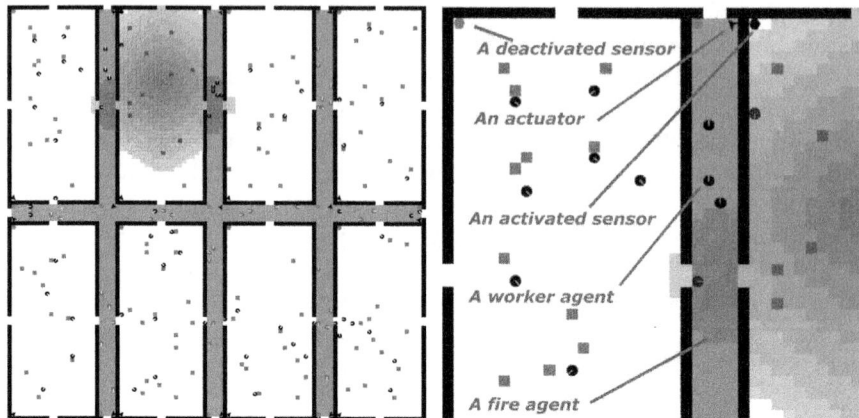

**Fig. 2.** On the left, a vectorial image of floor in Ubiksim with 100 agents. On the right, the zoom in the upper left corner of the floor.

In order to perform the study, the variables we logged were the number of died and saved agents. Later, we wanted to have much more information such as: agents exposed to fire, the space occupied by the fire at every time, the number of agents which used each stairs, the average time of escape for each floor, the speed of the agents, the positions where agents died more often, etc.

To perform this study, the initial approach was to flood the code with new variables for the subsequent registration without using AOP. The result was nothing short of chaotic because several developers were interested in different events to log, generating multiple versions of Ubiksim. Besides, the code necessary for the event log was spread throughout the simulation code, making maintenance costly. Finally, such dispersion made it difficult to reuse the code on other platforms or simulations in which we were working. Thanks to the ideas explained in this paper, the registration code was isolated in aspects of easy modification and localization solving the above problems. Capturing the inspectors of the MASON framework with aspects, the code to log elements of interest can be written even before these elements are defined. Furthermore, the use is not limited to Ubiksim, the code can be used in any other simulation implemented with MASON. The traces of the execution flow were also very useful in the debugging phase. These traces allow selecting agents of an execution, agents who are not having a good behavior, and show all methods and constructors that these faulty agents are calling. The simple code needed for these improvements is described in the previous section.

Furthermore, observing the code analysis centralized makes it easier to acquire a global view to suggest improvements. We realized that one of the best indicators to verify the performance of these inmotic applications was the number of agents which use or not the inmotic devices and if they die or not. You can see these results for the *evilApplication* and *simpleApplication* in figure 3. The figure shows the average of agents which: have fled because of seeing a fire,

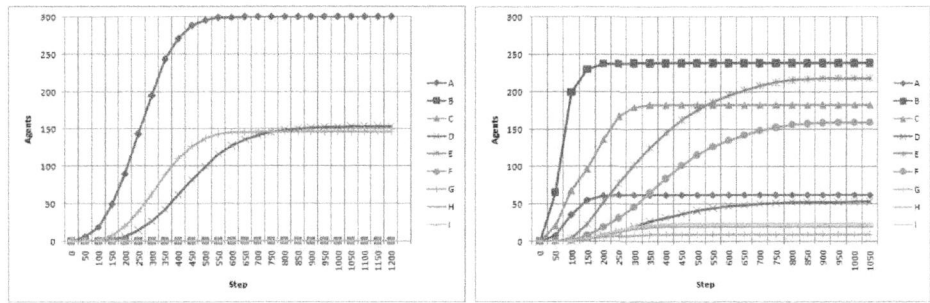

**Fig. 3.** On the left, the use of inmotic devices in the evilApplication. On the right, the use of inmotic devices in the simpleApplication. Legend: (A) Agents fleeing by a fire or other agents, (B) Agents fleeing by an actuator, (C) Agents following suggestion from actuators, (D) Agents in A which have been saved, (E) Agents in B which have been saved, (F) Agents in C which have been saved, (G) Agents in A which have died, (H) Agents in B which have died, (I) Agents in C which have died.

have fled because of seeing an actuator, and have fled following a path suggested by an actuator. It also provides for each of these groups the average of died and saved agents.

To test these applications Ubiksim was configured with a building of 3 floors inspired by the CEEIM building. The analysis was performed with 200 runs simulating 300 worker agents and random fires for each run. The results of the *evilApplication* (figure 3 on the left) show that there are no agents fleeing because of actuators or following suggestions from actuators. These results indicate a good performance for an application which hides the actuators. The chart also shows that, on average, almost 50% of the agents died using this application. Much more interesting are the results with the same conditions for the *simpleApplication* (figura 3 on the right) where it can be appreciated that almost all the agents fled because they observed an activated actuator. It is also showed that more than 50% of the agents escaped after following the directions indicated by the actuators. The deaths, obviously, are much lower than with the *evilApplication*. However, this application still has to be improved because there are a significant number of agents which do not follow suggestions of actuators, more than 100. This means that these agents were fleeing without information about where the fire was. This is because all the actuators of the building are activated when a sensor detects fire, but an actuator does not show indications if its floor still is not on fire. We are working on applications which scale the escapes. These applications deactivate the actuators when they are far enough from the fire in order to the agents near these actuators do not start fleeing crowding the exits.

The ideas of this paper raise two questions of great interest: what elements are there in common between the numerous MABS? and which of these elements are always interesting to be studied?. The answers to these questions are very difficult. The proposal explained in this paper try to work without answering these questions, which is not little. In concrete, the proposal delegates the developer to use the monitors of the framework and then these monitors are automatically recorded. In our experience, apart of agents that are created (and not necessarily destroyed), the element that is always present in MABS is the communication (between agents or between agents and environment). Therefore, one of our most promising future works is focused on the formal definition of interactions for MABS and the assistance for the analysis of these interactions.

# 6    Conclusions and Future Work

The paper introduces an infrastructure to assist the analysis, understanding and debugging of a *Multi-agent based simulation* (MABS) by adapting successful techniques which have been applied to *multi-agent systems* (MAS). The infrastructure consists of forensic analysis by *aspect oriented programming* (AOP). The infrastructure is flexible about the MABS framework used, the simulated model and how the model is programmed.

The paper explains how researchers in the field of MABS are not generally interested in the analysis phase, despite the fact that the success of a research in this field depends on it. All MABS platforms have approaches to the analysis, but they depend on the platform, the specific model, and the specific programming of the model. However, approaches to the analysis task which resolves these problems has been given in the field of MAS. That is why this paper aims to extrapolate the use of these approaches to MABS, specifically, a forensic analysis based on AOP is proposed. The key idea is to capture interesting elements of a simulation using AOP and store them in a RDB to allow consultations or to get simplified representations of the stored data. The proposal directly delegates the developers to discover what elements are interesting to register. Then, the developers must use the facilities of the MABS framework to show these elements. The use of AOP can isolate all the analysis code in a few classes called "aspects". In this way, the analysis code is flexible about changes in the chosen platform, the platform version, the model code, the analysis code, etc. With the adaptation to these situations, the maintenance cost is greatly reduced. The paper also gives the keys to the concrete implementation of the infrastructure for the MASON platform, providing MASON with a great power of analysis. The flexibility and genericity in the proposal is illustrated with only a few lines of AOP. Finally, the ideas of the paper are applied to a simulation called Ubiksim which is used for the development and testing of inmotic applications.

Regarding future work, the immediate one is to migrate the forensic analysis from MASON to Repast which has a large developer community. Another important work is to obtain, from the forensic analysis of MABS, representations to simplify the data and to provide an analysis of certain aspects of the agent society. Specifically, we want to use the graphs to reflect collaborative cores of agents and similarity among members of the society [23]. There is a great variety of representations in the field of MAS that can assist the analysis of the MABS. We also intend to investigate the automation of the analysis process (when it is possible). Once again, the field of MAS has many approaches to model interactions between agents and then, they can be automatically tested and validated.

However, understandable representations are always necessary to help humans to discover unexpected and not modeled elements as emergent behaviors.

## References

1. Netlogo 4.0.4 user manual, http://ccl.northwestern.edu/netlogo/docs/
2. Berryman, M.: Review of software platforms for agent based models. DSTO Defence Science and Technology Organisation, 2008. Australian Government, Department of Defence (2008)
3. Chen, C.-C., Nagl, S.B., Clack, C.D.: Specifying, detecting and analysing emergent behaviours in multi-level agent-based simulations. In: SCSC: Proceedings of the 2007 summer computer simulation conference, San Diego, CA, USA, pp. 969–976. Society for Computer Simulation International (2007)
4. Collier, N.: Repast: An extensible framework for agent simulation (2002)
5. Conte, R., Gilbert, N., Sichman, J.S.: Mas and social simulation: A suitable sommitment. In: Proceedings of the First International Workshop on Multi-Agent Systems and Agent-Based Simulation, London, UK, pp. 1–9. Springer, Heidelberg (1998)
6. Cost, R.S., Chen, Y., Finin, T.W., Labrou, Y., Peng, Y.: Using colored petri nets for conversation modeling. In: Issues in Agent Communication, London, UK, pp. 178–192. Springer, Heidelberg (2000)
7. David, N., Sichman, J.S., Coelho, H.: Towards an emergence-driven software process for agent-based simulation. In: 3rd International Workshop on Multi-Agent Based Simulation, MABS (2002)
8. Drogoul, A., Vanbergue, D., Meurisse, T.: Multi-agent based simulation: Where are the agents? In: Sichman, J.S., Bousquet, F., Davidsson, P. (eds.) MABS 2002. LNCS (LNAI), vol. 2581, pp. 1–15. Springer, Heidelberg (2003)
9. Fishwick, P.A.: Computer simulation: growth through extension. Trans. Soc. Comput. Simul. Int. 14(1), 13–23 (1997)
10. Gómez, J.J., Botia, J.A., Serrano, E., Pavón, J.: Testing and debugging of mas interactions with ingenias. In: Agent oriented software engineering. Workshop at AAMAS 2008, Estoril, Portugal (2008)
11. Harel, D., Politi, M.: Modeling Reactive Systems with Statecharts: The Statemate Approach. McGraw-Hill, Inc, New York (1998)
12. Laddad, R.: AspectJ in Action: Practical Aspect-Oriented Programming. Manning Publications Co., Greenwich (2003)
13. Luke, S., Cioffi-Revilla, C., Panait, L., Sullivan, K.: Mason: A new multi-agent simulation toolkit. In: Proceedings of the 2004 Swarmfest Workshop (2004)
14. Van Dyke Parunak, H.: Visualizing agent conversations: Using enhanced dooley graphs for agent design and analysis. In: Proc. Second Int'l Conf. Multiagent Systems, pp. 275–282. AAAI Press, Menlo Park (1996)
15. Paurobally, S.: Developing agent interaction protocols using graphical and logical methodologies. In: Dastani, M.M., Dix, J., El Fallah-Seghrouchni, A. (eds.) PROMAS 2003. LNCS (LNAI), vol. 3067, pp. 149–168. Springer, Heidelberg (2004)
16. Peisert, S.P.: A model of forensic analysis using goal-oriented logging. PhD thesis, La Jolla, CA, USA. Adviser-Karin, Sidney (2007)
17. Poutakidis, D., Padgham, L., Winikoff, M.: Debugging multi-agent systems using design artifacts: the case of interaction protocols. In: AAMAS 2002: Proceedings of the first international joint conference on Autonomous agents and multiagent systems, pp. 960–967. ACM, New York (2002)

18. Railsback, S.F., Lytinen, S.L., Jackson, S.K.: Agent-based simulation platforms: Review and development recommendations. SIMULATION 82(9), 609–623 (2006)
19. Remondino, M., Correndo, G.: Mabs validation through repeated execution and data mining analisys. International Journal of Simulation: Systems, Science & Technology 7(6) (2006)
20. Saleh, M., Arasteh, A.R., Sakha, A., Debbabi, M.: Forensic analysis of logs: Modeling and verification. Know.-Based Syst. 20(7), 671–682 (2007)
21. Serrano, E., Botia, J.A., Cadenas, J.M.: Construction and debugging of a multi-agent based simulation to study ambient intelligence applications. In: Cabestany, J., Sandoval, F., Prieto, A., Corchado, J.M. (eds.) IWANN 2009. LNCS, vol. 5517, pp. 1090–1097. Springer, Heidelberg (2009)
22. Serrano, E., Botia, J.A.: Infrastructure for forensic analysis of multi-agent systems. In: Proceedings of the Programming Multi-Agent Systems Workshop at AAMAS 2008, Estoril, Portugal (2008)
23. Serrano, E., Gómez-Sanz, J.J., Botía, J.A., Pavón, J.: Intelligent data analysis applied to debug complex software systems. Neurocomputing 72(13-15), 2785–2795 (2009)
24. Simon, H.A.: The architecture of complexity. Proceedings of the American Philosophical Society 106(6), 467–482 (1962)

# Representing Long-Term and Interest BDI Goals

Lars Braubach and Alexander Pokahr

Distributed Systems and Information Systems,
Computer Science Department, University of Hamburg, Germany
{braubach,pokahr}@informatik.uni-hamburg.de

**Abstract.** In BDI systems, agents are described using mentalistic notions such as beliefs and goals. According to the intentional stance this helps specifying and understanding complex behavior, because the system is made up of folk psychological concepts that humans naturally tend to use for explaining reasoning and behavior and therefore can easily grasp. To close the gap between the natural usage of the term goal and its operationalization within agent systems, BDI goals should reflect the typical characteristics of goals in the folk psychological sense, which is not completely the case for existing BDI goal representations. Hence, in this paper desirable features of BDI goals are presented and important aspects that are currently not covered in existing specifications are further elaborated. Concretely, the representation and processing of BDI goals is extended supporting also *long-term* and *interest* goals. The usefulness of the newly gained expressivity will be illustrated by an example application, implemented in the Jadex BDI agent system.

## 1 Introduction

A concise definition of the term goal is extraordinarily hard to find, so that it is used in many psychological and artificial intelligence articles without a strict definition and with partially different meanings [2]. The main difficulty of the definition problem arises from the fact that in order to be useful for a variety of application areas, a definition has to reveal the term's essence without being too strict. Typically, definitions in the context of planning [10] and also w.r.t. specific theories for intentional agents (cf. [7,20]) tend to be to be too narrow and often reduce the meaning of a goal to a desirable world state that needs to be achieved. A recent attempt in the area of multi-agent systems proposes the following definition: "a goal is a mental attitude representing preferred progressions of a particular multi-agent system that the agent has chosen to put effort into bringing about" [30]. Even though the definition is broader than the ones mentioned before and allows capturing different kinds of goals such as achievement or maintenance, it is already quite restrictive. Firstly, it uses the term "preferred progressions", which is not suitable for all kinds of goals. In case of e.g. avoidance goals [29] doing nothing could be better than doing any of the available actions, i.e. here the progression of actions is not an adequate means for characterizing the goal. Secondly, especially the last part of the definition limits its usability

L. Braubach, J.-P. Briot, and J. Thangarajah (Eds.): ProMAS 2009, LNAI 5919, pp. 201–218, 2010.

by requiring an agent to put effort into the goal achievement. If an agent has no means to pursue a goal at some moment in time, that doesn't mean that it cannot possess the goal. It could just sit and wait until it gets the possibility to act towards the goal or just wait passively for its achievement [2].

This paper proposes using a property-based view of goals. The rationale behind this view is to abandon the objective to introduce a strict separation of what is a goal and what is not a goal, but to see goals as a tool for analyzing and specifying systems. Considering a goal by its characteristics may further help understanding how it should be represented and processed and avoids definitions with limited applicability. Note, that a similar procedure led to the agreed upon characterizations of the term agent [24, p. 33], especially the weak/strong notion of agency [32], which is based on the characterizing properties autonomy, reactivity, proactivity, social abilities, and mentalistic notions.

In the next Section 2, the characteristics of BDI goals will be presented. Thereafter, in Section 3 existing goal representations will be extended under consideration of the uncovered aspects of the previous section. In this respect, special attention will be paid to long-term and interest goals, which have in common that they both might not lead to actions immediately respectively at all. In Section 4 the usefulness of the extended goal semantics will be illustrated by a booktrading example application. Finally, in Section 5 a conclusion is given and some aspects of future work are presented.

## 2     Characteristics of BDI Goals

After having shown the difficulties in defining the term goal precisely, in this section characteristics of goals will be discussed especially in the context of the belief-desire-intention (BDI) model, because it is one of the predominant agent architectures today [26]. In addition to identifying those properties we will examine the degree to which the existing PRS architecture addresses these issues and which deficiencies still exist. PRS have been chosen a reference architecture here, because it is the archetype of many PRS systems. Many existing systems adapt a strong PRS-based view (e.g. JACK, Jason, JAM, OpenPRS), even there are also BDI inspired systems improving the goal view (e.g. Practionist, GOAL).

Before concrete characteristics will be presented, the three different BDI perspectives – philosophical, logical and software technical – will be sketched, because they use slightly different terms. In the original work of Bratman [3] the most general meaning of the goal concept in the form of desires is introduced. A desire represents the motivational reasons for an agent's acting. Bratman allows desires to be quite vague and also conflicting so that an agent has to decide to commit to some of its desires making them concrete intentions, which are considered as conflict-free. In contrast to this perspective, in the logical interpretation of [21] no desires but only goals are considered. They are represented as logical formulae of a branching time logic. Here goals are seen as a subset of belief-accessible worlds and are therefore per se declarative and of type achieve. Hence, in this perspective the only difference between goals and beliefs is the optative vs. indicative interpretation of the logical expression. Considering the software engineering perspective the goal concept has been further simplified and reduced to be some kind of volatile event. In the procedural reasoning system (PRS) architecture [9] and AgentSpeak(L) [19] those kinds of goal events are only used for triggering suitable plans and do not posses an explicit representation.

In the following sections an initial attempt is made to identify the most important goal properties from the existing literature. The first five properties have already been identified in a seminal paper of Rao and Georgeff [23]. In addition to these basic properties several further desirable characteristics can be found in the agent as well as social science literature. Note that the further characteristics mainly aim to isolate goal properties that are useful for a software engineering perspective. The discussion in all sections will first explain the meaning of the property and will then discuss its support in the context of the original PRS architecture as well as recent advancements.

**Persistent.** Persistent goals are entities that have a persistent character, which means that they exist over a period of time. In volatile environments it is important for an agent to commit to its goals and give them up only for good reasons. Hence, the persistence of goals serves for stability in an agent's behavior [21].

The persistency of goals and intentions has not been defined exactly for the PRS architecture. Instead it has often been discussed in the context of commitment strategies [21,31,27], whereby such strategies determine to what extent an agent should keep pursuing its current goals. In the literature a distinction between blind (fanatical), single-minded and open-minded commitment strategies have been proposed. These strategies implement different strengths of commitments. The most committed agent is blindly committed and sticks to its intentions until they finally succeed. A single-minded agent can abandon intentions when believed unachievable and an open-minded agent keeps intentions only as long as they are in line with its goals [22]. Experiments have shown that the efficiency of those strategies is heavily dependent on the existing environmental dynamics, i.e. the faster an environment changes the more flexibility an agent has to adapt its goals [13]. Compared to human decision making, especially an open-minded strategy seems to be promising for truly goal-directed agents, because BDI agents should be enabled to reason about their goals (support goal deliberation) and drop them any time, if an important reason occurs.

**Consistent.** In order to describe the consistency property of goals it is necessary to distinguish between the actively pursued goals called adopted goals and the currently inactive goals called candidate goals resp. options [17,26]. The adopted goals of an agent should be consistent with each other at any point in time in the sense that all goals should be achievable concurrently. An agent should therefore refrain from pursuing a goal, which it thinks stays in conflict with some adopted goals. In case the agent wants to urgently adopt this new goal, a goal deliberation process has to decide if a conflict-free goal set can be found and possibly then has to drop some of the already adopted goals.

The original PRS architecture assumes goals to be always consistent and does not take into account the first phase of practical reasoning, i.e. goal deliberation [16]. This shifts the task for ensuring conflict-freeness to the application layer so that the developer has to cope with these tedious issues directly. This deficiency of the original architecture has been subject of intensive research yielding proposals for supporting also the goal deliberation phase [28,17].

**Possible.** An adopted goal should be possible to pursue, i.e. an agent should be convinced that it can achieve a goal and it does not contradict its current beliefs. This property ensures that an agent does not adopt goals it cannot achieve, but it does not guarantee that a goal can always be successfully pursued.

In PRS the conformance of goals and beliefs cannot be directly ensured due to the event-based character of goals. In an indirect way, the pre- and context conditions of plans help guaranteeing that a goal can only be (successfully) processed when those conditions are valid. Nonetheless, as plans could be applicable for different goal types this support is not fully adequate and should be complemented with checks on the goal level.

**Known/Explicit.** A rational agent should be aware of all its goals (candidate and adopted), because this is a necessary prerequisite for any kind of reasoning on its objectives [17].

In PRS an agent knows its goals as long as they are part of the means-end reasoning. The initialization of a goal normally results from a subgoal call within a plan and leads to the generation of a goal event. This event is saved within the corresponding intention of the calling plan, often called the intention stack [19]. During the processing of the goal via different plans the goal is kept in the stack and is e.g. used to save information about its execution state (e.g. which plans have already been tried) [12]. This event-based representation is not expressive enough for supporting goal deliberation and hence explicit goal representations have been proposed [5,30].

**Unachieved.** An agent should only pursue goals, which it assumes to be unachieved. This kind of behavior will ensure that no unnecessary actions will be initiated and resources will not be wasted. 'Unachieved' is a property, which is not applicable to all kinds of goals (e.g. maintain goals) and was mainly proposed by Rao and Georgeff with achievement goals in mind.

This property is realized by the PRS architecture via testing the achievement condition of a goal before plan processing is started. In case the condition is immediately true, the goal is considered as succeeded and no plans will be executed. Even though this mechanism ensures correct achieve goal processing, it cannot directly be applied to other goal kinds such as maintain. In order to support this property generically its meaning needs to be adapted to different goal kinds guided by the idea to avoid means-end reasoning if the goal does not require it. E.g. a query goal, that is responsible for information retrieval, should only initiate plan processing when the requested data cannot be directly extracted from the beliefbase [5].

**Producible/Terminable.** In order to be useful for agents, goals should be producible and terminable [8]. For the creation as well as the termination of goals, procedural as well as declarative means should be supported, i.e. an agent should be enabled to create/terminate a goal from a plan as well as due to situational reasons.

In PRS goals can typically be created only in a procedural way by issuing subgoal calls from within a plan. The ex post termination of goals is not possible at all due to their implicit representation. A plan is only allowed to issue one subgoal at a time (intention stack) and the subgoal call itself passivates the original plan and lets it wait until the subgoal processing has finished. Declarative means for creating and terminating goals have been introduced e.g. in [5] and rely on a generic representation for the various goal kinds.

**Suspendable.** In addition to the termination of goals it can be advantageous in certain situations to suspend the pursuit of a goal [8,5,25,30], e.g. if the agent has devoted considerable effort into bringing about the goal and cannot continue to pursue it due to a conflict with another possibly more important goal. Further use cases for goal suspension are detailed in [25]. The suspension of a goal should allow saving the current processing state of that goal and continue from there when it gets activated again [25].

The original PRS architecture does not support the suspension of goals. In [5] and [30] the suspension of goals has been addressed by introducing goal lifecycle states, which allow differentiating between active and suspended goals in an agent. The underlying concept is extended in [25] by also addressing the suspension of plans that are executed whilst their goal is suspended.

**Variable Duration.** Intelligent behavior is based on a combination of strategic and tactical action. Strategic behavior is based on long-term goals, which persist over longer time periods and are typically challenging to achieve, e.g. they need several milestones being reached before the goal as a whole can be tackled. Tactical behavior is in many cases based on short-term goals or even reflexes. Hence, short-term goals often only live for the short moment in which the reason for their creation, e.g. an environmental change, was detected. These kinds of goals are closely linked to (physical) actions and exhibit event-based character.

The PRS architecture focuses exclusively on means-end reasoning and therefore goals only exist during their execution phase, i.e. a goal is held as long as plans are executed for this goal. If no (more) plans are available for a goal the means-end reasoning phase has finished and the goal is considered as finished. This does not necessarily mean that goals are always short-term in PRS, because the corresponding plans could be long-lasting. Nevertheless, using long-term goals requires that goal processing can be immediately started, which is not always desired. Furthermore, goals in PRS are typically not of strategic nature, because conflicts between them cannot be detected and long-lasting goals would considerably increase the probability of goal clashes. Hence, the traditional PRS idea is more centered on realizing short-term goal-driven behavior.

**Action Decoupled.** Goals express and incarnate motivations with respect to a specific situation. This motivation can exist even if an agent cannot contribute actively to the goal achievement. These so called interest or passive goals do not directly lead to action execution, but should nonetheless be allowed to persist within an agent [2]. On the one hand, an agent might eventually gain new procedural knowledge for pursuing the goal [1] or on the other hand the goal might be fulfilled by a third party, e.g. other agents.

Due to the action-centeredness of PRS, interest goals cannot be represented. Instead goals are always part of an intention stack and cannot exist without that structure. The means-end reasoning of PRS ends as soon as no further plans can be executed. This also terminates the corresponding goal by popping the event from the intention stack.

## 2.1   Challenges

The aforementioned goal properties shape the complex nature of goals and also indicate in which directions the PRS architecture should be further extended to support the full gamut of goals. Previous works mainly tackled aspects of explicit goal representation [27,5,30] and goal deliberation aspects [17,16,28]. Goal processing was examined with respect to PRS means-end reasoning [21,6] and recently also concerning additional features such as goal suspension [25].

To our knowledge none of the existing works has tackled questions of long-term and interest goals for BDI agents, even though these kinds of goals represent a helpful extension for the conceptual canon of BDI agent programmers. Long-term and interest goals represent attitudes an agent preserves over a longer period and not only during the normally short phase of goal processing. They are different from options, because the agent pursues them and has to take them into account for its goal deliberation activities. The importance of interest goals is emphasized in the literature especially by the cognitive structure of emotions model (OCC - Ortony, Clore and Collins) [14], which assumes that three different goal types exist: "active goals" an agent can directly bring about by performing some actions (e.g. open a bottle), "interest goals" representing states of the world an agent would like to become reality but cannot do anything about pursuing them (e.g. make my favourite soccer team win) and finally "replenishment goals", which repeatedly spawn activities only on demand (e.g. keep healthy). The first and third OCC goal types are already covered by BDI achievement and maintenance goals [5], whereas no support for long-term and interest goals exists. Application cases for interest goals are all scenarios in which external factors (be it actors, processes or something else) are responsible for the agent's goal achievement. Examples include conversation handling, where one participant depends on its communication partners [15] and acting in competitive multi-agent settings, where the actions of one agent can contribute to or thwart the goals of another one [11]. Hence, this paper investigates how long-term and interest goals can be represented and how the PRS architecture needs to be modified in order to allow their processing.

# 3   Long-Term and Interest Goals

To meet the set out requirements and enable a representation of long-term and interest goals in BDI agent systems, two properties should be ensured. First, goals need to be represented explicitly and separately from other BDI constructs such as events or procedural plans. Only with such an explicit representation, the long-term and action-decoupled goals can exist independently of short-lived events and concrete plans resp. actions. Second, an agent should stay committed to these kinds of goals, even if a goal cannot (immediately) be achieved. Otherwise, the agent will not know when to start acting towards the goal when the time comes (long-term goal) or to refrain from counterproductive actions until the goal is achieved (interest goal).

In the following, an extended goal representation will be introduced that is based on existing work on explicit goal representation and adds the necessary property of *long-term, action-independent commitment*. First, a well-accepted goal lifecycle model from the literature will be described as it forms the basis for the new goal representation. It will be shown, how long-term and interest goals fit into this general model. Second, the detailed processing of long-term and interest goals will be discussed. Moreover, it will be shown how the long-term and interest state of goals can be embedded in different goal types, such as achieve, perform, maintain. The section closes with considerations about the usage of long-term and interest goals.

## 3.1   Goal Lifecycle Model

Figure 1 shows a basic goal lifecycle introduced in [5]. This lifecycle divides the set of adopted goals of an agent according to the three possible substates *option*, *active* and *suspended* in order to support the goal deliberation and means-end reasoning phases [31]. Thereby, the means-end reasoning of the agent operates

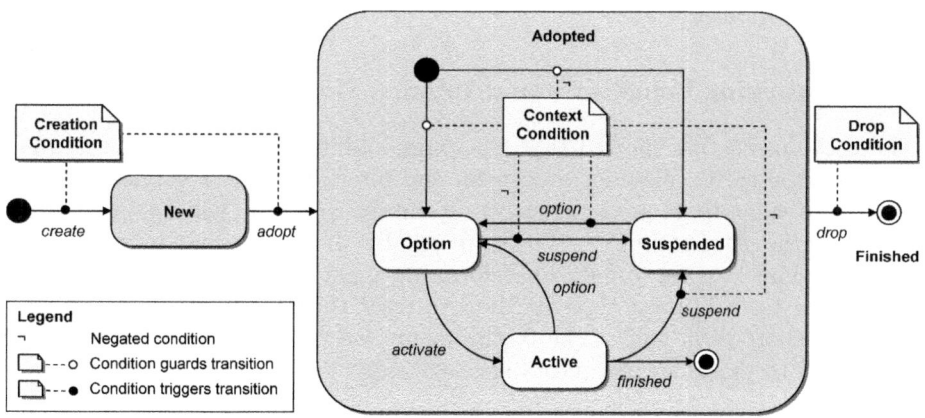

**Fig. 1.** Basic goal lifecycle

on active goals only, i.e. only active goals can lead to the execution of plans and actions. Moreover, suspended goals are goals, which currently cannot be pursued due to an invalid context condition, while options are those goals, which the agent's deliberation mechanism has decided not to pursue (e.g. in favor of other more important goals). Although each goal can only be in exactly one of the substates at any point in time, the state of a goal can change, e.g. when changes happen to beliefs or other goals of an agent.

Based on this generic goal lifecycle, the characteristics of long-term and interest goals can be defined. Whenever a goal enters the active state, the agent will start the means-end reasoning process in order to find suitable means for pursuing the goal. Unlike usual short-term goals, which immediately lead to actions, for a long-term or interest goal it might be an appropriate means to actually do nothing at all. *Therefore, a long-term or interest goal is a goal, which can be active even without executing any plans for it.* The distinction between long-term in contrast to interest goals is merely one of future expectations. For a long-term goal, the agent expects to find suitable means somewhere in the future, while for an interest goal, the agent does not expect to be able to contribute to goal achievement, but still expects that the goal might be (automatically) achieved in the future, if the agent refrains from doing counterproductive actions.

Allowing for goals to be active even without suitable actions leads to some important advantages with respect to goal deliberation processes. Because the goal is among the active goals of an agent, it will be considered as such during the agent's goal deliberation, e.g. in contrast to a suspended goal. Therefore, other conflicting goals will not be activated, unless they are considered more important than a currently active long-term or interest goal. This example also shows that sticking to a long-term or interest goal even without a suitable plan does not contradict an open-minded commitment (cf. section 2), as the agent still can decide to abandon the goal at any time. Another advantage with respect to long-term goals is that for an active goal, the agent can adopt any suitable plan as soon as it becomes available/viable, and does not have to enter complex goal deliberation processes.

## 3.2   Processing Long-Term and Interest Goals

The previous section showed that the expressibility of the goal lifecycle model can be extended to allow for long-term and interest goals by supporting active goals even when there are (currently) no suitable plans. In general, not all goals are of the long-term/interest type, but usually should be abandoned, when no suitable plans can be found. Therefore, an agent needs to know which goals are of long-term/interest type and how to treat these goals differently from the "normal" short-term goals. The requirements for this special treatment can be condensed to the following questions:

**When to stop, but not drop?** The usual behavior is to fail a goal, when no suitable plans can be found once the goal has become active. For long-term/interest goals, the agent programmer needs a mechanism for overriding this behavior in such a way that the agent will stop the means-end reasoning, but not drop the goal.

**When to continue processing?** Some time after a long-term goal has stopped processing, the agent should re-check the availability of plans. For efficiency and effectiveness the programmer should have fine-grained, yet simple control over the re-check activity for ensuring that the agent stays reactive in a changing environment, but avoiding the overhead of unnecessarily checking too frequently.

**When to succeed/finally fail?** Long-term as well as interest goals should not stay in the agent forever. For one, similar to short-term goals the agent should be able to detect when a goal has been achieved, e.g. because the environment has changed or some successful plan could finally be found. Moreover, because dropping unachievable long-term/interest goals is not done automatically, an agent programmer may want to explicitly state reasons for dropping a long-term or interest goal.

To capture the required functionality, a generic goal processing component is introduced (cf. Figure 2). This component is generic in the sense that it is independent of the concrete goal type (perform, achieve, maintain, etc.), but forms the conceptual and technical basis for processing of all goal types. The component is activated through the *in* edge, which is triggered depending on the goal type, e.g. when a goal becomes active (achieve) or a condition becomes violated (maintain). Regardless of how the component is activated, it will enter two nested loops, which are responsible for basic means-end reasoning and long-term/interest goal handling respectively. In the following sections it will be discussed, how this generic component gives answers to the questions raised above.

**When to stop, but not drop?** The inner loop is the "retry loop", which represents traditional PRS-style means-end reasoning as known from currently implemented BDI systems. This part is captured by the *In Process* state in the

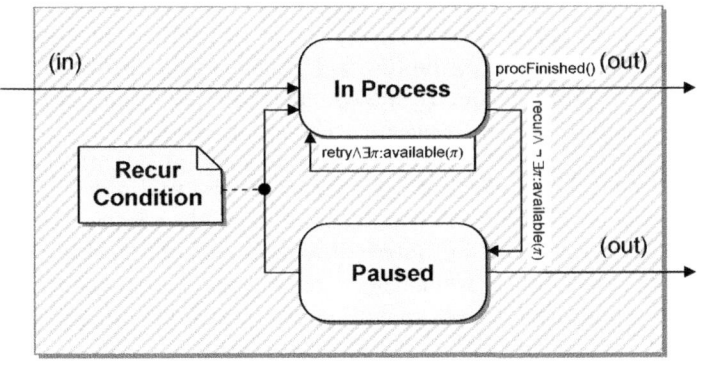

**Fig. 2.** Generic goal processing component

figure, in which usually the agent selects and executes a single plan for a goal.[1] If the goal is not finished after the plan has been executed ($procFinished()$), the retry loop continues, leading to the next plan being selected and executed. The retry loop iterates – unless retry behavior is disabled with the *retry* flag – until no more applicable plans are available for the goal ($retry \wedge \exists \pi : available(\pi)$).

To extend this basic means-end reasoning with the required functionality for handling long-term and interest goals, a new *Paused* state is introduced. This state effectively represents the means of "doing nothing" to achieve a goal. Extended means-end reasoning for long-term/interest goals therefore happens according to the outer "recur loop", which alternates between the *In Process* and *Paused* states. The first question posed above then becomes the question of when to move from the *In Process* to the *Paused* state. For this decision, the *recur* flag is introduced that an agent developer can set to true for a goal to be handled as a long-term/interest goal. Hence, the *Paused* state is entered, when the *recur* flag is set and no (more) plans are available ($recur \wedge \neg \exists \pi : available(\pi)$). Note that *Paused* and *In Process* are substates of the lifecycle state *Active* (cf. Figure 1), which means that paused goals suppress the execution of other conflicting, but less important goals e.g. according to the "easy deliberation strategy" [17].

**When to continue processing?** The continuation of processing forms the second part of the "recur loop", i.e. moving from the *Paused* state back to *In Process*. To allow fine-grained control over when an agent should reconsider the processing of long-term goals, three different specification means are supported – recur delay, recur condition, and recur action – that a developer can choose from or combine, depending on the application at hand. The recur delay of a goal is a simple mechanism for continuously looking for newly applicable plans becoming available. This allows the developer to specify a time interval, after which processing of the goal should be restarted. A more advanced way is the *Recur Condition*, illustrated in the figure. The recur condition allows the specification of a world state (based on the agent's beliefs) that should cause reprocessing of the goal. Therefore it provides a declarative way for specifying the conditions, under which a reconsideration of the goal becomes worthwhile. The most flexible, but least automated way is an explicit recur action that can be manually invoked on a goal. Therefore, the developer can provide arbitrary code (e.g. inside a procedural plan), to determine when certain goals should be reconsidered and explicitly invoke the recur action on these as needed.

**When to succeed/finally fail?** In Figure 2, the two *out* edges from the *In Process* as well as *Paused* state determine possible ways of exiting the goal processing. First, it should be noted that as illustrated in Figure 2, goal processing would never finish when the *recur* flag is set to true. The lower *out* edge has no guard and therefore will never actively trigger (as long as not

---

[1] For brevity, we do not cover detailed fine-tuning of the means-end reasoning process, such as caching vs. recalculation of the applicable plan list (APL) or parallel execution of plans for the same goal (post-to-all), even though these variations are supported by the proposed model as well.

refined in a concrete goal type), while the guard on the upper *out* edge is
*procFinished* $() = (\neg retry \lor \neg \exists \pi : available\ (\pi)) \land \neg recur$, i.e. processing is only
finished, when *retry* and *recur* are both false or when *recur* is false and no more
plans are available. An answer to the question above, therefore cannot be given
in the context of the generic goal processing component alone, but also needs to
consider the generic goal lifecycle (cf. Figure 1) and the specifics of the different
goal types, such as achieve and maintain.

The generic goal lifecycle of Figure 1 allows for several ways of exiting the
*Active* state, which would cause the substates like *In Process* and *Paused* to
be exited as well. First, the *Active* state can be exited due to goal deliberation
issues, e.g. moving to the *Option* state when a more important but conflicting
goal occurs or to the *Suspended* state, when the context of the goal becomes
invalid. In both cases, processing of the goal would be stopped regardless of
the goal being a short-term, long-term, or interest goal. Moreover, goals can be
abandoned at any time, e.g. when the *Drop Condition* triggers or the goal is
dropped manually. In the latter cases, the goal will finish before being achieved
and therefore can be considered as finally failed. How to determine goal success
depends on the specific goal type and will be discussed in the next section.

### 3.3  Realization of Specific Goal Types

The extended reasoning process has been embedded into the four goal types
perform, achieve, query, and maintain, as introduced in [5].

The simplest extension is the perform goal, which represents a purely procedural goal kind, i.e., it does not possess a declarative part. It is used to directly
initiate activities and refines the generic processing component only with respect
to several small details. It can be seen in Fig. 3 that the start and end states of the

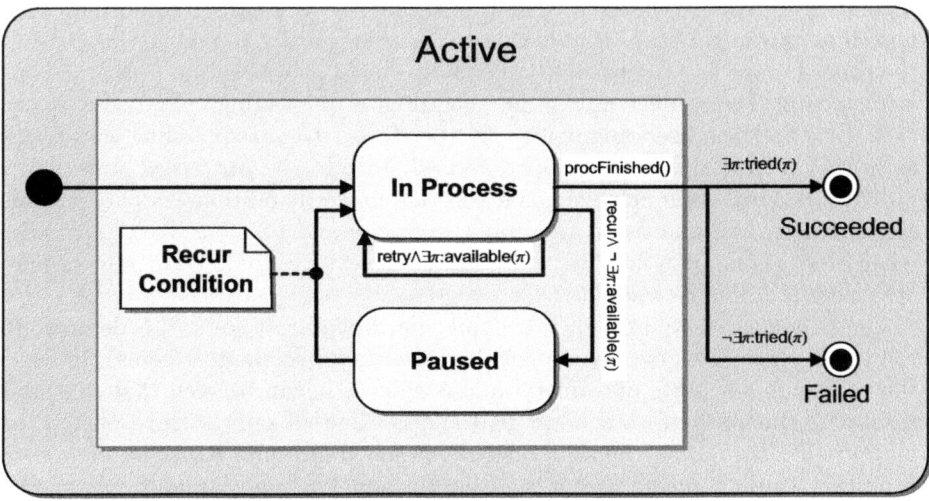

**Fig. 3.** Extended processing for perform goals

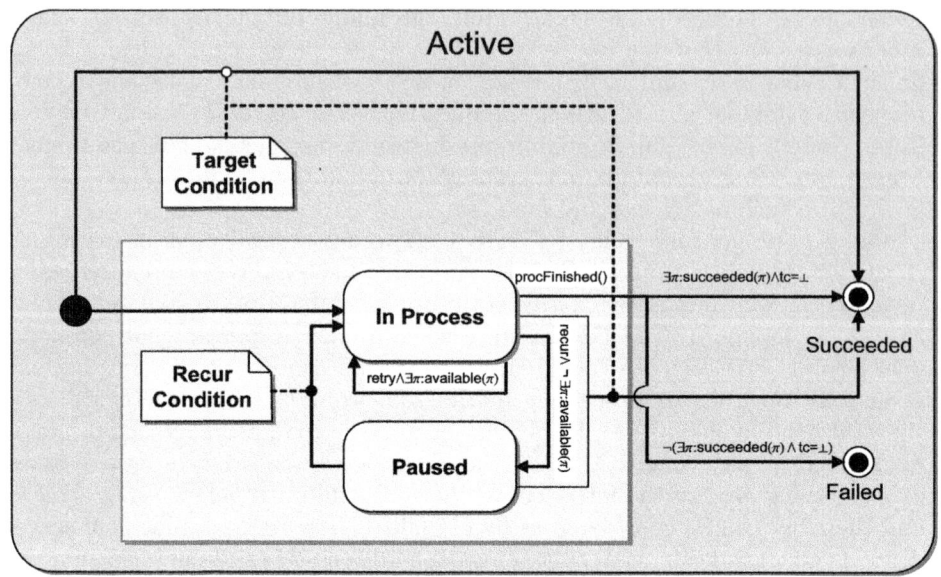

**Fig. 4.** Extended processing for achieve goals

perform goal have been directly connected to the in- and outputs of the processing component. The success state of a perform goal depends on the existence of a plan that could be executed for the goal. If at least one plan has been executed ($\exists \pi : tried\,(\pi)$) the goal is considered as succeeded, otherwise as failed.

Figure 4 shows the extended model for processing achieve goals. In contrast to a perform goal, an achieve goal can have declarative as well as procedural semantics. Normally, an achieve goal is defined with a target condition, which describes the world state that needs to be achieved by pursuing the goal. On the other hand this target condition can also be omitted leading to a procedural achieve goal. For achieve goals, the generic goal processing component is used as a basis and has been augmented by the *Target Condition*, which can trigger a transition from the *In Process* or *Paused* state to the *Succeeded* state. Moreover, procedural style achieve goals without target condition ($tc = \perp$) are also supported by two guards on the upper *out* edge and are considered succeeded, when at least one plan finishes successfully ($\exists \pi : succeeded\,(\pi) \wedge tc = \perp$) or failed otherwise ($\neg\,(\exists \pi : succeeded\,(\pi) \wedge tc = \perp)$).

Query goals can be used for retrieving specific information or for determining the truth value of an expression (in this case they become test goals). In Fig. 5 the refined active state of a query goal is shown. It can be seen that it is quite similar to the state of an achieve goal and is different only with respect to one major point. It replaces the achieve goal's target condition with an implicit result condition. Implicit means that it is part of the goal kind and cannot be changed by the agent programmer. The query itself is specified as goal parameters containing expressions that restrict the allowed goal parameter values. The result condition

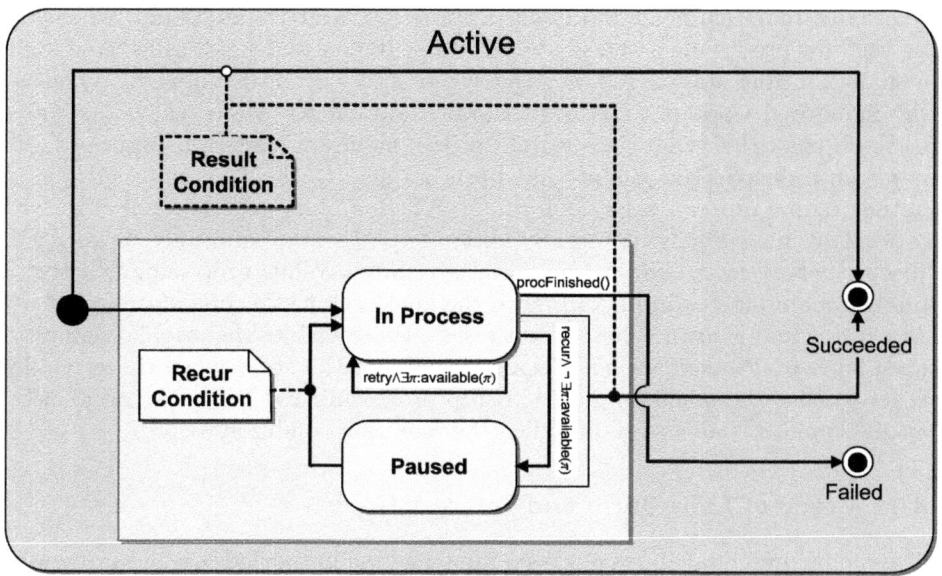

**Fig. 5.** Extended processing for query goals

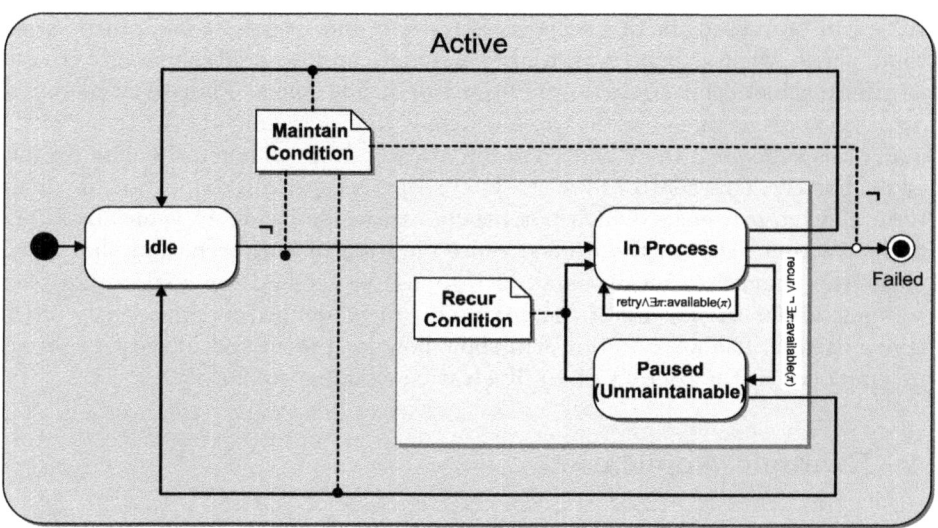

**Fig. 6.** Extended processing for maintain goals

states that all free variables in these parameter expressions have to be bound to values, i.e. the task of the goal is to find a valid substitution of values from the agent's beliefbase with respect to the query goal parameters. A query goal tries to answer the given query first on basis of the beliefbase. If the necessary information is not readily available, plans will be initiated to gather that information.

Finally, maintain goals represent a purely declarartive goal kind, which can be used for preserving a specific world state. In contrast to all other goal kinds a maintain goal stays adopted even when it is currently fulfilled. Whenever the monitored world state is not sustained any longer, plans will be activated to reestablish the violated world state. For maintain goals (cf. Figure 6), the newly introduced *Paused* state has been mapped to the *Unmaintainable* state of the original processing model from [5]. As a maintain goal does not start with processing immediately, it initially enters the *Idle* state and only moves to *In Process*, when the *Maintain Condition* is violated. While processing is active, a fulfilled maintain condition will move the goal back to the *Idle* state from both *In Process* and *Paused*. This semantics exactly resembles the original semantics from [5] (with *Unmaintainable* renamed to *Paused*), except when the *recur* flag is set to false the maintain goal will stop processing and fail, when none of the available plans is able to re-establish the maintain condition.

### 3.4   Usage of Long-Term and Interest Goals

The model presented above has been implemented in the Jadex agent framework [18]. One primary advantage of the model is that long-term and interest goals are represented just like other (short-term) goals. Therefore, their usage does not differ from these and the available mechanisms for creating and handling goals can be reused. In this respect, long-term and interest goals can be given to an agent, when it is born (initial goals) and can also be dynamically created at runtime based on creation conditions or inside plans. Plans can choose to dispatch goals as independent top-level goals that exist outside the scope of the plan or as subgoals, which will be automatically dropped when the plan finishes or is aborted. This control over the goal scope is especially important for long-term and interest goals, which potentially can reside inside an agent for a long period of time. Due to the unified representation of long-term and short-term goals, the plans that get executed in response to a long-term goal do not need to know about the nature of the goal and can be defined independently of the goal's nature. The next section will show how long-term and interest goals can be employed in the context of an illustrative example scenario.

## 4   Example Application

To illustrate how long-term and interest goals can be used in practice the book-trading scenario from [4] is used, where personal buyer and seller agents are responsible for trading books according to orders given by their principals. The participants use a market-based coordination strategy following the contract-net protocol for reaching agreements acceptable for both sides. It is assumed that buyers take the initiator role of the protocol, whereas sellers play the participant role. An order of a principal includes all relevant data needed for an agent to be able to buy resp. sell a book. Concretely, it contains the name of the book, the start and limit prices as well as a deadline at which the transaction has to be done at latest. The start price represents the acceptable price for an agent at the beginning of the negotiation. While time passes and the deadline approaches a linear price adaptation strategy is used to calculate the currently acceptable price between start and limit price.[2]

Buy or sell orders are entered by the principals through the user interface for each agent. For each of these orders the agents form purchase resp. sell goals, which express the motivations of the principals. For a buyer agent a purchase book goal represents the long-term goal for buying a book, according to the definitions in the order. It is of long-term nature, because initially there might be no seller available that offers the book at the desired price. Nevertheless, the agent should not drop the goal in this case, but instead wait for new sellers to appear or the book gets cheaper at the available sellers. The purchase book goal is therefore modeled as an active achieve goal, which has the purpose of initiating negotiations with potential sellers in fixed time intervals until the book could be bought or the deadline has passed. At the top of Figure 7 the concrete implementation of the *purchase_book* goal is illustrated. The *purchase_book* goal (lines 1-5) contains the principal's order in a corresponding parameter (line 2). It is defined as a long-term goal via the recur flag (line 1), which enables the long-term processing loop. In addition, it is made active by specifying the recurdelay, stating that each 10 seconds (10000 ms.) a new negotiation round is started. If the negotiation is successful, the state of the buy order will change to *DONE*, which is tracked by the goal's targetcondition (line 3). On the other hand, the dropcondition (line 4) monitors the deadline and lets the goal automatically fail, when no negotiation result could be achieved before the deadline ends.

The seller's *sell_book* goal (lines 7-11) is realized in a very similar way. The main difference here is that it is a pure interest goal, i.e. it is assumed that sellers passively wait for buy requests to come in and match them with their existing sell goals. An interest goal is specified by activating the recur flag without specifying means for recur initiation, i.e. no recur delay and no recur condition (line 7). The seller agent has no plans for achieving its *sell_book* goal. But the agent does have a plan for reacting to buy book requests from buyer agents and engaging in a corresponding negotiation. When such a negotiation comes to a result, the target condition (line 9) is fulfilled and the *sell_book* goal is achieved.

This example shows how long-term and interest goals can facilitate the high-level and natural modeling of BDI scenarios. The availability of these conceptual abstractions allows for a direct mapping of buy and sell orders to goals, which are present as long as the corresponding orders are relevant. Using only standard BDI goals would require additional error prone code: The buyer's long-term goal could be emulated using a long-term plan, which captures the recur semantics and initiates negotiations in certain intervals. The seller's interest goal would have to be mapped to other structures such as beliefs leading to a rather artificial design, which would also differ a lot from the buyer side.

---

[2] In case of a buyer the start price is lower than the limit price and is continuously increased. The opposite behavior is used by sellers.

```
1   <achievegoal name="purchase_book" recur="true" recurdelay="10000">
2     <parameter name="order" class="Order"/>
3     <targetcondition>Order.DONE.equals($goal.order.state)</targetcondition>
4     <dropcondition>$beliefbase.time > $goal.order. deadline </dropcondition>
5   </achievegoal>
6
7   <achievegoal name="sell_book" recur="true">
8     <parameter name="order" class="Order"/>
9     <targetcondition>Order.DONE.equals($goal.order.state)</targetcondition>
10    <dropcondition>$beliefbase.time > $goal.order. deadline </dropcondition>
11  </achievegoal>
```

**Fig. 7.** Purchase and sell book goals

## 5  Conclusion

This paper has tackled the representation and processing of long-term and interest goals. In order to understand goals in BDI agent systems, definitions of the term goal have been reviewed. This review mainly revealed that the essence of the term is very hard to capture, because on the one hand different perspectives on BDI exist – ranging from philosophical to implementational – and on the other hand many definitions tend to be too restrictive by overlooking important goal aspects. As a result, this paper has proposes characterizing goals according to their typical properties, similar to property-based definitions of the term agent. Such a specification is more practically useful as it has the aim of supporting the goal-oriented software specification and is not targeted towards a clear-cut separation of what is a goal and what isn't.

Based on the characterization of goals it has been shown that long-term and interest goals are not currently considered in the modeling and implementation of BDI systems. These goals are typically long-lasting, whereby they can be active without having plans executed for them. In the case of interest goals, an agent does not possess plans for their fulfillment, whereas in the case of long-term goals, plans could exist but not fit to the situation at activation time. Their main relevance can be seen in the more strategic nature of these goals allowing also long-lasting objectives to be expressed. Especially, in combination with goal deliberation mechanisms such strategic goals represent useful extensions to traditional BDI goals, which are of rather tactical, short-term nature.

The main contribution of this paper consists of providing a representation and processing mechanism for long-term and interest goals. The new mechanism builds on the explicit goal representation from [5], and introduces a generic goal processing component for short- and long-term means-end reasoning. This component introduces two control loops, one responsible for traditional plan selection and execution and one responsible for pausing the execution of long-term goals in the case where no processing is currently possible. This generic component can be used to support different goal kinds such as achieve and maintain. The concepts of long-term and interest goals have been implemented within the Jadex BDI agent system and already been used for building different example applications, such as the presented booktrading scenario.

In future work we plan to further extend the expressiveness of goal specifications available for describing BDI agent systems. In this respect one important goal type are soft-goals, which represent non-functional properties and have therefore been excluded from the implementation layer so far.

# References

1. Ancona, D., Mascardi, V., Hübner, J., Bordini, R.: Coo-AgentSpeak: Cooperation in AgentSpeak through Plan Exchange. In: Proceedings of AAMAS 2004, pp. 698–705. ACM press, New York (2004)
2. Beaudoin, L.: Goal Processing in Autonomous Agents. PhD thesis (March 1995)
3. Bratman, M.: Intention, Plans, and Practical Reason. Harvard Univ. Press (1987)
4. Braubach, L., Pokahr, A.: Goal-oriented interaction protocols. In: Petta, P., Müller, J.P., Klusch, M., Georgeff, M. (eds.) MATES 2007. LNCS (LNAI), vol. 4687, pp. 85–97. Springer, Heidelberg (2007)
5. Braubach, L., Pokahr, A., Moldt, D., Lamersdorf, W.: Goal Representation for BDI Agent Systems. In: Bordini, R.H., Dastani, M.M., Dix, J., El Fallah Seghrouchni, A. (eds.) PROMAS 2004. LNCS (LNAI), vol. 3346, pp. 44–65. Springer, Heidelberg (2005)
6. Busetta, P., Howden, N., Rönnquist, R., Hodgson, A.: Structuring BDI Agents in Functional Clusters. In: Jennings, N.R. (ed.) ATAL 1999. LNCS, vol. 1757, pp. 277–289. Springer, Heidelberg (2000)
7. Cohen, P.R., Levesque, H.J.: Intention is choice with commitment. Artificial Intelligence 42, 213–261 (1990)
8. Dignum, F., Conte, R.: Intentional Agents and Goal Formation. In: Proceedings of ATAL 1997, pp. 231–243 (1997)
9. Georgeff, M., Lansky, A.: Reactive Reasoning and Planning: An Experiment With a Mobile Robot. In: Proceedings of AAAI 1987, pp. 677–682. AAAI, Menlo Park (1987)
10. Ghallab, M., Nau, D., Traverso, P.: Automated Planning: Theory and Practice. Morgan Kaufmann Publishers, San Francisco (2004)
11. Johns, M., Silverman, B.G.: How Emotions and Personality Effect the Utility of Alternative Decisions: A Terrorist Target Selection Case Study. In: Proceedings of SISO 2001, pp. 55–64 (2001)
12. Kinny, D.: Algebraic specification of agent computation. Journal Applicable Algebra in Engineering, Communication and Computing 16(2-3), 77–111 (2005)
13. Kinny, D., Georgeff, M.: Commitment and effectiveness of situated agents. In: Proceedings of IJCAI 1991, pp. 82–88 (February 1991)
14. Ortony, A., Clore, G.L., Collins, A.: The Cognitive Structure of Emotions. Cambridge University Press, Cambridge (1988)
15. Pasquier, P., Dignum, F., Rahwan, I., Sonenberg, L.: Interest-based negotiation as an extension of monotonic bargaining in 3apl. In: Shi, Z.-Z., Sadananda, R. (eds.) PRIMA 2006. LNCS (LNAI), vol. 4088, pp. 327–338. Springer, Heidelberg (2006)
16. Pokahr, A., Braubach, L., Lamersdorf, W.: A Flexible BDI Architecture Supporting Extensibility. In: Proc. of IAT 2005, pp. 379–385. IEEE, Los Alamitos (2005)
17. Pokahr, A., Braubach, L., Lamersdorf, W.: A goal deliberation strategy for bdi agent systems. In: Eymann, T., Klügl, F., Lamersdorf, W., Klusch, M., Huhns, M.N. (eds.) MATES 2005. LNCS (LNAI), vol. 3550, pp. 82–94. Springer, Heidelberg (2005)

18. Pokahr, A., Braubach, L., Lamersdorf, W.: Jadex: A BDI Reasoning Engine. In: Multi-Agent Programming: Languages, Platforms and Applications, pp. 149–174. Springer, Heidelberg (2005)
19. Rao, A.: AgentSpeak(L): BDI Agents Speak Out in a Logical Computable Language. In: Perram, J., Van de Velde, W. (eds.) MAAMAW 1996. LNCS, vol. 1038, pp. 42–55. Springer, Heidelberg (1996)
20. Rao, A., Georgeff, M.: Asymmetry thesis and side-effect problems in linear-time and branching-time intention logics. In: Proc. of IJCAI 1991 (1991)
21. Rao, A., Georgeff, M.: BDI Agents: from theory to practice. In: Proceedings of ICMAS 1995, pp. 312–319. MIT Press, Cambridge (1995)
22. Rao, A.S., Georgeff, M.P.: Modeling rational agents within a BDI-architecture. Tech. Rep. 14, Australian AI Institute, Carlton, Australia (1991)
23. Rao, A.S., Georgeff, M.P.: An abstract architecture for rational agents. In: Proceedings of KR 1992, pp. 439–449 (1992)
24. Russell, S., Norvig, P.: Artifical Intelligence: A Modern Approach. Prentice-Hall, Englewood Cliffs (2003)
25. Thangarajah, J., Harland, J., Morley, D., Yorke-Smith, N.: Suspending and resuming tasks in bdi agents. In: Proc. of AAMAS 2008 (2008)
26. Thangarajah, J., Harland, J., Yorke-Smith, N.: A soft cop model for goal deliberation in a bdi agent. In: Proceedings of CP 2007 (September 2007)
27. Thangarajah, J., Padgham, L., Harland, J.: Representation and Reasoning for Goals in BDI Agents. In: Proc. of ACSC 2002 (2002)
28. Thangarajah, J., Padgham, L., Winikoff, M.: Detecting and Avoiding Interference Between Goals in Intelligent Agents. In: Proc. of IJCAI 2003 (2003)
29. van Lamsweerde, A.: Goal-Oriented Requirements Engineering: A Guided Tour. In: Proceedings of RE 2001, pp. 249–263. IEEE Press, Los Alamitos (2001)
30. van Riemsdijk, B., Dastani, M., Winikoff, M.: Goals in agent systems: a unifying framework. In: Proceedings of AAMAS 2008, pp. 713–720 (2008)
31. Wooldridge, M.: Reasoning about Rational Agents. MIT Press, Cambridge (2000)
32. Wooldridge, M.: An Introduction to MultiAgent Systems. Wiley & Sons, Chichester (2001)

# Introducing Relevance Awareness in BDI Agents

Emiliano Lorini[1] and Michele Piunti[2]

[1] Université de Toulouse, CNRS, Institut de Recherche en Informatique de Toulouse, France
[2] Università degli studi di Bologna - DEIS, Bologna, Italy

**Abstract.** Artificial agents engaged in real world applications require accurate allocation strategies in order to better balance the use of their bounded resources. In particular, during their epistemic activities, they should be able to filter out all irrelevant information and just consider what is relevant for the current task that they are trying to solve. The aim of this work is to propose a mechanism of relevance-based belief update to be implemented in a BDI cognitive agent. This is in order to improve the performance of agents in information-rich environments. In the first part of the paper we present the formal and abstract model of the mechanism. In the second part we present its implementation in the *Jason* programming platform and we discuss its performance in simulation trials.

## 1 Introduction

Realistic cognitive agents are by definition resource-bounded [6], hence they should not waste time and energy in reasoning, fixing and reconsidering their knowledge on the basis of every piece of information they get. For this reason, they require accurate allocation strategies in order to better balance the use of their bounded computational resources. In this paper we present a computational model of a mechanism of relevance-based belief update. This mechanism is responsible for filtering out all non-relevant information and for considering only what is *relevant* for the current task that an agent is trying to solve. We show how such a mechanism can be implemented in a BDI (Belief, Desire, Intention) agent [22]. BDI is a well-established framework which is aimed at describing an agent's mental process of deciding, moment by moment on the basis of current beliefs, which action to perform in order to achieve his goals. The mechanism we propose will accomplish the following general function in an agent reasoning process: (*i*) to signal the inconsistency between the agent's beliefs and an incoming input which is relevant with respect to the agent's current intentions and (*ii*) to trigger a process of belief update in order to integrate such a relevant input in the agent's belief base. More generally, we suppose that at each moment an agent is focused and allocates his attentive resources on a particular task that he is trying to fulfill and on a certain number of intentions which represent the pragmatic solution selected by the agent to accomplish the task [3]. In so doing, the agent ignores all incoming inputs which are not relevant with respect to the current task on which he is focused and only considers the information that is relevant. If a relevant input turns out to be incompatible with respect to the pre-existent beliefs of the agent, the agent reconsiders them.

The approach proposed in this paper is also intended to bridge the existing gap between formal and computational models of belief change and cognitive models of belief

L. Braubach, J.-P. Briot, and J. Thangarajah (Eds.): ProMAS 2009, LNAI 5919, pp. 219–236, 2010.

dynamics. Indeed, formal approaches to belief change implicitly assume that when an agent perceives some fact such a perception is always a precursor of a process of belief change. In contrast, we model here these precursors of a process of belief change and, in agreement with cognitive theories of bounded rationality (e.g. [24]), we show that implementing them in a resource-bounded agent can improve his performance in information-rich environments requiring massive perceptive activities.

This proposal is also intended to provide a novel insight in the design and programming of cognitive agents. Whereas in the context of Multi Agent Systems (MAS) mainstream agent platforms provide advanced mechanisms to process messages and Agent Communication Languages (ACLs), the perception of heterogeneous events and information is often shaped on the basis of technical constructs, which are typically designed in a domain-dependent fashion and implemented with constructs built at the language level. Mainstream programming models are often not flexible enough to integrate different perceptive abilities, nor to relate them with cognitive constructs such as the cognitive ones typical of BDI agents. Instead, we propose in this paper a programming model in which the relationship between perception and practical reasoning is clearly specified in terms of the pivotal notion of pragmatic relevance.

The paper is organized as follows. Section 2 abstractly describes the proposed approach and contextualizes it with respect to the related literature on the subject of relevance. Section 3 defines the abstract model of a cognitive agent. This includes informational attitudes (e.g. beliefs which change over time and stable causal knowledge) and motivational attitudes (e.g. intentions and desires). Section 4 applies the agent's abstract model to the formalization of a specific problem domain. In section 5 the cognitive architectures of two general typologies of BDI agents are formally defined—respectively implementing a traditional BDI interpreter and $BDI^{rel}$ with relevance awareness abilities. Section 6 describes a programming model for the $BDI^{rel}$ agent, discussing how it has been implemented by using the *Jason* platform [2]. Finally, Section 7 compares the performance of agents engaged in simulated experiments in the scenario previously described and Section 8 concludes with final remarks and future directions of research.

## 2    The Concept of Relevance: An Overview

The notion of information relevance is not new in the literature, as it has been extensively investigated in several domains like AI, philosophy and cognitive sciences.

Most theoretical works on relevance have been interested in modeling a particular form of *informational* relevance based on various forms of conditional in/dependence. According to [13,18], for instance, the concept of relevance coincides with the probabilistic concept of conditional dependence and, in particular, irrelevance is identified with conditional independence, and relevance is identified with the negation of irrelevance. Relevance logic [1] proposes alternatives to material implication where the antecedent and consequent are relevantly related.

In the area of belief revision, some authors [7,19] have introduced a primitive notion of relevance of an agent's belief base with respect to an incoming input $\chi$. These authors argue that during belief revision a rational agent does not change his entire belief corpus, but only the portion of it that is relevant to the new incoming information $\chi$, that is, only the portion that shares common propositional variables with the minimal language of the input $\chi$. Some computational systems, inspired by Information Theory [23], conceive relevance as a quantitative notion of informativeness that can be related to a given datum. Among others, such an approach gave rise to ranking mechanisms used for instance by web research engines, which are almost always based on a quantitative and possibly weighted analysis of the amount of links referable to a web document.

Differently from the above mentioned works, which are mostly interested in a notion of informational relevance, we are interested here in investigating a notion of *pragmatic relevance*[1] and in its application to agent programming. The notion of relevance discussed in this paper is closer to the one considered in several psychological theories of motivations and emotions [14,9], where relevance is related to the subjective appraisal of a certain event with respect to an agent's ongoing goals and intentions. In particular, according to these theories, an agent's perception of a fact which is relevant with respect to his goals and intentions might be responsible for triggering a certain emotion of the agent. For example, imagine an agent perceiving the fact "there is a lion in front of me" which is relevant with respect to his goal of survival. Then, the agent will feel an intense fear caused by the perception of this fact.

Such a notion of pragmatic relevance has been considered in some design models of active perception (see, e.g., [26]) and of low-level mechanisms in which relevance is related to action selection through classifier systems [25]. Some models exist explaining the relationship that exists between perceptive processes and agent reasoning. Among others, Pereira & Tettamanzi recently proposed a formal model of goal generation where both relevance and trustworthiness of information sources are involved in rational goal selection [8]. Few works deal with agent models which are capable of appraising incoming input on the basis of cognitive relevance: [12] proposed a model where percepts are filtered according to a programmable heuristic defined in a so called *impact function*, while in [16] a model relating relevant information to an internal value indicating unexpectedness and surprisingness of percepts is envisaged.

The aim of this work is to ground the concept of relevance on mental states such as beliefs, goals and intentions. Once grounded on mental states, the notion of pragmatic relevance can be easily integrated in the practical reasoning of an agent and, in particular, it can be operationalized in the widely adopted BDI (belief, desire, intention) computational model of cognitive agents [21] and then integrated into a programming model for intelligent agents and multi-agent systems.

Before introducing our computational model of pragmatic relevance and in order to ground it on agents' mental states, in the next section the adopted agent reasoning model is briefly described.

## 3   The Abstract Agent Model

In this section a definition of an agent's abstract model based on BDI is provided. At the programming level this includes constructs obtained by perceptions, static causal

---

[1] See, e.g., [10] for a discussion on the distinction between informational relevance and pragmatic relevance.

knowledge, volatile beliefs, desires and intentions, desire-generating and planning rules, and a repertoire of basic actions.

Let VAR$=\{X_1, \ldots, X_n\}$ be a non-empty set of random variables. We suppose that each random variable $X_i \in$ VAR takes values from a non-empty set of variable assignments $\mathrm{Val}_{X_i}$. For each set $\mathrm{Val}_{X_i}$ we denote by $\mathrm{Inst}_{X_i}$ the corresponding set of all possible instantiations of random variable $X_i$. For example, suppose that $\mathrm{Val}_{X_i} = \{x_1, \ldots, x_r\}$ then $\mathrm{Inst}_{X_i} = \{X_i = x_1, \ldots, X_i = x_r\}$. We denote by Inst the set of all possible instantiations of all random variables, that is: $\mathrm{Inst} = \bigcup_{X_i \in \mathrm{VAR}} \mathrm{Inst}_{X_i}$.

*Perceived data.* $\Gamma \subseteq$ Inst is a set of perceived data which fixes the value of certain variables that an agent perceives at a certain moment. For example, $\Gamma = \{X_i = x\}$ means "the agent perceives the event $X_i = x$". We denote by

$$\Gamma_{Var} = \{X_i \in \mathrm{VAR} \mid \exists\, x \in \mathrm{Val}_{X_i} \text{ such that } X_i = x \in \Gamma\}$$

the subset of VAR which includes the variables that an agent observes at a certain moment. Here we suppose that for all $X_i \in \Gamma_{Var}, \mathrm{Inst}_{X_i} \cap \Gamma$ is a singleton, that is, we suppose that an agent cannot perceive two different instantiations of the same variable. We use the notation $\Gamma(X_i)$ to denote this singleton for every $X_i \in \Gamma_{Var}$, that is, $\Gamma(X_i) = \mathrm{Inst}_{X_i} \cap \Gamma$.

*Stable causal knowledge.* K is a Bayesian network which represents the joint probability distribution over the set of random variables VAR. A Bayesian network is a directed acyclic graph (DAG) whose nodes are labeled by the random variables in VAR and the edges represent the causal influence between the random variables in VAR [18]. Given an arbitrary random variable $X$ (i.e. an arbitrary node) in the Bayesian network K we denote by $\mathrm{anc}(X)$ the set of ancestors of $X$. Formally, $Z$ is an *ancestor* of $X$ in the Bayesian network K if there is a directed path from $Z$ to $X$ in K.

Moreover, given an arbitrary random variable $X$ in the Bayesian network K, we denote by $\mathrm{par}(X)$ the set of parents of $X$ in the Bayesian network. Formally, $Z$ is a *parent* of $X$ in the Bayesian network K if $Z$ is an ancestor of $X$ in K which is directly connected to $Z$. Finally, we associate to each random variable $X$ in K a conditional probability distribution $P(X \mid \mathrm{par}(X))$. The Bayesian network K encodes the agent's causal knowledge of the environment. Here we suppose that this part of the agent's knowledge is stable and can not be reconsidered.

*Volatile beliefs.* The abstract agent model also includes beliefs that can change over time, i.e. the agent's volatile beliefs [5]. Given a random variable $X_i \in$ VAR, we denote by $\sum_{X_i}$ the set of all possible probability distributions over the random variable $X_i$. We denote by BEL the cartesian product of all $\sum_{X_i}$, that is $\mathrm{BEL} = \prod_{X_i \in \mathrm{VAR}} \sum_{X_i}$. BEL includes all possible combinations of probability distributions over the random variables in VAR. Elements in BEL are vectors $\mathrm{B} = \langle \mathrm{B}_1, \ldots, \mathrm{B}_n \rangle, \mathrm{B}' = \langle \mathrm{B}'_1, \ldots, \mathrm{B}'_n \rangle, \ldots$. Every vector B in BEL corresponds to a particular configuration of beliefs of the agent. In this sense, BEL includes all potential configurations of beliefs of the agent.

Suppose that $\mathrm{Val}_{X_i} = \{x_1, \ldots, x_r\}$. Then, every element $\mathrm{B}_i$ in a configuration of beliefs B is just a set $\{(X_i = x_1) = a_1, \ldots, (X_i = x_r) = a_r\}$ of probability assignments $a_1, \ldots, a_r \in [0, 1]$ to each possible instantiations of the variable $X_i$.

Given a specific configuration of beliefs $B=\langle B_1,\ldots,B_n\rangle$, we write $B(X_i=x)=a$ if and only if $(X_i=x)=a \in B_i$. For example, $B(X_i=x)=0.4$ means that given the configuration of beliefs $B=\langle B_1,\ldots,B_n\rangle$ the agent assigns probability 0.4 to the fact that variable $X_i$ takes value $x$. Moreover, we denote by $B(X_i=x)$ the number $a \in [0,1]$ such that $B(X_i=x)=a$.

*Intentions and desires.* We also model motivational attitudes by denoting with INT the set of potential intentions of an agent. Here we suppose that every instantiation of a variable in Inst is a potential intention of the agent, that is, INT = Inst. We denote by $I, I', \ldots \in 2^{INT}$ specific sets of intentions of the agent. Given a specific set of intentions of the agent I, we denote by $I_{Var}$ the subset of VAR which includes all intended variables, that is, all those variables which have (at least) one instantiation in I. Formally:

$$I_{Var}=\{X_i \in VAR \mid \exists\, x \in Val_{X_i} \text{ such that } X_i=x \in I\}.$$

We call *intention supports* all variables that are parents in the Bayesian network K of some intended variable. The set of intention supports is formally defined as follows:

$$SUPP_{Var}=\{X_i \in VAR \mid \exists\, X_j \in I_{Var} \text{ such that } X_i \in par(X_j)\}.$$

Note that the set of intention supports includes intention preconditions, that is, all conditions on which the achievement of an intended result of the agent depends.

DES is the set of all potential desires of the agent. As for intentions, we suppose that every instantiation of a variable in Inst is a potential desire of the agent, that is, DES=Inst. We denote by $D, D', \ldots \in 2^{DES}$ specific sets of desires of the agent.

*Desire-generating rules and planning rules.* We specify a set DG of desire-generating rules and a set PL of planning rules. A desire-generating rule in DG is a desire-generating rule in the style of [11] of the form:

$$\psi_1,\ldots,\psi_s \mid \lambda_1,\ldots,\lambda_j \Longrightarrow \varphi_1,\ldots,\varphi_t.$$

Such a rule is responsible for generating $t$ desires $\varphi_1,\ldots,\varphi_t$ when the agent has $s$ beliefs $\psi_1,\ldots,\psi_s$ and $j$ intentions $\lambda_1,\ldots,\lambda_j$.[2] The set of desire-generating rules DG corresponds to a function *options* : $BEL \times 2^{INT} \mapsto 2^{DES}$. This function returns a specific set D of desires, given a specific configuration B of beliefs and a specific set I of intentions.

A planning rule in the set of planning rules PL is a plan-generating rule of the form:

$$\psi_1,\ldots,\psi_s \mid \lambda_1,\ldots,\lambda_j \Longrightarrow \alpha_1,\ldots,\alpha_t.$$

Such a rule is responsible for generating $t$ plans $\alpha_1,\ldots,\alpha_t \in ACT$, where ACT is the repertoire of actions and plans of our agent, when the agent has $s$ beliefs $\psi_1,\ldots,\psi_s$ and $j$ intentions $\lambda_1,\ldots,\lambda_j$. The set of planning rules PL corresponds to a function *plan* : $BEL \times 2^{INT} \mapsto 2^{ACT}$.

This function returns a set $\pi$ of plans, given a specific set B of beliefs and specific set I of intentions. To summarize, an agent's abstract model is defined as a tuple $\langle \Gamma, K, B, D, I, DG, PL, ACT \rangle$, where each element in the tuple is defined as before.

---

[2] Our desire-generating rules correspond to the goal generation rules of the BOID framework [4].

# 4  Formalization of the Experimental Scenario

A simple experimental scenario is here introduced for testing relevance aware agents in a concrete problem domain. The scenario has been inspired by *Tileworld*, a simulation game originally introduced in [20]. Despite its simplicity, the experiment has been conceived as a testbed by introducing a highly parameterized environment that can be used to investigate and compare several performances in agents' reasoning processes. In this case, the environment layout is represented by the $12 \times 12$ grid in Fig. 1(a). An agent moves in the grid being driven by the goal of finding fruits of a certain color, according to the ongoing season. Indeed, agents look for fruits of different colors in different seasons of the year. We suppose that there are three different seasons and related colors of fruits and trees: the red season, the blue season and the green season. Agents are intrinsically motivated to look for and to eat red fruits during the red season, blue fruits during the blue season and green fruits during the green season. Environmental dynamics are characterized by periodic season cycles: after $s_t$ rounds the season changes on the basis of a periodic function and the intrinsic motivation of an agent changes accordingly. Fruits of any color occupy cells $(i, j)$ (with $1 \leq i \leq 16$ and $1 \leq j \leq 9$), where $i$ indicates the number of the macro-area in the grid and $j$ the number of the cell inside the macro-area. Trees of any color occupy macro-areas $i$ of size $3 \times 3$ (with $1 \leq i \leq 16$) in the grid depicted in Fig. 1(a). We suppose that at each moment for every color there is exactly one fruit and tree of that color in the grid. Moreover, we suppose an objective dependence between trees and fruits in the grid: a fruit of a certain color is a sign of the presence of a fruit of the same color in the immediate neighborhood. Agents exploit these signs during their search of fruits. We suppose that a tree of any color is randomly placed in a macro-area $i$ of size $3 \times 3$. Given a tree of a certain color in a macro-area $i$ of size $3 \times 3$, a fruit of the same color is randomly placed by the simulator in one of the nine cells inside the macro-area $i$. For example, if a red tree is in the macro-area 1 of the grid then for each cell $(1, i)$ with $1 \leq i \leq 9$, there is $\frac{1}{9}$ of probability that

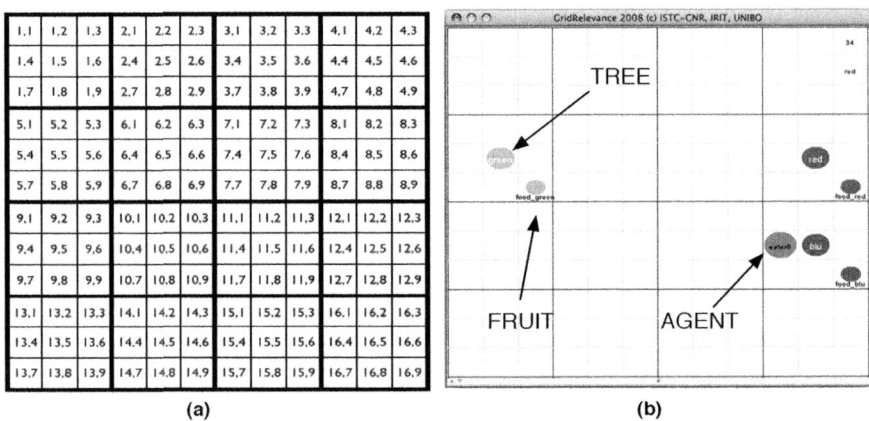

**Fig. 1.** Environment grid in agent's domain representation (a) and the running experiment (b)

a red fruit is located in that cell. Fruits and trees change periodically their positions. The dynamism factor $\delta$ indicates how many seasons have to pass before a tree location changes.

We impose constraints on the perceptual capabilities of agents by supposing that an agent sees only those fruits which are in the cells belonging to the same macro-area in which the agent is. For example, if the agent is in cell $(6, 1)$, he only sees those fruits which are in the cells belonging to the macro-area 6. Moreover we suppose that an agent sees only those trees which are situated in the same macro-area in which the agent is or in the four neighboring macro-areas on the left, right, up or down. For example, if the agent is in cell $(6, 1)$, he only sees those trees which are in macro-areas 2, 5, 7 or 10.

The knowledge of our agents is encoded by means of the following eight random variables VAR$= \{SEAS, POS, RF, BF, GF, RT, BT, GT\}$. The variables $RF$, $BF$, $GF$, $POS$ take values from the sets $\{(i, j) \mid 1 \leq i \leq 16, 1 \leq j \leq 9\}$, whilst the variables $RT$, $BT$, $GT$ take values from the set $\{i \mid 1 \leq i \leq 16\}$. Finally, $SEAS$ takes value from the set $\{r, b, g\}$. Variables $RF$, $BF$, $GF$ specify respectively the position of a red/ blue/ green fruit in the grid depicted in Fig. 1 (a). Variables $RT$, $BT$, $GT$ specify respectively the position of a red/blue/green tree in the grid. For example, $RT{=}13$ means "there is a red tree in the macro-area 13". Variable $SEAS$ specifies the current season. For example, $SEAS{=}blue$ means "it is time to look for blue fruits!". Finally, Variable $POS$ specifies the position of the agent in the grid.

The variables in VAR are organized in the Bayesian network K as follows: par$(POS){=} \{\emptyset\}$, par$(SEAS){=} \{\emptyset\}$, par$(RT){=} \{\emptyset\}$, par$(BT){=} \{\emptyset\}$, par$(GT){=} \{\emptyset\}$, par$(RF){=} \{RT\}$, par$(BF){=} \{BT\}$, par$(GF){=} \{GT\}$. Since there are 144 possible positions of a fruit and 16 possible positions of a tree in the grid, each conditional probability table associated with $P(RF \mid RT)$, $P(BF \mid BT)$ and $P(GF \mid GT)$ has $144 \times 16{=}2304$ entries. We suppose that the knowledge an agent has about the dependencies between trees and fruits perfectly maps the objective dependencies between trees and fruits. Hence, we only specify for each tree of a certain color – and arbitrary macro-area $i \in \{1, \ldots, 16\}$ in the grid in which a tree can appear – the 9 conditional probabilities that a fruit of the same color appears in one cell in that macro-area. We suppose for each of them the same probability value $\frac{1}{9}$. All other conditional probabilities have value 0, that is, given a tree of a certain color which appears in an arbitrary macro-area $i \in \{1, \ldots, 16\}$, the probability that there is a fruit of the same color outside that macro-area is zero. More precisely, we have that for all $1 \leq i, j \leq 16$ and $1 \leq z \leq 9$: (i) if $i{=}j$ then $P(RF{=}(j, z) \mid RT{=}i){=}\frac{1}{9}$; (ii) if $i \neq j$ then $P(RF{=}(j, z) \mid RT{=}i){=}0$.

Desire-generating rules in DG are exploited by agents for solving the general task of finding a fruit of a certain color in the grid. Agents are endowed with three general classes of desire-generating rules.

The first class includes desire-generating rules of the following form. For $i \in \text{Val}_{SEAS}$: $(SEAS{=}i){=}1 \implies SEAS{=}i$. These desire-generating rules are responsible for changing the intrinsic motivation of an agent, according to the season change, that is: if an agent is certain that it is time to look for fruits of kind $i$, then he should form the desire to look for fruits of kind $i$.

The second class includes desire-generating rules shown in Table 1 (DG *Group 1*). These are responsible for orienting the search toward a certain macro-area, according to

**Table 1.** Desire-generating rules governing agents' intention selection. At an implementation level (i.e. in *Jason*) the formuled expressions are stated in terms of context conditions and used for the applicability of related plans.

| DG **Group 1** | DG **Group 2** |
|---|---|
| For $1 \leq i \leq 16$: | For $1 \leq i \leq 16$ and $1 \leq j \leq 9$: |
| $(RT{=}i){=}1 \mid SEAS{=}r \Longrightarrow RT{=}i$ | $(RF{=}(i,j)){=}1 \mid SEAS{=}r \Longrightarrow RF{=}(i,j)$ |
| $(BT{=}i){=}1 \mid SEAS{=}b \Longrightarrow BT{=}i$ | $(BF{=}(i,j)){=}1 \mid SEAS{=}b \Longrightarrow BF{=}(i,j)$ |
| $(RT{=}i){=}1 \mid SEAS{=}g \Longrightarrow GT{=}i$ | $(RF{=}(i,j)){=}1 \mid SEAS{=}g \Longrightarrow GF{=}(i,j)$ |

the current season (i.e. an intention to find fruits of a certain color) and his beliefs about the position of trees in the grid. For instance, if an agent is certain that there is a red tree in the macro-area 3 of the grid (i.e. $(RT{=}3){=}1$) and desires to find a red fruit (i.e. $SEAS{=}red$), then he should form the intention to reach that position of a red tree (i.e. $RT{=}3$). Finally, agents are endowed with the kind of desire-generating rules shown in Table 1 (DG *Group 2*). These desire-generating rules are responsible for orienting the search of an agent toward a certain cell, according to the current season (i.e. an intention to find fruits of a certain color) and his beliefs about the position of fruits in the grid. For example, if an agent desires to find a blue fruit (i.e. $SEAS{=}blue$) and knows/ is certain that there is a blue fruit in cell $(10, 1)$ of the grid (i.e. $(BF{=}(10, 1)){=}1$), then he should form the intention to move toward that position of the blue fruit (i.e. $BF{=}(10, 1)$).

We suppose that agents have five basic actions in repertoire: *MoveDown*, *MoveUp*, *MoveLeft*, *MoveRight* and *EatFruit*. Indeed, at each round they can only move from one cell to the next one. Planning rules encode approaching policies which depend on the agent's current intentions and his actual position in the grid. Agents have both planning rules for reaching macro-areas in the grid (given their current positions) and planning rules for reaching cells in the grid (given their current positions). The latter planning rules are exploited for the local search of a fruit of a certain color inside a macro-area. An example of these planning rule is the following: $(POS{=}(15, 1)){=}1 \mid RT{=}3 \Longrightarrow MoveUp$. Thus, if an agent intends to reach position 3 of a red tree and is certain to be in cell $(15, 1)$ then he should form the plan to move one step up.

## 5   Pragmatic Relevance and Belief Update

In this section we present two different architectures and corresponding typologies of cognitive agents to be tested in the scenario described above. The first type of agent corresponds to a standard BDI agent whose control loop is described in the right column of Table 2. The second type of agent, whose control loop is described in the left column of Table 2, is a BDI agent endowed with a relevance-based mechanism of belief update. We call this second type of agent BDI$^{rel}$ agent.

The formal description of the control loop of the standard BDI agent is similar to [27,22]. In lines 1-2 the beliefs and intentions of the agent are initialized. The main

**Table 2.** Abstract interpreter implemented by the two typologies of agents

| $BDI^{rel}$ agent control loop | BDI agent control loop |
|---|---|
| 1. B:=$B_0$; | |
| 2. I:=$I_0$; | 1. B:=$B_0$; |
| 3. while (true) do | 2. I:=$I_0$; |
| 4. get new percept $\Gamma$; | 3. while (true) do |
| 5. if REL(I, $\Gamma$, B) $> \Delta$ then | 4. get new percept $\Gamma$; |
| 6. B:=$bu^*(\Gamma, B, I)$; | 5. B:=$bu(\Gamma, B)$; |
| 7. end-if | 6. D:=$options(B, I)$; |
| 8. D:=$options(B, I)$; | 7. I:=$filter(B, D, I)$; |
| 9. I:=$filter(B, D, I)$; | 8. $\pi$:=$plan(B, I)$; |
| 10. $\pi$:=$plan(B, I)$; | 9. $execute(\pi)$; |
| 11. $execute(\pi)$; | 10. end-while |
| 12. end-while | |

control loop is in lines 3-10. In lines 4-5 the agent perceives some new facts $\Gamma$ and updates his beliefs according to a function $bu$. In line 6 the agent generates new desires by exploiting his desire-generating rules. In line 7 he deliberates over the new generated desires and his current intentions according to the function $filter$.[3] Finally, in lines 8-9 the agent generates a plan for achieving his intentions by exploiting his planning rules and he executes an action of the current plan. The main difference between the standard BDI agent and the $BDI^{rel}$ agent is the belief update part in the control loop. We suppose that a process of belief update is triggered in the $BDI^{rel}$ agent only if the agent perceives a fact and evaluates this to be relevant with respect to what he intends to achieve (line 5 in the control loop of the $BDI^{rel}$ agent). In this sense, the $BDI^{rel}$ is endowed with a cognitive mechanism of relevance-based belief update. In fact, this mechanism filters out all perceived facts that are irrelevant with respect to the current intentions. Thus, the $BDI^{rel}$ agent only updates his beliefs by inputs which are relevant with respect to his current intentions. Differently, at each round the standard BDI agent updates his beliefs indiscriminately: for any fact he perceives, he updates his beliefs whether the perceived fact is relevant with respect to his intentions or not.

One might argue that the belief update strategy adopted by the $BDI^{rel}$ agent is somewhat shortsighted. Indeed, the $BDI^{rel}$ agent only considers inputs which are relevant with respect to his current intentions. We postpone to future work the analysis and the design of more sophisticated agents who consider in their belief update strategies also those inputs that they *expect* to be relevant for their future intentions.

In order to design the mechanism of relevance-based belief update, we define a notion of local relevance of an input $\Gamma$ with respect to an intention $Y=y \in I$, given the configuration of beliefs B. This is denoted by rel($Y=y$,$\Gamma$,B) and is defined as follows, where for every $c \in [-1, 1]$, Abs[$c$] returns the absolute value of $c$.

---

[3] Space restrictions prevent a formal description of the function $filter$ here (see [27] for a detailed analysis). Only notice that this function is responsible for updating the agent's intentions with his previous intentions and current beliefs and desires (i.e. $filter : B \times 2^I \times 2^D \mapsto 2^I$).

$$\mathrm{rel}(Y{=}y,\Gamma,\mathsf{B}){=} \begin{cases} \Rightarrow \text{ If } Y \in \Gamma_{Var}: \\ 1{-}\mathsf{B}(\Gamma(Y)) \\[4pt] \Rightarrow \text{ If } \mathrm{par}(Y) \subseteq \Gamma_{Var} \text{ and } Y \notin \Gamma_{Var}: \\ \mathrm{Abs}[\mathsf{B}(Y{=}y){-}P(Y{=}y \mid \{X_i{=}x \mid X_i \in \mathrm{par}(Y) \text{ and } X_i{=}x \in \Gamma\})] \\[4pt] \Rightarrow \text{ If } \mathrm{par}(Y) \not\subseteq \Gamma_{Var} \text{ and } Y \notin \Gamma_{Var}: \\ 0 \end{cases} \quad (1)$$

The degree of local relevance of the percept $\Gamma$ with respect to intended fact $Y{=}y \in \mathsf{I}$ (given the agent's configuration of beliefs B) is defined on the basis of three conditions.

According to the first condition, if the intended variable $Y$ is also a perceived variable in $\Gamma_{Var}$ (i.e. there exists an instantiation of $Y$ which is an element of $\Gamma$) then, $\mathrm{rel}(Y{=}y,\Gamma,\mathsf{B})$ is equal to the degree of unexpectedness of the percept $\Gamma$ (i.e. $1{-}\mathsf{B}(\Gamma(Y))$). The degree of unexpectedness of the percept $\Gamma$ is inversely proportional to the prior probability assigned by the agent to the perceived instantiation of the intended variable $Y$ (see [15] for an analysis of the notion of unexpectedness).

According to the second condition, if the intended fact $Y{=}y$ is not an instantiation of a perceived variable in $\Gamma_{Var}$ and the parents of $Y$ in the Bayesian network K are perceived variables in $\Gamma_{Var}$ then, $\mathrm{rel}(Y{=}y,\Gamma,\mathsf{B})$ is equal to the degree of discrepancy between the intended fact $Y{=}y$ and the percept $\Gamma$. The degree of discrepancy between the intended fact $Y{=}y$ and the percept $\Gamma$ is given by the absolute value of the difference between the probability assigned to $Y{=}y$ (i.e. $\mathsf{B}(Y{=}y)$) and the conditional probability that $Y{=}y$ is true given that the perceived instantiations of the parents of $Y$ are true (i.e. $P(Y{=}y \mid \{X_i{=}x \mid X_i \in \mathrm{par}(Y) \text{ and } X_i{=}x \in \Gamma\}))$.

According to the third condition, if the intended fact $Y{=}y$ is not an instantiation of a perceived variable in $\Gamma_{Var}$ and there is some parent of $Y$ in the Bayesian network K that is not a perceived variable in $\Gamma_{Var}$ then $\mathrm{rel}(Y{=}y,\Gamma,\mathsf{B})$ is zero. This third condition corresponds to the irrelevance of the incoming input $\Gamma$ with respect to the agent's intention $Y{=}y$. Under this third condition, the agent simply ignores the input.

Let us now define a notion of global relevance, noted $\mathrm{REL}(\mathsf{I},\Gamma,\mathsf{B})$, as the maximum value of local relevance for each intended fact $Y{=}y \in \mathsf{I}$:

$$\mathrm{REL}(\mathsf{I},\Gamma,\mathsf{B}){=} \max_{Y{=}y\in\mathsf{I}} \mathrm{rel}(Y{=}y,\Gamma,\mathsf{B}) \quad (2)$$

This notion of global relevance is used in the control loop of the $\mathrm{BDI}^{rel}$ agent: if the new percept $\Gamma$ is responsible for generating a degree of global relevance higher than $\Delta$ (with $\Delta \in [0,1]$) then a process of belief update is triggered and the $\mathrm{BDI}^{rel}$ agent adjusts his beliefs with the perceived data $\Gamma$ according to a function $bu^*$. The belief update function $bu^*$ of the $\mathrm{BDI}^{rel}$ agent takes in input the set of intentions $\mathsf{I}$, the belief configuration B and the percept $\Gamma$ and returns an update belief configuration B′, that is:

$$bu^* : 2^{\mathrm{Inst}} \times \mathrm{BEL} \times 2^{\mathrm{INT}} \mapsto \mathrm{BEL}.$$

More precisely, suppose that $bu^*(\Gamma,\mathsf{B},\mathsf{I}){=}\mathsf{B}'$. The set B′ is defined according to the following three conditions. For every $Y \in \mathrm{VAR}$ we have:

(A) If $Y \in \mathsf{I}_{Var}$ or $Y \in \mathrm{SUPP}_{Var}$, and $Y \in \Gamma_{Var}$ then:
    $\mathsf{B}'(\Gamma(Y)){=}1$ and for every $Y{=}x \in \mathrm{Inst}_Y \setminus \Gamma(Y), \mathsf{B}'(Y{=}x){=}0$.

(B) If $Y \in I_{Var}$ or $Y \in \text{SUPP}_{Var}$, and $\text{par}(Y) \subseteq \Gamma_{Var}$ and $Y \notin \Gamma_{Var}$ then:
for every $Y=y \in \text{Inst}_Y$, $B'(Y=y)=P(Y=y \mid \{X_i=x \mid X_i \in \text{par}(Y) \text{ and } X_i=x \in \Gamma\})$.

(C) Otherwise:
for every $Y=y \in \text{Inst}_Y$, $B'(Y=y)=B(Y=y)$.

According to the previous formal characterization of the function $bu^*$, the $\text{BDI}^{rel}$ agent only reconsiders the probability distributions over his intentions $Y \in I_{Var}$ and over his intention supports $Y \in \text{SUPP}_{Var}$. In fact, we suppose that the $\text{BDI}^{rel}$ agent only reconsiders those beliefs which are directly related with his intentions or with his intention supports, since he allocates his attention on the current task he is trying to solve. More precisely: if $Y$ is either an intended random variable in $I_{Var}$ or an intention support in $\text{SUPP}_{Var}$, and $Y$ is a perceived variable in $\Gamma_{Var}$, then the updated probability distribution over $Y$ assigns probability 1 to the perceived instantiation $\Gamma(Y)$ of variable $Y$ and probability 0 to all the other instantiations of variable $Y$ (condition A); if $Y$ is either an intended random variable in $I_{Var}$ or an intention support in $\text{SUPP}_{Var}$, $Y$ is not a perceived variable in $\Gamma_{Var}$, but $Y$'s parents in the Bayesian network are perceived variables in $\Gamma_{Var}$, then the updated probability distribution over $Y$ assigns to each instantiations $Y=y$ of variable $Y$ a probability which is equal to the conditional probability that $Y=y$ is true given that the perceived instantiations of the parents of $Y$ are true (i.e. $P(Y=y \mid \{X_i=x \mid X_i \in \text{par}(Y) \text{ and } X_i=x \in \Gamma\})$) (condition B). In all other cases the probability distribution over $Y$ is not updated (condition C).

Space restrictions prevent a formal description of the belief update function $bu$ of the standard BDI agent. Let us only say that function $bu$ (differently from the function $bu^*$ of the $\text{BDI}^{rel}$ agent) updates indiscriminately all beliefs of the agent, that is, at each round the standard BDI agent reconsiders the probability distributions over all random variables $Y \in \text{VAR}$. The function $bu$ has the same conditions of function $bu^*$ specified above. The only difference is that in $bu$ the requirement '$Y \in I_{Var}$ or $Y \in \text{SUPP}_{Var}$' is not specified.

## 6  Programming Model

This section introduces the programming model implementing the mechanism of relevance-based belief update described above. The experimental platform has been built on top of CArtAgO, a framework for developing MAS environments based on the abstraction of agents and artifacts [17]. Agents have been implemented by extending *Jason*, a programming platform for BDI agents based on AgentSpeak(L) [2].

*Environment.* The rationale behind the adoption of the Agents and Artifacts (A&A) meta-model for the design of the experimental platform resides in the particular interaction model provided by CArtAgO, where all the mechanisms related to agent's perception and action are regulated, at a system level, by the framework. Agents – independently from their internal model and technology– are allowed to play in CArtAgO environments by interacting with artifacts through operation of *use* which consists in exploiting the artifact's usage interface. Besides, agent's perceptive activities are defined through the notions of *observation* which consists in retrieving the information that artifacts display, and *perception*, enabling agents to sense signals and events coming from artifacts. In this perspective artifacts are conceived as a target for agents' overall activity, and thus exploited by agents either to execute their actions upon the environment, and to obtain information in a machine-readable format. To implement the scenario described in section 4, the environment has been instrumented with the following artifacts.

- Timer provides agents with timing information and enables the automatic mechanisms regulating the dynamism of the environment. Accordingly, it makes available two properties which are related to its internal state: ticktime (indicating the actual value of simulated time) and season (indicating the value of the ongoing season).
- GridBoard provides operations to be used as pragmatic actions by agents (i.e. $Move$, $Eat$) and feedback information in terms of percepts about the effects of these actions in the environment. In addition, based on the temporal signals generated by the Timer and on the actions performed by the agents, it provides the logic governing the dynamics and the physical consistency of the overall environment.
- GridboardGUI is linked to the previously described artifacts and is based on their internal states. It provides the graphical user interface for the system and allows the execution of experiment trials.

It is worth to remark that the adopted artifact-based environment promotes a principled design for agent perceptive activities. Thanks to the defined **A&A** interaction, events coming from artifacts can signal to the agent situations which require special attention. These signals are automatically sent back to the agent control system in order to be filtered and processed. For instance, once an artifact observable property or a signal is sensed by an agent, it can be filtered according to the given relevance function and possibly become a perceived datum (i.e. a percept). Following the basic idea provided in this work, only if such a percept is relevant it can be used to update the agent's belief base.

*Agents.* The overall goal for agents is to find and to eat fruit items. At any time step (i.e., round) agents can perfom only one pragmatic action (i.e., a move action in an adjacent cell) while, the score associated to the various fruit items depends on the ongoing season: a fruit of a given color (e.g. blue) provides a reward of $+1$ only if the ongoing season has the same color (e.g. the blue season), otherwise agents obtain no reward. In so doing, agents' performances are straightforwardly related to the environments dynamics. It is supposed that a tree changes its position at regular time intervals due to the ongoing dynamism $\delta$, hence agents need to adaptively govern their behavior with respect to the actual situation. In particular, an agent needs to maintain an updated knowledge of the overall environment in order to avoid wasting resources, thus a certain amount of agent resources need to be allocated to exploration and epistemic activities. Besides, looking for food items in an area which is actually related to a food type that is not consistent with the ongoing season is a disadvantageous behavior in terms of global performance. In these conditions, an effective strategy is to look for fruits by using trees as reference points. Once a tree which is related to the ongoing season is encountered, the agent can perform epistemic actions aimed at updating his beliefs about the presence of fruits in the macro-area in which the agent is located.

At an architectural level, a Bayesian network governing goal deliberation and intention selection has been realized. To have a seamless integration with the *Jason* programming language, the kernel units used by the reasoning engine to perceive and update beliefs have been extended (namely, the `architecture.AgArch` and `asSemantics.Agent` components). In particular, specialized data-types and methods allowing the dynamic query on the probability distribution of domain entities have been introduced. In addition, agent's representation of the problem domain has been realized with a series of dynamic hash-maps. Each hash-map is, in this case, a problem representation related to a given season type. At any given time step this working memory can be accessed by the agent by indicating the coordinates of a given cell, thus returning the content of the cell in terms of entities which are expected to be there. For instance, once a tree is perceived, the agent can control if any information relating to that location is present and possibly update it. Accordingly, when an agent updates his belief about the position of a certain tree, he will also update the belief about the position of the fruit of the same color, given a possibly known probability distribution (we assume that agents know which relation exists between the location of a certain tree and the probability to find food items in the cells belonging to the same area).

Thanks to their perceptive skills, once some particular signal is encountered, agents can exploit it for updating their beliefs, or for reconsidering their intentions. Therefore, after becoming aware of some relevant facts, agents can elicit belief update or an adaptive re-allocation of their computational resources. Artifacts provide, in this case, two kinds of signals: signals for temporal synchronization (agents rule their actions based on a clock signals perceived from the `Timer`) and signals belonging to the set $\Gamma_{Var}$, which in turn contains the percepts corresponding to visible entities. For instance, as shown in the following *Jason* cutout, once a clock signal is received from the focused `Timer`, an internal action `gridworld.perceptRel` interacts with the `GridBoard` to retrieve the list of percepts indicating all the visible entities.

```
+tick_time(X)[source("percept"), artifact("timer"), workspace("Relevance")]
  : actual_season(S)
  <- -+time(X);
     gridworld.perceptRel(S);
     !deliberateTarget.
```

The `gridworld.perceptRel` perceptive action has two different implementations respectively for the BDI agent and for the BDI$^{rel}$ agent. `gridworld.perceptRel` is supposed to realize the belief update functions $bu$ and $bu^*$. Percepts are inserted in the agent working memory and then filtered by the belief update function. In the case of the BDI$^{rel}$ agent, once these percepts are related to the current intention (i.e. actual season) they are stored in the agent memory as permanent belief facts. In particular, $bu^*$ is supposed to retrieve from the `GridBoard` the list of visible entities (these elements become percepts). Moreover, for each retrieved fact, $bu^*$ deletes the beliefs actually referring to entities which are not already present in the actual range of sight (trees and fruits can disappear due to the environment dynamism) and adds a new fact to the belief base only if the scrutinized percept in $\Gamma$ matches the current intention. For discriminating relevant and not relevant percepts a simple pattern matching is used. Hence, the function of local relevance $rel(Y{=}y, \Gamma, B)$ is greater than zero when the current season matches the entity

**Table 3.** Amount of achieved goals and performed belief updates measured at the end of the experiment series for BDI and $BDI^{rel}$ agents in environments with dynamism $\delta \in \{1, 2, 3\}$

|  | $\delta = 3$ | | $\delta = 2$ | | $\delta = 1$ | |
|---|---|---|---|---|---|---|
|  | BDI | $BDI^{rel}$ | BDI | $BDI^{rel}$ | BDI | $BDI^{rel}$ |
| Goal.eff | 42.375 | 42.375 | 38.185 | 37.625 | 33.937 | 33.875 |
| Cost.eff | 92.125 | 78.437 | 101.437 | 85.312 | 143.125 | 107.875 |
| cost.ratio | 2.381 | 2.012 | 2.882 | 2.252 | 4.379 | 3.214 |

type, otherwise $r = 0$. Notice that in the case of the described scenario (where actual agent's intention depends on the current season) the threshold $\Delta$ is set to 0.

After the execution of the `perceptRel`, the BDI agent has a complete knowledge of the actual state of its surroundings (i.e. the belief base is supposed to be consistent with the actual state of the visible area). On the other side, $BDI^{rel}$ only considers the information that is relevant with respect to the current situation. Then, to achieve their goals, both BDI and $BDI^{rel}$ agents can adopt the following plans to decide the next course of action.

```
+!deliberateTarget                    +!deliberateTarget
  : actual_season(S) & food(S,X,Y)     : actual_season(S) & not food(S,_,_)
  <- -+targetLoc(X,Y);                   & tree(S,X,Y)
     !doAction.                          <- -+targetLoc(X,Y);
                                            !doAction.
                                    +!deliberateTarget <- !doAction.
```

It is worth nothing that, according to the *Jason* transition system, the desire-generating rules described in Tab. 1 are here expressed by means of *context-conditions*, i.e. in form of expression of beliefs (*belief formulae*). The belief `targetLoc(X,Y)` can refer to a given fruit location only if the agent has already located a fruit and has stored a related fact in his belief base. If there are no facts in the belief base concerning fruits or trees related to the ongoing season, the agent will perform an epistemic action, i.e. by exploring the grid in order to discover some new relevant fact. Besides, once beliefs are canceled from the belief base by the internal belief update activities –ruled respectively by $bu$ for the standard BDI agent and $bu^*$ for the $BDI^{rel}$ agent– the agent reconsiders its intentions and selects a new target to be reached.

```
-food(T,X,Y) : targetLoc(X,Y)         -tree(T,X,Y) : targetLoc(X,Y)
          <- !deliberateTarget.                  <- !deliberateTarget.
```

In so doing, both the BDI agent and the $BDI^{rel}$ agent update their belief base in two circumstances: (*i*) when the actual belief base is wrong (not consistent with the perceived state of the environment), and (*ii*) when the actual belief base is incomplete (due to a lack of knowledge). Finally, by using the operations allowed by the `GridBoard` interface, and taking into account the planning rules discussed in section 4, a `!doAction` realizes the basic pragmatic actions (i.e., *eat* a fruit or *move* towards `targetLoc(X,Y)`).

## 7   Experiment

This section discusses a series of experiments comparing the performances of BDI vs. $BDI^{rel}$ agents engaged in in the scenario presented in section 4.

## 7.1  Experiment Setting

In our experimental setting we suppose for simplicity that agents have always access to their current position in the grid, and that they are always notified about simulation steps and season changes. Therefore, at the beginning of a new season, an agent always knows that it is time to look for fruits of a different color, and thus adopting the goal to look for fruits belonging to the ongoing color. In order to have a measure about the trade-off between effectiveness and efficiency, agents' performances have been evaluated according to a twofold metric. On the one hand, goal effectiveness ($Goal.eff$) represents the total amount of achieved goals during a trial (i.e., eaten fruits), while cost effectiveness ($Cost.eff$) is the total amount of update operations performed by the agent on his belief base. On the other hand, we define the $cost.ratio$ of an agent in terms of the agent's belief update cost divided by the total amount of achieved goals ($Cost.eff/Goal.eff$). This in particular gives a quantitative measure of efficiency, namely how many units of cost the agent needs to spend for each achieved goal. In other terms, a $cost.ratio = 1$ means that the agents has performed a belief update operation for each achieved goal (i.e., eaten fruit). Besides, since only one $Move$ action is allowed for each time step, the adopted metrics provide insights on how many pragmatic actions are needed for agents to achieve their goals.

The length of experiments has been set to 900 rounds in order to be long enough for the chosen metrics to become stable. The global performance of each agent is measured by averaging $cost.ratio$ of 16 trials in environments with different dynamism $\delta$. Season length $s_t$ is set at 15 rounds, while we consider $n=3$ seasons (respectively red, blue and green) with three associated types of tree and fruit. The initial placements of entities are randomly selected, while a fruit of a given color is generated at the beginning of each corresponding season. Finally, we assume that for any color at most one fruit is present in the grid at the same time.

## 7.2  Discussion

Fig. 1 (b) shows a snapshot of the running simulation. Experiments have been conducted using three different variables of dynamism $\delta$ for the environment. The first two columns in Tab.3 show the $cost.ratio$ respectively for the BDI agent and the BDI$^{rel}$agent operating in a static environment ($\delta = 3$, a tree changes its location every 3 seasons, 45 rounds). Both agents attain an average of 43.375 eaten fruits on their trials. However they have to pay quite different costs of belief update (BDI performs an average of 92.125 update operations, while BDI$^{rel}$78.437). Considering the $cost.ratio$, once agents have overcome their transitory phase they spend respectively 2.381 (BDI) and 2.012 (BDI$^{rel}$) costs for each eaten fruit.

The central columns show the performances of the two agents in environments with medium dynamism ($\delta = 2$, a tree changes its location every 2 seasons, 30 rounds). Here, due to the frequent tree changes, both agents rely on a less accurate knowledge model. In terms of eaten fruits the BDI agent attains a higher performances (38.185), clearly outperforming the BDI$^{rel}$agent (37.125). On the other hand, as far as costs of belief update are concerned, BDI$^{rel}$performs better: in fact, under the same conditions, BDI$^{rel}$does less belief update operations (85.312 vs. 101.437). As a consequence, BDI$^{rel}$considerably shows a better effectiveness with respect to the $cost.ratio$

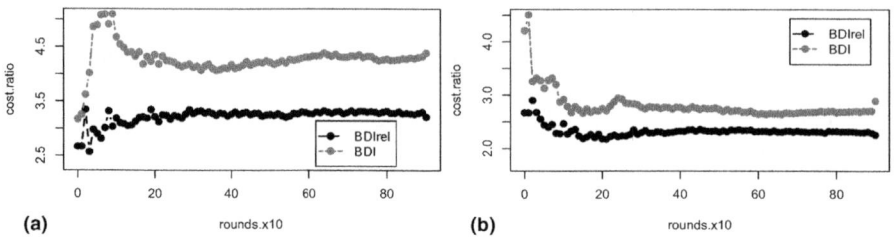

**Fig. 2.** Cost ratio in environments characterized by different dynamism: $\delta=1$ (a) and $\delta=2$ (b)

(see Fig.2.b) whose value converges, at the end of the experiments, at an average of 2.252 belief update operations per achieved goal (vs. 2.882 for the BDI agent).

The last two columns shows the results in a highly dynamic environment ($\delta = 1$, a tree changes its location every season change, 15 rounds). Here, due to the massive epistemic activities, the standard BDI agent is able to maintain a more consistent and complete knowledge of the environment. Therefore, he performs better than the $BDI^{rel}$ agent in terms of achieved goals (with an average of 33.937 number of eaten fruits against 33.875). In contrast, the BDI agent has to pay higher costs related to his epistemic activities, even beyond the initial transitory phase. In this case, the costs of belief update are 143.125 for the BDI agent and 107.875 for the $BDI^{rel}$ agent. As depicted in Fig.2.a, the *cost.ratio* reflects this difference by converging to a value of about 4.379 for the BDI and of 3.214 for the $BDI^{rel}$.

Despite the simplicity of the problem domain, the experiments show a noticeable effect of the relevance-based filter of belief update on the $BDI^{rel}$ performance. By reporting agent effectiveness both in terms of goal achieved and in terms of costs for belief update, *cost.ratio* is, indeed, a good indicator for analyzing the trade-off in agents performances (see Fig.2). As the results of the experimental analysis show, on the one side the BDI agent is always the best in terms of goal effectiveness, thus able to achieve an higher amount of goals. BDI agents are *passively* affected by all incoming information, hence they obtain a precise knowledge of their surroundings and result in a more acknowledged decision making. Consequently, we may argue that the more an agent spends his resources for belief update, the more his belief base will be correct and adequate with respect to the current state of the environment, and the more the agent will find fruits in the grid. On the other side, $BDI^{rel}$ agents adopt an active perception style and exploits their relevance-based mechanism to filter percepts: if the incoming input is not relevant with respect to the current intention, then the $BDI^{rel}$ agent simply ignores it. Besides a worse performance in terms of goal achieved, this mechanism allows the $BDI^{rel}$ agent to avoid wasting computational resources for belief update, thus resulting in a better global performance in terms of *cost.ratio*. This aspect is worth to be considered in cases where agents have bounded resources and environments are characterized by strong dynamicity or information richness. As the results show, the higher the dynamism of the environment is, the higher the computational costs which are paid by BDI agents for belief update processes. In these conditions, $BDI^{rel}$ agents have a concrete advantage in filtering noise and in considering only what is expected to be useful for achieving their current goals.

## 8  Conclusion

We have presented in this work a mechanism of relevance-based belief update providing a computational model for BDI agents, and implemented it using *Jason* platform. As the experimental results show, the costs for belief update are effectively reduced by using the mechanism for filtering relevant percepts. Despite the simple scenario adopted, the experimental results can be easily generalized as well as the computational model for relevance aware agents can be straightforwardly applied to more complex application domains. We think that a notion of pragmatic relevance is a pivotal one for the implementation of forthcoming agent-based systems, for instance in all the cases in which agents have to perform complex and resource demanding activities in highly dynamic and information-rich environments (i.e., the Web, as well as pervasive systems in the real world).

In this line, the directions for future works are manifold. We are actually working on a generalization of our model of pragmatic relevance which consists in adding a quantitative dimension for intentions. In this generalized model, the degree of relevance of a certain input with respect to an agent's intention will also depend on the utility/importance of the intended outcome. Besides, we will further investigate the relationships between the notion of relevance and intention reconsideration mechanisms. Since the persistence of an intention over time depends on the persistence of those beliefs which support this intention (i.e. beliefs are reasons for intending), we will study how the relevance-based filter of belief update discussed in this paper may affect the persistence of intentions in an indirect way. Moreover, we intend to develop in the future a more advanced model extending an agent's abilities to manage a probabilistic belief base (i.e., by introducing salience maps, dynamic Bayesian networks, influence diagrams, etc.).

Finally, as already noticed in section 5, we intend to extend our model to a more sophisticated type of agent than the $BDI^{rel}$ agent who also considers inputs that he expects to be relevant for his future intentions. For instance, if such an agent has the current intention to cook a meal and he expects that tomorrow morning he will have the intention to go from Paris to Rome by train, he will also consider information that are relevant with respect to his expected intention (e.g. the information "there will a train strike").

## References

1. Anderson, A.R., Belnap, N.D.: Entailment: the logic of relevance and necessity, vol. 1. Princeton University Press, Princeton (1975)
2. Bordini, R., Hübner, J.F., Wooldridge, M.: Programming Multi-Agent Systems in AgentSpeak Using Jason. John Wiley & Sons, Ltd., Chichester (2007)
3. Bratman, M.: Intentions, plans, and practical reason. Harvard University Press, Cambridge (1987)
4. Broersen, J., Dastani, M., Hulstijn, J., van der Torre, L.: Goal generation in the BOID architecture. Cognitive Science Quarterly 2(3-4), 428–447 (2002)

5. Casati, R., Pasquinelli, E.: How can you be surprised? the case for volatile expectations. Phenomenology and the Cognitive Sciences 6(1-2), 171–183 (2006)
6. Cherniak, C.: Minimal rationality. MIT Press, Cambridge (1986)
7. Chopra, S., Parikh, R.: Relevance sensitive belief structures. Annals of Mathematics and Artificial Intelligence 28(1-4), 259–285 (2000)
8. da Costa Pereira, C., Tettamanzi, A.G.B.: Goal generation with relevant and trusted beliefs. In: 7th International Conference on Autonomous Agents and Multiagent Systems (AAMAS 2008), pp. 397–404. ACM Press, New York (2008)
9. Ellsworth, P.C., Scherer, K.R.: Appraisal processes in emotion. In: Davidson, R.J., Goldsmith, H.H., Scherer, K.R. (eds.) Handbook of the affective sciences. Oxford University Press, Oxford (2003)
10. Floridi, L.: Understanding epistemic relevance. Erkenntnis 69, 69–92 (2008)
11. Kaelbling, L.P., Rosenschein, S.J.: Action and planning in embedded agents. In: Maes, P. (ed.) Designing autonomous agents, pp. 35–48. MIT Press, Cambridge (1990)
12. Koster, A., Koch, F., Sonenberg, L., Dignum, F.: Augmenting BDI with Relevance: Supporting Agent-based, Pervasive Applications. In: Mobile Interaction Devices (PERMID 2008) Workshop at Pervasive 2008, Sydney (2008)
13. Lakemeyer, G.: Relevance from an epistemic perspective. Artificial Intelligence 97(1-2), 137–167 (2004)
14. Lazarus, R.S.: Emotion and adaptation. Oxford University Press, New York (1991)
15. Lorini, E., Castelfranchi, C.: The unexpected aspects of surprise. International Journal of Pattern Recognition and Artificial Intelligence 20(6), 817–833 (2006)
16. Lorini, E., Piunti, M.: The Benefits of Surprise in Dynamic Environments: From Theory to Practice. In: Paiva, A.C.R., Prada, R., Picard, R.W. (eds.) ACII 2007. LNCS, vol. 4738, pp. 362–373. Springer, Heidelberg (2007)
17. Omicini, A., Ricci, A., Viroli, M.: Artifacts in the A&A meta-model for multi-agent systems. Autonomous Agents and Multi-Agent Systems 17(3) (2008)
18. Pearl, J.: Probabilistic reasoning in intelligent systems: networks of plausible inference. Morgan Kaufman, Cambridge (1988)
19. Peppas, P., Chopra, S., Foo, N.Y.: Distance semantics for relevance-sensitive belief revision. In: Proceedings of the Ninth International Conference on Principles of Knowledge Representation and Reasoning (KR 2004), pp. 319–328. AAAI Press, Menlo Park (2004)
20. Pollack, M.E., Ringuette, M.: Introducing the tileworld: Experimentally evaluating agent architectures. In: National Conference on Artificial Intelligence (1990)
21. Rao, A.S., Georgeff, M.P.: Modelling rational agents within a BDI-architecture. In: Fikes, R., Sandewall, E. (eds.) Proceedings of the 2nd International Conference on Principles of Knowledge Representation and Reasoning (KR 1991), San Mateo, CA, pp. 473–484. Morgan Kaufmann Publishers, San Francisco (1991)
22. Rao, A.S., Georgeff, M.P.: BDI agents: from Theory to Practice. In: Proceedings of the First International Conference on Multi-Agent Systems, ICMAS 1995 (1995)
23. Shannon, C.E.: A mathematical theory of communication. Bell System Technical Journal 27, 623–656 (1948)
24. Simon, H.: Models of thought, vol. 1. Yale University Press, New Haven (1979)
25. Weiß, G.: Learning the goal relevance of actions in classifier systems. In: Proc. of the Tenth European Conference on Artificial intelligence (ECAI 1992), pp. 430–434 (1992)
26. Weyns, D., Steegmans, E., Holvoet, T.: Model for active perception in situated multi-agent systems. Special Issue of Journal on Applied Artificial Intelligence 18, 200–204 (2003)
27. Wooldridge, M.: An Introduction to Multiagent Systems. John Wiley & Sons, Chichester (2002)

# Modularity and Compositionality in Jason

Neil Madden and Brian Logan

School of Computer Science
University of Nottingham, UK
{nem,bsl}@cs.nott.ac.uk

**Abstract.** In this paper, we present our experiences using the *Jason* agent-oriented programming language to develop a complex multi-agent application. We highlight a number of shortcomings in the current design of the language when building complex agents, and propose revisions to the language to allow the development of modular programs that facilitate code reuse and independent development. In particular, we propose a mechanism for modular construction of agents from functionally encapsulated components, and discuss alterations to the belief base language to enable more robust software engineering.

## 1 Introduction

Agent-oriented programming languages (AOPLs), such as *Jason* [1] and 2APL [2], have been the subject of a great deal of research and development in recent years. Building on the foundations of logic programming and theories of agency—in particular, the BDI (belief-desire-intention) model [3]—they aim to raise the level of abstraction used in constructing complex modern software applications. However, while they have been successfully applied in a number of interesting problem domains, the literature contains relatively few reports of attempts to apply such languages to large-scale software development efforts.

In this paper we present our experiences of applying the agent-oriented programming language *Jason* to the development of a large-scale multi-agent system consisting of (relatively) complex *witness narrator agents* which report on events occurring in online persistent game environments [4]. Witness-narrator agents are embodied in a virtual environment and observe and narrate activities occuring within that environment. The deployed system consisted of a team of 100 agents which reported on events in a medium-scale persistent virtual environment over a period of several weeks. The agents had to handle a number of complex tasks during this period, including activity recognition, multi-agent coordination, generation of prose stories describing activities, and interaction with human participants. The system makes use of a range of technologies, including ontological reasoning, plan and activity recognition, and multi-agent coordination and teamwork. The architecture of the agents is organised as a collection of functionally encapsulated 'capability' modules to handle distinct tasks, such as low-level activity recognition, editing of reports from multiple agents, and generation of prose text for a particular output medium.

Our experiences with *Jason* indicate that it is a useful and flexible language which provides a clean, high-level approach to defining complex agent logic. However, we

L. Braubach, J.-P. Briot, and J. Thangarajah (Eds.): ProMAS 2009, LNAI 5919, pp. 237–253, 2010.
© Springer-Verlag Berlin Heidelberg 2010

also found the language to be lacking in some respects, particularly in relation to the development of more complex agents. In this paper we describe the problems that we encountered, and propose revisions to the language to allow the development of modular programs that facilitate code reuse and independent development. In particular, we propose a mechanism for modular construction of agents from functionally encapsulated components, and discuss alterations to the both the belief base language and plan execution to enable more robust software engineering.

While this paper concentrates on our experiences with *Jason* in order to focus the discussion and motivate practical recommendations, many of the problems we identify also apply to other (BDI) agent programming languages, such as 2APL. The discussion therefore separates general concerns of modularity and compositionality from the specific issues in relation to *Jason*.

The remainder of the paper is organised as follows. In section 2 we first give a brief introduction to the *Jason* programming language. Section 3 then discusses the problems of developing modular agent programs with *Jason*, motivated by our experiences. We then use this experience to develop a set of requirements that should be satisfied by an agent-oriented programming language in order to support modular agent construction. These requirements, which are generally applicable to other BDI AOPLs, are discussed in section 4. We then look in further depth at two proposals for alterations to *Jason* to better support these requirements. Firstly, the choice of Prolog for the default belief-base language in *Jason* and other AOPLs, is investigated in section 5 and found lacking with respect to the requirement for compositionality of beliefs. An alternative based on Datalog is proposed. Secondly, in section 6, a simple module system is proposed that allows the development of functionally-encapsulated, independent components, which can be composed to create more complex agents. Finally, we conclude with a look at related work in section 7 and some general conclusions in section 8.

## 2   Jason

*Jason* [1] is a Java-based interpreter for an extended version of AgentSpeak(L). AgentSpeak(L) is a high-level agent-oriented programming language [5] that incorporates ideas from the BDI (belief-desire-intention) model of agency [3]. The language is loosely based on the logic programming paradigm, exemplified by Prolog, but with an operational semantics based on plan execution in response to events and beliefs rather than SLD resolution as in Prolog. *Jason* extends AgentSpeak(L) with support for more complex beliefs, default and strong negation, and arbitrary internal actions implemented in Java. The belief base of AgentSpeak(L) consists simply of a set of ground literals, whereas *Jason* supports a sizeable subset of Prolog for the belief base, including universally-quantified rules (Horn clauses). The syntax of *Jason* plans essentially consists of a single triggering event (such as a goal or belief addition or deletion, or a percept), a belief context pattern, and then a sequence of actions to perform if the plan is selected.[1] During execution, *Jason* first processes any events and updates the belief base. The interpreter then selects a single event to process and matches it against the

---

[1] In the interests of brevity, we have slightly simplified the presentation of *Jason* syntax and semantics.

1. Perceive the environment;
2. Update the belief base;
3. Receive communication from other agents;
4. Select socially acceptable messages;
5. Select an event;
6. Retrieve relevant plans;
7. Determine applicable plans;
8. Select one applicable plan;
9. Select an intention for execution;
10. Execute an action.

**Fig. 1.** *Jason* interpreter cycle

plan library to select one or more plans to handle the event. Of these plans, a single plan is then selected to become an intention. Finally, one of the currently active intentions is selected and allowed to perform an action, before the cycle repeats. The complete cycle is shown in Fig. 1, adapted from [1], Chap. 4.

The process of constructing software using *Jason* proceeds at two levels. At a high-level, the problem domain is broken down in terms of a society of autonomous and cooperating (or competing) agents. Agents in *Jason*, as in other agent-oriented programming languages, are autonomous encapsulated processes that communicate with each other by sending messages (speech acts). In the BDI paradigm, programming in the large thus involves decomposition of the system into entities (agents) to which belief and other propositional attitudes can most naturally be ascribed. At a lower level, individual agents are authored in terms of their beliefs and goals, and plans which specify how to achieve the agent's goals and how to react to events. The primary mechanism for structuring a *Jason* program in the small is therefore the plan.[2] Issues arise when a natural decomposition of the system into (intentional) agents results in entities with large numbers of plans. In such cases, a modular approach to agent development is often desirable.

## 3   Problems of Modular Agent Programming

An agent-oriented approach to constructing large software has several advantages, such as encouraging separation of concerns, loose coupling between components, and extending relatively naturally to a distributed environment in which messages are sent over a network to other remote agents. *Jason* provides good support for constructing multi-agent systems at this level, providing natural and easy to use speech-act based communications, and abstracting away from many of the details of the underlying infrastructure. At the level of constructing an individual agent, the BDI model of *Jason* and the sophisticated plan and belief base facilities it provides allow the developer to express complex logic in a concise and clear fashion. However, our experience with

---

[2] Although traditional Prolog-style rules in the belief base can also form a significant part of the codebase.

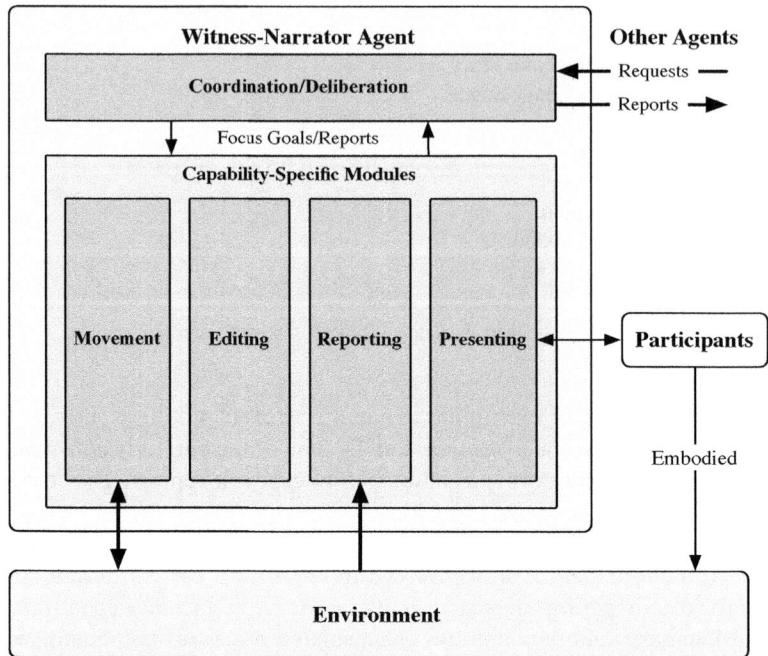

**Fig. 2.** Architecture of witness-narrator agent

using *Jason* to develop a large and complex application indicates that there is a gap between these two levels that becomes more apparent as individual agents grow in complexity. In particular, *Jason* lacks any mechanism for decomposing an individual agent into constituent components or modules. Figure 2 shows the overall architecture of one of the agents in the system we developed, known as a *witness-narrator agent*. The witness-narrator agents have a quite complex internal structure, consisting of a number of different competences ('capabilities') that are conceptually independent of one another to a large degree and which communicate only through clearly defined interfaces. Each capability module consists of a set of *Jason* plans, along with some beliefs and rules, that are used to implement that particular competence. For instance, the reporting module contains plans for detecting and recording activity occurring within an environment, while the presenting module has plans and rules for formatting a report for a particular output medium (HTML, Atom [6]). A separate coordination module handles communication and interaction with other agents, such as team formation. The current implementation of witness-narrator agents in *Jason* implements such modules simply as a set of files which are included one at a time into a main agent program. There are a number of drawbacks with this approach:

- there is the possibility of name clashes between belief and goal relations defined in separate modules;
- it may be desirable for plans in different modules to react to the same triggering event;

– the order in which modules are included can have surprising effects on the execution of the agent.

The first problem is one of namespace management, and can be addressed to a certain degree by adopting coding guidelines to ensure that beliefs and goals in separate modules have different names, for instance using a simple unique prefix for each module. However, this issue becomes more important when we consider third-party modules that are developed independently by different organisations. While guidelines can be adopted to try to ensure that unique prefixes are chosen (e.g., incorporating the institution name into the prefix), such approaches can be cumbersome to use. The possibility that agents may dynamically locate and acquire new modules at runtime (e.g., OWL ontologies) also suggests that good namespace management should be built in to the language itself.

The second and third drawbacks present more serious problems. The semantics of plan execution in *Jason* require a single plan to be selected to respond to any particular triggering event. This prevents multiple modules from responding to the same event in different ways, and introduces a form of implicit coupling between modules that must be explicitly resolved by the agent developer. For instance, in the development of the witness-narrator agents, certain events were of interest to both the reporting and general movement modules. If an agent is attacked, for example, this is both a cause for the movement module to take action (to evade the attack), but also presents a potentially interesting event that the reporting module may want to record. In the current implementation, this is achieved by having one module handle the event, and then to generate a secondary event purely for the other module to be notified. This requires both explicit cooperation between the modules (and corresponding effort from the developer), and also introduces extra code whose purpose can be obscure to a reader of the program.

The third problem stems partly from the second, in that if two modules attempt to react to the same triggering event (and the developer hasn't noticed this), then which plan gets to run depends on the plan selection function, which by default is based on the order in which plans are defined. This can lead to some surprising and difficult to understand behaviour where one plan appears not to be triggering correctly as a consequence of another plan in an entirely unrelated module. The problem also occurs if one module included earlier in the sequence includes a plan that effectively matches many or all triggering events, for instance if an unbound variable is used for the trigger. This then takes precedence over any subsequent plans introduced by later modules.

## 4    Requirements for Modularity

The problems discussed in the last section can be seen as stemming from the overall problem of how to construct an agent by composing independent functional units. Ideally, an agent could be constructed by glueing together independent reuseable modules. Two general requirements immediately become apparent from this description:

1. *compositionality*: the behaviour of the overall system should be predictable from the combination of components, regardless of the specific order in which they are combined;

2. *modularity*: components should be independent and functionally encapsulated—
it should be possible to understand the behaviour of each component in isolation
without reference to the rest of the system.

We discuss each of these requirements in turn.

## 4.1 Compositionality

The most important property that such a module system should address is that the behaviour of an agent composed of separate modules should not depend on the order in which those modules are composed. Given modules $A$, $B$, and $C$ and a module composition operator $\otimes$, we would like the following laws to hold:

$$(A \otimes B) \otimes C = A \otimes (B \otimes C) \tag{1}$$
$$A \otimes B = B \otimes A \tag{2}$$

In other words, we would like composition of modules to be both associative (1) and commutative (2), so that the order in which modules are combined does not affect the resulting behaviour. This property of compositionality is particularly important in an event-driven architecture such as *Jason*, where plan execution in response to events can sometimes be difficult to predict. Minimising effects caused by code refactoring helps to reduce the opportunities for confusion when constructing sophisticated software.

The requirements for associative and commutative composition of modules have a number of implications for the design of *Jason* and related AOPLs. Firstly, we must ensure that the composition of beliefs from all included modules has the same meaning, and produces the same runtime inference behaviour, regardless of the order in which those beliefs are added to the belief base of the agent. This has an impact on the choice of belief representation language and reasoning strategy employed in the belief base. Similar considerations must be taken into account for goals. Secondly, in order to minimise conflicts between modules, it is important to support encapsulation of beliefs, goals and plans that are internal implementation details of a module, while exposing those that form part of its interface. This includes avoiding simple name clashes, but also more important issues of belief and goal scope and visibility.

## 4.2 Modularity

In addition to requiring that agent components should be compositional, we can also describe some general requirements that the components themselves should exhibit. These requirements partly ensure that compositionality is maintained, but also allow a system as a whole to be understood in simpler terms, as a decomposition into a number of independent parts. The requirements for modularity we have identified are as follows:

1. *packaging* of functionally related areas of code, including beliefs, goals, and plans, into reuseable units;
2. *encapsulation* of such units with a clear separation between interface and implementation;

3. *protection* against name clashes and other adverse interactions when different components are combined;
4. *independence* of components, allowing each a chance to respond to relevant events.

These requirements are sufficient to address the immediate problems that were experienced during construction of the witness-narrator agent system, and more generally are prerequisites for robust software engineering in any AOPL. We do not consider more advanced functionality, such as parameterisation of modules, instantiation of multiple instances of a particular component, or customisation of plan selection or intention execution functions on a per-module basis.

## 5   Belief Base Compositionality

One of the enhancements of *Jason* over AgentSpeak(L) is the support for a substantial subset of Prolog in the belief base language, including backward-chaining rules. This considerably increases the expressive power of the language, and allows for succinct descriptions of some problems, while also allowing the *Jason* developer to take advantage of the large amount of existing Prolog code. However, despite these advantages, it is not clear whether Prolog is in fact the most appropriate choice for a belief language.

– The order in which clauses are added to the belief base has an explicit effect on execution in Prolog (and hence *Jason*), with clauses defined earlier in a program having precedence over later clauses. In some cases, reversing the order of two clauses can lead to incorrect behaviour or even nontermination of a previously correct definition. This clearly violates the requirements for compositionality of beliefs.
– The backtracking execution strategy of Prolog may not be the most efficient way of handling large numbers of beliefs, particular when these may be stored in a relational database system, or other persistent store. For example, the agents used in our software used a MySQL database for persistent beliefs (archives of generated reports and previous activity), and over the several weeks the system was running, acquired many thousands of ground facts.
– Prolog is a computationally complete language, capable of expressing nonterminating algorithms. This is an undesireable property for a belief language, the purpose of which is largely to perform limited inferences to determine if a plan is currently applicable. The possibility that such a belief context check may in fact not terminate has consequences for the rest of the plan execution semantics, and indeed could entirely halt the agent or even the entire MAS depending on the implementation and infrastructure in use. This problem is particularly important when beliefs (including rules) may be acquired dynamically from potentially unreliable sources.

The sensitivity to belief addition order is particularly important for agents in dynamic environments, where the agents are continually acquiring (and possibly revising) their beliefs over time. This is also a concern with regard to the modularity issues discussed in the previous section: if two modules add facts or rules to the same belief relation, we would like the order in which they are added to not affect the resulting behaviour. For example, the witness-narrator agents combined default rules for classifying observations together with dynamically acquired knowledge regarding individuals. For instance, an agent may have a default rule for determining whether an animal can fly, perhaps by reasoning about its anatomy or species, but then can also record instances where it has directly observed individuals flying. The default rule is likely to be defined when the agent is created, whereas the specific instances are added to the belief base as they are observed. In *Jason*, depending on the belief-base implementation, this can result in the observations being ordered after the default rule.[3] Due to the execution strategy of Prolog, this will lead to the inefficient and surprising behaviour that the agent will spend time trying to infer if a particular individual is capable of flight when it already has an explicit fact recording this information in its belief base. Another area where the use of Prolog caused some difficulties was in the translation of ontological rules from an OWL ontology into equivalent belief base rules. While a number of such translations have been described in the literature for Prolog-like rule languages (in particular, Datalog) [7,8], the details of the translation for Prolog itself are complicated by the sensitivity to ordering of rules, and naïve translations can easily result in rules that do not terminate on certain inputs.

In the implementation of the witness-narrator agents, we worked around these problems by providing a custom persistent belief base implementation which implemented slightly different semantics to that of Prolog, by always preferring ground facts to rules, regardless of the order in which they were added to the belief base. This was sufficient to ensure correct operation of the software in a wide range of cases, but the possibility for encountering a non-terminating query could not be entirely ruled out.

### 5.1  Datalog as a Belief Base Language

A better solution to the problem would be to replace Prolog with a more appropriate knowledge representation language. There are a number of candidates, including restricted versions of Prolog designed for interfacing with relational databases, such as Datalog [9], or a description logic based language [10], such as OWL. Current description logic languages, however, are unable to express many interesting rules that are (easily) expressible in Datalog. In addition, restricting the belief base language to unary and binary predicates (concepts and roles, respectively) makes some problems rather clumsy to express, and can lead to difficulties keeping track of all the information associated with an individual, e.g., when performing belief revision.

Datalog offers many of the advantages of Prolog (the entire belief base used in our witness-narrator agent framework could have been expressed in Datalog with very few changes) while affording more efficient implementation. In particular, the properties of Datalog that make it suitable as a belief language include:

- the order of clauses in a Datalog program does not affect the semantics of query answering;

---

[3] The description of belief updates in the *Jason* documentation and formal semantics [1] state only that a belief is 'added' to a belief base, and that subsequent to this addition the belief base entails the new belief; the ordering of this belief wrt. the previous beliefs is not specified. In practice, the default in-memory belief base adds dynamically acquired beliefs before existing beliefs, whereas the supplied JDBC (database) belief base we were using left this decision up to the particular database driver, which in all cases we tested made the opposite choice.

- the limitations on the language allow all queries to be answerable in polynomial time;[4]
- more efficient query answering, particularly for larger sets of beliefs.

As Datalog was designed to be a database query language, it should also provide better support for large belief bases, such as those backed by a relational database management system. The non-recursive subset of Datalog has a natural translation into the relational algebra, allowing for efficient and direct compilation of Datalog belief rules into equivalent SQL queries or views. As a further benefit, there also exist translations from various description logics into Datalog. The use of Datalog as a belief base language would therefore go some way towards supporting efficient ontological reasoning in *Jason*, in particular supporting efficient ABox queries over large ontologies.

# 6 Encapsulating Beliefs, Goals and Plans

The problems described in section 3 indicate that some mechanism for modular decomposition of individual agents is needed in *Jason*, addressing the requirements described in section 4.2. Such a mechanism could take a number of forms, ranging from a relatively simple module or namespace mechanism, up to a complex object-oriented solution, complete with component instantiation, inheritance, and encapsulation. It could be argued that the agent abstraction could also be used at this level: an individual agent in a society being itself composed of a society of simpler agents. Such an approach is intuitively appealing, but it is not clear whether the advantages of agent-oriented programming in the large also hold for development of agents themselves. In addition, the capabilities within our system do not naturally fit with the usual notion of an 'agent', and it seems unnatural to try and shoe-horn the architecture into layered societies of agents.

For *Jason*, the requirements for a module system are relatively modest, as the agent level already provides many of the more sophisticated features required for agent development, such as dynamic instantiation of agents and communication interfaces. We therefore concentrate on developing a relatively simple module system that addresses the core requirements of encapsulation and independence that we have identified.

## 6.1 A Module System for *Jason*

Based on the requirements outlined above, we describe a proposal for a module system for *Jason*. A *Jason module* consists of the following elements:

1. a local belief base, containing any beliefs that are private to the module;
2. a local goal base;
3. a plan library, implementing the functionality of the module;
4. a local event queue, for belief and goal update events that are local to the module;
5. a list of exported belief and goal predicates;
6. a unique identifier (URI) that acts as a prefix for all belief and goal symbols in the module, based on XML namespaces;
7. a mapping from simple string prefixes to imported module URIs.

---

[4] Although this isn't true for various extensions to support negation or disjunctive heads in rules.

A module is therefore a subset of the functionality of an agent, encapsulated into a functional unit, along with a URI for identification. An agent is then defined as a composition of modules, together with an interpreter based on the original *Jason* BDI interpreter. Composition of modules within an agent is a flat one-level hierarchy, with the agent as the root. Nested sub-modules are not permitted in this scheme. This implies that there is only a single copy of each module within each agent, and references to that module are shared between all other modules that import it. This approach greatly simplifies the treatment of beliefs and events, while still addressing all of the requirements that we have described.

We adopt the XML approach to namespaces [11], where each module is considered as a separate namespace, identified by a URI. To ease the use of such a system, we also adopt the XML mechanism of allowing each module to declare a set of simple string prefixes that expand into the full URI reference for another module. For example, a module defining beliefs concerning relationships between members of a family might be given a URI such as `http://example.com/family#`. A predicate symbol denoting the 'parent-of' relationship defined in this module would then be given a fully-qualified name consisting of the module URI followed by the predicate symbol, such as `http://example.com/family#parentOf`. When this module is imported into another *Jason* module, this URI can be given a convenient string name. For example, an importing module might define the following mapping, which would allow the 'parent-of' relation to be referred to as simply `family:parentOf` within the scope of the importing module:

$$\{\text{"family"} \Rightarrow \text{"http://example.com/family#"}\}$$

The implementation of this mechanism in *Jason* can make use of the existing annotation mechanism, which allows arbitrary terms to be associated with belief literals and then used to restrict which literals match a belief query. Thus, the atom `family:parentOf(X, Y)` would expand into the annotated belief literal `parentOf(X, Y)[module("http://example.com/family#")]`. Goal symbols can be scoped in an identical fashion.

The URI used for a module, as well as the prefix mappings used by that module, are defined in a *Jason* source file using simple directives:

```
{ module("family", "http://example.com/family#");
  import("friend", "http://example.com/friend#");
  export(["fatherOf/2","brotherOf/2","!birthday/1"]); }
```

This example declares that the source file implements a module that is identified by the URI `http://example.com/family#`, and which imports a 'friend' module with a similar URI. Both modules are given simple string names that can be used within the source file in place of the full URIs (here, the strings 'family' and 'friend' are used respectively). Note that the string prefixes are just a convenience within this source file, and only the URIs are significant outside of the module. The `import` directive would also ensure that the specified module is loaded (once) into the agent, if it has not already been loaded[5]. Imported modules are not nested, but conform to the flat module

---

[5] We do not specify how module URIs are used to locate implementations.

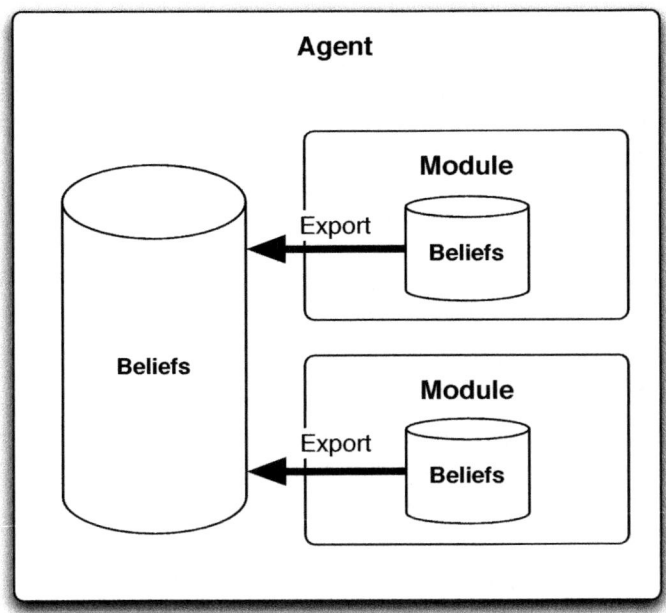

**Fig. 3.** Scoping of beliefs within modules with export

hierarchy. Importing one module into another does not expose the private beliefs or goals of the imported module, but merely ensures that the module is loaded into the agent and sets up a convenient short name for it within the context of the importing module. Finally, an `export` directive specifies which belief and goal predicates should be exported from this module, as discussed below.

Each module is considered to contain its own independent belief base. Belief additions or revisions performed by a module can only be performed on either the module's own belief base, or the main agent belief base: no module can alter the belief base of any other module, as required for encapsulation. By default, belief updates are applied to the module-local belief base. A mechanism is provided to override this behaviour, by allowing some belief (and goal) predicates to be declared as *exported*. Exported beliefs are not added to the module's own belief base, but are instead promoted to the belief base of the agent itself, as shown in Fig. 3. The same approach is used for goals, in that each module has a private goal base, while exported goal symbols are added to the agent's main goals. This partitioning of beliefs and goals into module-private areas also has implications for the generation and propagation of events arising from addition or deletion of beliefs and goals (so-called 'internal events'). A belief or goal predicate that is considered to be private to a module can be seen as an implementation detail of that module, and so events relating to beliefs or goals matching that predicate should not be visible outside of that module. Otherwise, other modules might become reliant on these events, and therefore subject to errors if those implementation details are changed in future updates to a module. However, it is clearly desireable for a module to be able to respond to events arising from changes in its own internal state. We therefore also include a mechanism for scoping of events on a per-module basis. Each module has a private event queue.[6] Events arising from changes to beliefs or goals in a per-module belief or goal base are added only to that module's event queue. Events arising from changes to the agent's main belief or goal base (i.e., from exported beliefs or goals) are added to the agent's main event queue, as in the current *Jason* implementation, and thus are visible to all modules.

Each module inherits the beliefs, goals and events of the main agent interpreter. This means that plans within a module can respond to events that occur either within that module, or in the main agent event queue. Likewise, the context of a plan can refer to belief predicates that are private to the module in which that plan is defined, or those which are added to the main agent belief base.

## 6.2  Interpreter Cycle Changes

The changes we have described to incorporate modules into *Jason* imply a number of changes to the *Jason* BDI interpreter cycle, shown previously in Fig. 1. We here describe the changes to the interpreter cycle that are required for our proposal. Items without comments are assumed to be identical to the current *Jason* implementation.

1. *Perceive the environment.*
2. *Update the belief base.* Belief updates must now take into account the scoping of beliefs, as described above. Belief updates from external sources (such as percepts) are added to the agent's main belief base.
3. *Receive communication from other agents.*
4. *Select socially acceptable messages.*
5. *Select an event.* The set of events to choose from is taken as the union of all of the pending event queues for each module and the agent's main event queue.
6. *Retrieve relevant plans.* The set of potentially relevant plans depends on the scope of the triggering event. For events that are local to a module, then only that module's plan library should be considered. For events scoped at the level of the overall agent, the set of potentially relevant plans is the union of the plan libraries of all modules. Determining whether a plan matches a triggering event is done by first expanding any URI references in both into *Jason* annotations, as described previously, and then performing matching as in the current implementation.
7. *Determine applicable plans.* As for relevant plans, determining applicable plans (i.e., those whose belief context is satisfied), must also respect scoping of those beliefs and expanding URI references.
8. *Select one applicable plan.* As described in Sec. 3, one of the motivating justifications for this work, and a key compositionality requirements, is that each module should be able to respond independently to events. It therefore seems sensible to change this step in the cycle so that up to one applicable plan is selected *per module*. However, this approach is more complicated than it immediately appears. The problem is that belief and goal events resulting from an existing intention cause any responding plans to become part of that same intention structure. Clearly this

---

[6] Alternatively, per-module events could be added to the main event queue, appropriately annotated. We consider these two approaches to be essentially equivalent.

presents a problem if multiple plans are selected, as only one can become part of the intention (without much more drastic changes to the structure of intentions). We discuss how to tackle this problem below.

9. *Select an intention for execution.*
10. *Execute an action.*

As described, the problem of allowing multiple modules to respond to the same event is more complex than it initially appears, due to interactions with the BDI model of *Jason*. In determining a solution to this problem, it is worth considering the types of events that can occur, and what an appropriate behaviour should be in each case. *Jason* currently distinguishes between so-called 'internal' events, arising from changes to the agent's internal state (beliefs and goals) caused by executing intentions, and 'external' events, caused by the arrival of new percepts and messages from other agents. External events always cause a new intention structure to be created, whereas internal events reuse the intention structure that generated the event. One solution, then, would be to only allow multiple modules to react to external events (creating a new intention for each module), and treat internal events as before, in which case only one module would get to respond. However, this seems overly restrictive, as it is reasonable for multiple modules to respond to *belief* updates caused by an executing intention, whereas a *goal* update should only result in one course of action being taken, to avoid conflicting or incoherent behaviour. Belief change events are largely *incidental* rather than intentional, and therefore should not put such strong constraints on resulting behaviour. For instance, an agent may want to perform various house-keeping tasks in response to a belief change: inferring further conclusions (forward-chaining), informing other agents of the change, and so on, but this is much less likely for goals. Indeed, the current behaviour of *Jason* makes little distinction between goals and beliefs with respect to how events are processed, whereas the purpose and meaning of these events may (indeed, should) be quite different.

It therefore seems more sensible to distinguish events not by an internal/external distinction, but rather by a belief/goal distinction. We therefore propose reverting to the approach taken in the original Procedural Reasoning System (PRS) [12] (Sec. 8.2), in which plans responding to belief update events always create new intention structures, allowing multiple modules to respond to the same event, whereas goal update events follow the current behaviour in *Jason*: only a single plan can respond to the event and this plan becomes part of the same intention that caused the event (if one exists). This addresses the compositionality requirements for beliefs, but still requires some coordination between module authors wishing to respond to the same goal event. We believe this is a correct division of responsibility. Conflicts between multiple plans reacting to the same *goal* are properly the concern of the agent's usual practical reasoning and plan selection functions. Allowing multiple modules to respond to the same goal event would increase the possibility of incoherent or conflicting responses, and therefore requires some explicit coordination mechanism. In practice, these changes address all of the issues that we encountered in the witness-narrator agent framework.

## 7    Related Work

Most popular current programming languages support some form of module system allowing for decomposition of large programs into functionally encapsulated components. Approaches range from simple namespace mechanisms, to sophisticated module systems supporting parameterisation, instantiation, and complex nested module structures. Within the realm of BDI agent-oriented programming languages and frameworks, a number of proposals have been presented in the literature [13,14,15,16,17,18,19,20,21]. In the following discussion we highlight those approaches that are most directly relevant to the approach presented here.

A form of modularity based on the notion of 'roles' in multi-agent systems was introduced in [14]. A *role* encapsulates the beliefs, goals, plans and social norms or obligations that are required for an agent to fulfill a particular role in a society. Roles can be 'enacted' at runtime, in which case the beliefs of the role are added to the agent's beliefs and the goals and plans are also adopted. Only a single role can be enacted at any one time, in contrast to most other modularity proposals. This approach would not have sufficed for the witness-narrator agent system, in which agents can be assigned multiple roles simultaneously, either within a single team or in multiple teams.

The notion of modules as 'capabilities' was developed within the context of the JACK™ agent framework [15] and has been extended in the JADEX framework [16]. A *capability* in this proposal is a collection of plans, beliefs, and events together with some scoping rules to determine which of these elements are visible outside of the module, and which are encapsulated. Like the proposal described here, capabilities represent a middle layer between that of an agent and the level of individual plans and beliefs. Capabilities address the concerns of avoiding name clashes and hiding of implementation details, while also supporting multiple instances of the same module to be created. The later work with JADEX extends the concept to include a more flexible notion of scoping for beliefs and events, as well as allowing capabilities to be parameterised and dynamically instantiated. However, capabilities do not address the problems of plan selection and execution that we have described, i.e., to allow plans from different modules to each have a chance to react to an event.

A proposal for incorporating a similar notion of modules has been described for an extended version of the 2APL programming language [18]. As with capabilities, extended 2APL modules can be instantiated multiple times, or can be declared as *singleton* modules, for which a single instance of the module is shared within an agent. 2APL modules can contain any elements that an agent can contain, including plans, beliefs, goals, and action specifications, and are similar to agents in many respects. Each module can be executed by the module (or agent) that instantiated it, and can receive and generate belief updates, goal revisions, and other events. Another approach to modularity has been described for the related 3APL language [19], in which a module encapsulates just the plans related to a particular goal, or set of goals. A module must be explicitly 'called' with a goal to pursue, after which that module (and only that module) will use its plans to try and achieve the goal. This avoids issues with conflicting plans (assuming each module is internally coherent), but at the cost of requiring more explicit programming from the agent author—deciding not only what goals to adopt, but which modules should be used to achieve them. The notion of modules as 'policy-based intentions' in GOAL [20] relaxes this restriction by allowing the module to specify a context condition on beliefs and goals that determines when it is activated. However, to the best of our knowledge, the implementations of these languages do not address the issues of belief compositionality we have described.

For *Jason*, a simple module system has been developed as part of the work on integrating ontological reasoning in the JASDL system [21]. However, this work concentrates on allowing per-module customisation of the various plan and intention selection functions in *Jason*, and does not address the modularity concerns described in the current paper. The changes described in Sec. 6.2 to the processing of events are based on the original scheme used in the Procedural Reasoning System (PRS) [12] (Sec. 8.2), in which belief change events cause new intentions to be created, whereas goal changes reuse the current intention structure. Given AgentSpeak's (and therefore *Jason*'s) historical basis in the PRS architecture, it seems natural to revert to this scheme.

While many agent programming languages use Prolog as a belief base language, e.g., *Jason*, 2APL, GOAL[22], there has been some work on alternative belief representation languages. For example, an alternative knowledge representation language for the belief base of *Jason* agents has been investigated in [23,21] in the context of adding support for ontological reasoning and OWL. However, this work has concentrated on extending the Prolog facilities of *Jason* with support for ontological reasoning, rather than replacing the existing belief base language. In [24] an approach to abstracting an agent language from any particular knowledge representation format is presented. While the authors note that Datalog and SQL meet their requirements for a *Knowledge Representation Technology*, the focus of the paper is on translations between knowledge representation technologies rather than the practicalities of any specific technology. Most agent programming frameworks (including the implementation of *Jason*) allow customising or replacing the default belief base to a certain degree. While such customisation can facilitate the integration of application specific or legacy belief bases, there remains a need for a practical knowledge representation formalism, even if only as a default, and we feel that Datalog is a more appropriate choice than Prolog for a default belief-base language.

# 8   Summary

In this paper we identified a number of problems with the *Jason* agent-oriented programming language arising from our experience of building a moderately large and complex piece of software using *Jason*. While *Jason* provides a clean and elegant framework for building sophisticated multi-agent systems, it provides less support for developing complex agents with diverse, interacting capabilties. We identified two key problems: a lack of support for modular software development, and an order-dependence in the semantics of the belief representation language which makes it hard to compose modules and to author plans within a module. To address these problems we proposed revisions to the language to simplify the construction of agents from functionally encapsulated components, and changes to the belief base language and plan execution to support more robust software engineering.

While the presentation of this work has been grounded in our experiences building software with *Jason*, much of the material is relevant to other agent-oriented programming languages, particularly those building on the BDI model. For example, our discussion of the requirements for modularity and compositionality in section 4 are generally applicable, and the discussion of choice of belief representation language in section 5 should be broadly applicable to similar languages and frameworks.

In future work, we plan to investigate further revisions to *Jason* suggested by our experiences developing the witness narrator agents system, including changes to the triggering conditions of plans and the semantic characterisation of percepts.

# References

1. Bordini, R.H., Hübner, J.F., Wooldridge, M.: Programming Multi-Agent Systems in AgentSpeak using Jason. John Wiley & Sons Ltd., Chichester (2007)
2. Dastani, M.: 2APL: a practical agent programming language. Autonomous Agents and Multi-Agent Systems 16, 214–248 (2008)
3. Rao, A.S., Georgeff, M.P.: Modeling rational agents within a BDI-architecture. In: Proceedings of the 2nd International Conference on Principles of Knowledge Representation and Reasoning, pp. 473–484 (1991)
4. Madden, N., Logan, B.: Collaborative narrative generation in persistent virtual environments. In: Proceedings of the AAAI Fall Symposium on Intelligent Narrative Technologies, Arlington, Virginia, USA (November 2007)
5. Rao, A.S.: AgentSpeak(L): BDI agents speak out in a logical computable language. In: Perram, J., Van de Velde, W. (eds.) MAAMAW 1996. LNCS, vol. 1038, pp. 42–55. Springer, Heidelberg (1996)
6. Gregorio, J., de hOra, B.: The Atom Publishing Protocol. Technical Report RFC 5023, Internet Engineering Task Force (October 2007)
7. Hustadt, U., Motik, B., Sattler, U.: Reducing SHIQ-description logic to disjunctive Datalog programs. In: Proceedings of the 9th International Conference on Knowledge Representation and Reasoning (KR 2004), Whistler, Canada, pp. 152–162 (June 2004)
8. Volz, R., Decker, S., Oberle, D.: Bubo—implementing OWL in rule-based systems. In: Proceedings of WWW 2003, Budapest, Hungary (May 2003)
9. Ceri, S., Gottlob, G., Tanca, L.: What you always wanted to know about Datalog (and never dared to ask). IEEE Transactions on Knowledge and Data Engineering 1(1), 146–166 (1989)
10. Baader, F., Calvanese, D., McGuiness, D., Nardi, D., Patel-Schneider, P. (eds.): The Description Logic Handbook. Cambridge University Press, Cambridge (2003)
11. Bray, T., Hollander, D., Layman, A., Tobin, R.: Namespaces in XML 1.0, 2nd edn. Technical report, W3C (2006)
    http://www.w3.org/TR/2006/REC-xml-names-20060816.
12. Myers, K.L.: Procedural reasoning system user's guide. Technical report, Artificial Intelligence Center. SRI International, Menlo Park, CA (1997)
13. Kakas, A., Mancarella, P., Sadri, F., Stathis, K., Toni, F.: The KGP model of agency. In: Proceedings of ECAI 2004 European Conference on Artificial Intelligence, Valencia, Spain, pp. 33–37 (August 2004)
14. Dastani, M., van Riemsdijk, M.B., Hulstijn, J., Dignum, F., Meyer, J.J.C.: Enacting and de-acting roles in agent programming. In: Odell, J.J., Giorgini, P., Müller, J.P. (eds.) AOSE 2004. LNCS, vol. 3382, pp. 189–204. Springer, Heidelberg (2005)
15. Busetta, P., Howden, N., Rönnquist, R., Hodgson, A.: Structuring BDI agents in functional clusters. In: Jennings, N.R., Lespérance, Y. (eds.) ATAL 1999. LNCS(LNAI), vol. 1757, pp. 277–289. Springer, Heidelberg (2000)

16. Braubach, L., Pokahr, A., Lamersdorf, W.: Extending the capability concept for flexible BDI agent modularization. In: Bordini, R.H., Dastani, M.M., Dix, J., El Fallah Seghrouchni, A. (eds.) PROMAS 2005. LNCS (LNAI), vol. 3862, pp. 139–155. Springer, Heidelberg (2006)
17. Haridi, S., Franzén, N.: Modules and interfaces. In: Tutorial of Oz (2008),
    `http://www.mozart-oz.org/documentation/tutorial/`
    `node7.html#chapter.modules`
18. Dastani, M., Mol, C.P., Steunebrink, B.R.: Modularity in agent programming languages: An illustration in extended 2APL. In: Bui, T.D., Ho, T.V., Ha, Q.T. (eds.) PRIMA 2008. LNCS (LNAI), vol. 5357, pp. 139–152. Springer, Heidelberg (2008)
19. van Riemsdijk, M.B., Dastani, M., Meyer, J.J.C., de Boer, F.S.: Goal-oriented modularity in agent programming. In: Nakashima, H., Wellman, M.P., Weiss, G., Stone, P. (eds.) Proceedings of the Fifth International Joint Conference on Autonomous Agents and Multiagent Systems (AAMAS 2006), Hakodate, Japan, May 8-12, pp. 1271–1278. ACM, New York (2006)
20. Hindriks, K.V.: Modules as policy-based intentions: Modular agent programming in GOAL. In: Dastani, M.M., El Fallah Seghrouchni, A., Ricci, A., Winikoff, M. (eds.) ProMAS 2007. LNCS (LNAI), vol. 4908, pp. 156–171. Springer, Heidelberg (2008)
21. Klapiscak, T., Bordini, R.H.: JASDL: a practical programming approach combining agent and semantic web technologies. In: Baldoni, M., Son, T.C., van Riemsdijk, M.B., Winikoff, M. (eds.) DALT 2008. LNCS (LNAI), vol. 5397, pp. 91–110. Springer, Heidelberg (2009)
22. Hindriks, K.V., de Boer, F.S., van der Hoek, W., Meyer, J.J.C.: Agent programming with declarative goals. In: Castelfranchi, C., Lespérance, Y. (eds.) ATAL 2000. LNCS (LNAI), vol. 1986, pp. 228–257. Springer, Heidelberg (2001)
23. Moreira, A.F., Vieira, R., Bordini, R.H., Hübner, J.: Agent-oriented programming with underlying ontological reasoning. In: Baldoni, M., Endriss, U., Omicini, A., Torroni, P. (eds.) DALT 2005. LNCS (LNAI), vol. 3904, pp. 132–147. Springer, Heidelberg (2006)
24. Dastani, M., Hindriks, K.V., Novák, P., Tinnemeier, N.A.M.: Combining multiple knowledge representation technologies into agent programming languages. In: Baldoni, M., Son, T.C., van Riemsdijk, M.B., Winikoff, M. (eds.) DALT 2008. LNCS (LNAI), vol. 5397, pp. 60–74. Springer, Heidelberg (2009)

# A MultiAgent System for Monitoring Boats in Marine Reserves

Giuliano Armano and Eloisa Vargiu

Dept. of Electrical and Electronic Engineering, University of Cagliari, Italy
{armano,vargiu}@diee.unica.it
http://iasc.diee.unica.it

**Abstract.** Setting up a marine reserve involves access monitoring, with the goal of avoiding intrusions of unauthorized boats – also considering that, typically, marine reserves are located in areas not easily accessible. Nowadays, intrusion detection in marine reserves is carried out by using radar systems or suitable cameras activated by movement sensors. In this chapter, we present a multiagent system aimed at monitoring boats in marine reserves. The goal of the proposed system is to discriminate between authorized and unauthorized boats – the formers being equipped with GPS+GSM devices. Boats are tracked by a digital radar that detects their positions. A prototype of the system has been experimented in a marine reserve located in the North of Sardinia. Results show that adopting the proposed approach facilitates the system administrator, as well as staff operators, in the task of identifying intrusions.

## 1   Introduction

Nowadays, the agent research community provides powerful theories, algorithms and techniques with great potential in the design, implementation, and deployment of real world applications. Several research and industrial experiences have already put into evidence the advantages of using agents in manufacturing processes [18], in web services and web-based computational markets [10], as well as in distributed network management [6]. Moreover, further studies suggest to exploit agents and MASs as enabling technologies for a variety of novel scenarios, such as autonomic computing [16], grid computing [9], and semantic web [5].

According to [13], the main bottlenecks that prevent a fast and massive adoption of agent-based solutions in real world applications are: (i) limited awareness about the potentials of agent technology; (ii) limited publicity of successful industrial projects carried out with the agent technology; (iii) misunderstandings about the effectiveness of agent-based solutions, characterized by over-expectations of the early industrial adopters and subsequent frustration; (iv) risks for adopting a technology that has not been already proven in large scale industrial applications; as well as (v) lack of design and development tools mature enough for industrial deployment.

In our opinion, the multiagent technology is already effective for deploying real applications from both a software engineering [21] and a technological perspective [4]. In fact, some applications of multiagent systems have been developed

L. Braubach, J.-P. Briot, and J. Thangarajah (Eds.): ProMAS 2009, LNAI 5919, pp. 254–265, 2010.

by commercial organizations or by research institutions as a result of specific industrial requirements. Let us recall here, the Shipboard Automation system deployed by Rockwell Automation, Inc. [20], the multiagent solutions applied in mass-production planning of car engines for Skoda Auto [14], and an agent-based demonstrator that provides an experimental testbed for various UAV collision avoidance strategies deployed by the Gerstner Laboratory, together with the Air Force Research Laboratory [15].

In this chapter, we present a multiagent system aimed at monitoring boats in marine reserves. A prototype of the system has been implemented by using X.MAS, a generic multiagent architecture devised to implement information retrieval and information filtering applications [2]. The corresponding scenario requires to discriminate between authorized and unauthorized boats – the formers being equipped with GPS+GSM devices. Boats are tracked by a digital radar that detects their positions. The prototype has been experimented in a marine reserve located in the North of Sardinia. Results show that adopting the proposed approach allows system administrator and staff operators to easily identify intrusions. It is worth mentioning that, to our best knowledge, no agent-based solutions have been proposed in the literature to monitor and signal intrusion in marine reserves.

The remainder of the chapter is organized as follows: first, selected related work on agent-based systems for monitoring and surveillance is recalled. Then, the scenario concerning boat monitoring is sketched. Subsequently, the adopted MAS solution is described, focusing on the prototype that has been implemented and on the macro-architecture from which it originates. After illustrating and discussing experimental results, conclusions end the chapter.

## 2 Agent-Based Systems for Monitoring and Surveillance

Applying agent methodologies in process monitoring and control is a relatively new approach, particularly suitable for distributed and dislocated systems. In particular, agent-based solutions have been proposed to monitor: (i) control systems [8], (ii) distant control experimentation systems [19], and forest fires [7]. In [8], a methodology for designing agent-based production control systems is described, focusing on a design method for identifying the agents of a production control system. In so doing, the designer can move from pure domain concepts (such as production processes) to agent-oriented concepts (such as agents and decision responsibilities). The identification of agents provides a basis for all other subsequent design steps, such as interaction design and agent programming. In [19], an approach for implementing distant control experimentation systems has been described, the main task being to monitor temperature and humidity and to control experiments with the possibility of video monitoring the experimental area. The underlying idea is to integrate a laboratory greenhouse model with a video system. The approach is then experimented by developing a multiagent system that involves specific software agents, responsible of all operations –from user-system communication to telecontrol and video monitoring.

In [7], a TCP/IP-based system is presented, which embeds sensor networks and server units for collecting, processing and storing data. Each sensor network has several monitoring units, which in turn embed video cameras (connected to a video web server), mini meteorological stations (connected to data web servers), and wireless communication units. Agents designed for forest fire monitoring strictly follow these guidelines, each module of the system being autonomous, aware of its environment and capable of active behavior if alarmed. Environment awareness is accomplished by connecting numerous meteorological sensors to a network-embedded microcontroller unit –responsible for collecting data from sensors and passing them to a central server agent.

Agent-based solutions have also been proposed to develop video surveillance systems. In this field, researchers are concerned with detection and tracking problems, with the goal of enforcing security. In [1], a video-based multi-agent system for traffic surveillance, called Monitorix, is presented. Agent interactions are controlled by a BDI-like architecture. Agents communicate using FIPA-ACL messages with SL contents. Vehicles are tracked across cameras by a suitable agent, using a traffic model whose parameters are continuously updated by learning algorithms. The classification of mobile objects uses competitive learning algorithms, whereas the computation of typical trajectories uses statistical adaptation. The tracking of mobile objects, from one camera into the next one, updates the parameters of its prediction model, using a combination of symbolic learning and genetic algorithms. In [12], an architecture aimed at performing scene understanding in the visual surveillance domain has been presented. The agent paradigm is adopted to provide a framework in which inter-related and event-driven processes can be managed to achieve a high level description of events observed by multiple cameras. Each camera is associated to an agent, entrusted with detecting and tracking moving regions of interest. Agents store a hidden Markov model of learned activity patterns. In [11], a coordinated video surveillance system is presented, able to precisely extract the 3D position of objects. The system embeds agents that control video cameras and perform image processing. An additional support module is devoted to handle communications among camera agents.

## 3   Monitoring Boats in Marine Reserves: The Scenario

In the summertime, in Sardinia and in its small archipelago, tourists sometimes sail in protected or forbidden areas close to the coast. Monitoring such areas with the goal of discriminating between authorized and unauthorized boats, is quite complicated. In fact, along Sardinian coasts, there are two-hundred tourist harbors with about thirteen thousand places available for boats and several services for boat owners. Monitoring large areas without suitable resources (such as radars) can be highly uneconomic, since staff operators would be (and typically are) compelled to directly patrol them over time. A typical solution consists of using a radar system controlled by a central unit located ashore in a strategical position. Radar signals allow to detect the positions of the boats that sail in the controlled area.

With the goal of monitoring and signaling intrusion in marine reserves, we experimented a mutiagent solution in which authorized boats are equipped with suitable devices able to transmit (through the GSM technology) their position (through the GPS technology). In this way, the corresponding scenario encompasses two kinds of boats: authorized, recognizable by the GPS+GSM devices, and unauthorized. Both kinds of boats are expected to be identified by a digital radar able to detect their position in the protected area. Comparing the positions sent by boats with those detected by the radar allows to identify unauthorized boats.

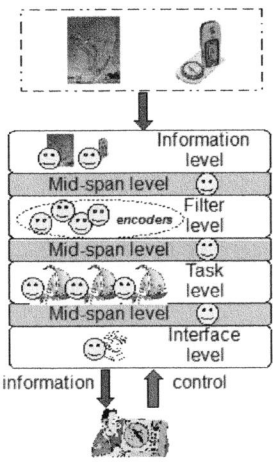

**Fig. 1.** SEA.MAS macro-architecture

## 4   SEA.MAS - The Proposed System

The multiagent system aimed at monitoring boats in marine reserves described in this chapter has been called SEA.MAS, to highlight the fact that it stems from X.MAS [2] –a generic multiagent architecture built upon JADE [3] devised to make it easier the implementation of information retrieval and information filtering applications. The adoption of X.MAS comes from the fact that the problem of monitoring and signaling intrusions in marine reserves can be seen as a particular information retrieval task, in which radar and GPS+GSM devices are information sources, whereas authorized and unauthorized boats are categories to be discriminated.

Let us point out in advance that the X.MAS generic architecture is designed to host a society of agents stratified in a hierarchy of four main levels: 1. information, 2. filter, 3. task, and 4. user interface. Additional middle-span levels take care of enacting communication between adjacent levels. Figure 1 gives a schematic representation of the SEA.MAS system, highlighting at the same time the correspondence with the design pattern that inspired the X.MAS generic architecture.

From an operational perspective X.MAS (thus SEA.MAS) agents are agents that can interact by exchanging FIPA-ACL messages, share a common ontology in accordance with the actual application, and exhibit a specific behavior according to their role. From a design-oriented perspective, information and interface agents are designed to embody information sources and specific devices, respectively, filter and task agents encompass actuators that depend on the specific application being implemented, whereas middle agents contain a dispatcher aimed at handling interactions among requesters and providers. From an implementation-oriented perspective, the X.MAS generic architecture is built upon JADE [3], and is in fact a Java library that provides an abstract class for each kind of agent made available. Furthermore (see Figure 2), each agent encompasses a scheduler devoted to handle the information and control flow that occurs along adjacent levels in the hierarchy (in particular the information flow goes from level 1. to 4., whereas the control flow goes from level 4. to 1.).

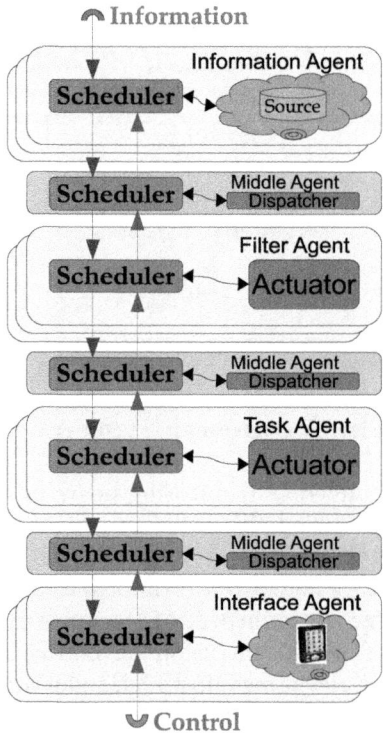

**Fig. 2.** Agent internals, level by level

## 4.1   SEA.MAS as Customization of X.MAS

The first step for customizing X.MAS to a specific application consists of extending each abstract class with the goal of providing the required features and capabilities. Let us summarize them level by level:

**Information level.** At this level, X.MAS agents are entrusted with extracting data from the information sources. Each information agent wraps a specific information source. In SEA.MAS, information sources are the digital radar and GPS+GSM devices. For each information source, a suitable information agent has been devised to embody the information provided therein. In particular, we implemented a wrapper for the digital radar and a wrapper for the GPS+GSM devices. The information generated by wrappers becomes available to other agents by invoking the middle agent corresponding to the middle-span level "Information-Filter".

**Filter level.** At this level, X.MAS agents are entrusted with selecting and encoding information deemed relevant to the users, and with preventing information from being overloaded and/or redundant. In SEA.MAS, filter agents are aimed at encoding the information extracted by the information agents. The encoding activity consists of creating events containing the position of the detected boats and their identification code, when available. Moreover, filter agents are devoted to avoid two kinds of redundancy: information detected more than once from the same device (caching) or throughout different devices (information overloading). Then, the middle agent corresponding to the middle-span level "Filter-Task" forwards the event to the corresponding task agent, assuming the role of yellow pages if the identification code is available or the role of broker otherwise. If a detected event is not related to an authorized boat, the middle agent creates a task agent able to handle the event.

**Task level.** At this level, X.MAS agents are entrusted with arranging data according to user personal needs and preferences. To achieve user goals task agents typically exhibit cooperation and adaptation abilities. In SEA.MAS, a task agent is created for each boat, the underlying motivation being the need to centralize the knowledge regarding the position of a boat and its state. As for the position, events are classified as belonging either to anonymous sources or to known sources. For known sources the state reports their identification code and –when available– further information (i.e. a description of the boat and/or owner's data). The main tasks of the agents belonging to this level are: (i) to follow a boat position during its navigation, also dealing with any temporary lack of signal; (ii) to promptly alerting the interface agents in the event that unauthorized boats are identified; and (iii) to handle messages coming from the interface level (e.g. false alarm notification).

**Interface level.** At this level, different X.MAS agents can be associated with different kinds of profiles (e.g. supervisor, administrator, client) and user interfaces (e.g. pc, pda, mobile phone). In SEA.MAS, suitable interface agents allow the system administrator and staff operators to interact with the system. In both cases, the corresponding interface agent is aimed at getting a feedback from the user, for instance to inform relevant agents about changes occurred in the environment or about faults that might occur in devices located on the authorized boats. User feedback can also be used to improve the overall ability of

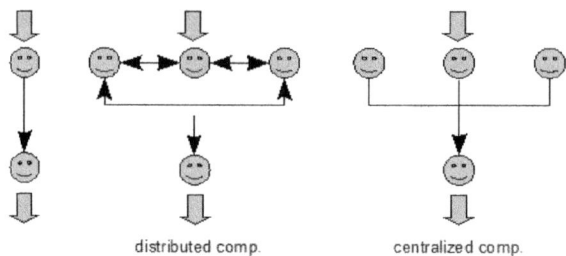

distributed comp.                centralized comp.

**Fig. 3.** Cooperation modes

discriminating among authorized and unauthorized boats. Currently, this kind
of user feedback is performed through a simple solution based on the k-NN technology[1]. When either a false positive or a false negative is evidenced by the
user, it is immediately embedded in the training set of the k-NN classifier that
implements the feedback.

### 4.2   Capabilities of SEA.MAS Agents

Some X.MAS (thus SEA.MAS) agent capabilities are common features that do
not depend on a specific level. The most relevant ones are: (i) cooperation, (ii)
mobility, (iii) personalization, and (iv) adaptivity.

**Cooperation.** In SEA.MAS cooperation may occur according to the modes devised for X.MAS, i.e. horizontally and vertically. The former kind of cooperation
occurs among agents belonging to a specific level, in particular it is implemented
in accordance with the following patterns: pipeline, centralized composition, and
distributed composition (see Figure 3). Pipelines are typically used to process
information at different levels of abstraction, so that data can be increasingly
refined and adapted to the user needs. Centralized composition is typically used
for integrating different capabilities, so that the resulting behavior actually depends on the combination activity. Distributed composition is typically used
to model a cooperation among the involved components aimed at processing
interlaced information (in other words, distributed composition encompasses a
generic cooperation that may occur among agents, plus a forwarder that upon
completion will be in charge of handling the result of the overall activity). On the
other hand, vertical cooperation is performed –across levels– throughout middle
agents, which support communication among requesters and providers belonging to adjacent levels of the architecture. As already pointed out, in SEA.MAS
agents at the middle-span level are implemented as matchmakers or brokers,
depending on the specific need.

---

[1] The k-nearest neighbor is a classification method based upon observable features.
The algorithm selects a set which contains the k nearest neighbors and assigns the
class label to the new data point based upon the most numerous class with the set.

**Mobility.** All involved agents can be mobile, if needed. In fact, in case of a large number of agents (i.e. boats) this requirement becomes mandatory in order to handle the computational complexity. Thus, mobility permits the run-time deployment of agents in a distributed architecture. Let us recall that X.MAS agents are in fact JADE agents; for this reason, it is very easy to build mobile agents able to migrate or copy themselves across a network –as JADE mobile agent can navigate across different containers and platforms. Of course, mobile agents must be location aware in order to decide when and where to move.

**Personalization.** In X.MAS personalization can be provided at the interface level thanks to hand-coded or adaptive algorithms. In SEA.MAS only hand-coded personalization has been implemented according to the types of involved operators (e.g., system administrator and staff operators). Although mainly stored by agents belonging to the interface level, part of the information concerning hand-coded user profiles is also forwarded to the filter and task level (throughout the corresponding middle-span levels). Furthermore, middle agents take care of avoiding potential inconsistencies.

**Adaptivity.** Currently, SEA.MAS agents exhibit a simple adaptive capability. Task agents, in fact, are able to adapt their behavior in order to avoid losing boats in case of signal absence (i.e., areas devoid of GSM signal).

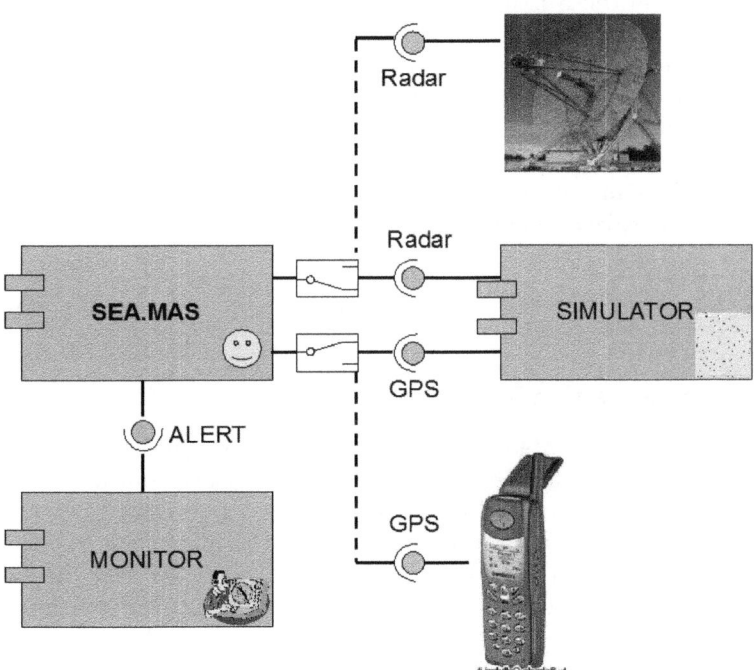

**Fig. 4.** Schema of the overall system

## 5   Experiments and Results

SEA.MAS involves a number of agents that in practice strictly depends on the number of boats being monitored. In fact, whereas the number of middle-, information-, filter-, and interface-level agents is fixed (i.e., one agent for each middle-span level, two agents at the information level, one agent at the filter level, and typically one agent at the interface level), a task agent is instantiated for each boat. It is worth pointing out in advance that this fact does not generate any scalability problem for two main reasons: the number of boats sealing in marine reserves is typically less than a hundred at a time and, if needed, agents could be distributed on several nodes.

Figure 4 highlights the overall architecture of the system used to run experiments. Two kinds of experiments have been performed to assess the capability of SEA.MAS in the task of intrusion detection: in a simulated and in a real scenario. To test SEA.MAS in the former setting, a simulator has been implemented, able to simulate both the radar and the GPS+GSM devices. In particular, it is able to generate signals virtually originated by the radar. The simulator provides randomization of temporal displacement and detection errors. Furthermore, it is able to mimic also the real world behavior of boats, such as accelerations and changing course. The presence of GPS devices on the boats have also been simulated. After being tested in a virtual scenario, the simulator has been switched off and SEA.MAS has been experimented in a real scenario, i.e. in a marine reserve located in the North of Sardinia.

To measure the error in distinguishing among authorized and unauthorized boats, we will refer to a confusion matrix where true positives (TP) are intruders, true negatives (TN) are authorized boats, false positives (FP) are authorized boats recognized as intruders; and false negatives (FN) are intruders recognized as authorized boats. Starting from the confusion matrix, we calculated some standard performance measures –such as accuracy ($\alpha$), precision ($\pi$), and recall ($\rho$) [17]. For the sake of completeness, let us recall hereafter their definitions:

$$\alpha = \frac{TP + TN}{P + N} \qquad \pi = \frac{TP}{TP + FP} \qquad \rho = \frac{TP}{TP + FN}$$

### 5.1   Experiments in a Virtual Scenario

We performed experiments with a number of boats varying from 10 to 100, considering first a scenario in which boats are suitably spaced out (see Table 1), and then a scenario in which boats have a high degree of overlapping (see Table 2).

Experimental results point out that, overall, the filter agent is able to easily distinguish among authorized and unauthorized boats, so that task agents are correctly instantiated and the system is able to signal detected intrusions. In particular, in the former scenario, the system accuracy with a typical number of boats involved (i.e. from 10 to 20) ranges from 95 to 93%. As for precision and recall, the system exhibits, on average, the same propensity to make mistakes in FP and FN, and the overall error is satisfactorily low. It is worth pointing out

**Table 1.** Experimental results obtained in virtual scenarios – no overlap

| TN | FP | FN | TP | $\alpha$ | $\pi$ | $\rho$ |
|----|----|----|----|------|------|------|
| 10 | 0 | 1 | 9 | 0.95 | 1 | 0.9 |
| 19 | 1 | 1 | 19 | 0.95 | 0.95 | 0.95 |
| 29 | 1 | 2 | 28 | 0.95 | 0.97 | 0.93 |
| 37 | 3 | 2 | 38 | 0.94 | 0.93 | 0.95 |
| 46 | 4 | 3 | 47 | 0.93 | 0.92 | 0.94 |

**Table 2.** Experimental results obtained in virtual scenarios – with overlap

| TN | FP | FN | TP | $\alpha$ | $\pi$ | $\rho$ |
|----|----|----|----|------|------|------|
| 9 | 1 | 2 | 8 | 0.85 | 0.89 | 0.8 |
| 17 | 3 | 6 | 14 | 0.78 | 0.82 | 0.7 |
| 24 | 6 | 8 | 22 | 0.77 | 0.79 | 0.73 |
| 30 | 10 | 12 | 28 | 0.73 | 0.74 | 0.7 |
| 36 | 14 | 15 | 35 | 0.71 | 0.71 | 0.7 |

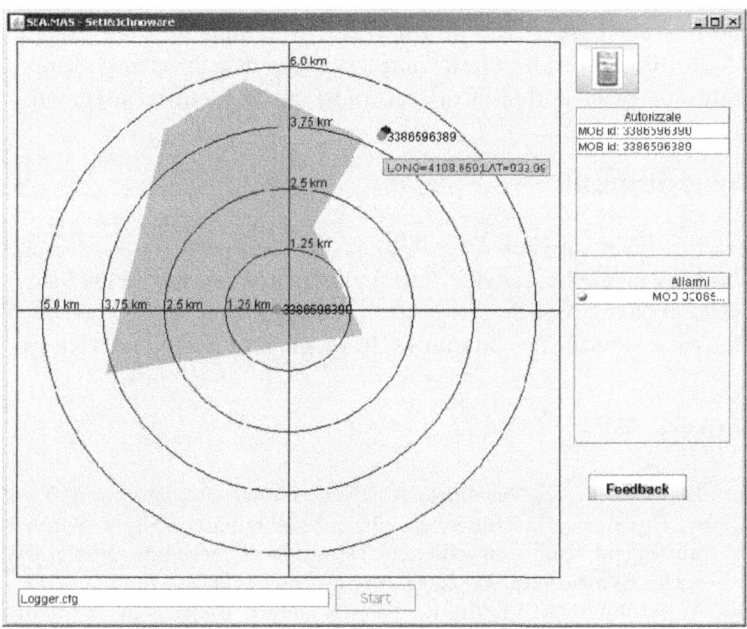

**Fig. 5.** A snapshot of the user interface

that the system exhibits a good degree of robustness to overloading conditions, as reported in Table 2. Performances put also into evidence that the system has a good behavior in terms of robustness. In fact, even considering 100 boats, it is able to signal intrusions –in real time– with a minimal loss of performances.

## 5.2    Experiments in a Real-World Scenario

In a real-world scenario, GPS- and radar-signals are retrieved by suitable information agents, devised to extract the actual position according to GPS and NMEA standards. The interface agent (see Figure 5) represents in different colors different states: authorized, unauthorized, not-detected, under verification. In case of intrusion, an acoustic sound is generated together with the position of unauthorized boats (such signal can be forwarded to the security patrol, whose primary goal is to catch intruders). The maximum number of boats in the selected marine reserve was 20. Experiments performed on the real scenario show results comparable with those obtained during the simulation.

# 6    Conclusions

In this chapter, SEA.MAS, a multiagent system for monitoring boats in marine reserves, has been presented. A prototype of the system has been built upon X.MAS, a generic multiagent architecture devoted to support the implementation of information retrieval and information filtering applications. The prototype has been used to monitor boats in a marine reserve located in the North of Sardinia. Results show that adopting the proposed approach allows system administrator and staff operators to easily identify intrusions.

## Acknowledgments

This work has been supported by Regione Autonoma della Sardegna, under the project "A Multiagent System for Monitoring Intrusions in Marine Reserves" (POR Sardegna 2000/2006, Asse 3 - Misura 3.13). The prototype has been developed and deployed together with the companies SETI snc and ICHNOWARE sas.

## References

1. Abreu, B., Botelho, L., Cavallaro, A., Douxchamps, D., Ebrahimi, T., Figueiredo, P., Macq, B., Mory, B., Nunes, L., Orri, J., Trigueiros, M., Violante, A.: Video-based multi-agent traffic surveillance system. In: Proceedings of the IEEE, Intelligent Vehicles Symposium, IV 2000, pp. 457–462 (2000)
2. Addis, A., Armano, G., Vargiu, E.: From a generic multiagent architecture to multiagent information retrieval systems. In: AT2AI-6, Sixth International Workshop, From Agent Theory to Agent Implementation, pp. 3–9 (2008)
3. Bellifemine, F., Caire, G., Greenwood, D.: Developing Multi-Agent Systems with JADE (Wiley Series in Agent Technology). John Wiley and Sons, Chichester (2007)
4. Bergenti, F., Rimassa, G., Poggi, A., Turci, P.: Middleware and programming support for agent systems. In: Proceedings of the 2nd International Symposium from Agent Theory to Agent Implementation, pp. 617–622 (2002)
5. Berners-Lee, T., Hendler, J., Lassila, O.: The semantic web. Scientific American Magazine (2001)

6. Bieszczad, A., White, T., Pagurek, B.: Mobile agents for network management. IEEE Communications Surveys 1(1), 2–9 (1998)
7. Bodrozic, L., Stipanicev, D., Stula, M.: Agent based data collecting in a forest fire monitoring system. In: International Conference on Software in Telecommunications and Computer Networks, 2006. SoftCOM 2006, October 1, pp. 326–330 (2006)
8. Bussmann, S., Jennings, N.R., Wooldridge, M.: On the identification of agents in the design of production control systems. In: Ciancarini, P., Wooldridge, M.J. (eds.) AOSE 2000. LNCS, vol. 1957, pp. 141–162. Springer, Heidelberg (2001)
9. Foster, I., Kesselman, C.: The Grid: Blueprint for a New Computing Infrastructure. Morgan Kaufmann, San Francisco (1999)
10. Kephart, J.O.: Software agents and the route to the information economy. Proc. Natl. Acad. Sci. 99(3), 7207–7213 (2002)
11. Kim, N., jae Kim, I., gon Kim, H.: Video surveillance using dynamic configuration of mutiple active cameras. In: IEEE International Conference on Image Processing 2006, October 2006, pp. 1761–1764 (2006)
12. Orwell, J., Massey, S., Remagnino, P., Greenhill, D., Jones, G.A.: A multi-agent framework for visual surveillance. In: ICIAP 1999: Proceedings of the 10th International Conference on Image Analysis and Processing, Washington, DC, USA, IEEE Computer Society, Los Alamitos (1999)
13. Pěchouček, M., Marik, V.: Industrial deployment of multi-agent technologies: review and selected case studies. Journal Autonomous Agents and Multi-Agent Systems 17(3), 397–431 (2008)
14. Pěchouček, M., Rehak, M., Charvat, P., Vlcek, T., Kolar, M.: Multi-agent planning in mass-oriented production. IEEE Transactions System, Man and Cybernetics, Part C 37(3), 386–395 (2007)
15. Pěchouček, M., Šišlák, D., Pavlíček, D., Uller, M.: Autonomous agents for air-traffic deconfliction. In: AAMAS 2006: Proceedings of the fifth international joint conference on Autonomous agents and multiagent systems, pp. 1498–1505. ACM, New York (2006)
16. Quitadamo, R., Zambonelli, F.: Autonomic communication services: a new challenge for software agents. Journal Autonomous Agents and Multi-Agent Systems 17(3), 457–475 (2008)
17. Sebastiani, F.: Machine learning in automated text categorization. ACM Computing Surveys (CSUR) 34(1), 1–55 (2002)
18. Shen, W., Norrie, D.H.: Agent-based systems for intelligent manufacturing: a state-of-the-art survey. Knowledge and Information Systems, an International Journal 1(2), 129–156 (1999)
19. Stipanicev, D., Stula, M., Bodrozic, L.: Multiagent based greenhouse telecontrol system as a tool for distance experimentation. In: Proceedings of the IEEE International Symposium on Industrial Electronics, ISIE 2005, vol. 4, pp. 1691–1696 (2005)
20. Tichý, P., Slechta, P., Maturana, F.P., Balasubramanian, S.: Industrial mas for planning and control. In: Mařík, V., Štěpánková, O., Krautwurmová, H., Luck, M. (eds.) ACAI 2001, EASSS 2001, AEMAS 2001, and HoloMAS 2001. LNCS (LNAI), vol. 2322, pp. 280–295. Springer, Heidelberg (2002)
21. Zambonelli, F., Omicini, A.: Challenges and research directions in agent-oriented software engineering. Journal of Autonomous Agents and Multiagent Systems 9, 253–283 (2004)

# Agent-Oriented Control in Real-Time Computer Games

Tristan M. Behrens

Department of Informatics, Clausthal University of Technology
Julius-Albert-Straße 4, 38678 Clausthal, Germany
behrens@in.tu-clausthal.de

**Abstract.** We introduce a new methodology that allows to apply techniques and methods from agent-oriented programming (AOP) to computer games. To this end, we introduce an underlying model based on *agents*, *controllable entities*, and an *agents-entities-relation*. Then we elaborate on a method how to steer several controllable entities through an environment with a single agent. Finally, we show how AOP can be used to implement several agents based on the method.

## 1   Introduction

Multi-agent systems programming is a promising software engineering paradigm. It is especially suited for the development of systems operating in dynamic environments. Examples for AOP [3,4] languages are the BDI-based 2APL, GOAL, Jadex, and Jason. 2APL realizes an effective implementation of both declarative and imperative programming. GOAL Jadex is Jason is an implementation of an AgentSpeak(L) extension.

In this paper we present a new methodology on how to apply AOP as a means to implement artificial intelligence for entities in real-time computer games. We believe that AOP languages are suitable to function as the high-level control of entities in games (which usually contain a large number of entities).

Why are we interested in computer games as platforms for the application of AOP? First of all computer games are a challenging compromise between toy examples and real world applications. Furthermore computer graphics cease to be the main drive of the industry and it is highly probable that the focus will shift to AI. Additionally many computer games make the cooperation of entities (optionally with a human player) desirable.

One goal of AOP is to control robots. The fact that robots are embodied agents and thus are situated in the real world, implies at least two requirements: the agent needs (1) sensors for perceiving its environment and (2) actuators for acting in the environment. Of course, both requirements can be challenges for researchers. Computer games – especially those of the newest generation – have complex game worlds and sophisticated physics, that make them quite realistic. It is straightforward to create sensors and actuators for agents that are situated in a game world. Sensors can be used to query the game state and

L. Braubach, J.-P. Briot, and J. Thangarajah (Eds.): ProMAS 2009, LNAI 5919, pp. 266–283, 2010.
© Springer-Verlag Berlin Heidelberg 2010

actuators can be used to update it. But how to perceive? There seem to be two extremes: (1) agents have direct access to the game-state and (2) agents perceive exactly the same data as the human player. The first extreme leads to (undesired) omniscience of the agents – they know for example about the positions of all the entities in the game world, whereas a human player might only be aware of the visible entities. That is something that is not desired in computer games, because it can quickly give rise to frustration on the side of the human player. The second extreme would require the application of (visual) recognition systems. Both extremes make it desirable to create *virtual sensors*, that simulate visibility (and audibility et cetera) for the agents. Those sensors are a necessary abstraction over the game state, once you decide not to allow omniscience as it has been explained before.

In this paper we propose

- a *new model* that is based on the notions of *agents*, *controllable entities*, and *agents-entities-relation*,
- a *navigational approach* for RTS-games based on entities (units and potential-fields) and artifacts (maps), and
- an implementation based on the AOP language 2APL.

In Section 2 we motivate the use of AI for computer games. In Section 3 we explain our approach. We then elaborate on our implementation in Section 4. Finally, we discuss similar work and conclude with future work.

## 2   Computer Games

In a typical computer game architecture, three integral components can be distinguished (see Fig. 1):

- the *game world simulator* that manages the *game-state*,
- the *visual/accoustic renderer* that renders the *current* game-state, and
- the *controllers* that allow to manipulate the *entities* in the game world.

The core of a computer game is usually the *game world simulator*. The game world simulator contains the *game state*, which consists of the game's entities (player, obstacles, items, opponents et cetera) and the environment in which the objects are situated, and the *game state transformer* which lets the game state evolve over time. A typical example for an integral component of a game state transformer is a *physics engine* which moves the entities in accordance to given laws of physics and deals with collision detection.

Another important component is the *visual/accoustic renderer*, which is responsible for the optical and aural representation of the game state for the human player.

Finally, a set of *controllers* manipulates the entities in the game world. Controllers can be employed both by the human player and the computer player.

All three components constitute the axes of game-development. The bulk of game history was characterized by advances in computer graphics. The renderer

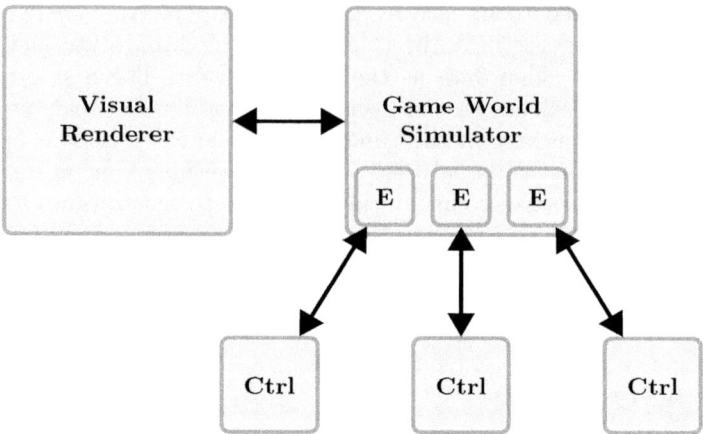

**Fig. 1.** The typical game architecture, with the tree components visual renderer (computer graphics), the game world simulator (physics) and the controllers (artificial intelligence)

has been the main focus of attention for decades. Now, at the dawn of realistic and hyperrealistic graphics, it is more than probable that the focus will shift to artificial intelligence, which has been quite neglected in the past.

Also, it is an observable trend that game AI is more and more applied to creating teams of entities. Entities cooperate and coordinate their actions in order to beat the human player and entities form teams to *support* the human player as well. This is where the social component of agents come in handy. Here cooperation is necessary if the summation of the agents capabilities lead to the success of the whole team.

The state-of-the art of game AI is the combination of *finite state machines* and *pathfinding* [17]. A state machine represents the state of an entity and distinguishes between different behaviors.

## 3    Our Approach to Real-Time Strategy Games

Although our approach is aimed at a general class of computer games – in which the game world is populated by many entities that are controlled by some kind of AI – we focus on *real-time strategy* (RTS) games in this paper. Real-time strategy games are not turn-based and usually incorporate some of the following concepts:

- **exploration:** the map is usually unknown territory at the beginning of each mission.
- **resource-gathering and -management:** resources are located in the environment and have to be gathered, usually in order to gain credits.

- **base building:** in order to establish and defend one's position in the territory and to produce armed units, a base has to be set up.
- **combat-oriented action:** usually the main goal is to overpower an opponent that is situated in the environment as well.
- **abstract unit control:** armed units are not controlled directly. Instead they are given orders that they act out.
- **technological development:** technological advances support performing the previous concepts.

The main focus of the RTS game play lies in base building and combat, usually in that order. Mission goals can be the following:

- complete destruction of the forces of the enemy,
- selective destruction of the opponent's structures,
- special operations, and
- object defense.

RTS games are usually quite complex. They feature a plethora of different armed units with different and task-dependent features, as well as a multitude of buildings with different functions. We omit, for our purposes, many of the features that increase the fun and excitement for the player but hinder the analysis from the AI perspective, and concentrate on the most interesting aspects instead. In this paper we only focus on navigation and interaction.

We use agents programmed in an AOP language to control entities in a game world. We also employ A* for navigation and potential-fields for collision avoidance.

### 3.1   Agents, Entities, and the Agents-Entities-Relation

Our approach is based on three notions: *agents*, *controllable entities*, and the *agents-entities-relation*. An agent in our work is a software agent. More precisely it is a 2APL-agent-program that is being executed. A controllable entity is in general any abstract thing that is situated in the environment and that can be controlled by external agents. More precisely: controllable entities provide agents with for example *effectoric* and *sensory* capabilities. This way they facilitate the situatedness of agents. Agents themselves are not entities. Instead they are capable of controlling entities by accessing the sensors and effectors. The agents-entities-relation is any subset of the Cartesian product $\mathcal{AG} \times \mathcal{EN}$, where $\mathcal{AG}$ is the set of agents and $\mathcal{EN}$ is the set of entities (see Fig. 2). Per default we allow one agent to control several entities, and even one entity being controlled by several agents. Special properties of the relation depend on the environment that is considered. If it makes sense to allow only a one-agent-one-entity-relation, the relation will be restricted in the implementation respectively. Finally, the agents-entities-relation is assumed to be *dynamic*, it can change over time: agents can register to and unregister from an evironment, entites can be created and removed, and agents can transfer their control over entities to other agents.

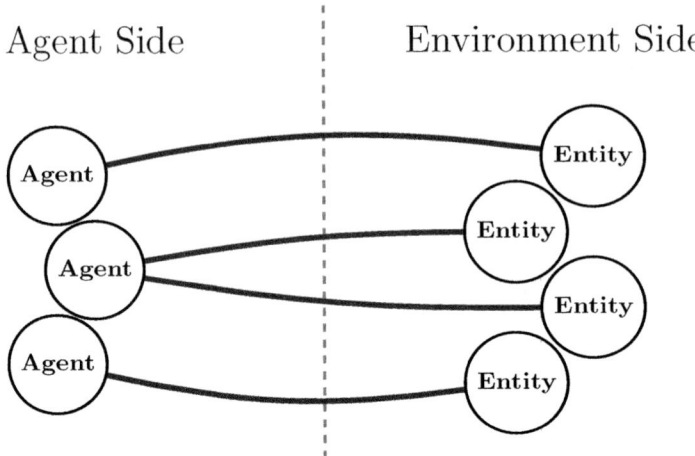

**Fig. 2.** Agents, controllable entities, and the agents-entities-relation. In general one agent can control several entities, and one entity can be controlled by several agents. This is restricted by the environment.

*Example 1 (multi-agent contest)*
The multi-agent contest [7] is a competitive set-up for comparing approaches to agent-oriented programming. Essentially, it is a heterogeneous multi-agent system. The environment is a grid-like world that is populated by cows. Cowboys are controllable entities. The agents-entities-relation is restricted to one-agent-one-entity. Cowboys can scare cows. The goal is to push cows as many cows as possible into corrals, Agents have to cooperate and coordinate their actions.

Why does it make sense to associate on agent with several entities instead of using a one-to-one approach?
    We believe it is beneficial to do so when dealing with groups of entities. If a group should fulfill a specific goal, a single agent could be employed to steer and coordinate the entities. Partitioning the overall goal of beating an opponent into subgoals that are solved by different agents, would make sense. Given a set of controllable entities (units, tanks et cetera) having one agent controlling one entity would absolutely be possible, but facing a lot of entities there would be performance issues, which could be optimized by partitioning the entities into sets with shared goals For example, if a group shall engage a given target, the entities – considered individually – will have similar plans to reach that goal. It does make sense to have a single agent manage the execution of such a plan that is shared by the entities. This approach would be the basis for an AOP-control of a massive number of entities, in the sense of having few agents control many entities. Agents could also transfer the responsibility for its entities or a subgroup to other agents. This could be employed for example if a group should be split up.

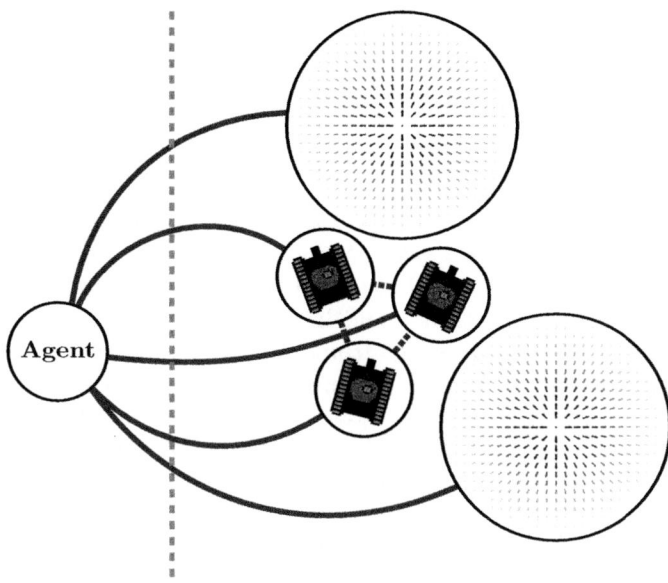

**Fig. 3.** One agent controls several, different entities. Units move influenced by potential-fields. Obstacles could be represented by repelling fields.

In this paper we consider different types of entities:

- **units** that consist of a body, sensors, and actuators for moving and shooting;
- **force fields** that influence units and make them move into certain directions; and
- **ad-hoc nets** that represent the spatial relation of units.

Fig. 3 shows on agent that is associated with several units and several force fields. The force fields influence the movement of the units as we will explain later.

Furthermore we utilize artifacts to coordinate agents:

- **maps** for representing the world and determining shortest paths.

## 3.2   Entities: Units, Potential Fields, and Ad-Hoc Nets

In the last subsection, we have agreed that in some scenarios it makes sense to refrain from the one-agent-one-entity approach. Now we discuss why it make sense in the RTS-scenario as well.

The first entity-type that we take into account are *units*. In RTS, since there are usually a lot of units (e.g. tanks, hum-vees, soldiers) involved in the game-play, it is regularly the case that several units would have the same goals and plans. For example it would happen often that several units would have the goal of eliminating the same target – we use the games-specific language here. Their plan would be moving towards the target and attacking it if it is in firing-range. These units could be controlled by one agent, but then a problem would arise: with several units under its control the agent has to deal with the movement of the units on a micro-level. It has to be aware of the positions, directions and speeds in order to coordinate the units. By applying the potential-fields-method the agent is relieved from the burden of micro-management. The method is a unified approach to steering units without the associated agent having to deal with micro-actions, that scales up very well with the number of associated units.

Now we consider *potential-fields*. A very good analogy to potential-fields is the idea of an electron moving through an electromagnetic field of non-uniform structure. The moving electron would interact with the sources of the field by being diverted through forces of *attraction* and *repellence*. This idea can be applied to navigating entities in a game as well. Imagine an entity having a certain goal to reach. On top of that, the entity should not bump into obstacles. It is easy to model the goal as an attractive and all obstacles as a repelling field each. The combination of all the fields would then steer the entity to the goal on an obstacle avoiding path.

There are a lot of different types of potential-fields. Good examples are:

- the **Gaussian repeller** that makes units avoid a specific position, the closer the entity is to the position, the stronger the repelling force is;
- the **sink attractor** that makes units move towards a specific position;
- the **square repeller** that makes units avoid an area that is a square in shape; and
- the **circle attractor** that makes units move towards a specific position, if close enough the units will circle the position.

Of course, the potential-fields method opens all doors of creativity when it comes to shapes, sizes and structures of special types of potential-fields. In this work, however, we only deal with the Gaussian repeller and the sink attractor in order not to confuse the reader with way too many different types. We use potential-fields to model the topology of an environment in a way that allows for steering sets of units.

Let us now introduce the potential-fields methodology formally. A potential-field is a function $f \in \mathbb{R} \times \mathbb{R}^{\mathbb{R} \times \mathbb{R}}$ that maps a two-dimensional vector to another one. Usually the input-vector represents a position on the Euclidean plane and the output vector a force that is effective at that position.

*Example 2 (potential-fields).* Any function

$$f_{gauss} : [x, y] \mapsto \frac{[x - x_0, y - y_0]}{|| [x - x_0, y - y_0] ||} \cdot a \cdot \exp \left( -\frac{|| [x - x_0, y - y_0] ||^2}{2s^2} \right)$$

is called a *Gaussian repeller* potential-field. The constant vector $[x_0, y_0]$ represents the *center*, and the constants $a$ and $s$ represent the *amplitude* and the *spread* of the field respectively.

The repelling force is strongest at the center and steeply falls off, converging to 0. An entity approaching a Gaussian repeller will be affected once it gets close to that force. The amplitude $a$ determines the maximum strength of the force. The spread $s$ determines the width of the Gaussian bell and thereby the range of influence of the field.

Another potential-field is the sink attractor:

$$f_{sink} : [x, y] \mapsto \frac{[x - x_0, y - y_0]}{||\,[x - x_0, y - y_0]\,||} \cdot g_{sink}(x, y)$$

with

$$g_{sink} : [x, y] \mapsto a \cdot \exp\left(-\frac{||\,[x - x_0, y - y_0]\,||^2}{2s^2}\right) - g \cdot ||\,[x - x_0, y - y_0]\,|| - a$$

The constant vector $[x_0, y_0]$ represents the *center*. The constants $a$ and $s$ represent the *amplitude* and the *spread* respectively. The constant $g$ represents the grade. In the sink attractor the attractive force is stronger the farther away the target is. It is the combination of a conical potential-field and a Gaussian one. Fig. 4 shows the two potential-fields as vector fields in the Euclidian plane.

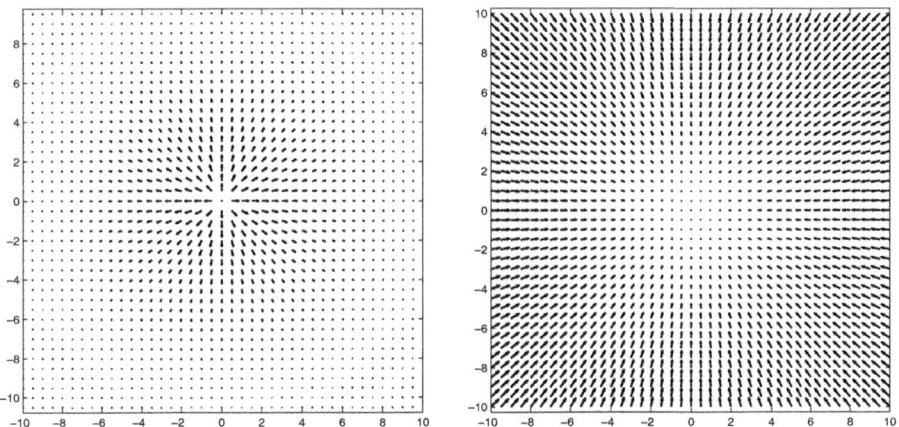

**Fig. 4.** Two potential-fields shown as vector fields. The left one shows the Gaussian repeller. The upper right one shows the sink attractor.

The set $F_{ag} := \{f_{ag,1}, \ldots, f_{ag,n}\}$ of potential-fields is overall potential-field of an agent $ag$. The force at a given position is $F_{ag}(x, y) := \sum_{f_{ag,i} \in F_{ag}} f_{ag,i}(x, y)$, which is just the sum of all forces that have an effect at that position. An agent would firstly come up with the set of all fields that are relevant for its entities, and would then let them follow the force vectors that are effective at the entities' positions.

If, for example, the agent has the goal of steering all associated entities to a given position, detected obstacles (static ones and enemy units) could be associated with a repeller each, and the goal position could be represented by an attractor. The sum of all potential-fields of the agent is the overall force field. The entities affected by that force-field would move away from obstacles towards the goal position. If on the other hand the entities should show the behavior of engaging a target, the target would be associated with an attractor as well.

Note that a potential-field does not influence all units in the environment. Rather it influences only those ones that are associated with the same agent as the field is.

Now, we consider the third entity-type: *ad-hoc nets*. Ad-hoc are self-configuring networks. The topology is arbitrary and the nodes are allowed to move and arrange themselves arbitrarily. Nodes in our case are units. We have decided to use triangulations for the network-structures. A triangulation is a graph that is planar and has the maximum number of edges. Triangulations cut down the complexity of the structure immensely. We use ad-hoc nets in order to reflect the spatial relation between units. This relation can be exploited for example for collision avoidance.

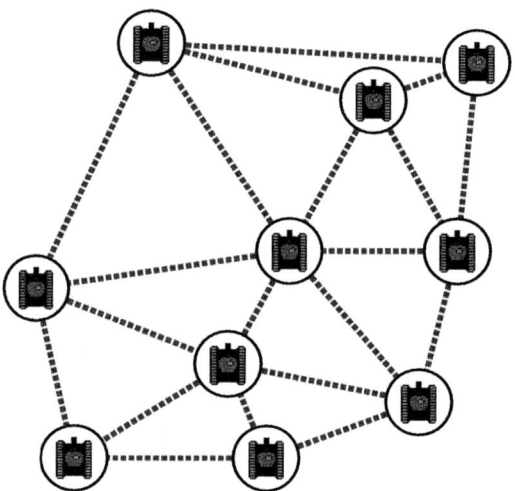

**Fig. 5.** A triangulation of set of units. The triangulation is an ad-hoc net. Its topology changes over time.

### 3.3   Artifacts: Maps

Artifacts are first class *mediating* tools [4]. They are used in lieu of traditional interaction models, that are based on direct communication like speech-acts and conversation-protocols. Artifacts are non autonomous and function-oriented, they can be controlled and used by agents, but they are not agents themselves. Where agents represent the goal-oriented part of a MAS, artifacts represent the functional one. They are applied to cope with the scaling up of social interactions by providing means for interactions in form of building blocks that can be manipulated and shared by agents while they perform their goal-oriented tasks. Examples for artifacts are calendars, blackboards, and shared knowledge-bases.

In this subsection we introduce a agent-interaction mechanism. That is a map artifact that will later be layered upon by potential-fields. For each player (human player or computer player) there is one map-artifact that can be accessed only by the agents of the respective team. The map represents the (continuous) topology of the environment as a grid. Each cell of the grid can either be marked as *free*, *blocked* or *unknown* (reminder: we deal with unexplored terrain). Agents can explore the terrain by steering their associated units through it and updating the map-artiface with properties of explored cells. Furthermore the agents can query the map-artifacts for shortest paths, which are calculated on request by the artifact using the established A*-algorithm. The A* algorithm is an informed search algorithm for finding shortest paths in graphs [16]. The algorithm it is quite common in computer games development. We assume that a reachability-graph can easily be derived from the world-representation that is a two-dimensional, rectangular navigational space. The cells of the map serve as nodes for the algorithm. Cells that are marked blocked will not be expanded.

At this point, we have do discuss why the potential-fields are not artifacts. One might be tempted to assume that the opposite is the case. Potential fields are used to facilitate the movement of units. But fields are not used to coordinate different agents, they are not a means for agent-interaction. Thus they are not artifacts.

## 3.4   Using Both Artifacts and Entities

In this subsection we explain how agents can combine artifacts and entities. The main problem of the potential-fields method is that it easily gets stuck in local optima, never reaching the goal. To ease this problem we apply the A* algorithm on top of the potential-fields.

How do A* and potential-fields combine? First of all, an agent that intends to steer its associated units to a specific destination queries the map-artifact for a shortest path, which is calculated using the A* algorithm. Then the agent associates an attractive field with the first node of the path. The agent then lets its associated units follow the overall potential-field. Once the node is reached, which is indicated by a specific criterion, it is removed from the path and the agent continues with the next one until the goal is reached. Local optima in the

---

**Algorithm 1.** Simple Navigation Algorithm

$P := calculatePath()$; //invoke A* (via map-artifact)
**while** $P \neq \emptyset$ **do**
    $p := removeFirst(P)$; //get and remove the first element
    $f := toField(p)$; //convert to field
    $F := F \cup \{f\}$; //add to overall field
    $moveTo(p, F)$ //move to $p$ following $F$
    $F := F/\{p\}$; //remove from overall field
**end while**

---

potential-fields method are ruled out as good as possible by the A* algorithm, which helps to avoid static obstacles. Of course, the probability of getting stuck is only reduced to a small value but not to zero. But in the case of getting stuck the path can be replanned. Algorithm 1 implements the proposed navigational method.

## 4    Implementation

Our implementation is based on the 2APL platform, that has kindly been made available to us by the developers in Utrecht. 2APL agents are cognitive agents and consist of *beliefs, goals, actions, plans* and *rules*. Beliefs model the information the agent has about its environment, goals denote the states the agent wants to achieve, actions are the agent's means to manipulate the environment, and rules – if applied – instantiate plans based on the agent's current goals and beliefs.

We have extended the 2APL platform a bit to serve our needs. One thing that we did was the introduction of two *special actions*, that allow the addition and the removal of agents during runtime. In its current implementation the 2APL platform only allows for multi-agent systems that are static in that respect. This extension deemed to be necessary after the analysis that many computer games are highly dynamic in respect to the number of entities. An agent is now able to create one or several agents by loading the specification from a file. Also each agent is able to terminate itself.

Our scenario's game world (the physical model) is an extension of the standard 2APL environment. Agents are capable of interacting with the environment via two ways: *external actions* and *external events*. External actions allow the agents to contribute to the state-change of the environment and events are issued by the environment to inform the agent.

The initial state of the MAS consists of one default agent and the environment. The default agent can instantiate more agents if necessary. Each agent can create new entities in the environment by invoking an external action. This consumes resources. Another external action can be used to transfer the responsibility over a set of entities from one agent to another. Entities cannot be directly removed by the agents. Instead they can be destroyed. Table 1 shows the actions that facilitate the described dynamics.

**Table 1.** The actions that change the set of agents, the set of entities and the agent-entities association. The first two are special actions, the last two are external actions.

| Action | Description |
| --- | --- |
| addAgent(File, N) | adds a number of agents loaded from a file |
| terminate() | lets an agent terminate itself |
| createUnit(T,X,Y) | creates a unit of a given type at a given position |
| transfer(Ag, Ens) | transfers the responsibility to another agent |

The 2APL platform is extremely flexible when it comes to the *execution model* of the agents. In its standard implementation, the multi-agent system is executed in a multi-threaded way. Each agent is executed in its own thread. In computer games development the tradition has been established to implement the whole project in a single thread [17]. Using a single thread makes it easy to keep the frame-rate (number of scenes rendered per second) on an adequate level that does not ruin the player's user-experience. We have refrained from following that approach. Instead we have two threads: the game world thread and the artificial intelligence thread. The first thread implements the evolution of the game world, it moves objects in real time, manages collisions, implements the game's logics and renders the scene. The second thread evolves the agents, each agent is allow to deliberate by one step in each cycle of the thread.

## 4.1   Scripting Language

In our approach 2APL can be considered a kind of "scripting language" for agents on top of a custom API.

Table 2 shows some exemplary external actions, that can be used to act and perceive in the game world and to manipulate the potential-fields Based on that API, different behaviors can be implemented. Here is an example for navigating through the environment.

**Table 2.** TODO rewrite Some external actions for perceiving, acting and manipulating the potential-fields

| Action | Description |
| --- | --- |
| getPath(X,Y) | invokes A* and returns a shortest path |
| senseMovingObstacles() | returns a list of moving obstacles that are visible |
| senseStaticObstacles() | return a list of static obstacles that are visible |
| addAttractor(I, X,Y,R) | adds an attractor to the potential-field |
| addRepeller(I, X,Y,R) | adds a repeller to the potential-field |
| removeForce(I) | removes a force from the potential-field |
| followPotentialField() | moves all entities along the potential-field |
| getNet() | calculates and returns an ad-hoc net |
| getNearestNeighbors() | returns the nearest neighbors |

*Example 3 (path-finding and -following).* Consider this code fragment:

```
PG-rules:
  beAt(X,Y) ← true | {
    @env( getPath(X,Y), P); // invoke A*
    followPath(P)  // follow the path
  }

PC-rules:
  followPath(Path) ← true | {
    B(Path = [pos(GX,GY)|R]); // get the next goal position
    @env( addAttractor(GX,GY), _ ); // add attractor
    @env( followPotentialField(),); // be affected by the field
```

```
B( isAt(GX,GY) ); // wait for goal to be reached
@env( removeAttractor(GX,GY), _ ); // remove the attractor
if B( not(R = [])) then // continue with next goal position
{
    followPath(R)
}
}
```

Rules in 2APL are used to instantiate plans in respect to beliefs, goals and events. Here we have two rules. The first rule is a *PG-rule*. PG-rules in 2APL instantiate plans in respect to the goal-base and the belief-base. The considered rule instantiates the plan if the agent has the goal to steer its entities to a certain position (beAt(X,Y)) and if true is implied by the belief-base, which is always the case. The plan consists of two statements. At first a path to the goal is calculated by invoking the external action getPath. Then the path is followed by raising the procedural event followPath. The second rule is a *PC-rule*. PC-rules instantiate plans in respect to the event-base and the belief-base. The plan in the example is instantiated once an event followPath(P) has been raised and true is implied by the belief-base. The first statement of the plan separates the path into its first element pos(GX,GY) and the rest R. The coordinates of that first element are then used to add an attractor to the potential-field by invoking the external action addAttractor. The agent then follows the potential-field executing followPotentialField. Once the first element of the current path is reached (once the agent believes being at the desired position) the attractor is removed via removeAttractor and the rest of the list is processed recursively.

This example shows a very simple navigational routine. A path is calculated and then followed by adding and removing attractors to and from the potential-field. An agent executing that behavior does not take obstacles into account and thus the associated entities would bump into them. Such a stubborn behavior might be desired in a computer game for the user experience. Nevertheless we improve the example a bit.

*Example 4 (obstacle avoidance).* Consider the following code:

```
PG-rules:
  avoid(obstacles) ← true | {
    @env( senseMovingObstacles(), M); // sense obstacles
    addRepellentFields(M) // add fields recursively
  }

PC-rules:
  addRepellentFields(Units) ← true | {
    B( Units = [obstacle(Id,X,Y)|R] ); // get the first obstacle
    @env( addRepeller(Id,X,Y), _ ); // add a repellent force
    if B( not(R = [])) then // add the rest if rest not empty
    {
      addRepellentFields(R) // proceed recursively
    }
  }
```

The first rule implements the following: if the agent has the goal of avoiding the visible obstacles the respective plan is instantiated. Firstly the moving obstacles are sensed and secondly they are added as repellers to the potential-field. The second rule implements the addition of the repellers in a recursive fashion. The first element is determined and added as a a repeller. After that the rest of the list is processed until the list is empty.

Internally each attractor/repeller is associated with a unique identifier. This is very useful for updating forces of moving obstacles. Also, if an agent finds out that an obstacle has been destroyed, the force can be easily removed from the overall potential-field.

The final example depicts a routine that makes units keep their distance, avoiding that entities get too close. The ad-hoc net is updated and the shortest edge is associated with a repellent potential-field.

*Example 5 (units made to keep their distance).* Consider this code fragment:

```
PG-rules:
  keep(distance) <- true | {
    while B(true) do {
      @env( getNet(), Net );
      @env( getShortestEdge(Net), T);
      if B( T = edge(E1,E2,X,Y,L) ) then {
        if B( L < 100) then {
          @env( addRepeller(triangle,X,Y,50), _ ) // add a repeller
        }
        else {
          @env( removeForce(triangle), _ ) // remove repeller
        }
      }
    }
  }
}
```

If the agent has the goal of making its associated agents keeping their distance it instantiates the respective plan. Firstly, the ad-hoc net is generated and re-trieved. Secondly, the shortest edge is determined. If the length of that edge is below a given margin, an attractive potential-field is put at the position of its baricentre.

What is the benefit from our approach of layering AOP in top of entities? We preserve the agents' autonomy. This way agents can reason about the potential fields and decide their behavior according to the results. Agents could for example decide to omit certain repellers or add attractors. They could for example decide to only take friendly entities into account as obstacles. This would lead to a behavior of avoiding friendly entities and bumping into enemies. Furthermore agents can decide when to update the data-structures. An agent might chose to not update its potential-field if it is busy doing something more important. An agent could also manipulate the representation of the potential-field. For example if it comes to the conclusion that an obstacle is extremely threatening, its repelling force could be increased. Our approach allows to easily implement and combine different behaviors to enhance the user experience.

To conclude this section we elaborate on an other issue that has been left undiscussed until now: human-agent interaction. How does the human player interact with the entities under his command? The environment allows the se-lection of one or several entities. The commands traditional to RTS games ("go there", "attack this", "guard that") are interpreted and sent to the agents as messages. To this¡ end we use to the message-passing facilities underlying 2APL.

# 5   Related Work

The potential-fields method was developed by Krogh [12] and Khatib [10] for obstacle avoidance control. Krogh borrowed the terminology from analytical mechanics. He determined a collision free path to transfer a system to a work-space. Khatib concentrated on a real-time obstacle avoidance approach for manipulators and mobile robots. Arkin in his book [1] describes the potential-fields methodology as a functional mapping from stimuli to motor-responses, in order to encode a continuous navigational space through the sensed world. Massari et al. in their paper [14] use potential-fields to steer planetary rovers. In their paper[11], Koren and Borenstein discuss problems inherent to the potential-fields method. They identify four significant problems: trap situations due to local optima, no passage between closely spaced obstacles, oscillations in the presence of obstacles, and oscillation in narrow passages. Mamei and Zambonelli[13] apply potential-fields to the computer game Quake 3 Arena.

Hagelbäck and Johansson in their paper [9] illustrate an application of potential-fields on the research platform ORTS [5]. The main difference between their approach and ours is that they rely on complete information, whereas we work with incomplete information. They have full access to the state of the world and we rely on the (limited) local view of the agents. The difference is the reason why they can afford to calculate a discretized potential-field for the complete map and we are forced to use local ones. Our approach is suited to deal with group of agents with different goals. The main aim of Hagelbäck and Johansson seems to be AI that wins, we are more interested in the user experience. They have no high-level path planning, we employ A*. Finally, we resort to AOP for the high-level control of the entities.

Davies and Mehdi present a prototype application [8] that implements a BDI agent system (based on Jadex) within the first person shooter Unreal Tournament, based on the GameBots and JavaBots technology. Their agents are capable of creating an internal representation of the three-dimensional world, navigate in it and show some basic behaviors. Our approach differs in two ways: we concentrate on a completely different world model and we are interested in a massive number of agents/entities.

Conceicao et al. introduce in their paper [6] a realistic mobile connectivity model for vehicular sensor networks in urban environments. They focus on the evolution of the average node degree in the graph and provide a characterization of the connectivity of a vehicular sensor network operating in an urban environment. Muhammad [15] presented a fully distributed algorithm to compute a planar graph and a geometric routing algorithm. His results are based on idealized unit disk graph model, that assumes that the communication range is the same for all the nodes. We do not share that assumption. The algorithm that we use to generate planar graphs is a simple one. Muhammad, on the other hand, generates Delaunay triangulations.

In his book [17] Schwab summarizes the state of the art of computer games AI that he rightly distinguishes from academic AI that has been applied in the industry.

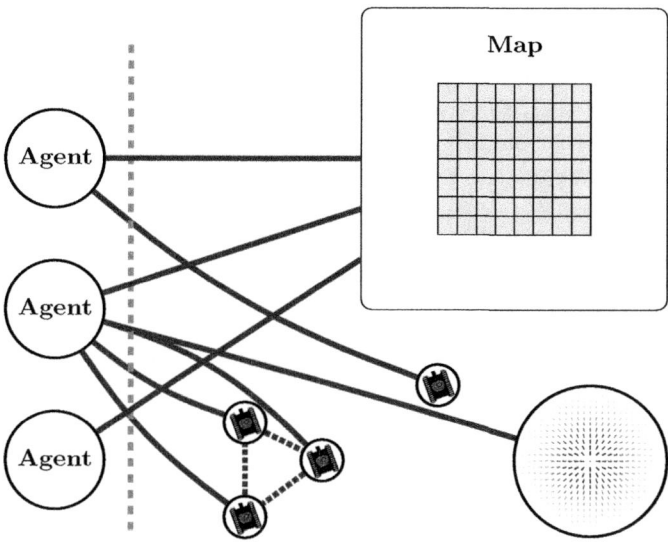

**Fig. 6.** This figure reflects our approach. There is a clear separation between agents and entities/artifacts. An agent controls several entities: unit consists of bodies, sensors and actuators; potential-fields move units; and ad-hoc nets represent the spatial relation of units. Also there is a map-artifact that agent-coordination.

## 6   Conclusion and Future Work

In this paper we have explained an approach to AI in computer games that feature a lot of entities. The approach is the result of a software-engineering experiment. To that end we have used the RTS scenario. RTS games usually contain a lot of entities that are controlled by issuing orders. AOP serves as a high-level control of the entities. The entities navigate using the A* algorithm for path planning and potential-fields for obstacle avoidance. Our approach is based on the notions *agents*, *controllable entities*, and the *agents-entities-relation*. Agents control entities in the environment and the relation determines which agent controls which entities. We have introduced two kinds of *entities*: units which can move through the environment and potential-fields which move units like charged particles in an electromagnetic field. One agent can control several units and several potential-fields. Furthermore, we have added a map-*artifact* to coordinate agents. Fig. 6 reflects our approach.

We are interested mostly in the two extremes of using agents to control entities in computer games. One extreme is associating one agent with exactly one entity in the game world. The other extreme is to have one agent that steers all entities. We would like to investigate the "in between" and find out, when does it make sense to associate one agent with several entities.

Also, we believe it would be fruitful to apply our approach to other games that feature a massive number of entities. God games, in which entities are steered indirectly by influencing the environment, come to mind immediately.

Our ultimate goal is to provide helper AI (that supports the human player) and opponent AI (the computer player) for computer games, by creating a society of heterogenous agents.

In parallel, we are working on a project called *Environment Interface Standard* (EIS), that is a Java-standard for implementing interfaces to arbitrary environments [2]. The EIS is based on a meta-model, that consists of an agent-model (software entities), an environment model (controllable entities), and an agents-entities-relation, which is the main feature. We intend to port our prototype to that standard and thus to all APL platforms that support it.

# References

1. Arkin, R.C.: Behavior-Based Robotics (Intelligent Robotics and Autonomous Agents). MIT Press, Cambridge (1998)
2. Behrens, T.M., Hindriks, K., Dix, J.: Towards an environment interface standard for AOP. Technical Report Ifi-09-09, Clausthal University of Technology (2009)
3. Bordini, R., Dastani, M., Dix, J., El Fallah Seghrouchni, A. (eds.): Programming Multi Agent Systems: Languages, Platforms and Applications. Multiagent Systems, Artificial Societies and Simulated Organizations, vol. 15. Springer, Berlin (2005)
4. Bordini, R.H., Dastani, M., Dix, J., El Fallah-Seghrouchni, A. (eds.): Multi-Agent Tools: Languages, Platforms and Applications. Springer, Berlin (2009)
5. Buro, M.: ORTS: A hack-free RTS game environment. In: Schaeffer, J., Müller, M., Björnsson, Y. (eds.) CG 2002. LNCS, vol. 2883, pp. 280–291. Springer, Heidelberg (2003)
6. Conceiçao, H., Ferreira, M., Barros, J.: On the urban connectivity of vehicular sensor networks. In: Nikoletseas, S.E., Chlebus, B.S., Johnson, D.B., Krishnamachari, B. (eds.) DCOSS 2008. LNCS, vol. 5067, pp. 112–125. Springer, Heidelberg (2008)
7. Dastani, M., Dix, J., Novák, P.: Agent contest competition - 3rd edition. In: Dastani, M.M., El Fallah Seghrouchni, A., Ricci, A., Winikoff, M. (eds.) ProMAS 2007. LNCS (LNAI), vol. 4908, pp. 221–240. Springer, Heidelberg (2008)
8. Davies, N.P., Mehdi, Q.: BDI for intelligent agents in computer games. In: Proceedings of CGAMES 2006 (2006)
9. Hagelbäck, J., Johansson, S.J.: Using multi-agent potential fields in real-time strategy games. In: AAMAS (2), pp. 631–638 (2008)
10. Khatib, O.: Real-time obstacle avoidance for manipulators and mobile robots, vol. 2, pp. 500–505 (1985)
11. Koren, Y. (Senior member), Borenstein, J.: Potential field methods and their inherent limitations for mobile robot navigation. In: Proc. IEEE Int. Conf. Robotics and Automation, pp. 1398–1404 (1991)
12. Krogh, B.: A generalized potential field approach to obstacle avoidance control (1984)
13. Mamei, M., Zambonelli, F.: Field-based motion coordination in quake 3 arena. In: AAMAS, pp. 1532–1533. IEEE Computer Society, Los Alamitos (2004)

14. Massari, M., Giardini, G., Bernelli-Zazzera, F.: Autonomous navigation system for planetary exploration rover based on artificial potential fields. In: Proceedings of Dynamics and Control of Systems and Structures in Space (DCSSS) 6th Conference (2005)
15. Muhammad, R.B.: A distributed graph algorithm for geometric routing in ad hoc wireless networks. JNW 2(6), 50–57 (2007)
16. Russell, S.J., Norvig: Artificial Intelligence: A Modern Approach, 2nd edn. Prentice-Hall, Englewood Cliffs (2003)
17. Schwab, B.: AI Game Engine Programming (Game Development Series). Charles River Media, Inc., Rockland (2004)

# Author Index

GPSR Compliance

*The European Union's (EU) General Product Safety Regulation (GPSR)*
*is a set of rules that requires consumer products to be  safe and our*
*obligations to ensure this.*

*If you have any concerns about our products, you can contact us on*
*ProductSafety@springernature.com*

In case Publisher is established outside the EU, the EU authorized
representative is:

Springer Nature Customer Service Center GmbH
Europaplatz 3
69115 Heidelberg, Germany


**Batch number: 09490872**


Printed by Printforce, the Netherlands